PERFORMING FEMINISMS
Feminist Critical Theory and Theatre

Edited by Sue-Ellen Case

The Johns Hopkins University Press
Baltimore and London

The Johns Hopkins University Press
2715 North Charles Street
Baltimore, Maryland 21218-4319
The Johns Hopkins Press Ltd., London

Library of Congress Cataloging-in-Publication Data

Performing feminisms: feminist critical theory and theatre/edited
  by Sue-Ellen Case.
      p.   cm.
   Includes bibliographical references.
   ISBN 0-8018-3968-8 — ISBN 0-8018-3969-6 (pbk.)
   1. Feminism and theatre.   2. Feminist literary criticism.
I. Case, Sue-Ellen.
PN1590.W64P4   1990
792´.082—dc20   89-24602
                                                          CIP

A catalog record for this book is available from the British Library.

Contents

PERFORMING FEMINISMS

Introduction

Sue-Ellen Case

"Performing feminisms" has been configured in particular ways in the 1980s. Situated among feminist debates around critical practices, including the romance with psychoanalytic theory, the uses of postmodernist strategies, the pitfalls of essentialism, and the centricity of differences, these articles consider performance and feminism in ways that represent many of the significant motive forces in the decade. Below, I would like to consider, in some detail, what I believe these forces to be and how they appear in these works. Appearing at the end of the decade, this anthology marks what became specific to theatrical critical practice within the circulation of feminist strategies.

The Institutional Project

These articles, with the exception of two, were selected from issues of *Theatre Journal* published from 1984 to 1989. The institutional project represented here, during the editorships of both Timothy Murray and myself, was to publish the feminist critique in theatre studies and even more broadly, to publish critical theory in theatre studies. Both projects were contested by the parent organization (ATHE) and are still deeply contested within the field itself.[1]

Sue-Ellen Case is an Associate Professor in the School of Drama, University of Washington. She has published a book, Feminism and Theatre, *and numerous articles in the areas of both feminist theory and German theatre. Her present projects include an anthology of plays by contemporary German women playwrights and a book on a feminist analysis of mimesis. She is the former editor of* Theatre Journal.

This introduction was written, in part, at the Wolf Pen Writers Colony, funded by Sallie Bingham's Kentucky Foundation for Women. The fortunate circumstances of being on retreat with Elin Diamond, Jill Dolan, Janelle Reinelt, and Vicki Patraka fostered many of the considerations in this work.

[1]As editors of the journal, Murray and I were severely criticized for the predominance of articles that incorporated theory and specifically political theory into their content. This move was interpreted as a move away from what was perceived as the center of theatre studies—the traditional uses of theatre history. This so-called schism between theory and history beleaguered the journal, its parent organization and theatre departments during the decade of the 1980s. In 1989, both Murray and I took part in panels at the national conference designed to heal this breach entitled "History/Theory/Revolution: the New Convergence." Moreover, the very interdisciplinarity of this approach was viewed by certain factions as a move away from theatre studies and its parent organizations and departments.

The articles represent the initial phase of the impact of feminist critical theory on the field of theatre. Published in a journal that represents the national organization of theatre in higher education, they are situated within the exclusionary and inclusionary academic practices that institutionalize, through departmental organization and genre biases, feminist critical theory and feminist stage practice. Although these institutional markings may not be directly articulated in the articles, they account for certain aspects of these works. The organization of ideas, the topics covered, the strategies employed, and the tone of the discourse all reflect both the position of the study of theatre in the academy as well as its uses of feminist theory.

Theatre studies has come "later" to the feminist critique than work in other genres. Several factors account for this "tardiness." Primary among them is the status theatre studies inhabits in the university at large. Theatre departments are relatively new to the university.[2] Prior to their founding, the study of theatre was located within English departments. This location meant that the study of theatre was regarded primarily as the analysis of playtexts, isolating them from practice, and employing the devices common to literary studies. When theatre departments were founded, their primary focus was and still is, in training practitioners. As the study of theatre within theatre departments developed, it was dominated by the history of theatre, rather than its criticism. Theatre criticism still resides primarily in English departments, where it focuses on Renaissance studies, with only marginal attention to contemporary theatre. Thus, current critical strategies applied to contemporary texts and practices, such as those of feminist theory, inhabit a severely marginal position in both theatre and English departments.

The history and status of theatre studies are configured several ways in these articles. First, many articles, although written in the 1980s, still pioneer the translation of feminist critical theory (from applications to the cinema and the novel) to the theatre, sounding an introductory tone not found in works by these same authors in other venues. For this reason, the articles often follow the format of first translating theoretical strategies in general and then applying them to specific theatrical texts and practices—a format that has marked the style of this initial phase. Second, these articles on Renaissance texts, arranged according to period rather than approach, illustrate how the work on that period has developed its own set of specialists and problems, based on its dominant status within the field. Third, the analysis of textual, rather than performative strategies still predominates. Few articles consider theories of performance, or performative elements and those, in particular the articles by Lorraine Helms and Glenda Dickerson, continue to develop in regard to texts. Perhaps Jeanie Forte's article on Performance Art best illustrates the theorizing of performance as its own kind of text—derived from purely theatrical considerations of feminist strategies. Further, this textual bias, developed in part because of the institutional history of these studies, has produced an interest in Lacan—a critique of discourse

[2]Although the first theatre program in the country began at Carnegie in 1914, that institution did not grant the PhD until as late as the mid-1960s. The first professional graduate program in Theatre was founded in 1926 at Yale. The first PhD in Drama granted in this country was completed by George Kernodle at Yale in 1937. Significantly, it was in the area of Renaissance Drama.

in its linguistic mode that saturates several of these articles—particularly those in the Renaissance section. The title of that section, "Reconfiguring the Fathers," refers both to the male playwrights and Lacan, in foregrounding the patriarchal roots of such a project.

What theory in general, but particularly feminist theory, has brought to the academy and a journal such as *Theatre Journal*, with its genre bias, is interdisciplinary work and a necessary bridging of scholarly study with the feminist social movement. The translation of strategies from psychoanalytic systems, philosophical traditions, and critical semiotics as well as their applications to cinema and the novel heralds the interdisciplinary site of the work itself. These articles are from many disciplines, from French psychoanalytic theory at the University of Paris to film theory from the History of Consciousness at UC Santa Cruz. The feminist social movement informs the site of critique, from rape considered in its specific historical moments, to prostitution within stage traditions, to the work of women in the South African liberation movement. The breadth of this scope has shaken departmental and genre assumptions in the academy, and the national organizations, threatening the tradition of departmental ownership of expertise and the foundations of expertise itself. Feminist critical theory raises the questions of what constitutes scholarship and more, what constitutes epistemology. The feminist critique also challenges the bourgeois code of manners that controls the kind of issues and materials that are suitable for study, bringing from the margins a variety of social transgressions into the halls of academia: Dolan's study of lesbian representation, Forte's study of performance artists who unscroll texts from their vaginas and sit in garbage dumps, Hermann's sense of transvestism, Dickerson's folk theory from Aunt Jemima, and Yung-Hee Kim Kwon's prostitutes. These same examples push out the walls of the institution of theatre to a notion of performance (particularly Butler's theory of the "act") that blurs disciplinary and performative practices, metaphorizes practices, literalizes linguistic codes, and begs the very notion of what constitutes the topic of theatre. I think the reader of these texts can, in their subtexts, read the tensions that these institutional pressures have produced and find, as well, the concentration of force in developing resistive strategies in their incipient form.

The Pleasures of the Texts

The pleasures in the texts and their intertextuality are many and varied. There is the pleasure in reading the words of activism that carry to the reader of the article, or to the audience of a performance, the experience of resistance and the imaginative space of liberation acted out in social gestures. Glenda Dickerson's article brings the voice of Winnie Mandela: "I have been threatened with my life; I am completely at their mercy. But I am not going to move from here because this is my home. It was a criminal act on the part of the government to arrest me in the first place. Imagine the audacity of it. If anybody should leave, it's not me, it is the settler government. There is only one person who is oppressed in this country. That person is Black . . . We are determined to fight to the bitter end for the liberation of our people." Dickerson amplifies the audacity of that voice and its strength within a critique of the form of the drama—its predilection for heroes—particularly heroes of a certain gender and class: "liberation is not accomplished by the heroes who flash like lightning or the royalty who sit upon the throne. It is achieved by the drylongso folk, the ordinary folk." From the pleasures of those audacious roots, Dickerson creates a theatre, as a director, and a theory of the theatre, as a feminist theorist.

Dickerson's move illustrates one way in which the social movement and the feminist theorist/theatre practitioner traverse a common terrain—the pleasure of a historical moment, a material condition moving within the gestures of the stage and the dynamics of performative forms. Margaret Wilkerson reads this relationship as the theatre's "double," in which struggles for civil rights operate within the narrative and characters in *Raisin in the Sun*, not as historical background, but as a received dimension of the play: the melding of Rosa Parks's refusal to move to the back of the bus to Lena Younger's "apolitical decision" to live in Clybourne Park. Wilkerson reveals political hope and resistance in the use of female stereotypes: "Lena Younger is not the accommodating Mammy who chooses the passive, safe path, but rather the folk figure, the courageous spirit that lends credence and power to the militant struggle." In the play, Ruth contemplates abortion in a dramatic moment charged for women today who are faced with the political struggles for the rights of poor women to determine their own lives. This theatre's double is not Artaud's metaphysical "splitting of forms," but one of feminist political action, especially for women of color who are, as Dickerson writes, "fixed on the fangs of the two-headed serpent."

The economy and grace with which feminist critical theory traverses historical, material circumstances and theoretical strategies is indeed pleasurable. When compared to the efforts, the puffing "projects" of unaligned postmodern theorists to refigure such objects of study, or history itself in the New Historicism, the feminist moves in these articles, proceeding from homologous sites, the certitude of "doubles," and the centricity of what other critical strategies are currently stretching out to include, provide a discourse of inclusion and social specificity that brings new dimensions to the project of theatre. The pleasure of such social/theatrical convergences is not limited to contemporary work, but envelops historical projects as well, refiguring the way classic texts mean. Carol Cook, in her treatment of *Troilus and Cressida* finds in the construction of the patriarchal narrative "violent impulses, a rage articulated in images of a fragmentation of the woman's body." Laurie Finke reads the way in which the very tropes of the classics align with actual violence to women: "Addressing Yorick's skull, Hamlet commands, 'get you to my lady's chamber and tell her, let her paint an inch thick, to this favor she must come' . . . Indeed this connection between women's vanity and death, evoked also by Vendice's Act III soliloquy to Gloriana's painted skull, is not entirely gratuitous since the effects of mercury based cosmetics available to Renaissance women included gradual decomposition." Finke's feminist critique enables her to move easily from a playtext to a medical one—the kind of move for which some New Historicists must make lengthy preparations to execute before daring it.[3] Finke quotes from a Seventeenth century

---

[3]See, for example, Stephen Greenblatt's *Renaissance Self-Fashioning: From More to Shakespeare* (Chicago: University of Chicago Press, 1980).

medical account: "they tremble (poor wretches) as if they were sick of the staggers, reeling, and full of quicksilver . . . it dries up and consumes the flesh underneath."

As well as locating the social in the theatrical, Judith Stephens traces the mutual interaction of social and theatrical ideologies between nineteenth-century moral reforms and melodrama. Kim Kwon reveals historical effects performance has had on the social life of some women. The *asobi* lost their status at court when the "Buddhist establishment which consisted mostly of males" took over their ceremonial rights, forcing them into an itinerant life, finally putting their performance into the service of prostitution. The singers, now singing to lure their sexual clients, worked on small boats: three women, the principle performer who sang and slept with the men, her aide, and an elderly performer who rowed the boat. Kwon: ". . . the totality of the issue of *asobi* is linked to far deeper questions about the dynamics involving women and entertainment, power structure and prostitution, and ritual and performing arts, and finally to the overarching question about the role and position of women stipulated by these powerful variables." These medieval performers signal the still contemporary practice that conflates women performing with sexual labor. The contemporary situation of the Geisha still images these power dynamics, a point that feminist activists are literally demonstrating against in the streets of Japan. This complex oppression informs classic performance in the West as well. I have written elsewhere about the critical phenomenon of the term "actress-courtesan" in this tradition.[4] The location of the woman performer as situated on the boundaries of notions of the sacred, public performance, and state politics provides a nexus of theory, state practice and patriarchal assumptions that delimits not only classical performers, such as the *devadasi* of India, but also Marilyn Monroe, in a less formal way, raising the theoretical issue of the codes and meanings of the female body on stage—as a performance site and as a social determinant. The pleasure of these texts is not in the oppression they record, but in their construction of a discourse that can accurately account for it and trace its dynamics—a discourse that moves in and out of oppressive operations, marking the perspective of the critique and the liberative distance the feminist critic is able to inhabit from collusion with its causes.

The powers of convergence in this discourse accompany a new kind of agency and motility in the feminist subject position that follows the inclusionary model. In fact, one of the most remarkable features of feminist critical theory in the 1980s is its configuration of heterogeneity and heteronomy in the subject position. Here, Yvonne Yarbro-Bejarano sketches a "culture-, class-, and 'race'-specific" desiring subject position "in dialectical relationship to a collective way of imagining sexuality" in Cherrìe Moraga's *Giving Up the Ghost*. Yarbro-Bejarano celebrates Moraga's subject in its heterogeneity and motility within: the juxtaposition of past and present, travelling the bipolar axes of masculine/feminine, active/passive, subject/object, and penetrator/penetrated "defined in Chicano-specific cultural terms." Yarbro-Bejarano's critical study not only accommodates this subject, but operates deconstructively at the same time. This subject's itineration "eschews the ordering of meaning through narrative history," operating within the culture-specific *teatropoesia* form.

[4]See this author's *Feminism and Theatre* (New York: Methuen, 1988).

Teresa de Lauretis also celebrates the motility of differences the subject position inhabits in Moraga's play, further broadening the spectrum: "The character Marisa, however, I would add, has moved away from the hommo-sexuality of Corky (her younger self at age 11 and 17); and with the ambiguous character of Amalia, who loved a man almost as if he were a woman and who can love Marisa only when she (Amalia) is no longer one, the play itself has moved away from any opposition of 'lesbian' to 'heterosexual' and into the conceptual and experiential continuum of female, Chicana subjectivity from where the question of lesbian desire must finally be posed." Judith Butler, in this volume, describes this move as "off the ground of a substantial model of identity to one that requires a conception of a constituted *social temporality.*" Not only does this new subject position move crab-wise to include the range of differences among women, it sweeps backwards, in the deconstructive mode, as it proceeds. The motility of this agency is lacquered with deconstructive operations. These pleasures of the text problematize taxonomies of feminism and "crystallize" them (to borrow an image from the grass-roots movement), on the one hand, while subverting the traditional strategies of textual production and representation on the other.

A different kind of pleasure in the texts resides in the community of feminist scholarship created in the citations. For example, Yarbro-Bejarano cites de Lauretis, de Lauretis cites Yarbro-Bejarano and Jill Dolan, who also cites de Lauretis. Jeanie Forte cites Jill Dolan and Dolan, Forte, and so on. This intercitation signals not only the community of scholars in the field, but also their direct interest in one another's work. Thus, a kind of dialogue is signalled in the citations that marks a sense of nourishment and dialectic. The dialectic, or contradictory status of many of the citations evidences several tendencies in feminist theory: to engage in dialectical thinking, to perform a kind of self-criticism, and to become positional. The practice of the dialectic and self-criticism are, in part, ghostings of earlier, less effective versions of a materialist analysis—vestigial processes from Marxism, which produced a much stabler analysis than the feminist one.[5] The dialectic and self-criticism maintain a kind of mobility in the dialogue, aligned with a materialist analysis and also create a sense of agency that continually tests itself within the context of dominant and collective ideology. These practices have produced the mode of address of positionality.

Positionality addresses the position from which the feminist critic writes. How does she situate, or delimit, or begin to inscribe her "project" or set of "strategies" upon the theoretical terrain of agency? For she, herself, inscribes a certain kind of agency in "approaching" her own combination of theory and theatre. Materialist analysis has taught how the critic inscribes her own gendered socio-economic and sexual compound, either self-consciously, or by formation of her critical apparatus. In earlier feminist criticism, the device for locating the voice was often an introductory testimonial, such as, "I am a white, heterosexual, middle-class academic." Although

---

[5]This discussion of citation developed, in part, in response to collective work done at the Wolf Pen Writer's Colony on this topic. The ideas of Diamond, Dolan, Patraka, and Reinelt are also operating here.

there may be political contexts in which such a statement remains effective, its theoretical assumptions, in regard to writing overlook certain key issues. In the generality and stability of such identifications, a certain essentialism appears that has been corrected by later, more materialist strategies of positionality. As quoted above, de Lauretis has moved the homo-hetero-sexual identity to a historically and socially specific position. In other words, sexual preference is bound to certain ethnic, class, historical practices and does not inhabit a changeless, self-enclosed, essentialist positional model. Likewise, Judith Butler, in her work here, destabilizes gender identity. She establishes that delimiting the sign 'woman' as some kind of stable referent, requires a performance of gender as a "repeated corporeal project." Butler further destabilizes even that concept: "The notion of a 'project', however, suggests the originating force of a radical will, and because gender is a project which has cultural survival as its end, the term 'strategy' better suggests the situation of duress under which gender performance always and variously occurs." In other words, gender becomes a performative strategy within a specific historical and material condition.

Thus, these intercitational moves perform the feminist critical dialogue through revised forms of the dialectic, self-criticism, and positionality that both insist upon the positioning of agency and its materialist deconstruction. In this way, the critical discourse gains accuracy and therefore efficacy. However, these adjustments of the discourse do not proceed through theoretical analysis alone, but through the proximity of the theorizing to the social movement. The criticism raised by women of color against the feminist movement as white and middle-class prompted a revision of its positionality and its material relations.

It should be noted, however, that there is not agreement among feminists upon this kind of discourse. While Butler suggests the more materially specific use of the word "strategy" other cultural feminists criticize what they describe as the rise of "militarist" terminology such as "strategy," "deploy," etc.[6] They would seek a discourse based on a more utopian sense of women's potentials. I find that accusation in itself essentialist, but will defer the treatment of essentialism/poststructuralism to the following section of this article, since it is hardly suitable as a "pleasure of the text."

The Essentialist/Poststructuralist Strife and Stall

To this critic, there appears to be a crucial stall in feminist theory in the late 1980s between the materialist poststructuralist (sometimes called postmodernist) critique and others that have been considered essentialist. The dialectic between these two critiques, or version of self-criticism, or posing of positionalities is the motive force behind much theory in the 1980s as well as what has produced the stall. As a stall, this split seems to have produced a crab-like, sideways-scurrying motility that cannot effectively advance against the increasingly hegemonic attacks by the Right in the late 1980s. It would seem that, on the one hand, praxis is unavailable to the materialist

[6]See Joyce Van Dyke, "Performance Anxiety," *The Women's Review of Books* 6:4 (1989): 1–3.

poststructuralist critique and, on the other, that essentialist praxis is based on an exclusionary critique. While the essentialist maneuvers fail in their exclusionary practices, they do succeed in inhabiting certain concepts such as "women," "lesbian," etc. that are increasingly endangered by dominant society in the 1980s—concepts that the materialist poststructuralists have either abandoned, or continue to modify at the price of an actively resistant praxis.

In this volume, I would like to use the prevalence and position of the psychoanalytic critique to represent transcendental or essentialist qualities in contemporary theory.[7] The materialist critique is lodged primarily (both in this volume and historically) in the articles on ethnicity and class as well as in elements in the articles of de Lauretis and Butler. It should also be noted that Janelle Reinelt's article stands alone as based entirely on Socialist Feminism. The isolation of this critique may also be found in the feminist community-at-large within the United States.

At this historical juncture, and toward this contemporary stall, it seems most appropriate to introduce a consideration of psychoanalytic theory through a critique of it. Laura Kipnis, in "Feminism: The Political Conscience of Postmodernism?"[8] describes the feminist use of psychoanalytic theory this way: ". . . the appropriation of psychoanalysis in . . . current feminism could be seen as an epiphenomenon of a regressive tendency toward modernism, problematic inasmuch as it is part of a larger impetus toward the aestheticization of the political . . . psychoanalytic theory can, in this reading, be seen as filling a certain hiatus between politics and aesthetics . . ." (153–54). Kipnis continues that in such critical theory ". . . the text itself comes to operate as a transcendental signified, as an ultimate meaning" (160) with a "modernist refusal of reference" (162).

Outside of the debate of whether or not it is modernist, the "transcendental" status of psychoanalytic theory, along with its "refusal of reference" are two attacks generally launched against its essentialist tendencies. Some of the authors in this volume correct that tendency by adding elements of a historical critique to the psychoanalytic one. Elin Diamond, though setting out with Kristeva, soon notes that the playwrights she discusses "as feminists . . . are also concerned with the historical human activity." In fact, she continues, "The issue for each dramatist is to represent history" without reinscribing a romanticization of woman in the subject position. What Lacan brings to Diamond's project is a way to dismantle notions of identity in discourse that reinscribe woman within a phallocratic system. Diamond, through Lacan, gets to what Barbara Freedman calls "the frame up" in representation. Yet Diamond, in this system, moves history to within textual operations, duplicating what Kipnis calls the transcendental status of the text. This move implies that "history," as Diamond would consider it, resides within the text.

Likewise, Sharon Willis uses Lacan to dismantle notions of identity in her article on *Dora*, amplifying the critique with a sense of the social "uses" of hysteria. Willis,

---

[7]Although the prevalence of Lacan in this volume reflects its prevalence within the feminist critique, it also reflects the expertise of Timothy Murray in this field and his work as editor.

[8]Laura Kipnis, "Feminism: The Political Conscience of Postmodernism?," *Universal Abandon?*, ed. Andrew Ross (Minneapolis University of Minnesota Press, 1988), 149–66.

with Barbara Freedman uses the Lacanian critique to move beyond the borders of the text to a consideration of spectatorship as what she terms "social practice." In defining this social practice, Willis theorizes the spectacle of the female body through the Lacanian apparatus. She employs the critique to dismantle "the stable instance of reception" and the notion of spectacle itself, thereby both "embodying" the spectator and mapping discontinuities in representation. Yet the "social space" that she carefully configures appears as if totally determined by the spectacle situated within psychosemiotic operations. Though less "transcendent," while less stable and continuous, spectatorship still falls outside of historical and material considerations. Although a critique of the sight/site of the female body linked to scopophilic strategies is crucial to a feminist configuration of oppression, the assimilation of the "social" into this limited frame of stage/audience may be precisely what Kipnis earlier called the "aestheticization of the political."

Yet, to reverse the dialectic, this reconfiguration of history as a textual operation and the notion of social as spectatorial exemplifies the way in which the psychoanalytic critique destabilizes the materialist notions of these same elements. Feminist critical theory has repositioned notions of history and its production through such studies, producing antinomies such as Phyllis Rackin's notion of women as "anti-historians." Rackin asserts that "The incorporation of the feminine can only take place at a point where history stops" in a "world in which history cannot be written." This assertion implies that more traditional materialist notions of history cannot account for the lives of women. Nor can prior notions of the social account for the psychosexual oppressions practiced in what was considered the private domestic sphere. Traditional history, as narrative, is then a textual operation, and the social thus reconfigured resides, in part, in spectatorship. The dialectics of this inversion are immanent in feminist uses of history and reflect the interplay between the poststructuralist/essentialist positionalities.

Kipnis makes another point about the psychoanalytic critique that may appear to be the case in this volume as well as in the larger context of feminist criticism. She argues that writers such as Kristeva, Cixous, Irigaray and Wittig in "their repudiation of representation, subjectivity, and history clearly set up the same antinomies with the popular that constituted aesthetic modernism from its inception" and what she calls the "late reception of Frankfurt school theory in France" (154). Does it mean, then, that within this approach, the texts that seem most promising as feminist are in the elitist tradition of the study of the avant-garde? Reviewing the articles here on Cixous, Benmussa, and performance art it would seem that the authors might just appear to be feminist Adornos.

Certainly, Kipnis registers that the initial romance with the postmodern has abated. The excitement that heralded the notion of a way to intervene in discourse, to think through the great brainwash has given way to a critique of its problems. Still, for intellectuals and artists in a political movement, the invention of a form, tied to a critical methodology that enables the perception of the masks of dominant ideology and tactics will always have an important function. Psychosemiotic criticism, certain varieties of deconstruction, and certain stage practices do just that with the phallic discourse, performing: the revelation of the absence of woman, her erasure in league with her sexualization, and representational practices that inscribe that erasure. Avant-garde forms, if they do not reach out to a majority of women as effectively as popular culture, do adequately perform feminism for some members of the movement.[9]

Moreover, in theatre, popular culture has often been allied with the well-made realistic play. In this volume, Glenda Dickerson refutes that form for African-American women: ". . . Aunt Jemima tapped my shoulder and told me that 'well-made'—in my case—was a phrase which modified beds" instead of plays. Aunt Jemima knows her Plato, with his famous bed analogy setting up the notion of a well-made mimesis based on the Father/Real, and revealing his fear of the "unmade bed" that reveals the woman/origin he wants to re-press. Aunt Jemima has taken away his iron. Further, Aunt Jemima perceives how the "well-made" relationship between the stage and social experience keeps the spectators mired in the glue of that binding ontological/mimetic bond—the site of reification. The spectators thus reify their own gendered, oedipalized material conditions. This petrification explains how the role of realism has become so fixed, so permanent, so lasting in the theatre—even in the seemingly resistant practice of socialist realism. No feminist wants to sleep (or perform even more stimulating acts) in that well-made bed.

The feminist resistance to patriarchal mimesis, however cannot become what Elin Diamond has called a "mom and pop mimesis"—one that simply trades the Mother for the Father.[10] This is to reject, in theatrical terms, the essentialist feminist position that maintains an origin of the Real, simply substituting the Mother origin for the Father one, that is, the mimetic play that re-presents Woman instead of Man. Here, Jill Dolan sketches out the way that such well-made mimesis petrified the potentially revolutionary lesbian theatre. The contradiction seems to remain lodged between the tradition of avant-garde resistances, with their elitist limitations as well as their transcendent performative and critical practices and a wider-reaching practice that accounts for race and class in form and in spectators as well as a critique that figures in those social and historical practices, equal to the transcendent text. One key consideration here, is the address of the critical and stage practice. Why does the feminist community need the deconstruction? What about a practice that provides precise alternatives rather than precise deconstructions?

While defending the avant-garde practice on the grounds of a community-specific address, it must be noted that one of the strengths of the psychosemiotic approach has been its strategies that enable an interaction directly with the frightening world of the fathers in which the feminist must negotiate with violent mysogynistic inscriptions, or the devastating effects of total absence. The power and accuracy of its

---

[9]I am reminded here of Brecht's invention of the Learning Play, specifically *The Measures Taken*, in terms of how it performed the elements of dialectical materialism specifically for agitators. It was both avant-garde in its form and designed for a limited audience, while remaining politically effective.

[10]Elin Diamond, "Mimesis, Mimicry and the 'True-Real,' " *Modern Drama* 32:1 (1989): 58–72. Apparently, as Diamond has informed me, the term "mom and pop mimesis," which I read in the manuscript was cut by the editors of the journal. Nevertheless, the point is still made.

dismantling apparatus seem adequate to the project of surviving the destructive forces in patriarchal social practices and discourse. For example, Carol Cook, in tracing the evacuation of the site of woman in *Troilus and Cressida*, along with the phallic, Oedipalized tropes that enable it, creates her own feminist Komos, abandoning the paters to the "violent embrace" of arms found in the concomitant "eroticization of combat." The Lacanian critique mobilizes the critic to move among the devices of dominant representation and reception and to thus "disarm" the gendering and oedipalizing operations within it that are key to its oppression of women.

I would like to back off for a moment from the scrutiny of forms to a broader viewpoint at which another locus of labor appears, common to both critiques, that influences the above dialectic. In part, the current situation proceeds from the critical focus on the subject position. Although this concern has been characterized by Gayatri Spivak as a First World one,[11] reflecting its own elite subject position on the international scene, it has nevertheless promised the feminist critique a new hope for agency. Woman-as-subject moves away from the prior focus on woman-as-object that inscribed passivity onto the position. The reconfiguration of the subject position promised motility and agency in discursive and experiential systems.

Yet the Lacanian critique, in its focus on woman as Other returns to the focus on woman as object. Although the psychosemiotic critique seems to address woman-as-subject, that subject position still operates solely within the patriarchal economy, reinscribing the Othering process on woman as she, at best, inscribes it upon herself with a vengeance of excess. This move, though seeming to advance the cause, actually produces a kind of stasis—a redefinition of the subject position in the specificity of its objecthood. Judith Butler contradicts this psychosemiotic configuration of the body by insisting that: "The body is not passively scripted with cultural codes, as if it were a lifeless recipient of wholly pre-given codes." Although Jeanie Forte points out that Rachel Rosenthal performs just that resistance in her "Bonsoir Dr. Schön," isn't there a kind of stasis produced in locating agency within that oppression? Additionally, the critic's focus remains on oppression and absence.

The "objecthood" inscribed on the subject position has also been configured in the materialist inscription of "differences." There, as illustrated in articles by Yvonne Yarbro-Bejarano and Vicki Patraka, the subject has become the specific conglomerate of one's oppressed object positions, negotiated with other oppressed, or "different" positionalities within that field. As Patraka illustrates, in her careful eschewing of essentialist notions of "Jewishness" in contrast to its historical uses, in working out the specificities of such a dialectical self-criticism, the analysis has not yet inhabited a feminist notion of a resistant agency.

The motility of the subject among "differences," then, has become its specific, historical movement along the axis of inclusionary/exclusionary practices. While the subject moves to broader and more specific inclusionary positions, it does little else.

[11]Gayatri Chakravorty Spivak, "Can the Subaltern Speak?" *Marxism and the Interpretation of Culture*, eds. Nelson, Grossberg (Urbana: University of Illinois Press, 1988), 271–2.

Moreover, the revision of simpler terms into more complex, heterogeneous ones has caused the evacuation of key sites. At this point in time, some feminist theorists acknowledge the necessity for reinhabiting in some way, the term "women" for political praxis as well as terms such as "lesbian." The Right has no trouble mobilizing forces against legalized abortion, Civil Rights measures, etc. employing just those terms the feminists have abandoned. Yet can they be re-inhabited only through Spivak's sense of "strategic essentialism?"[12] Spivak, a deconstructionist, herself admits that there is something in the deconstructive "not-not," i.e. one can-not-not want "women" to have abortion rights, that sounds obscenely crabbed in terms of social processes, in spite of her continuation of just such a practice. However, there is something in the term "strategic essentialism" that reminds this critic of the New Economic Policy instituted after the Revolution in the Soviet Union in 1921 that introduced "limited capitalism," with negative historical results.

Linda Alcoff addresses this same problem in her article "Cultural Feminism versus Post-Structuralism: The Identity Crisis in Feminist Theory."[13] As she puts it "post-structuralism deconstructs the position of the revolutionary in the same breath as it deconstructs the position of the reactionary" (418). Likewise, Nancy Hartsock asserts that the poststructural terminology is empty of any content that configures change. She further contends that such terminology is written from the perspective of dominant ideology: "One might ask, from whose perspective change appears as . . . disruptive?"[14] The emphasis in poststructuralist terminology on "strategies" such as disruption is portrayed by Hartsock as perceived from the perspective of the dominant, emptying out the articulation of what the process might really be—stalling the theoretical or practical discovery of alterity. Alterity itself, it may be noted, is a similar kind of term that simply configures a distance from the dominant. To what effect, then, is the construction of agency and motility if it figures only a "negative feminism?" This seems to be the stall in both the psychoanalytic and the materialist poststructuralist critique.

Some critics have attempted to work their way through this stall—Alcoff cites primarily de Lauretis in this regard. Here, de Lauretis works out a class-specific, lesbian-specific, or ethnic-specific critical and cinematic practice as well as a resistant spectator who reads the representational codes against dominant values. Still, de Lauretis's heterogeneous model only moves along the axis of inclusion/exclusion. In her "correction" here of an earlier article by Jill Dolan she characterizes Dolan's figuration of "lesbian desire" as "dependent on the presumption of a unified lesbian viewer/reader, gifted with undivided and non-contradictory subjectivity, and every bit as generalized and universal as the female spectator both Dolan and Davy impute (and rightly so) to the anti-pornography feminist performance art." De Lauretis,

---

[12]Gayatri Chakravorty Spivak, "Subaltern Studies: Deconstructing Historiography," in *In Other Worlds* (New York: Methuen, 1987), 205.

[13]Linda Alcoff, "Cultural Feminism versus Poststructuralism: The Identity Crises in Feminist Theory," *Signs* 13:3 (1988): 405–36.

[14]Nancy Hartsock, "Foucault: The Evanescence Of Power," *Feminism/Postmodernism*, ed. Linda Nicholson (London: Routledge, Kegan, Paul), forthcoming.

however, leaves the reader within the negative stasis of what cannot be seen. As feminism has moved to feminisms, and lesbian might move to lesbianS, one still finds, in feminist practice, the need to assert, somehow, the visible categories of "women" and "lesbian" and there comes the stall.

In this era of "differences," it is also necessary to find some notion of the "same" that allows coalition politics and united fronts to form in resistance to the increasing attacks on women's rights, civil rights for people of color, and lesbian and gay rights. A notion of the same need not become the Platonic notion of same-ness. For example, only after de Lauretis's article, it must be noted, but nevertheless following it, one might configure the same within the lesbian position. Ironically, de Lauretis figures homo-sexuality (same-sex sexuality) primarily upon differences. What about the seduction of the same? Elsewhere, when I argued for the performance of the butch/ femme roles, the masquerade of difference, I neglected to explore how the joke of that, the base that makes the camp masquerade operative is the base of the same.[15] One part of this task would be to untie the notion of the seduction of the same from Freud's idea of narcissism which so dominates that figuration. At the same time, such a lesbian critique would reveal how Freud's notion of narcissism displays his heterosexual anxiety before the seduction of the same.

This exploration of the same might lead back to the ghetto—in this case, the lesbian bar, where a closed-off utopia of the same was formed. In its windowless darkness— perhaps it really "cannot be seen"—the ghetto/bar transgresses the scopophilic trope. It is particularly difficult at this historical moment in the feminist critique to find the permission to explore that space—it seems fraught with the essentialist threat. Perhaps some way in which differences and the same operate in tandem could offer a way to proceed. Perhaps one could articulate same-sex seduction alongside class and ethnic differences. After all, the same doesn't necessarily need to denote the opposite of difference. The feminist critic might negotiate her way out of the bipolarity of definitions—the Aristotelian taxonomies of hierarchical difference. If she could retain the transgression of the seduction of same within the heterosexist social prescription, while remaining cognizant of the heterogeneity being constructed in the feminist critical community, she might move past the present stall to a motile feminist subject both within critical theory and political praxis.

[15]See my "Toward a Butch-Femme Aesthetic," in *Making a Spectacle: Feminist Essays of Contemporary Women's Theatre*, ed. Lynda Hart (Ann Arbor: University of Michigan Press, 1989).

Part I

The Margins of Sexuality

Sexual Indifference and Lesbian Representation

Teresa de Lauretis

> If it were not lesbian, this text would make no sense
> —Nicole Brossard, *L'Amèr*

There is a sense in which lesbian identity could be assumed, spoken, and articulated conceptually as political through feminism—and, current debates to wit, *against* feminism; in particular through and against the feminist critique of the Western discourse on love and sexuality, and therefore, to begin with, the rereading of psychoanalysis as a theory of sexuality and sexual difference. If the first feminist emphasis on sexual difference as gender (woman's difference from man) has rightly come under attack for obscuring the effects of other differences in women's psychosocial oppression, nevertheless that emphasis on sexual difference did open up a critical space—a conceptual, representational, and erotic space—in which women could address themselves to women. And in the very act of assuming and speaking from the position of subject, a woman could concurrently recognize women as subjects *and* as objects of female desire.

It is in such a space, hard-won and daily threatened by social disapprobation, censure, and denial, a space of contradiction requiring constant reaffirmation and painful renegotiation, that the very notion of sexual difference could then be put into question, and its limitations be assessed, both *vis-à-vis* the claims of other, not strictly sexual, differences, and with regard to sexuality itself. It thus appears that "sexual difference" is the term of a conceptual paradox corresponding to what is in effect a real contradiction in women's lives: the term, at once, of a sexual *difference* (women are, or want, something different from men) and of a sexual *indifference* (women are, or want, the same as men). And it seems to me that the racist and class-biased practices legitimated in the notion of "separate but equal" reveal a very similar paradox in the liberal ideology of pluralism, where social difference is also, at the same time, social indifference.

Teresa de Lauretis, Professor of the History of Consciousness at the University of California, Santa Cruz, is the author of Alice Doesn't: Feminism, Semiotics, Cinema *and the editor of* Feminist Studies/Critical Studies. *She is also general editor of the series "Theories of Representation and Difference" for Indiana University Press. Her most recent book is* Technologies of Gender: Essays on Theory, Film, and Fiction.

The psychoanalytic discourse on female sexuality, wrote Luce Irigaray in 1975, outlining the terms of what here I will call sexual (in)difference, tells "that *the feminine occurs only within models and laws devised by male subjects.* Which implies that there are not really two sexes, but only one. A single practice and representation of the sexual."[1] Within the conceptual frame of that *sexual indifference,* female desire for the self-same, an other female self, cannot be recognized. "That a woman might desire a woman 'like' herself, someone of the 'same' sex, that she might also have auto- and homo-sexual appetites, is simply incomprehensible" in the phallic regime of an asserted sexual difference between man and woman which is predicated on the contrary, on a complete indifference for the "other" sex, woman's. Consequently, Irigaray continues, Freud was at a loss with his homosexual female patients, and his analyses of them were really about male homosexuality. "The object choice of the homosexual woman is [understood to be] determined by a *masculine* desire and tropism"—that is, precisely, the turn of so-called sexual difference into sexual indifference, a single practice and representation of the sexual.

> So there will be no female homosexuality, just a hommo-sexuality in which woman will be involved in the process of specularizing the phallus, begged to maintain the desire for the same that man has, and will ensure at the same time, elsewhere and in complementary and contradictory fashion, the perpetuation in the couple of the pole of "matter."[2]

With the term *hommo-sexuality* [*hommo-sexualité*]—at times also written *hom(m)osexuality* [*hom(m)osexualité*]—Irigaray puns on the French word for man, *homme,* from the Latin *homo* (meaning "man"), and the Greek *homo* (meaning "same"). In taking up her distinction between homosexuality (or homo-sexuality) and "hommo-sexuality" (or "hom(m)osexuality"), I want to remark the conceptual distance between the former term, homosexuality, by which I mean lesbian (or gay) sexuality, and the diacritically marked hommo-sexuality, which is the term of sexual indifference, the term (in fact) of heterosexuality; I want to re-mark both the incommensurable distance between them and the conceptual ambiguity that is conveyed by the two almost identical acoustic images. Another paradox—or is it perhaps the same?

> There is no validation for sodomy found in the teaching of the ancient Greek philosophers Plato or Aristotle.
>
> —Michael Bowers, Petitioners Brief in *Bowers v. Hardwick.*

To attempt to answer that question, I turn to a very interesting reading of Plato's *Symposium* by David Halperin which (1) richly resonates with Irigaray's notion of sexual indifference (see also her reading of "Plato's Hystera" in *Speculum*), (2) emphasizes the embarrassing ignorance of the present Attorney General of the State of

---

[1]Luce Irigaray "Così fan tutti," in *This Sex Which Is Not One,* trans. Catherine Porter (Ithaca: Cornell University Press, 1985), 86. The phrase "sexual indifference" actually appeared in Luce Irigaray, *Speculum of the Other Woman* [1974], trans. Gillian C. Gill (Ithaca: Cornell University Press, 1985), 28.
[2]Irigaray, *Speculum,* 101–103.

Georgia in matters of classical scholarship, which he nevertheless invokes,[3] and (3) traces the roots of the paradoxes here in question to the very philosophical foundation of what is called Western civilization, Plato's dialogues. For in those master texts of hommo-sexuality, as Halperin proposes, it is the female, reproductive body that paradoxically guarantees true eros between men, or as Plato calls it, "proper paederasty."[4]

"Why Is Diotima a Woman?," Halperin argues, is a question that has been answered only tautologically: because she is not or cannot be a man. It would have been indecorous to imply that Socrates owed his knowledge of erotic desire to a former paederastic lover. But there is a reason more stringent than decorum why Socrates's teacher should have been a woman. Plato wanted to prescribe a new homoerotic ethos and a model of "proper paederasty" based on the reciprocity of erotic desire and a mutual access to pleasure for both partners, a reciprocity of eros whose philosophical import found ultimate expression in the dialogue form. His project, however, ran against the homoerotic sexual ethos and practices of the citizens of classical Athens, "locked as they were into an aggressive, phallic sexuality of domination—and, consequently, into a rigid hierarchy of sexual roles in their relations with males and females alike." For an adult male citizen of Athens could have legitimate sexual relations only with his social inferiors: boys, women, foreigners, and slaves. Plato repudiated such erotic asymmetry in relations between men and boys and, through the teaching of Socrates/Diotima, sought to erase "the distinction between the active and the passive partner—according to Socrates, both members of the relationship become active, desiring lovers; neither remains a merely passive object of desire."

Hence the intellectual and mythopoetic function of Diotima: her discourse on erotic desire, unlike a man's, could appear directly grounded in the experiential knowledge of a non-hierarchical, mutualistic and reproductive sexuality, i.e., female sexuality as the Greeks construed it. It is indeed so grounded in the text, both rhetorically (Diotima's language systematically conflates sexual pleasure with the reproductive or generative function) and narratively, in the presumed experience of a female character, since to the Greeks female sexuality differed from male sexuality precisely in that sexual pleasure for women was intimately bound up with procreation. Halperin cites many sources from Plato's *Timaeus* to various ritual practices which represented, for example, "the relation of man to wife as a domestic form of cultivation homologous to agriculture whereby women are tamed, mastered, and made fruitful. . . . [I]n the absence of men, women's sexual functioning is aimless and unproductive, merely a form of rottenness and decay, but by the application of male pharmacy it becomes at once orderly and fruitful."

---

[3]See Petitioner's Brief in *Bowers v. Hardwick*, cited by Mary Dunlap, "Brief *Amicus Curiae* for the Lesbian Rights Project et al.," *Review of Law and Social Change* 14 (1986): 960.

[4]David M. Halperin, "Why Is Diotima a Woman?," in Halperin, *One Hundred Years of Homosexuality and Other Essays on Greek Love* (forthcoming); subsequent references to this work, which is still in manuscript form, will have no page number. See also Halperin, "Plato and Erotic Reciprocity," *Classical Antiquity* 5:1 (1986): 60–80.

After remarking on the similarity between the Greek construction and the contemporary gynaecological discourses on female eroticism, Halperin raises the question of Plato's politics of gender, noting that "the interdependence of sexual and reproductive capacities is in fact a feature of male, not female, physiology," and that male sexuality is the one in which "sexual pleasure and reproductive function cannot be separated (to the chagrin of Augustine and others)." His hypothesis is worth quoting at length:

> Plato, then, would seem to be interpreting as feminine and allocating to men a form of sexuality which is masculine to begin with and which men had previously alienated from themselves by constructing it as feminine. In other words, it looks as if what lies behind Plato's doctrine is a double movement whereby men project their own sexuality onto women only to reabsorb it themselves in the guise of a feminine character. This is particularly intriguing because it suggests that in order to facilitate their own appropriation of the feminine men have initially constructed femininity according to a male paradigm while creating a social and political ideal of masculinity defined by the ability to isolate what only women can *actually* isolate—namely, sexuality and reproduction, recreative and procreative sex.

Let me restate the significance of Halperin's analysis for my own argument here. Plato's repudiation of asymmetrical paederasty and of the subordinate position in which that placed *citizen* boys who, after all, were the future rulers of Athens, had the effect of elevating the status of all male *citizens* and thus of consolidating *male citizen* rule. It certainly was no favor done to women or to any "others" (male and female foreigners, male and female slaves). But his move was yet more masterful: the appropriation of the feminine for the erotic ethos of a male social and intellectual elite (an ethos that would endure well into the twentieth century, if in the guise of "heretical ethics" or in the femininity ["*dévenir-femme*"] claimed by his most deconstructive critics)[5] had the effect not only of securing the millenary exclusion of women from philosophical dialogue, and the absolute excision of non-reproductive sexuality from the Western discourse on love. The construction and appropriation of femininity in Western erotic ethos has also had the effect of securing the heterosexual social contract by which all sexualities, all bodies, and all "others" are bonded to an ideal/ ideological hierarchy of males.[6]

The intimate relationship of sexual (in)difference with social (in)difference, whereby, for instance, the defense of the mother country and of (white) womanhood has served to bolster colonial conquest and racist violence throughout Western history, is nowhere more evident than in "the teaching of the ancient Greek philosophers," *pace* the Attorney General. Hence the ironic rewriting of history, in a female-only

---

[5]I am thinking in particular of Julia Kristeva, "Stabat Mater" (originally published as "Héréthique de l'amour") in *Tales of Love*, trans. Leon Roudiez (New York: Columbia University Press 1987), and Jacques Derrida, *Spurs: Nietzsche's Styles*, trans. Barbara Harlow (Chicago: University of Chicago Press, 1979).

[6]For a related reading of Aristotle and theatre, see Sue-Ellen Case, "Classic Drag: The Greek Creation of Female Parts," *Theatre Journal* 37:3 (1985): 317–327. I have developed the notion of heterosexual contract (originally suggested in Monique Wittig, "The Straight Mind," *Feminist Issues* 1:1 [1980]: 103–111) in my "The Female Body and Heterosexual Presumption," *Semiotica* 67:3/4 (1987): 259–79.

world of mothers and amazons, by Monique Wittig and Sande Zeig in *Lesbian Peoples: Material for a Dictionary.*[7] And hence, as well, the crucial emphasis in current feminist theory on articulating, specifying, and historicizing the position of the female social subject in the intricate experiential nexus of (often contradictory) heterogeneous differences, across discourses of race, gender, cultural, and sexual identity, and the political working through those differences toward a new, global, yet historically specific and even local, understanding of community.[8]

Pardon me, I must be going!

—Djuna Barnes, *The Ladies Almanack*

Lesbian representation, or rather, its condition of possibility, depends on separating out the two contrary undertows that constitute the paradox of sexual (in)difference, on isolating but maintaining the two senses of homosexuality and hommo-sexuality. Thus the critical effort to dislodge the erotic from the discourse of gender, with its indissoluble knot of sexuality and reproduction, is concurrent and interdependent with a rethinking of what, in most cultural discourses and sociosexual practices, is still, nevertheless, a gendered sexuality. In the pages that follow, I will attempt to work through these paradoxes by considering how lesbian writers and artists have sought variously to escape gender, to deny it, transcend it, or perform it in excess, and to inscribe the erotic in cryptic, allegorical, realistic, camp, or other modes of representation, pursuing diverse strategies of writing and of reading the intransitive and yet obdurate relation of reference to meaning, of flesh to language.

Gertrude Stein, for example, "encrypted" her experience of the body in obscure coding, her "somagrams" are neither sexually explicit or conventionally erotic, nor "radically visceral or visual," Catharine Stimpson argues.[9] Stein's effort was, rather, to develop a distinguished "anti-language" in which to describe sexual activity, her "delight in the female body" (38) or her ambivalence about it, as an abstract though intimate relationship where "the body fuses with writing itself" (36), an act "at once richly pleasurable and violent" (38). But if Stein does belong to the history of women writers, claims Stimpson, who also claims her for the history of lesbian writers, it is not because she wrote out of femaleness "as an elemental condition, inseparable from the body" (40), the way some radical feminist critics would like to think; nor because her writing sprung from a preoedipal, maternal body, as others would have it. Her language was not "female" but quite the contrary, "as genderless as an atom of platinum" (42), and strove to obliterate the boundaries of gender identity.

---

[7]Monique Wittig and Sande Zeig, *Lesbian Peoples: Material for a Dictionary* (New York: Avon Books, 1979).

[8]See Biddy Martin and Chandra Mohanty, "Feminist Politics: What's Home Got to Do with It," in *Feminist Studies/Critical Studies,* ed. Teresa de Lauretis (Bloomington: Indiana University Press, 1986), 191–212, and Teresa de Lauretis, "Eccentric Subjects: Feminist Theory and Historical Consciousness," forthcoming in *Poetics Today.*

[9]Catharine R. Stimpson, "The Somagrams of Gertrude Stein," in *The Female Body in Western Culture: Contemporary Perspectives,* ed. Susan Suleiman (Cambridge: Harvard University Press, 1986), 34.

Djuna Barnes's *Nightwood*, which Stimpson calls a "parable of damnation,"[10] is read by others as an affirmation of inversion as homosexual difference. In her "Writing Toward *Nightwood*: Djuna Barnes's Seduction Stories," Carolyn Allen reads Barnes's "little girl" stories as sketches or earlier trials of the sustained meditation on inversion that was to yield in the novel the most suggestive portrait of the invert, the third sex.

> In that portrait we recognize the boy in the girl, the girl in the Prince, not a mixing of gendered behaviors, but the creation of a new gender, "neither one and half the other" . . . . In their love of the same sex [Matthew, Nora and Robin] admire their non-conformity, their sexual difference from the rest of the world.[11]

That difference, which for the lesbian includes a relation to the self-same ("a woman is yourself caught as you turn in panic; on her mouth you kiss your own," says Nora), also includes her relation to the child, the "ambivalence about mothering one's lover," the difficult and inescapable ties of female sexuality with nurture and with violence. In this light, Allen suggests, may we read Barnes's personal denial of lesbianism and her aloofness from female admirers as a refusal to accept and to live by the homophobic categories promoted by sexology: man and woman, with their respective deviant forms, the effeminate man and the mannish woman—a refusal that in the terms of my argument could be seen as a rejection of the hommosexual categories of gender, a refusal of sexual (in)difference.

Thus the highly metaphoric, oblique, allusive language of Barnes's fiction, her "heavily embedded and often appositional" syntax, her use of the passive voice, indirect style, and interior monologue techniques in narrative descriptions, which Allen admirably analyzes in another essay, are motivated less by the modernist's pleasure in formal experimentation than by her resistance to what *Nightwood* both thematizes and demonstrates, the failure of language to represent, grasp, and convey her subjects: "The violation [of reader's expectation] and the appositional structure permit Barnes to suggest that the naming power of language is insufficient to make Nora's love for Robin perceivable to the reader."[12]

> "Dr. Knox," Edward began, "my problem this week is chiefly concerning restrooms."
>
> —Judy Grahn, "The Psychoanalysis of Edward the Dyke"

Ironically, since one way of escaping gender is to so disguise erotic and sexual experience as to suppress any representation of its specificity, another avenue of

---

[10]Catharine R. Stimpson, "Zero Degree Deviancy: The Lesbian Novel in English," *Critical Inquiry* 8:2 (1981): 369.

[11]Carolyn Allen, "Writing Toward *Nightwood*: Djuna Barnes' Seduction Stories," forthcoming in *Silence and Power: A Reevaluation of Djuna Barnes*, ed. M. L. Broe (Carbondale: Southern Illinois University Press, 1987).

[12]Carolyn Allen, " 'Dressing the Unknowable in the Garments of the Known': The Style of Djuna Barnes' *Nightwood*," in *Women's Language and Style*, ed. Butturft and Epstein (Akron: L&S Books, 1978), 116.

escape leads the lesbian writer fully to embrace gender, if by replacing femaleness with masculinity, as in the case of Stephen Gordon in *The Well of Loneliness*, and so risk to collapse lesbian homosexuality into hommo-sexuality. However, representation is related to experience by codes that change historically and, significantly, reach in both directions: the writer struggles to inscribe experience in historically available forms of representation, the reader accedes to representation through her own historical and experiential context; each reading is a rewriting of the text, each writing a rereading of (one's) experience. The contrasting readings of Radclyffe Hall's novel by lesbian feminist critics show that each critic reads from a particular position, experiential but also historically available to her, and, moreover, a position chosen, or even politically assumed, from the spectrum of contemporary discourses on the relationship of feminism to lesbianism. The contrast of interpretations also shows to what extent the paradox of sexual (in)difference operates as a semiotic mechanism to produce contradictory meaning effects.

The point of contention in the reception of a novel that by general agreement was the single most popular representation of lesbianism in fiction, from its obscenity trial in 1928 to the 1970s, is the figure of its protagonist Stephen Gordon, the "mythic mannish lesbian" of the title of Esther Newton's essay, and the prototype of her more recent incarnation, the working-class butch.[13] Newton's impassioned defense of the novel rests on the significance of that figure for lesbian self-definition, not only in the 1920s and 1930s, when the social gains in gender independence attained by the New Woman were being reappropriated via sexological discourses within the institutional practices of heterosexuality, but also in the 1970s and 1980s, when female sexuality has been redefined by a women's movement "that swears it is the enemy of traditional gender categories and yet validates lesbianism as the ultimate form of femaleness" (558).

Newton argues historically, taking into account the then available discourses on sexuality which asserted that "normal" women had at best a reactive heterosexual desire, while female sexual deviancy articulated itself in ascending categories of inversion marked by increasing masculinization, from deviant—but rectifiable—sexual orientation (or "homosexuality" proper, for Havelock Ellis) to congenital inversion. Gender crossing was at once a symptom and a sign of sexual degeneracy.[14] In the terms of the cultural representations available to the novelist, since there was no image of female sexual desire apart from the male, Newton asks, "Just how was Hall to make the woman–loving New Woman a sexual being?. . . . To become avowedly

[13]Esther Newton, "The Mythic Mannish Lesbian: Radclyffe Hall and the New Woman," *Signs* 9:4 (1984): 557–575. See also Madeline Davis and Elizabeth Lapovsky Kennedy, "Oral History and the Study of Sexuality in the Lesbian Community: Buffalo, New York, 1940–1960," *Feminist Studies* 12:1 (1986): 7–26; and Joan Nestle, "Butch-Fem Relationships: Sexual Courage in the 1950s," *Heresies* 12 (1981): 21–24, now reprinted in Joan Nestle, *A Restricted Country* (Ithaca: Firebrand Books, 1987), 100–109.

[14]See the discussion of Krafft-Ebing, Ellis, and others in George Chauncey, Jr., "From Sexual Inversion to Homosexuality: Medicine and the Changing Conceptualization of Female Deviance," *Salmagundi* 58–59 (1982–83): 114–146, and in Carroll Smith-Rosenberg, "The New Woman as Androgyne," in *Disorderly Conduct: Visions of Gender in Victorian America* (New York: Oxford University Press, 1985), 245–349.

sexual, the New Woman had to enter the male world, either as a heterosexual on male terms (a flapper) or as—or with—a lesbian in male body drag (a butch)" (572–73). Gender reversal in the mannish lesbian, then, was not merely a claim to male social privilege or a sad pretense to male sexual behavior, but represented what may be called, in Foucault's phrase, a "reverse discourse": an assertion of sexual agency and feelings, but autonomous from men, a reclaiming of erotic drives directed toward women, of a desire for women that is not to be confused with woman identification.

While other lesbian critics of *The Well of Loneliness* read it as an espousal of Ellis's views, couched in religious romantic imagery and marred by a self-defeating pessimism, aristocratic self-pity, and inevitable damnation, what Newton reads in Stephen Gordon and in Radclyffe Hall's text is the unsuccessful attempt to represent a female desire not determined by "masculine tropism," in Irigaray's words, or, in my own, a female desire not hommo-sexual but homosexual. If Radclyffe Hall herself could not envision homosexuality as part of an autonomous female sexuality (a notion that has emerged much later, with the feminist critique of patriarchy as phallic symbolic order), and if she therefore did not succeed in escaping the hommo-sexual categories of gender ("Unlike Orlando, Stephen is trapped in history; she cannot declare gender an irrelevant game," as Newton remarks [570]), nevertheless the figure of the mannish female invert continues to stand as the representation of lesbian desire against both the discourse of hommo-sexuality and the feminist account of lesbianism as woman identification. The context of Newton's reading is the current debate on the relationship of lesbianism to feminism and the reassertion, on the one hand, of the historical and political importance of gender roles (e.g., butch-femme) in lesbian self-definition and representation, and on the other, of the demand for a separate understanding of sex and gender as distinct areas of social practice.

The latter issue has been pushed to the top of the theoretical agenda by the polarization of opinions around the two adverse and widely popularized positions on the issue of pornography taken by Women Against Pornography (WAP) and by S/M lesbians (Samois). In "Thinking Sex," a revision of her earlier and very influential "The Traffic in Women," Gayle Rubin wants to challenge the assumption that feminism can contribute very much to a theory of sexuality, for "feminist thought simply lacks angles of vision which can encompass the social organization of sexuality."[15] While acknowledging some (though hardly enough) diversity among feminists on the issue of sex, and praising "pro-sex" feminists such as "lesbian sadomasochists and butch-femme dykes," adherents of "classic radical feminism," and "unapologetic heterosexuals" for not conforming to "movement standards of purity" (303), Rubin nonetheless believes that a "theory and politics specific to sexuality" must be de-

---

[15]Gayle Rubin, "Thinking Sex: Notes for a Radical Theory of the Politics of Sexuality," in *Pleasure and Danger: Exploring Female Sexuality*, ed. Carole S. Vance (Boston: Routledge & Kegan Paul, 1984), 309; "The Traffic in Women: Notes on the 'Political Economy' of Sex," in *Toward an Anthropology of Women*, ed. Rayna R. Reiter (New York: Monthly Review Press, 1975), 157–210. On the feminist "sex wars" of the 1970s and 1980s, see B. Ruby Rich, "Feminism and Sexuality in the 1980s," *Feminist Studies* 12:3 (1986): 525–561. On the relationship of feminism to lesbianism, see also Wendy Clark, "The Dyke, the Feminist and the Devil," in *Sexuality: A Reader*, ed. *Feminist Review* (London: Virago, 1987), 201–215.

veloped apart from the theory of gender oppression, that is feminism. Thus she goes back over her earlier feminist critique of Lacan and Lévi-Strauss and readjusts the angle of vision:

> "The Traffic in Women" was inspired by the literature on kin-based systems of social organization. It appeared to me at the time that gender and desire were systematically intertwined in such social formations. This may or may not be an accurate assessment of the relationship between sex and gender *in tribal organizations*. But it is surely not an adequate formulation for sexuality *in Western industrial societies*. (307, emphasis added)

In spite of Rubin's rhetorical emphasis (which I underscore graphically in the above passage), her earlier article also had to do with gender and sexuality in Western industrial societies, where indeed Rubin and several other feminists were articulating the critique of a theory of symbolic signification that elaborated the very notion of desire (from psychoanalysis) in relation to gender as symbolic construct (from anthropology)—a critique that has been crucial to the development of feminist theory. But whereas "The Traffic in Women" (a title directly borrowed from Emma Goldman) was focused on women, here her interest has shifted toward a non-gendered notion of sexuality concerned, in Foucault's terms "with the sensations of the body, the quality of pleasures, and the nature of impressions."[16]

Accordingly, the specificity of either female or lesbian eroticism is no longer a question to be asked in "Thinking Sex," where the term "homosexual" is used to refer to both women and men (thus sliding inexorably, it seems, into its uncanny hommo-sexual double), and which concludes by advocating a politics of "theoretical as well as sexual pluralism" (309). At the opposite pole of the debate, Catharine MacKinnon argues:

> If heterosexuality is the dominant gendered form of sexuality in a society where gender oppresses women through sex, sexuality and heterosexuality are essentially the same thing. This does not erase homosexuality, it merely means that sexuality in that form may be no less gendered.[17]

I suggest that, despite or possibly because of their stark mutual opposition and common reductivism, both Rubin and MacKinnon collapse the tension of ambiguity, the semantic duplicity, that I have tried to sort out in the two terms homosexual and hommo-sexual, and thus remain caught in the paradox of sexual (in)difference even as they both, undoubtedly, very much want to escape it, one by denying gender, the other by categorically asserting it. As it was, in another sense, with Radclyffe Hall, Newton's suggestive reading notwithstanding. I will return to her suggestions later on.

---

[16]Michel Foucault, *The History of Sexuality* (New York: Pantheon, 1978), 106, cited by Rubin, "Thinking Sex," 307. For a critical reading of the relevance and limitations of Foucault's views with regard to female sexuality, see Biddy Martin, "Feminism, Criticism, and Foucault," *New German Critique* 27 (1982): 3–30, and Teresa de Lauretis, *Technologies of Gender: Essays on Theory, Film, and Fiction* (Bloomington: Indiana University Press, 1987), chapters 1 and 2.

[17]Catharine A. MacKinnon, *Feminism Unmodified: Discourses on Life and Law* (Cambridge: Harvard University Press, 1987), 60.

A theory in the flesh

—Cherríe Moraga, *This Bridge Called My Back*

It is certain, however, as Rubin notes, that "lesbians are *also* oppressed as queers and perverts" (308, emphasis added), not only as women; and it is equally certain that some lesbians are also oppressed as queers and perverts, and *also* as women of color. What cannot be elided in a politically responsible theory of sexuality, of gender, or of culture is the critical value of that "also," which is neither simply additive nor exclusive but signals the nexus, the mode of operation of *interlocking* systems of gender, sexual, racial, class, and other, more local categories of social stratification.[18] Just a few lines from *Zami*, Audre Lorde's "biomythography," will make the point, better than I can.

> But the fact of our Blackness was an issue that Felicia and I talked about only between ourselves. Even Muriel seemed to believe that as lesbians, we were all outsiders and all equal in our outsiderhood. "We're all niggers," she used to say, and I hated to hear her say it. It was wishful thinking based on little fact; the ways in which it was true languished in the shadow of those many ways in which it would always be false.
> ....
> It was hard enough to be Black, to be Black and female, to be Black, female, and gay. To be Black, female, gay, and out of the closet in a white environment, even to the extent of dancing in the Bagatelle, was considered by many Black lesbians to be simply suicidal. And if you were fool enough to do it, you'd better come on so tough that nobody messed with you. I often felt put down by their sophistication, their clothes, their manners, their cars, and their femmes.[19]

If the black/white divide is even less permeable than the gay/straight one, it does not alone suffice to self-definition: "Being Black dykes together was not enough. We were different. . . . Self-preservation warned some of us that we could not afford to settle for one easy definition, one narrow individuation of self" (226). Neither race nor gender nor homosexual difference alone can constitute individual identity or the basis for a theory and a politics of social change. What Lorde suggests is a more complex image of the psycho-socio-sexual subject ("our place was the very house of difference rather [than] the security of any one particular difference") which does not deny gender or sex but transcends them. Read together with the writings of other lesbians of color or those committed to antiracism (see note 8 above), Lorde's image of the house of difference points to a conception of community not pluralistic but at once global and local—global in its inclusive and macro-political strategies, and local in its specific, micro-political practices.

I want to propose that, among the latter, not the least is the practice of writing, particularly in that form which the *québecoise* feminist writer Nicole Brossard has

---

[18]Combahee River Collective, "A Black Feminist Statement," in *This Bridge Called My Back: Writings by Radical Women of Color*, ed. Cherríe Moraga and Gloria Anzaldúa (New York: Kitchen Table: Women of Color Press, 1983), 210.

[19]Audre Lorde, *Zami: A New Spelling of My Name* (Trumansburg, New York: The Crossing Press, 1982), 203 and 224.

called *"une fiction théorique,"* fiction/theory: a formally experimental, critical and lyrical, autobiographical and theoretically conscious, practice of writing-in-the-feminine that crosses genre boundaries (poetry and prose, verbal and visual modes, narrative and cultural criticism), and instates new correlations between signs and meanings, inciting other discursive mediations between the symbolic and the real, language and flesh.[20] And for all its specific cultural, historical, and linguistic variation—say between francophone and anglophone contemporary Canadian writers, or between writers such as Gloria Anzaldúa, Michelle Cliff, Cherríe Moraga, Joanna Russ, Monique Wittig, or even the Virginia Woolf of *Three Guineas* and *A Room of One's Own*—the concept of fiction/theory does make the transfer across borderlines and covers a significant range of practices of lesbian (self-)representation.

Lesbians are not women

—Monique Wittig, "The Straight Mind"

In a superb essay tracing the intertextual weave of a lesbian imagination throughout French literature, the kind of essay that changes the landscape of both literature and reading irreversibly, Elaine Marks proposes that to undomesticate the female body one must dare reinscribe it in excess—as excess—in provocative counterimages sufficiently outrageous, passionate, verbally violent and formally complex to both destroy the male discourse on love and redesign the universe.[21] The undomesticated female body that was first *concretely* imaged in Sappho's poetry ("she is suggesting equivalences between the physical symptoms of desire and the physical symptoms of death, not between Eros and Thanatos," Marks writes [372]) has been read and effectively recontained within the male poetic tradition—with the very move described by Halperin above—as phallic or maternal body. Thereafter, Marks states, no "sufficiently challenging counterimages" were produced in French literature until the advent of feminism and the writing of a lesbian feminist, Monique Wittig.

"Only the women's movement," concurred the writer in her preface to the 1975 English edition of *The Lesbian Body*, "has proved capable of producing lesbian texts

---

[20]"Writing. It's work. Changing the relationship with language. . . . Women's fictions raise theoretical issues: women's theorizing appears as/in fiction. Women's writing disturbs our usual understanding of the terms fiction and theory which assign value to discourses. . . . Fiction/theory has been the dominant mode of feminist writing in Québec for more than a decade," states Barbara Godard for the editorial collective of *Tessera* no. 3, a Canadian feminist, dual-language publication that has appeared annually as a special issue of an already established magazine ("Fiction/Theory: Editorial," *Canadian Fiction Magazine* 57 [1986]: 3–4). See Nicole Brossard, *L'Amèr ou Le Chapitre effrité* (Montréal: Quinze, 1977) and *These Our Mothers Or: The Disintegrating Chapter*, trans. Barbara Godard (Toronto: Coach House, 1983). On Brossard and other Canadian writers of fiction/theory, see Shirley Neuman, "Importing Difference," and other essays in *A Mazing Space: Writing Canadian Women Writing*, ed. Shirley Neuman and Smaro Kamboureli (Edmonton: Longspoon Press and NeWest Press, 1986).

[21]Elaine Marks, "Lesbian Intertextuality," in *Homosexualities and French Literature*, ed. George Stambolian and Elaine Marks (Ithaca: Cornell University Press, 1979), 353–377.

in a context of total rupture with masculine culture, texts written by women exclusively for women, careless of male approval."[22] If there is reason to believe that Wittig would no longer accept the designation lesbian-feminist in the 1980s (her latest published novel in English, *Across the Acheron*, more than suggests as much), Marks's critical assessment of *The Lesbian Body* remains, to my way of seeing, correct:

> In *Le corps lesbien* Monique Wittig has created, through the incessant use of hyperbole and a refusal to employ traditional body codes, images sufficiently blatant to withstand reabsorption into male literary culture. . . . The J/e of *Le corps lesbien* is the most powerful lesbian in literature because as a lesbian-feminist she reexamines and redesigns the universe. (375–76)

Like Djuna Barnes's, Wittig's struggle is with language, to transcend gender. Barnes, as Wittig reads her, succeeds in "universalizing the feminine" because she "cancels out the genders by making them obsolete. I find it necessary to suppress them. That is the point of view of a lesbian."[23] And indeed, from the impersonal *on* [one] in *L'Opoponax*, to the feminine plural *elles* [they] replacing the generic masculine *ils* [they] in *Les guérillères*, to the divided, linguistically impossible *j/e* [*I*], lover and writing subject of *The Lesbian Body*, Wittig's personal pronouns work to "lesbianize" language as impudently as her recastings of both classical and Christian myth and Western literary genres (the Homeric heroes and Christ, *The Divine Comedy* and *Don Quixote*, the epic, the lyric, the *Bildungsroman*, the encyclopaedic dictionary) do to literary history.[24] What will not do, for her purposes, is a "feminine writing" [*écriture féminine*] which, for Wittig, is no more than "the naturalizing metaphor of the brutal political fact of the domination of women" (63) and so complicit in the reproduction of femininity and of the female body as Nature.

Thus, as I read it, it is in the garbage dump of femininity, "In this dark adored adorned gehenna," that the odyssey of Wittig's *j/e-tu* in *The Lesbian Body* begins: "Fais tes adieux m/a très belle," "say your farewells m/y very beautiful . . . strong . . . indomitable . . . learned . . . ferocious . . . gentle . . . best beloved to what they call affection tenderness or gracious abandon. No one is unaware of what takes place here, it has no name as yet."[25] Here where?—in this book, this journey into the body of Western culture, this season in hell. And what takes place here?—the dismemberment and slow decomposition of the *female* body limb by limb, organ by organ, secretion by secretion. No one will be able to stand the sight of it, no one will come to aid in this awesome, excruciating and exhilarating labor of love: dis-membering

---

[22]Monique Wittig, *The Lesbian Body*, trans. David LeVay (New York: William Morrow, 1975), 9, cited by Marks, 373.

[23]Monique Wittig, "The Point of View: Universal or Particular," *Feminist Issues* 3:2 (1983): 64.

[24]See Hélène Vivienne Wenzel, "The Text as Body/Politics: An Appreciation of Monique Wittig's Writings in Context," *Feminist Studies* 7:2 (1981): 264–287, and Namascar Shaktini, "Displacing the Phallic Subject: Wittig's Lesbian Writing," *Signs* 8:1 (1982): 29–44, who writes: "Wittig's reorganization of metaphor around the lesbian body represents an epistemological shift from what seemed until recently the absolute, central metaphor—the phallus" (29).

[25]Monique Wittig, *Le corps lesbien* (Paris: Minuit, 1973), 7. I have revised the English translation that appears in *The Lesbian Body*, 15.

and re-membering, reconstituting the body in a new erotic economy, relearning to know it ("it has no name as yet") by another semiotics, reinscribing it with invert/inward desire, rewriting it otherwise, other-wise: a *lesbian* body.

The project, the conceptual originality and radical import of Wittig's lesbian as subject of a "cognitive practice" that enables the reconceptualization of the social and of knowledge itself from a position eccentric to the heterosexual institution, are all there in the first page of *Le corps lesbien*.[26] A "subjective cognitive practice" and a practice of writing as consciousness of contradiction ("the language you speak is made up of words that are killing you," she wrote in *Les guérillères*); a consciousness of writing, living, feeling, and desiring in the noncoincidence of experience and language, in the interstices of representation, "in the intervals that your masters have not been able to fill with their words of proprietors."[27] Thus, the struggle with language to rewrite the body beyond its precoded, conventional representations is not and cannot be a reappropriation of the female body as it is, domesticated, maternal, oedipally or preoedipally en-gendered, but is a struggle to transcend both gender and "sex" and recreate the body other-wise: to see it perhaps as monstrous, or grotesque, or mortal, or violent, and certainly also sexual, but with a material and sensual specificity that will resist phallic idealization and render it accessible to women in another sociosexual economy. In short, if it were not lesbian, this body would make no sense.

> Replacing the Lacanian slash with a lesbian bar
>
> —Sue-Ellen Case, "Towards a Butch Femme Aesthetic"

At first sight, the reader of *The Lesbian Body* might find in its linguistically impossible subject pronoun several theoretically possible valences that go from the more conservative (the slash in *j/e* represents the division of the Lacanian subject) to the less conservative (*j/e* can be expressed by writing but not by speech, representing Derridean *différance*), and to the radical feminist ("*j/e* is the symbol of the lived, rending experience which is *m/y* writing, of this cutting in two which throughout literature is the exercise of a language which does not constitute m/e as subject," as Wittig is reported to have said in Margaret Crosland's introduction to the Beacon paperback edition I own). Another reader, especially if a reader of science fiction, might think of Joanna Russ's brilliant lesbian-feminist novel, *The Female Man*, whose protagonist is a female genotype articulated across four spacetime probabilities in four characters whose names all begin with J—Janet, Jeannine, Jael, Joanna—and whose sociosexual practices cover the spectrum from celibacy and "politically correct" monogamy to

---

[26]The concept of "subjective, cognitive practice" is elaborated in Wittig, "One Is Not Born a Woman," *Feminist Issues* 1:2 (1981): 47–54. I discuss it at some length in my "Eccentric Subjects" (note 8 above).

[27]Monique Wittig, *Les Guérillères*, trans. David LeVay (Boston: Beacon Press, 1985), 114.

live toys and the 1970s equivalent of s/m.[28] What Wittig actually said in one of her essays in the 1980s is perhaps even more extreme:

> The bar in the *j/e* of *The Lesbian Body* is a sign of excess. A sign that helps to imagine an excess of "I," an "I" exalted. "I" has become so powerful in *The Lesbian Body* that it can attack the order of heterosexuality in texts and assault the so-called love, the heroes of love, and lesbianize them, lesbianize the symbols, lesbianize the gods and the goddesses, lesbianize the men and the women. This "I" can be destroyed in the attempt and resuscitated. Nothing resists this "I" (or this *tu* [you], which is its name, its love), which spreads itself in the whole world of the book, like a lava flow that nothing can stop.[29]

Excess, an exaltation of the "I" through costume, performance, *mise-en-scène*, irony, and utter manipulation of appearance, is what Sue-Ellen Case sees in the discourse of camp. If it is deplorable that the lesbian working-class bar culture of the 1950s "went into the feminist closet" during the 1970s, when organizations such as the Daughters of Bilitis encouraged lesbian identification with the more legitimate feminist dress codes and upwardly mobile lifestyles, writes Case, "yet the closet, or the bars, with their hothouse atmosphere [have] given us camp—the style, the discourse, the *mise-en-scène* of butch-femme roles." In these roles, "recuperating the space of seduction,"

> the butch-femme couple inhabit the subject position together. . . . These are not split subjects, suffering the torments of dominant ideology. They are coupled ones that do not impale themselves on the poles of sexual difference or metaphysical values, but constantly seduce the sign system, through flirtation and inconstancy into the light fondle of artifice, replacing the Lacanian slash with a lesbian bar.[30]

The question of address, of who produces cultural representations and for whom (in any medium, genre, or semiotic system, from writing to performance), and of who receives them and in what contexts, has been a major concern of feminism and other critical theories of cultural marginality. In the visual arts, that concern has focused on the notion of spectatorship, which has been central to the feminist critique of representation and the production of different images of difference, for example

---

[28]Joanna Russ, *The Female Man* (New York: Bantam, 1975). See also Catherine L. McClenahan, "Textual Politics: The Uses of Imagination in Joanna Russ's *The Female Man*," *Transactions of the Wisconsin Academy of Sciences, Arts and Letters* 70 (1982): 114–125.

[29]Monique Wittig, "The Mark of Gender," *Feminist Issues* 5:2 (1985): 71.

[30]Sue-Ellen Case, "Towards a Butch-Femme Aesthetic," in *Feminist Perspectives on Contemporary Women's Drama*, ed. Lynda Hart (Ann Arbor: University of Michigan Press, forthcoming). The butch-femme couple, like Wittig's *j/e-tu* and like the s/m lesbian couple—all of whom, in their respective self-definitions, are one the name and the love of the other—propose a dual subject that brings to mind again Irigaray's *This Sex Which Is Not One*, though they all would adamantly deny the latter's suggestion that a non-phallic eroticism may be traced to the preoedipal relation to the mother. One has to wonder, however, whether the denial has more to do with the committedly heterosexual bias of neo-Freudian psychoanalysis and object relations theory, with their inability to work through the paradox of sexual (in)difference on which they are founded but perhaps not destined to, or with our rejection of the maternal body which phallic representation has utterly alienated from women's love, from our desire for the self-same, by colonizing it as the "dark continent" and so rendering it at once powerless and inaccessible to us and to all "others."

in women's cinema.[31] Recent work in both film and performance theory has been elaborating the film-theoretical notion of spectatorship with regard to what may be the specific relations of homosexual subjectivity, in several directions. Elizabeth Ellsworth, for one, surveying the reception of *Personal Best* (1982), a commercial man-made film about a lesbian relationship between athletes, found that lesbian feminist reviews of the film adopted interpretive strategies which rejected or altered the meaning carried by conventional (Hollywood) codes of narrative representation. For example, they redefined who was the film's protagonist or "object of desire," ignored the sections focused on heterosexual romance, disregarded the actual ending and speculated, instead, on a possible extratextual future for the characters beyond the ending. Moreover, "some reviewers named and illicitly eroticized moments of the film's 'inadvertent lesbian verisimilitude' [in Patrice Donnelly's performance] . . . codes of body language, facial expression, use of voice, structuring and expression of desire and assertion of strength in the face of male domination and prerogative."[32]

While recognizing limits to this "oppositional appropriation" of dominant representation, Ellsworth argues that the struggle over interpretation is a constitutive process for marginal subjectivities, as well as an important form of resistance. But when the marginal community is directly addressed, in the context of out-lesbian performance such as the WOW Cafe or the Split Britches productions, the appropriation seems to have no limits, to be directly "subversive," to yield not merely a site of interpretive work and resistance but a representation that requires no interpretive effort and is immediately, univocally legible, signalling "the creation of new imagery, new metaphors, and new conventions that can be read, or given new meaning, by a very specific spectator."[33]

The assumption behind this view, as stated by Kate Davy, is that such lesbian performance "undercut[s] the heterosexual model by implying a spectator that is not the generic, universal male, not the cultural construction 'woman,' but lesbian—a subject defined in terms of sexual similarity . . . whose desire lies outside the fundamental model or underpinnings of sexual difference" (47). Somehow, this seems too easy a solution to the problem of spectatorship, and even less convincing as a representation of "lesbian desire." For, if sexual similarity could so unproblematically replace sexual difference, why would the new lesbian theatre need to insist on gender, if only as "the residue of sexual difference" that is, as Davy herself insists, worn in the "stance, gesture, movement, mannerisms, voice, and dress" (48) of the butch-

---

[31]See, for example, Judith Mayne, "The Woman at the Keyhole: Women's Cinema and Feminist Criticism," and B. Ruby Rich, "From Repressive Tolerance to Erotic Liberation: *Maedchen in Uniform*," in *Re-vision: Essays in Feminist Film Criticism*, ed. Mary Ann Doane, Patricia Mellencamp, and Linda Williams (Frederick, Md.: University Publications of America and the American Film Institute, 1984), 49–66 and 100–130; and Teresa de Lauretis, "Rethinking Women's Cinema: Aesthetics and Feminist Theory," in *Technologies of Gender*, 127–148.

[32]Elizabeth Ellsworth, "Illicit Pleasures: Feminist Spectators and *Personal Best*," *Wide Angle* 8:2 (1986): 54.

[33]Kate Davy, "Constructing the Spectator: Reception, Context, and Address in Lesbian Performance," *Performing Arts Journal* 10:2 (1986): 49.

femme play? Why would lesbian camp be taken up in theatrical performance, as Case suggests, to recuperate that space of seduction which historically has been the lesbian bar, and the Left Bank salon before it—spaces of daily-life performance, masquerade, cross-dressing, and practices constitutive of both community and subjectivity?

In an essay on "The Dynamics of Desire" in performance and pornography, Jill Dolan asserts that the reappropriation of pornography in lesbian magazines ("a visual space meant at least theoretically to be free of male subordination") offers "liberative fantasies" and "representations of one kind of sexuality based in lesbian desire," adding that the "male forms" of pornographic representation "acquire new meanings when they are used to communicate desire for readers of a different gender and sexual orientation."[34] Again, as in Davy, the question of lesbian desire is begged; and again the ways in which the new context would produce new meanings or "disrupt traditional meanings" (173) appear to be dependent on the presumption of a unified lesbian viewer/reader, gifted with undivided and non-contradictory subjectivity, and every bit as generalized and universal as the female spectator both Dolan and Davy impute (and rightly so) to the anti-pornography feminist performance art. For, if all lesbians had one and the same definition of "lesbian desire," there would hardly be any debate among us, or any struggle over interpretations of cultural images, especially the ones we produce.

What is meant by a term so crucial to the specificity and originality claimed for these performances and strategies of representation, is not an inappropriate question, then. When she addresses it at the end of her essay, Dolan writes: "Desire is not necessarily a fixed, male-owned commodity, but can be exchanged, with a much different meaning, between women" (173). Unless it can be taken as the ultimate camp representation, this notion of lesbian desire as commodity exchange is rather disturbing. For, unfortunately—or fortunately, as the case may be—commodity exchange does have the same meaning "between women" as between men, by definition—that is, by Marx's definition of the structure of capital. And so, if the "aesthetic differences between cultural feminist and lesbian performance art" are to be determined by the presence or absence of pornography, and to depend on a "new meaning" of commodity exchange, it is no wonder that we seem unable to get it off (our backs) even as we attempt to take it on.

> The king does not count lesbians
>
> —Marilyn Frye, *The Politics of Reality*

The difficulty in defining an autonomous form of female sexuality and desire in the wake of a cultural tradition still Platonic, still grounded in sexual (in)difference, still caught in the tropism of hommo-sexuality, is not to be overlooked or willfully

---

[34]Jill Dolan, "The Dynamics of Desire: Sexuality and Gender in Pornography and Performance," *Theatre Journal* 39:2 (1987): 171.

Lois Weaver and Sheila Dabney in *She Must Be Seeing Things* (1987),
directed by Sheila McLaughlin. Photo, Anita Bartsch.

bypassed. It is perhaps even greater than the difficulty in devising strategies of representation which will, in turn, alter the standard of vision, the frame of reference of visibility, of *what can be seen*. For, undoubtedly, that is the project of lesbian performance, theatre and film, a project that has already achieved a significant measure of success, not only at the WOW Cafe but also, to mention just a few examples, in Cherríe Moraga's *teatro*, *Giving Up the Ghost* (1986), Sally Potter's film *The Gold Diggers* (1983), or Sheila McLaughlin's *She Must Be Seeing Things* (1987). My point here is that redefining the conditions of vision, as well as the modes of representing, cannot be predicated on a single, undivided identity of performer and audience (whether as "lesbians" or "women" or "people of color" or any other single category constructed in opposition to its dominant other, "heterosexual women," "men," "whites," and so forth).

Consider Marilyn Frye's suggestive Brechtian parable about our culture's conceptual reality ("phallocratic reality") as a conventional stage play, where the actors—those committed to the performance/maintenance of the Play, "the phallocratic loyalists"—visibly occupy the foreground, while stagehands—who provide the necessary labor and framework for the material (re)production of the Play—remain invisible in the background. What happens, she speculates, when the stagehands (women, feminists) begin thinking of themselves as actors and try to participate visibly in the performance, attracting attention to their activities and their own role in the play? The loyalists cannot conceive that anyone in the audience may see or focus their attention on the stagehands' projects in the background, and thus become "disloyal"

Sheila Dabney in *She Must Be Seeing Things* (1987), directed by Sheila McLaughlin.
Photo: Chris Boas.

to the Play, or, as Adrienne Rich has put it, "disloyal to civilization."[35] Well, Frye suggests, there are some people in the audience who do see what the conceptual system of heterosexuality, the Play's performance, attempts to keep invisible. These are lesbian people, who can see it because their own reality is not represented or even surmised in the Play, and who therefore reorient their attention toward the background, the spaces, activities and figures of women elided by the performance. But "attention is a kind of passion" that "fixes and directs the application of one's physical and emotional work":

> If the lesbian sees the women, the woman may see the lesbian seeing her. With this, there is a flowering of possibilities. The woman, feeling herself seen, may learn that she *can be* seen; she may also be able to know that a woman can see, that is, can author perception. . . . The lesbian's seeing undercuts the mechanism by which the production and constant reproduction of heterosexuality for women was to be rendered *automatic.* (172)

And this is where we are now, as the critical reconsideration of lesbian history past and present is doing for feminist theory what Pirandello, Brecht, and others did for the bourgeois theatre conventions, and avant-garde filmmakers have done for Hol-

---

[35]"To Be and Be Seen," in Marilyn Frye, *The Politics of Reality: Essays in Feminist Theory* (Trumansburg, New York: The Crossing Press, 1983), 166–173; Adrienne Rich, "Disloyal to Civilization: Feminism, Racism, Gynephobia," in *On Lies, Secrets, and Silence: Selected Prose 1966–1978* (New York: Norton, 1979), 275–310.

lywood cinema; the latter, however, have not just disappeared, much as one would wish they had. So, too, have the conventions of seeing, and the relations of desire and meaning in spectatorship, remained partially anchored or contained by a frame of visibility that is still heterosexual, or hommo-sexual, and just as persistently color blind.

For instance, what are the "things" the Black/Latina protagonist of McLaughlin's film imagines seeing, in her jealous fantasies about her white lover (although she does not "really" see them), if not those very images which our cultural imaginary and the whole history of cinema have constructed as the visible, what can *be seen*, and eroticized? The originality of *She Must Be Seeing Things* is in its representing *the question of* lesbian desire in these terms, as it engages the contradictions and complicities that have emerged subculturally, in both discourses and practices, through the feminist-lesbian debates on sex-radical imagery as a political issue of representation, as well as real life. It may be interestingly contrasted with a formally conventional film like Donna Deitch's *Desert Hearts* (1986), where heterosexuality remains off screen, in the diegetic background (in the character's past), but is actively present nonetheless in the spectatorial expectations set up by the genre (the love story) and the visual pleasure procured by conventional casting, cinematic narrative procedures, and commercial distribution. In sum, one film works *with and against* the institutions of heterosexuality and cinema, the other works *with* them. A similar point could be made about certain films with respect to the novels they derive from, such as *The Color Purple* or *Kiss of the Spider Woman*, where the critical and formal work of the novels against the social and sexual indifference built into the institution of heterosexuality is altogether suppressed and rendered invisible by the films' compliance with the apparatus of commercial cinema and its institutional drive to, precisely, commodity exchange.

So what *can* be seen? Even in feminist film theory, the current "impasse regarding female spectatorship is related to the blind spot of lesbianism," Patricia White suggests in her reading of Ulrike Ottinger's film *Madame X: An Absolute Ruler* (1977).[36] That film, she argues, on the contrary, displaces the assumption "that feminism finds its audience 'naturally' "(95); it does so by addressing the female spectator through specific scenarios and "figures of spectatorial desire" and "trans-sex identification," through figures of transvestism and masquerade. And the position the film thus constructs for its spectator is not one of essential femininity or impossible masculinization (as proposed by Mary Ann Doane and Laura Mulvey, respectively), but rather a position of marginality or "deviance" *vis-à-vis* the normative heterosexual frame of vision.[37]

Once again, what *can* be seen? "When I go into a store, people see a black person and only incidentally a woman," writes Jewelle Gomez, a writer of science fiction

[36]Patricia White, "Madame X of the China Seas," *Screen* 28:4 (1987): 82.

[37]The two essays discussed are Mary Ann Doane, "Film and the Masquerade: Theorising the Female Spectator," *Screen* 23:3–4 (1982): 74–87, and Laura Mulvey, "Afterthoughts on 'Visual Pleasure and Narrative Cinema' Inspired by *Duel in the Sun*," *Framework* 15/16/17 (1981): 12–15. Another interesting discussion of the notion of masquerade in lesbian representation may be found in Sue-Ellen Case, "Toward a Butch-Femme Aesthetic."

and author of at least one vampire story about a black lesbian blues singer named Gilda. "In an Upper West Side apartment building late at night when a white woman refuses to get on an elevator with me, it's because I am black. She sees a mugger as described on the late night news, not another woman as nervous to be out alone as she is."[38] If my suspicion that social and sexual indifference are never far behind one from the other is not just an effect of paranoia, it is quite possible that, in the second setting, the elevator at night, what a white woman sees superimposed on the black image of the mugger is the male image of the dyke, and both of these together are what prevents the white woman from seeing the other one like herself. Nevertheless, Gomez points out, "I can pass as straight, if by some bizarre turn of events I should want to . . . but I cannot pass as white in this society." Clearly, the very issue of passing, across any boundary of social division, is related quite closely to the frame of vision and the conditions of representation.

"Passing demands quiet. And from that quiet—silence," writes Michelle Cliff.[39] It is "a dual masquerade—passing straight/passing lesbian [that] enervates and contributes to speechlessness—to speak might be to reveal."[40] However, and paradoxically again, speechlessness can only be overcome, and her "journey into speech" begin, by "claiming an identity they taught me to despise"; that is, by passing black "against a history of forced fluency," a history of passing white.[41] The dual masquerade, her writing suggests, is at once the condition of speechlessness and of overcoming speechlessness, for the latter occurs by recognizing and representing the division in the self, the difference and the displacement from which any identity that needs to be claimed derives, and hence can be claimed only, in Lorde's words, as "the very house of difference."

Those divisions and displacements in history, memory, and desire are the "ghost" that Moraga's characters want to but cannot altogether give up. The division of the Chicana lesbian Marisa/Corky from the Mexican Amalia, whose desire cannot be redefined outside the heterosexual imaginary of her culture, is also the division of Marisa/Corky from herself, the split produced in the girl Corky by sexual and social indifference, and by her internalization of a notion of hommo-sexuality which Marisa now lives as a wound, an infinite distance between her female body and her desire for women. If "the realization of shared oppression on the basis of being women and Chicanas holds the promise of a community of Chicanas, both lesbians and heterosexual," Yvonne Yarbro-Bejarano states, nevertheless "the structure of the play does not move neatly from pain to promise," and the divisions within them remain

[38]Jewelle Gomez, "Repeat After Me: We Are Different. We Are the Same," *Review of Law and Social Change* 14:4 (1986): 939. Her vampire story is "No Day Too Long," in *Worlds Apart: An Anthology of Lesbian and Gay Science Fiction and Fantasy*, ed. Camilla Decarnin, Eric Garber, and Lyn Paleo (Boston: Alyson Publications, 1986), 215–223.

[39]"Passing," in Michelle Cliff, *The Land of Look Behind* (Ithaca: Firebrand Books, 1985), 22.

[40]Michelle Cliff, "Notes on Speechlessness," *Sinister Wisdom* 5 (1978): 7.

[41]Michelle Cliff, "A Journey into Speech" and "Claiming an Identity They Taught Me to Despise," both in *The Land of Look Behind*, 11–17 and 40–47; see also her novel *No Telephone To Heaven* (New York: E. P. Dutton, 1987).

unresolved.[42] The character Marisa, however, I would add, has moved away from the hommo-sexuality of Corky (her younger self at age 11 and 17); and with the ambiguous character of Amalia, who loved a man almost as if he were a woman and who can love Marisa only when she (Amalia) is no longer one, the play itself has moved away from any simple opposition of "lesbian" to "heterosexual" and into the conceptual and experiential continuum of a female, Chicana subjectivity from where the question of lesbian desire must finally be posed. The play ends with that question—which is at once its outcome and its achievement, its éxito.

> What to do with the feminine invert?
>
> —Esther Newton, "The Mythic Mannish Lesbian"

Surveying the classic literature on inversion, Newton notes that Radclyffe Hall's "vision of lesbianism as sexual difference and as masculinity," and her "conviction that sexual desire must be male," both assented to and sought to counter the sociomedical discourses of the early twentieth century. "The notion of a feminine lesbian contradicted the congenital theory that many homosexuals in Hall's era espoused to counter the demands that they undergo punishing 'therapies' " (575). Perhaps that counter-demand led the novelist further to reduce the typology of female inversion (initially put forth by Krafft-Ebing as comprised of four types, then reduced to three by Havelock Ellis) to two: the invert and the "normal" woman who misguidedly falls in love with her. Hence the novel's emphasis on Stephen, while her lover Mary is a "forgettable and inconsistent" character who in the end gets turned over to a man. However, unlike Mary, Radclyffe Hall's real-life lover Una Troubridge "did not go back to heterosexuality even when Hall, late in her life, took a second lover," Newton points out. Una would then represent what *The Well of Loneliness* elided, the third type of female invert, and the most troublesome for Ellis: the "womanly" women "to whom the actively inverted woman is most attracted. These women differ in the first place from normal or average women in that . . . they seem to possess a genuine, though not precisely sexual, preference for women over men."[43] Therefore, Newton concludes, "Mary's real story has yet to be told" (575), and a footnote after this sentence refers us to "two impressive beginnings" of what could be Mary's real story, told from the perspective of a self-identified, contemporary femme.[44]

The discourses, demands, and counter-demands that inform lesbian identity and representation in the 1980s are more diverse and socially heterogeneous than those

---

[42]Yvonne Yarbro-Bejarano, "Cherríe Moraga's *Giving up the Ghost*: The Representation of Female Desire," *Third Woman* 3: 1–2 (1986): 118–119. See also Cherríe Moraga, *Giving Up the Ghost: Teatro in Two Acts* (Los Angeles: West End Press, 1986).

[43]Havelock Ellis, "Sexual Inversion in Women," *Alienist and Neurologist* 16 (1895): 141–158, cited by Newton, "The Mythic Mannish Lesbian," 567.

[44]Joan Nestle, "Butch-Fem Relationships" (see note 13 above) and Amber Hollibaugh and Cherríe Moraga, "What We're Rollin' Around in Bed With," both in *Heresies* 12 (1981): 21–24 and 58–62.

Lois Weaver in *She Must Be Seeing Things* (1987), directed by Sheila McLaughlin.
Photo: Anita Bartsch.

of the first half of the century. They include, most notably, the political concepts of oppression and agency developed in the struggles of social movements such as the women's movement, the gay liberation movement, and third world feminism, as well as an awareness of the importance of developing a theory of sexuality that takes into account the working of unconscious processes in the construction of female subjectivity. But, as I have tried to argue, the discourses, demands, and counter-demands that inform lesbian representation are still unwittingly caught in the paradox of socio-sexual (in)difference, often unable to think homosexuality and hommo-sexuality at once separately *and* together. Even today, in most representational contexts, Mary would be either passing lesbian or passing straight, her (homo)sexuality being in the last instance what can not be seen. Unless, as Newton and others suggest, she enter the frame of vision *as or with* a lesbian in male body drag.[45]

[45]For many of the ideas developed in this essay, I am indebted to the other participants of the student-directed seminar on Lesbian History and Theory sponsored by the Board in Studies in History of Consciousness at the University of California, Santa Cruz in Fall 1987. For support of various kinds, personal and professional, I thank Kirstie McClure, Donna Haraway, and Michael Cowan, Dean of Humanities and Arts.

" 'Lesbian' Subjectivity in Realism: Dragging at the Margins of Structure and Ideology"[1]

Jill Dolan

When lesbian subjectivity became part of the feminist theoretical discourse, discussions about its construction were located staunchly in an alternative performance tradition. The postmodernist, camp, collectivist performances of Split Britches and the WOW Cafe became the space of debate on the radical implications of lesbian desire's disruption of conventional paradigms of spectatorship. The lesbian work at WOW is very specific about the audience it addresses—an ad hoc lesbian community culled mostly from its East Village New York neighborhood.[2] The lesbian subcultural context and mode of production often make these performances illegible to the heterosexual reader/spectator.[3]

Jill Dolan is an assistant professor of Theatre and Drama and Women's Studies at the University of Wisconsin–Madison. She is the author of The Feminist Spectator as Critic *and numerous articles on feminist performance theory.*

[1]This article was written during a July 1989 residency at the Wolf Pen Women Writer's Colony in Prospect, Kentucky, funded by the Kentucky Foundation for Women. The residency was shared with Sue-Ellen Case, Elin Diamond, Janelle Reinelt, and Vivian Patraka, with whom I engaged in continual discussion around the issues I am presenting here. Their insights ghost my own in this article and their inquiries always provoked me. I am indebted to them for the support and encouragement they provided in the context of this writing. I am also indebted to Sallie Bingham for making our residency possible, and for the supportive, stimulating atmosphere she provided for feminist theoretical thinking.

[2]For work on the history of the WOW Cafe, see Alisa Solomon's "The WOW Cafe," *The Drama Review* 29:1 (1985): 92–101. See Jill Dolan, *The Feminist Spectator as Critic* (Ann Arbor: UMI Research Press, 1988), Kate Davy, "Reading Past the Heterosexual Imperative: *Dress Suits to Hire*," *The Drama Review* 33:1 (1989): 153–70, Kate Davy, "Constructing the Spectator: Reception, Context, and Address in Lesbian Performance," *Performing Arts Journal* 10:2 (1986), 74–87, and Sue-Ellen Case, "From Split Subject to Split Britches," in Enoch Brater, ed. *Feminine Focus* (New York: Oxford University Press, 1989) for writing on Split Britches and the WOW Cafe, as well as the issue of lesbian desire and representation.

[3]See Davy, "Reading Past the Heterosexual Imperative," for a discussion of *Dress Suits for Hire* in which she argues that the semiotics of lesbian representation is intentionally organized to thwart heterosexual readings. Davy proposes a somewhat essentialist position for the lesbian performers

40

Partially because of the increased theoretical writing on lesbian performance, the work has gained a notoriety that enhances its marketplace value. As lesbian work is brought out of its marginalized context and traded as critical currency in heterosexual academic and theatre venues, the question of the performance's "readability" becomes complicated.[4] What does it mean for lesbian texts to circulate on the heterosexual marketplace? Is a lesbian performance transported to a heterosexual context readable, or is it illegible because it is inflected with subcultural meanings that require a lesbian viewer to negotiate? Is the intentional obtuseness of its postmodern structure frustrating for the uninitiated spectator? Which is more frustrating, its lesbian content, or its postmodern form? If lesbian performance is now being created for mixed audiences, will the new context prompt a return to more conventional forms and their meanings?

These questions raise the issue of realism's efficacy as a political strategy in lesbian representation. My task here is to return to realism, which has been eclipsed by the postmodern performance work in discussions of lesbian representation. My theoretical project is to explore how lesbian positions are constructed under realism's formal constraints, and to answer revisionist feminist critics who suggest that dabbling in traditional forms might be an effective method of insinuating social change. The realist plays examined below cross a historical spectrum, from plays written by heterosexuals for heterosexuals to those written by lesbians and performed in lesbian, alternative, and mainstream venues.

These texts also address the theoretical problem of constructing lesbian subject positions. Much of the work on lesbian subjectivity in representation has been deconstructive, pointing to the possibilities of the lesbian position as excessive to representation's conventional codes. In the process of deconstructing representation, the lesbian subject position within it was unwittingly posited as essential and whole, unproblematized in the transcendent, unified position it had assumed. Teresa de Lauretis, in a 1988 *Theatre Journal* article, took the next step in the theoretical debate

---

in the piece, and Case, in a forthcoming letter to *The Drama Review*, reads it as Shepardesque, transposing traditional tropes of the Old West to a lesbian context without radically changing their meanings. The question of this piece's legibility to heterosexual audiences is an important tangent to the discussion of lesbian realism that follows here. Additional debates about its production venues are set forth in *The Drama Review* 33:1 (1989).

[4]The performance narrative and production context of Holly Hughes's latest solo piece, *World Without End* (1988), is somewhat revealing in this regard. In "Polymorphous Perversity and the Lesbian Scientist," (*The Drama Review* 33:1 (1989): 171–83), an interview with Hughes, Rebecca Schneider remarked that Hughes's piece is "in some ways flavored by the recent appearances of lesbian theatre before more diverse audiences" (172). The mix of heterosexual and lesbian spectators might be the condition that allows Hughes to bring her bisexuality out of the closet in *World*. The piece is a long, autobiographical monologue about Hughes's relationships with her mother, other women and men. Her usual maniacal, unpredictable stage presence is exchanged for the high-heeled, prettily dressed, lugubrious politeness of the family drama. Her adamant flaunting of her "polymorphous perversity" (173) constructs her as sexually autonomous, but in the process, unmoors her from the lesbian community that fostered her early work. Hughes has been domesticated by her own bisexual, bourgeois narrative.

by explicitly deconstructing the lesbian subject position into a heterogeneous site of differences.[5]

The most politically and theoretically appropriate lesbian subject position now seems to be a deconstructive one. But the term "lesbian" seems evacuated, its meaning eternally deferred. For theorists who would continue to write from within a lesbian position—if only provisionally, and if only one among many—the challenge becomes to reconstruct lesbian subject positions without reinstating essentialisms. While theorists teeter between the deconstructive possibilities and the essentialist problems of writing on lesbian subjectivity, representations of lesbians in realism continue to construct their conditions of objecthood.[6] The realist structure offers unhappy positionalities for lesbians, the ideological inflections of which are crucial to mark. My project, then, includes an investigation of how realism constructs the term "lesbian."

Realism and the Case for Readability

Janelle Reinelt, in a historical overview of feminist theory and performance, describes the first phase of feminist criticism as one which believed optimistically that realism "seemed capable of reflecting the 'true' (her) story of women's lives in a direct, unmediated manner."[7] Those were halcyon days, when the project of feminist criticism seemed simply to agitate for more positive images of women within traditional theatrical forms. Since then, the Marxist critique of representation, as well as poststructuralism and postmodernism, have been pressed into service for feminism to explode the notion of coherent texts whose transparent language is capable of projecting a stable meaning.

The "new poetics" have thrown into doubt the project of inserting a feminist agenda into the realist guise.[8] "Unmediated" realism has since been theorized as a site in which ideology intervenes in a very material way to inflect the meanings of the text. The mystification of the author, and his or her singular authority over the construction of meaning in the text; the position of the spectator as the competent interpreter of the realist text; and the mimetic function of realism as a mirror that truthfully records an objective social portrait, have all been analyzed as elements of the pernicious operation of a form with dire consequences for women.[9]

---

[5]Teresa de Lauretis, "Sexual Indifference and Lesbian Representation," *Theatre Journal* 40:2 (1988): 155–77. See also de Lauretis, "Issues, Terms, Contexts," in de Lauretis, ed., *Feminist Studies/Critical Studies* (Bloomington: Indiana University Press, 1986), 1–19.

[6]The notion of "objecthood" evolved in discussions with the women at Wolf Pen about the deconstructed lesbian position and the pitfalls of "strategic essentialism." I am indebted to them for their observations.

[7]Janelle Reinelt, "Feminist Theory and the Problem of Performance," *Modern Drama* 32:1 (1989): 48.

[8]See Sue-Ellen Case, *Feminism and Theatre* (New York: Methuen, 1988), particularly chapter seven, "Towards a New Poetics," 112–32.

[9]Sue-Ellen Case, for example, in "Towards a Butch/Femme Aesthetic," in Lynda Hart, ed., *Making a Spectacle: Feminist Essays on Contemporary Women's Theatre* (Ann Arbor: University of Michigan Press, 1989) proposes that realism is deadly for women: "The violence released in the continual zooming in on the family unit, and the heterosexist ideology linked with its stage partner, realism, is directed

Materialist feminist performance critics have profited from Catherine Belsey's work on classical realism, in which she states, in a much-quoted passage:

> Classical realist narrative . . . turns on the creation of enigma through the precipitation of disorder which throws into disarray the conventional cultural and signifying systems . . . [T]he story moves inevitably towards closure which is also disclosure, the dissolution of enigma through the re-establishment of order, recognizable as a reinstatement or a development of the order which is understood to have preceded the events of the story itself.[10]

The events that precede the story are the authorized narratives of the dominant culture, and the enigma that disrupts the social order is usually one that threatens its ideological fabric. As Jeanie Forte remarks, "In light of this definition, it becomes evident that classic realism, always a reinscription of the dominant order, could not be useful for feminists interested in the subversion of a patriarchal social structure."[11]

Forte, however, questions whether subversive texts in turn "give rise to politicized action on the part of the newly constructed reader."[12] She suggests that because of its structural recognizability, or "readability," realism might be able to politicize spectators alienated by the more experimental conventions of non-realistic work. Forte cites Terry Baum's and Carolyn Meyer's lesbian revue, *Dos Lesbos*, as a case of "pseudo-realism." By tempering its realism with Brechtian distancing and foregrounding strategies, Forte feels the text is able to thwart the ideological impositions of the traditional form.

Forte chooses *Dos Lesbos* to illustrate how its pseudo-realism might move spectators away from homophobia, but her own heterosexist ideology slips out in the moments of textual overstatement which belie the seamless argument of her text.[13] Forte says the play's "ribald humor . . . endears the audience to the characters, who are then able to communicate some of the not-so-humorous problems for lesbians to a sym-

---

against women and their hint of seduction . . . the closure of [the] realist narrative chokes women to death and strangles the play of symbols, the possibility of seduction. . . . Cast realism aside—its consequences for women are deadly" (297).

[10]Catherine Belsey, "Constructing the Subject, Deconstructing the Text," in Judith Newton and Deborah Rosenfelt, eds., *Feminist Criticism and Social Change: Sex, Class and Race in Literature and Culture* (Methuen, 1985), 53, quoted in Jeanie Forte, "Realism, Narrative, and the Feminist Playwright—A Problem of Reception," *Modern Drama* 32:1 (1989): 116.

[11]Forte, 116.

[12]Forte, 117. See also Laura Kipnis, "Feminism: The Political Conscience of Postmodernism?" in Andrew Ross, ed., *Universal Abandon? The Politics of Postmodernism* (Minneapolis: University of Minnesota Press, 1989), 149–66, in which, in the context of a complex discussion, she argues against modernist countercinematic practice as a political program in terms similar to Forte's argument for realism: "If the analysis of scopophilia in dominant cinema produces remedial cultural practices whose only audience is the traditional audience of high culture, it seems to suggest somehow luring the masses to *Riddles of the Sphinx* as a future political program" (156).

[13]This description of the overstatement of realist narratives belying their ideological base is borrowed from Vivian M. Patraka, "Lillian Hellman's *Watch on the Rhine*: Realism, Gender and Historical Crisis," *Modern Drama* 32:1 (1989): 128–45.

pathetic audience."[14] Such a formulation positions the audience as charitable toward lesbian pathos.

Forte goes on to propose that the "realist elements serve to promote enough illusion of 'real experience in the world' . . . that the audience can identify (in a manner which has been culturally conditioned) with [the lesbian characters] as people who are just trying to achieve a measure of happiness . . ."[15] Forte's point actually illustrates that the realist elements in *Dos Lesbos* threaten to elide the lesbians's difference from the heterosexual norm.

The play's realist elements construct them as palatable only if they can be seen as humorous, pitiful, or as no different from heterosexuals. In fact, Forte says, "Many readers find *Dos Lesbos* somewhat palatable, even if the content disturbs them, precisely because of its relative readability, its quiescent realism."[16] The readability Forte champions for realism makes difference acceptable only by constructing it as sameness. Lesbians disappear under the liberal humanist insistence that they are just like everyone else. Difference is effectively elided by readability.

Rather than the deconstructive possibilities of the lesbian position provided through critical theory, bourgeois realism reinstates the unitary, transcendent lesbian caught in a binary opposition with heterosexuality. Realism is not recuperable for lesbian theorists, because its ideology is so determined to validate dominant culture that the lesbian position can only be moralized against or marginalized. The lesbian subject most readable in realism is either dead or aping heterosexual behavior.

Lesbian Positions in Heterosexual Realism

To explore the pernicious effects of bourgeois realism on the lesbian subject, a comparison of significant texts at contrasting historical moments will be useful. John Clum's work on gay male drama makes a distinction between plays written from an "outside/heterosexual" and an "inside/homosexual" perspective that can be transposed productively to a lesbian setting.[17] Lillian Hellman's *The Children's Hour* (1934) is written from outside of lesbian experience. The text is paradigmatic of the manner in which the structural codes of realism operate to mark and finally purge the lesbian

---

[14]Forte, 118.

[15]Forte, 118.

[16]Forte, 119. She goes on to argue that the readability of realism might produce a political response in some spectators by allowing them to recognize similar life experiences, and raise their consciousness about difference. Recognition, however, might be problematized as an adequate pre-condition for political action and as effective feminist dramaturgy. Helene Keyssar, for example, in *Feminist Theatre* (New York: Grove Press, 1985) proposes that recognition is key to traditional dramatic theory, and that perhaps transformation is the benchmark of the new feminist drama (xiii–xiv).

[17]John Clum, " 'A Culture That Isn't Just Sexual': Dramatizing Gay Male History," *Theatre Journal* 41:2 (1989): 169–89. The inside versus outside distinction is helpful, but also threatens a reinstatement of the essentialism that lurks when writing about marginalized communities. Because a lesbian writes from within the marginalized experience, are her truths "authorized" and therefore essentialized? This is a theoretical problem to worry at another time, but one that hovers on the margins of my text nonetheless.

enigma from its bourgeois, moral midst. On a superficial level, the narrative describes the emotional and economic ruin of two young women teachers by a psychopathic student who accuses them of lesbianism. The realist structure, however, damns Martha Dobie as an unsettling influence even before the lie about her sexuality has begun to circulate.

Hellman's description of the Wright-Dobie School for Girls presents the inevitable drawing room that demarcates the bourgeois family boundaries in which realism lodges its moral dilemmas. In the first scene, Martha's eccentric aunt, Mrs. Mortar, instructs the girls in sewing and elocution.[18] Mrs. Mortar's flamboyant behavior is a parody of proper femininity, but the scene exemplifies the domestic normalcy in which these girls are inculcated before the threat of perversion disrupts their lives. Mary's entrance marks the first disorder in this otherwise socially regimented scene. Her dishonesty about her whereabouts and her easy manipulation of Mrs. Mortar's affections establish her as morally impure and frighteningly powerful, instituting the binary opposition of goodness and evil that frames the realist plot.

The presentation of the structural enigma, however, occurs with Martha's entrance. Hellman quickly establishes Martha's displeasure with her partner Karen's pending marriage to Dr. Joe Cardin. The playwright loads her stage directions with subtext that implicates Martha as "unnatural": "MARTHA: (*Looking at* [*Karen*].) You haven't talked about marriage for a long time" (15). The binary "natural and unnatural" is set up alongside that of good and evil, as Karen responds impatiently to Martha's fears, "For God's sake, do you expect me to give up my marriage?" (16). Heterosexuality is naturalized and unassailable.

The discourse of heterosexuality is further authorized by Cardin's entrance. He has stopped on the way to the school to look at a bull a neighbor recently bought, and predicts, "There's going to be plenty of good breeding done in these hills" (16). His proximity to animal procreation casts him as a virile—if domesticated—man whose marriage to Karen will be equally (re)productive. Late in Act Two, Cardin is again inscribed within a natural, reproductive site, when he tells his aunt, Mrs. Tilford, "We're getting the results from the mating season right about now" (45). When he loses his resolve to marry Karen after the trial, Cardin's manhood seems deflated by the authorized verdict of "unnatural" sexuality which taints his procreative scene.

Since Martha rarely gets to speak for herself throughout the play, her motivations and emotions remain accessible to the spectator only through other characters' interpretations. Her silenced position invites spectators—with their longing for information and their desire to know encouraged by the play's realism—to side with the narrative constructed against Martha. Although Mrs. Mortar has been established as an unreliable source of information, the spectator is able to believe her insinuations about Martha's sexuality through witnessing Martha's earlier emotionally ambivalent scene with Karen.

[18]See Lillian Hellman, *The Children's Hour*, in *Six Plays by Lillian Hellman* (New York: Vintage Books, 1979). All other references will appear in the text.

When Mary fabricates her story for Mrs. Tilford, she is able to persuade her grandmother of its truth by harping on Mrs. Mortar's reading of Karen and Martha's "unnatural" relations. Mrs. Tilford insists Mary "stop using that silly word" (37), but clever Mary knows she is making progress when she senses her grandmother's fear. Whispering her description of the alleged sexual crime into the older woman's ear, Mary doesn't even understand herself, but the spectator, directed by Mrs. Tilford's response, is voyeuristically invited to imagine the horrors of a lesbian encounter. The scene, which is never named aloud, is unravelled for their disapproval, and for their prurient interest. In a climate of sexual repression, imagination breeds pornography.

Truth and justice weave their way through *The Children's Hour* thematically, but also serve as tropes for its realist structure. If there is an enigma in realism, its structural shape is bent toward unravelling and expunging it. Evil young Mary functions as a metaphor for the inexorable push of realism toward knowing and ordering its truths through the discourse of power. Mary's power at the Wright-Dobie School, for example, comes from her ability to collect and use information. People's secrets become fodder for her manipulations.

Mary is somewhat aligned with Martha in the text's two binary systems. She is evil incarnate and, given the gendered ideology the play authorizes, Mary's aggressive, manipulative behavior seems vaguely masculine. Mary is bad because good girls don't act as she does, but her pathological evil is contained at the narrative's end, easily managed compared to Martha's unnatural affections. Good and evil are familiar oppositions, but the threat of sexual perversity threatens not just moral probity but the heterosexual base of an economic system badly shaken by the 1930s stock market crash and ensuing depression.

Martha's position threatens Karen and Cardin's heterosexual emotional and economic union. In effect, after the trial, Cardin will be forced to marry both women. Persuading Martha to stay with him and Karen, he says, "You stay with us now. . . . I'll buy you good coffee cakes and take you both to Ischl for a honeymoon" (65). To spectators in the 1930s, the prospect of supporting two women must have been perceived as daunting, and worked to convince them of Martha's status as an albatross.

In her final scene with Cardin, Karen tries to retain her place in heterosexual discourse, claiming she can have a baby like everyone else (68). But the taint of lesbianism makes her a social outcast until after Martha's death, when the possibility of a heterosexual reunion is reinstated. Mrs. Tilford insists, "You must go back to [Joe]." Karen protests, but admits "perhaps" when Mrs. Tilford amends, "Perhaps later, Karen?" (77).

Martha, on the other hand, is allowed no such resurrection. She internalizes the guilt thrust on her by the culture. "I've got to tell you how guilty I am," she pleads with Karen. ". . . I couldn't call it by a name . . ." (71). The social sphere gives her a name by which she acquiesces to the ideological pressure of her unnaturalness and dies. The enigma is purged and the social order reinstated.

Martha's story could be read through a 1980s perspective, as the tragic isolation of a lesbian forced to deal with her sexuality through the distortions of the dominant culture. However, such a literal reading too easily remains on the level of plot, and does not adequately indict the form that narrates Martha's position. Martha merely fulfills the requisites of the realist plot, which is to create truths that serve its ideology. The play is not Martha's play and is not accurately about lesbianism.[19] The realist structure inscribes Martha as the problem to be purged. Her death is inevitable and serves the order of morality that informs the play's structural movement. The lesbian position is a convenient, expedient pawn in a narrative that insists on its own moral justice.

The realist structure's manipulation of the lesbian position becomes more complex in Frank Marcus's *The Killing of Sister George* (1965). Although the play falls within Clum's "outside" designation, its subcultural references and focus mark it more explicitly as a "gay" play.[20] The death of the lesbian is metaphorical in this case, since the lesbian position is carved into two levels through which representation itself intervenes.

Sister George is a character in a BBC radio drama located in the fictitious community of Applehurst, which exemplifies the traditional values of English life.[21] Some of the text's tension derives from the implosion of representation and reality, shaded by the irony of loyal Sister George's "real life" as a monstrous butch lesbian named June Beckwith. June fears for the life of Sister George, who is in fact eventually killed off from the series because her ratings have dropped. The dominant culture, represented by the BBC's Mrs. Mercy Croft, intervenes in June's personal life to reclaim her infantilized lover Alice—called "Childie"—back into the bosom of the family life that the BBC radio program enshrines. June is eventually punished and ostracized by the disjuncture between her real and representational lives, left loverless and drunk.

Alice and June's relationship is described as butch/femme, not through the definitions of a lesbian community that throws gender enculturation into spin, but through the censoring, moralizing eye of the heterosexual mores the relationship is constructed to imitate.[22] June/George expresses her masculinity through vicious sado-masochistic power plays. The binary operative alongside good and evil in Marcus' play is that of masculine and feminine behaviors as inscribed over female sexuality. George, the butch, is described as cruel, evil, and irredeemable because her masculinity is a perversion of heterosexual manhood and of femininity. Alice is allied with dominant cultural values—she gets up before dawn to queue up for ballet tickets—and is described as appropriately feminine. Her sexuality is ambivalent;

---

[19]Hellman insisted the play was about a lie, not about lesbians.

[20]See William Hoffman's introduction to his edited anthology *Gay Plays* (New York: Avon, 1979), in which *The Killing of Sister George* is described as "probably the most famous play about lesbians ever written" (xxxviii).

[21]Frank Marcus, *The Killing of Sister George*, in William Hoffman, ed., *Gay Plays*, 340–41. All other references will appear in the text.

[22]See Case, "Toward a Butch/Femme Aesthetic," for a feminist theoretical discussion of butch/femme behavior in social and performative settings.

George casts aspersions on Alice's ability to faithfully refrain from liaisons with men. The possibility of her return to heterosexuality threatens George's hegemony.

Mrs. Mercy's intrusion into this distorted domestic scene displaces George into the enigma position and, with Mrs. Mercy as the narrative agent of dominant cultural values, the text moves inexorably toward George's exile from the social order. Mrs. Mercy creates the narrative of Sister George's death—"leave it to the BBC, we know best" (381)—and refuses June the pleasure of revealing herself as the character's creator, since "that would spoil the illusion" (382).

Since June is robbed of Sister George, whose persona is June's only entree into dominant discourse, she is pushed closer and closer to her metaphorical social death. Mrs. Mercy offers to resurrect June Beckwith in a children's series called "The World of Clarabelle Cow," in which June would play the title role (403), but the half-hearted effort to recuperate June into femininity fails.

Once again, the lesbian is positioned as external to the discourse of dominant culture by the realist structure. Sister George mounts her motorbike—an ironic reference to lesbian subculture—and is hit by a truck. June listens to Sister George's radio death with a morbid fascination. The fictitious community and the BBC's listeners mourn Sister George while the actor who played her sits alone mooing plaintively. Marcus describes her final utterance as "a heart-rending sound" (411), painful since June cannot enter the role dominant culture has marked for her, and is therefore purged from it. The social order is restored and June/George joins Martha in the graves of the dispossessed. The play's subcultural references and its levels of gendered characterization could be read as referring ironically to constructions of both gender and sexuality in a heterosexual culture, but the vicious portrait of the butch lesbian makes such a revisionist reading difficult. *The Killing of Sister George* premiered in the United States in 1966, before the Stonewall riots of 1969 had begun the public uprising of gay liberation.

The lesbian plays discussed below are located in the post-Stonewall ideology of the gay liberation movement and are inflected by the growing influence of the second wave of United States feminism. Both movements reconfigure the position of the butch lesbian. When described through realist plays written in the mid-1970s, her narrative position remains consistent to the marginalized, immoral place constructed for all lesbians in the "outside" texts.

Lesbian Subjectivity and the Exiled Butch

Historians John D'Emilio and Estelle Freedman describe the radical contours of the early movement for gay liberation, citing tracts that launched attacks against the restrictive gender and sexuality assignations of the nuclear family. "Coming out" became the gay liberation movement's rallying cry, an act of "public avowal" that would help gay men and lesbian women "shed much of the self-hatred they had internalized."[23] Coming out, inflected with feminism's intersection of public choices

---

[23]John D'Emilio and Estelle B. Freedman, *Intimate Matters: A History of Sexuality in America* (New York: Harper and Row, 1988), 322.

and personal politics, represented "not simply a single act, but the adoption of an identity in which the erotic played a central role."[24]

The assertion of the erotic for lesbians became taboo when liberal feminism's analysis was imposed on lesbian existence in the early 1970s. "Sensitive to the reaction that the [feminist] movement was eliciting in the minds of Americans," D'Emilio and Freedman write, "many feminists sought to keep the issue quiet, to push lesbians out of sight."[25] The homophobia of liberal feminism prompted lesbians to splinter into separate groups, which combined an analysis of gender and sexuality oppressions.

The modifying adjective "feminist," however, tended to focus the new lesbian analysis on gender and away from alternative descriptions of sexuality. While the new radical lesbian-feminists identified their sexual practice along a continuum of "woman-identification," the butch/femme behavior that marked lesbian subcultures in the 1950s and 1960s was erased and moralized against.[26] By the mid-1970s, the sexual lesbian who engaged in butch behavior as a subcultural resistance to the dominant culture's gender and sexual ideology was silenced by feminism, her transgressive sexual desire "feminized" through the woman-identification that neatly elided active sexuality as a pre-condition for lesbianism.

At the same historical moment, D'Emilio and Freedman document that the "gay movement adapted to the times, for the most part pulling back from its radical critique of the effects of sexual repression and instead recasting itself as a movement in the

---

[24] D'Emilio and Freedman, 323. Coming out still plays a crucial thematic role in lesbian realist dramatic literature, although eventually, the focus on such a transitional moment within the realist text traps the lesbian in a negative relation to heterosexual culture and disallows a full exploration of alternative lifestyles and sexuality. *Dos Lesbos*, in Kate McDermott, ed., *Places, Please! The First Anthology of Lesbian Plays* (Iowa City: Aunt Lute, 1985), for example, worries the issue of coming out at work and in the family so exclusively that the oppressions of the dominant culture outweigh the pleasures of lesbian life. Jane Chambers's *Last Summer at Bluefish Cove*, discussed below, although focused within a Long Island lesbian community, is distracted by Eva's coming out story, her transition away from heterosexual choices. Sarah Dreher's *8x10 Glossy* (in McDermott, ed., *Places, Please!*) displaces its lesbian feminist heroine's traumas to solicit empathy for her married sister Julie and her divorced friend Dana, who are contemplating a lesbian affair. The coming out story, as represented in the realist tradition, is a fait accompli, the problem resolved, the deed completed by the narrative's end. Such a formulation elides the fact that for most lesbians, coming out narratives lack closure, since the dominant culture operates under a heterosexual assumption that forces lesbians to continually reassert their resistant identities.

[25] D'Emilio and Freedman, 316.

[26] See Adrienne Rich, "Compulsory Heterosexuality and Lesbian Existence," *Signs* 5:4 (1980) for a radical feminist analysis of lesbianism as woman-identification. Case, in "Towards a Butch/Femme Aesthetic," writes that "the middle-class upward mobility of the lesbian feminist identification shifts the sense of community from one of working-class, often women-of-color lesbians in bars to that of white, upper-middle-class, heterosexual women who predominated in the early women's movement" (285). She also points out that the "ghosting of the lesbian subject" in feminism is a result of moralizing crusades such as the anti-porn movement (284). See also Dolan, "The Dynamics of Desire: Sexuality and Gender in Pornography and Performance," *Theatre Journal* 39:2 (1987): 157–74 for writing on the relationship between lesbian subjectivity and pornography.

long tradition of American reform."[27] The focus on transgression shifted to one on equal civil rights. Rather than asserting the radical difference of their lives and their critique, gays began to insist they were like everyone else, and could imitate the heterosexual model in same-sex couples.

In such a setting, the butch lesbian retains her difference and presents a dangerous threat to heterosexual, gay-assimilationist, and lesbian-feminist ideology. The butch in lesbian realist plays inflected by these ideologies remains ghosted as an anachronism from an unenlightened time, whom feminism has been unable to recuperate. Her isolation and the moral judgments launched against her by other characters place the butch in the position once defined for all lesbian subjects by heterosexuality. She becomes the enigma to be purged from the lesbian realist text.

Jane Chambers's *A Late Snow* (1974), for example, is a lesbian identity play inflected with the complementary demands of gay liberation as civil rights and early feminism's notion that the personal is political but not sexual for lesbians.[28] The play takes place in a secluded cabin at which, through a contrived series of events, a literature professor named Ellie is forced to scrutinize her alliances with four other women.

The realist narrative constructs Ellie's ex-lover, Pat, as a masculine, sexually rapacious, disruptive influence, a woman who is constitutionally incapable of maintaining a monogamous relationship. Pat's five-year relationship with Ellie dissolved when an affair Pat was having ended in tragedy and the other woman was killed. Chambers's choice to embed the butch in such a melodramatic narrative helps to elicit a moral stance against Pat. Not only is she an inveterate womanizer and a violent drunk, she is guilty of manslaughter.

Quincey, Ellie's new lover, is a much younger woman to whom Chambers assigns the rhetoric of gay liberation. "Somebody has to make change happen," she intones. "Somebody who believes in the goodness of themselves and what they are" (306). Quincey insists that Ellie come out as the only proof of her self-love. Ellie argues, through pre-Stonewall knowledge, that she arrived at her sexual identity within a different historical era: "When I was your age, 'lesbian' was a dictionary word used only to frighten teenage girls and parents. Mothers fainted, fathers became violent, landlords evicted you, and nobody would hire you. A lesbian was like a vampire: she looked in the mirror and there was no reflection" (308).[29] Chambers sketches a continuum of lesbian identities inflected by history, and slowly shifts each character toward the public avowal and self-acceptance gay liberation and liberal feminism demand be inscribed within monogamous relationships.

Only Pat is left at the far end of the continuum as irredeemable. The text's dim view of non-monogamous sexuality allows Ellie to accuse Pat of hating women and

[27]D'Emilio and Freedman, 323.

[28]Jane Chambers, *A Late Snow*, in William Hoffman, ed., *Gay Plays*, 281–335. All other references will appear in the text.

[29]See Sue-Ellen Case, "Femimesis," an unpublished paper presented at the New Languages for the Stage conference in Lawrence, Kansas, October 1988, for a recuperation of vampire mythology in the context of lesbian representation.

hating herself (302). Compared to the romanticism of Ellie's relationship with Quincey and her budding attraction to Margo, Pat is staunchly pragmatic. All her anniversaries are celebrated on the same day, the date of which corresponds to the first three digits of her social security number (286). Her choice of gender roles is also pragmatic. "I never wanted to be a woman," she says. "It's a crappy thing to be" (323). While her mobster father travelled the world, Pat watched her mother's circumscribed domestic life play out among babies, laundry, and groceries. Pat prefers the independence and mobility of a life that for a pre-Stonewall, pre-feminism lesbian, could only be theorized as butch.

Chambers strains to win reasoned sympathy for Pat's choices, but is ultimately swayed by the exigencies of the realist form and its production context. Pat remains the embattled transgressor in the context of a polite skirmish for equal lesbian rights, and the realist structure exiles her to the margins of its moral center. Happily riding off into the sunset of its liberal humanist ideology, *A Late Snow* leaves Pat adrift.

Last Summer at Bluefish Cove (1980) distances the nascent feminism that serves as the agent of the butch's demise in *A Late Snow*.[30] The text focuses on a lesbian community in which women are paired across age and class lines. Difference is implicit in their couplings. But Lil, the butch, remains the sacrificial victim of this realist text. Because she is dying of cancer, the narrative allows more sympathy for Lil's position, but it also insists on recuperating her into monogamy before she dies.

Bluefish opens on an inscription of Lil's butchness within her fishing expertise. Dangling her pole by the water, Lil seduces the fish:

> I see you circling down there. . . . if you were a person, you know what we'd call you? A C.T. You nuzzle the bait but you don't put out. Now, I'm going to try a different approach, it's called courting. You're going to love it. . . . You're a terrific looking fish, you know that, sweetheart? You're a real knockout. Now, don't get me wrong, it's not just your body I'm after. I love your mind, your sense of humor, your intellect, your politics. . . . I respect you, darling. I love you. Now bite, baby, bite.
>
> [8]

Lil is obviously adept at seduction, and even this one, witnessed by Eva, the unwitting heterosexual, is successful. Lil and Eva fall in love.

Months before her death, Lil is ready to settle into what the dominant culture constructs as a legitimate relationship. She tells Eva, "I love you more than I have ever loved anyone. For the first time in my life, I understand why knights rode miles to slay a dragon for their lady's hand" (77). Lil's butch aesthetic is still tinted with a chivalric code, but she is seduced into accepting the discourse of monogamous love. Eva's coming out story, however, prevails over the narrative, and Lil's death becomes the necessary pre-condition to Eva's independence.

[30]Jane Chambers, *Last Summer at Bluefish Cove* (New York: JH Press, 1982). All other references will appear in the text. Kitty Cochrane, for example, the famous feminist in Bluefish Cove, is constructed as self-serving and self-righteous, her rhetoric belied by her life. Her best-selling book is a feminist tract in which she encourages women to "seize their sexuality" (18), but her fame requires that she keep her lesbianism closeted, since "the public is not ready" (27) to see it disclosed.

If Chambers mourns the butch's passing in *Bluefish Cove*, she resurrects her in her last play, *Quintessential Image* (1983).[31] The play is the most self-referential of Chambers's work, referring directly to the realist conventions that dominate and control her early texts. The short piece is set in a television studio, in which cameras and monitors loom over the scene, providing layers of constructed representations.

Margaret Foy, a superficial, self-involved talk show host, has invited award-winning photographer Lacey Lanier to be interviewed. The presumption of a studio audience allows Foy to address the spectators in the theatre directly, and the levels of spectatorship become implicit in the play's production of meanings. Enormous enlargements of Lacey's photographs, which appear to capture key moments in American history, hang on the set. The interview eventually deconstructs the images into the scene lurking like a palimpsest behind their creation—each image captures Lacey Lanier's failed attempt to photograph Belinda Adams, a woman she loved unrequitedly most of her life.

As Chambers focuses more directly on lesbian representation, the liberal and radical feminist analysis imposed on her earlier plays disappears. Lacey Lanier, with her wild hair, sensible shoes, "no-nonsense appearance" and tough vulnerability (3) is Chambers's resurrection of the butch lesbian back into the center of her own narrative. Her moment in the studio is a failed attempt to reconstruct her lesbian truths. The eye of the culture pervades the set, and through the closeted Margaret Foy, enforces its readings of her work, keeping her lesbian desire safely exiled from the frame.

Representation becomes a trope in the play, which allows Chambers to comment on the dominant culture's manipulation of images and the ideology they bear. Foy explains that the interview can be cut and edited, and interpolates editorial remarks throughout her exchange with Lacey about which of the photographer's comments will be retained and which excised. Lacey eventually realizes that her appearance on television may be as misunderstood as her photographs, and insists, "I don't want you clipping moments out" (17).

Trying to circulate her story from within dominant discourse, however, proves difficult, as Lacey learns that the image of herself on the tape can in fact do "something different" than she is doing (9). Lacey learns the tape is not strictly mimetic, but constructs her position in a discourse over which she has no control. But as she exits the set, Lacey goes off not to die, mute and marginalized, but to share the narrative of her life with Foy's lesbian lover, who wants to write a book about Lacey.

Only by commenting on the ideological codes of dominant representation can Chambers reconstruct a lesbian position outside of radical or liberal feminist ideology. *Quintessential Image* allows Chambers to break productively from the realist, Hellmanesque model of her earlier plays, in which bourgeois realism's inevitable moralizing finds its target in the transgressive butch lesbian.

---

[31]Jane Chambers, *Quintessential Image*, unpublished manuscript, 1983. See also Case, *Feminism and Theatre*, 78–79, and Dolan, *Toward a Critical Methodology of Lesbian Feminist Theatre*, unpublished MA thesis, Performance Studies Department. New York University, 1983, for further analysis of the play.

These examples of lesbian realist plays follow the legacy of *The Children's Hour* and *The Killing of Sister George*, which epitomize the position of lesbians in realism as marginalized and moralized against by the narrative structure that surrounds them. The lesbians who survive in realism are the ones who look straight, who don't spin the sign system into the excess of butch/femme or other subcultural transgressions of sexual display. While lesbian performance in the post-modernist style works at constructing what has been called a "collective subject," realism isolates, marginalizes, and sometimes murders the lone lesbian, whose position is untenable.[32] The lesbian subject in realism is always singular, never adequately a site of the differences between or among lesbians, never described within the divided identity of the deconstructive mode.

A challenge for lesbian theory in the 1990s will be to reconstruct a tenable lesbian subject position outside of realist moralizing and somewhere between deconstruction and essentialism. Elin Diamond calls realism mimesis at its most naive, positivist moment, and argues that it can be detached from the pernicious effects of its truth-value to "suggest ways in which feminist practitioners might avail themselves of realism's referential power without succumbing to its ideological conservatism."[33] Diamond argues that rather than dismissing mimesis, feminism should "militate for the complex, different referents we want to see, even as we work to dismantle the mechanisms of patriarchal modeling."[34]

Reconstructing a variable lesbian subject position that will not rise like a phoenix in a blaze of essentialism from the ashes of deconstruction requires emptying lesbian referents of imposed truths, whether those of the dominant culture or those of lesbian radical feminist communities which hold their own versions of truth. The remaining, complex, different referent, without truth, remains dependent on the materiality of actual lesbians who move in and out of dominant discourse in very different ways because of their positions within race, class, and variant expressions of their sexuality—dragging at the margins of structure and ideology.

---

[32]See Case, "From Split Britches to Split Subject," and Reinelt, "Feminist Theory and the Problem of Performance," for theories of the collective subject.

[33]Elin Diamond, "Mimesis, Mimicry, and the 'True-Real,' " *Modern Drama* 32:1 (1989): 61, 68.

[34]Diamond, 62.

Frame-Up: Feminism, Psychoanalysis, Theatre

Barbara Freedman

> In the dark I orient myself in a familiar room when I can seize on a single object whose position I can remember. Here obviously nothing helps me except the capacity of determining positions by a subjective ground of distinction. For I do not see the objects whose position I should find, and if someone had played a joke on me by putting on the left what was previously on the right while still preserving their relationships to each other, I could not find my way in a room with otherwise indistinguishably equal walls. But I soon orient myself through the mere feeling of a difference between my left and right sides.
> —Kant, *Critique of Practical Reason*, 295

Was it always so difficult to orient oneself, to place oneself, to choose sides, to step into a frame? Consider the scene of *The Taming of the Shrew.* A woman surveys the scene. A page, dressed up as a woman, surveys the scene. A boy, dressed up as a page, dressed up as a woman, surveys the theatre of which s/he is a part. The character beside him lusts for him. It is, we are told, his part. And so, and yet, "we" lust for the page/woman, the page of woman, the scripted woman. We entertain the sexual longing, enjoy the masquerade of femininity, deny our own construction within this carnivalesque version of aristocratic/sexist/sadistic theatre which gazes at itself and fondles its own power relations. And as we watch these characters watching these plays within plays located somewhere within the always elusive boundaries of *The Taming of the Shrew,* as we sit silently in the protective darkness and fulfill our role as sanctioned voyeurs, our gaze always returns to that enigmatic construction of a construction otherwise known as Sly's "madam wife." Is s/he not a part of the play s/he observes, since it concludes at the same time as the spectacle in which s/he appears as audience, in which we appear as audience, erasing distinctions between play and reality? And yet is not this ambiguous goddess—both audience and character, male and female, servant and mistress—who reigns over this laby-

Barbara Freedman is Associate Professor of English at Saint John's University. This essay appears in substantively revised form in her forthcoming Staging the Gaze: Psychoanalysis, Postmodernism, and Shakespearean Comedy *(Cornell University Press, 1990).*

rinthine theatre the true guardian of *Shrew* and its enshrined shrew, the comptroller of the cultural law of difference and the protector of that animal within its confines who remains unconquered?

How uncanny a figure s/he is, calling to mind both how easily we are fooled and how quickly we deny the differences that we know. It is certain that at some level gender uncertainty is engaged by this figure, much as it was when we first disavowed, after having perceived, genital difference. Freud would read in this page proof of the male subject's perception of the little girl as castrated, and so of the woman as always already a man in drag—the little girl as a little man.[1] We may read altogether differently, and find in this character the character of sexual difference itself, a surplus as well as a lack. The guardian of the "truth" of sexuality—which is always withheld because always an imposture—the page flirtatiously, fraudulently suggests consummation and tantalizes with the fiction of difference. Inasmuch as we all mistake, misrecognize sexual identity, we are all, like Sly, taken in by the play. Yet the drama of the page is the drama of language itself, which suggests not only the masquerade that is femininity, but the inevitability of the law of form, the mediation of sexuality by cultural representation, and the power of language to inscribe the raw energy of the drives.

Is the relation of the sexes the quintessential *trompe l'oeil?* Most of us are familiar with the story Lacan tells of the engendering of the subject through language: a little boy and little girl are seated in a train facing each other and so see opposing sides of the station which they are approaching. " 'Look,' says the brother, 'we're at Ladies!', 'Idiot!' replies his sister, 'Can't you see we're at Gentlemen.' " As Lacan observes: "For these children, Ladies and Gentlemen will be henceforth two countries towards which each of their souls will strive on divergent wings, and between which a truce will be the more impossible since they are actually the same country and neither can compromise on its own superiority without detracting from the glory of the other."[2] Lacan here suggests how language and sexual difference are intertwined; perhaps less important than the misdirection of these little souls is the arbitrary identification of these bodily egos and so the misdirection of their libidinal energies, yet another form of *méconnaissance*. Lacan draws two identical doors with the words "ladies" and "gentlemen" written under them to remind us that the signifier does not "stand for" the thing, but only makes sense in relationship to another signifier. Similarly, male and female, regardless of biological differences, are products of a linguistic signifying system, so that male is necessarily "not female" and female "not male." As Jacqueline Rose observes: "In Lacan's account, sexual identity operates as a law—it is something

[1] See Freud's *The Ego and the Id, The Standard Edition of the Complete Psychological Works of Sigmund Freud*, Vol. 19, trans. James Strachey (London: Hogarth Press, 1923) in which, after the little girl sees "her lack of a penis as being a punishment personal to herself and has realized that the sexual character is a universal one, she begins to share the contempt felt by men for a sex which is the lesser in so important a respect, and, at least in holding that opinion, insists on being like a man" (253).

[2] Lacan, "Agency of the letter in the unconscious, "*Écrits,* trans. Alan Sheridan (New York: Norton, 1977), 152.

enjoined on the subject. For him, the fact that individuals must line up according to an opposition (having or not having the phallus) makes that clear."[3]

As identity demands the fiction of closure, so sexual identity requires a fiction which, however fostered by biology or in its service, is essentially linguistic, ideological, and fetishistic. At issue is the representation of sexuality—the way in which libidinal energy is parceled up and channeled through socially appropriate bodily zones. For Lacan, the assumption of a sexual identity is accompanied by the sacrifice of free libidinal energy necessitated by signification itself, which demands that we be one thing and not another. What Lacan refers to as "castration" is the loss in sexuality resulting from the inevitable mediation of desire by signification. The problem, Rose observes, is that we have "failed to see that the concept of the phallus in Freud's account of human sexuality was part of his awareness of the problematic, if not impossible, nature of sexual identity itself" as a result of which we "lost sight of Freud's sense that sexual difference is constructed at a price and that it involves subjection to a law which exceeds any natural or biological division. The concept of the phallus stands for that subjection, and for the way in which women are very precisely implicated in its process."[4] Yet another problem, however, is the price we pay for subjection to a discourse which enframes us; how are feminists who pass on a discourse of the phallus implicated in this process, and framed in turn?

My question regards the implacability of the law of place and frame; the potential of theatre for revisioning it and/or the complicity of theatre in this frame-up. Given feminist rethinkings of narrative—particularly psychoanalytic narratives—and feminist reviewings of cinema, especially as seen through a Lacanian lens[5]—we come at last to the question of how theatre figures difference. At issue is the problem of the frame and framing behavior as intrinsic to theatre, the extent to which theatre is always already determined by the frames it puts onstage, and the extent to which theatre provides a means for reframing. Given the longstanding debt of psychoanalysis to classical drama and the centrality of the Oedipus to both disciplines, is a feminist, anoedipal theatre possible, or possibly a contradiction in terms? Given the phallocentric vocabulary of contemporary psychoanalytic theory, is feminist theory which employs Lacan not framed in turn? In question is the potential of feminism, psychoanalysis, and theatre to reflect and effect change—to insert a difference in our construction of the subject and so to make a difference.

Let us break the field with a quotation that by misunderstanding nonetheless gets us to the root of the problem. Jane Gallop writes: "This problem of dealing with difference without constituting an opposition may just be what feminism is all about

---

[3] Jacqueline Rose, "Introduction—II," in *Feminine Sexuality: Jacques Lacan and the École Freudienne*, ed. Juliet Mitchell and Jacqueline Rose, trans. Jacqueline Rose (New York: Norton, 1985), 29.

[4] Rose, "Introduction," 28.

[5] See Laura Mulvey, "Visual Pleasure and Narrative Cinema," *Screen* 16, no. 3 (1975): 6–18; Kaja Silverman, *The Subject of Semiotics* (Oxford: Oxford University Press, 1983); E. Ann Kaplan, *Women and Film: Both Sides of the Camera* (New York: Methuen, 1983); Teresa de Lauretis, *Alice Doesn't: Feminism, Semiotics, Cinema* (Bloomington: Indiana University Press, 1984); and Jacqueline Rose, *Sexuality and the Field of Vision* (London: Verso, 1986).

(might even be what psychoanalysis is about). Difference produces great anxiety. Polarization, which is a *theatrical* representation of difference, tames and binds that anxiety. The classic example is sexual difference which is represented as a polar opposition (active-passive, energy-matter). All polar oppositions share the trait of taming the anxiety that specific differences provoke"[6] (italics added).

Gallop succinctly assesses the shared goals of feminism, psychoanalysis, and de-construction in the postmodernist enterprise, insofar as all are similarly predicated upon subverting the figuration of difference as binary opposition. Structuralism and semiotics, the twin harbingers and now culprits of postmodernist theory, process experiences into polar oppositions which offer an Illusion of Alternatives—nature/culture, passive/active, male/female—rather than a continuum of differences. The deciding gesture for the avant-garde theorist remains Derrida's critique of the met-aphysical basis of the division of the sign into signifier and signified, form and content, writing and speech, representation and presence, as well as his critique of the tran-scendental signified or *sujet supposé savoir*—whether Man, God, or History—who stands outside them and guarantees their stability. The problem here is not only the pretense that the signified is somehow immune from commutability, from being transformed into another signifier, but the way in which such oppositions depend as well on a subject who conceives or perceives of these differences while standing somehow outside them. Further, this organization of experience is not only ideo-logically coerced but coercive, insofar as it tames and binds a larger field of differences through repressive and repressing tactics, and in turn privileges and procures one term at the expense of the other, be it Male versus female or Consciousness versus the unconscious. Deconstructive techniques function to unsteady if not dismantle such oppositions, and the revival of feminist and psychoanalytic theory owes much to their success.

What surprises in Gallop's formulation is her use of the word "theatrical." Why is polarization "a *theatrical* representation of difference"? Whereas the relationship of ideology and genre is hardly Gallop's subject here, the identification of theatre with a defensive, ideologically complicit ordering of difference constitutes a serious challenge to those for whom theatre offers an epistemological model or mode of inquiry. Is theatre the guarantor of polarities—part and parcel of the "great semiol-ogical myth of the versus"—or, as Barthes contends, designed to subvert them?[7] Is deconstruction theatre's enemy or its double? Is a feminist theatre possible, or possibly a contradiction in terms?

Those in search of the poor monster, dramatic theatre, will discover it miming the role of the scapegoat for Western humanism in a new-fangled postmodern morality play. Accused and found guilty as a machine of the state and an enemy of the people, drama is charged with the job of carrying away the fourfold sins of phallocentrism, humanism, individualism, and representation along with its demise. In this contest

[6] Jane Gallop, *The Daughter's Seduction, Feminism and Psychoanalysis* (Ithaca: Cornell University Press, 1982), 93.

[7] Roland Barthes, *Roland Barthes by Roland Barthes*, trans. Richard Howard (London: Macmillan, 1977), 69, 177.

of the avant-garde with itself on the field of representation, theatre has indeed been hoist on its own petard.[8] Long derided as one of the last bastions of humanism in literary studies, one of the few free zones where character, plot, and even presence itself could travel undisturbed, unsuspected, and unsuspecting, theatre is only now in the process of saving itself by denying itself. Traveling incognito as Performance, denying any relation to the tradition of *dramatic* theatre upon which it preys, theatre, now *sous rature*, has become avant-garde. Aristotle is changed for Artaud, *Hamlet* for *Screens*. It would seem that such theatre, even *sous rature*, is going to have difficulty making a comeback.

Postmodernist attacks on traditional dramatic theatre are not wholly unfounded at this point in the western cultural revolution. As with our political party system and our gender system, traditional Western theatre offers us only two stages, comic and tragic, upon which are always playing some version of *Oedipus* or its sister play, *The Taming of the Shrew*. A set-up is therefore always being staged as well—one that places its spectators in the position of Kate, Oedipus, and one Christopher Sly, all of whom "cannot choose" but accept the interpellation or hailing that indoctrinates the subject into a confusing and limiting identity, a *méconnaissance*, a delusion.

If traditional Western theatre rests upon and remains obsessed with the Oedipus— the scene of a founding crime of sexuality and a payment which decisively orders sexuality and gender, *Shrew* rewrites that scenario for women. To participate in *Shrew* is to identify the achievement of civilization itself with the domination of women through patriarchal exogamy rites, physical violence, and doublebinding mind games. If we conflate the complementary myths of *Oedipus* and *Shrew*, we have the tragedy of the man who discovers his sexuality and the woman who learns to disavow her own in the very apprehension of a repressive patriarchal law. One scenario identifies civilization with male payment for his own sexuality, the other identifies it with male control over disordered female sexuality. Both not only record but promulgate the values of a repressive patriarchal culture.

Tragedy and comedy alike therefore champion what Freudians and Lacanians like to think of as civilization-as-"castration"—a phallocentric concept which equates the organization of human sexuality and gender with the birth of language and repression, and so with a psychic displacing-as-ordering which alienates the subject even as it guarantees it a place in the symbolic order. Whereas cinema is associated with the pre-Oedipal look, and the desire to see oneself seeing, theatre replaces the desiring eye with the blinded eye g(l)azed over. Theatre is an Oedipal affair, the scene of the cut or wound, of the crown that burns its wearer. Theatre enacts the costs of assuming the displacing image returned back by society—the mask which alienates as it procures entry into society. In short, theatrical looking assumes a gaze which is a looking back, if not a staring down.

The Oedipal narrative—which places incestuous desire in the context of a communal law which condemns it—offered Freud a locus for his theories of childhood

[8] Julia Kristeva, "Modern Theater Does Not Take (a) Place," trans. Alice Jardine and Thomas Gora, *Sub-Stance* 18/19 (1977): 131–34.

sexuality and male castration anxiety. In the so-called Oedipal period, the male child's fantasies of being with the mother sexually are accompanied by fears of castration for such desires. These fears signify the internalization of social taboos, whether we term the effect superego development or the ordering and repression of sexuality. When *Twelfth Night's* "I would you would you were as I would have you be," is replaced by the motto, "that that is, is," we see how comedy as well as tragedy promotes the interpretation of identity as destiny.

As a psychoanalyst and teacher of Freudian theory, Lacan's reading of human psychic development also relies heavily upon traditional narratives of Western drama, and so is colored by the same sense of transcendent law or necessity which limits its potential for envisioning change. Lacan's primary interest is in the splitting and so procuring of the subject in language as it impinges on human psychic functioning. This leads him to be as interested in the instability of sexual identity as ego identity, and to see both as a function as division and repression, of the ordering fictions by means of which the ego as supplement gets set into place. Lacanian theory has proven especially useful for describing how masculinity depends upon woman as both the castrated Other and as externalized lack. And this model of woman as lack constituted the basis of the early analyses by feminist theorists of traditional phallocentric narrative and cinema.

The most influential feminist analyses of cinema and narrative have been set forth by Laura Mulvey and Teresa de Lauretis, both of whom expose the way in which the pleasure of these genres depends upon and in turn develops coercive identifications with a position of male antagonism toward women. Insofar as theatre incorporates many of the scopic and narrative pleasures as cinema, these formulations — however limited — also apply to theatre, and yet may also help to clarify the differences between the ways in which theatre and cinema stage difference. Since the male is traditionally envisioned as the bearer of the gaze, the woman represented as the fetishized object of the gaze (Mulvey), the gaze itself emerges as a site of sexual difference. The classic cinematic gaze splits us into male (voyeur) and female (exhibitionist). Seeing, according to this staging of the cinematic apparatus, is always already a matter of sexual difference. Insofar as classic theatre incorporates not only spectacle but narrative — so that the male is represented as a mobile agent as well as a bearer of the gaze, the female as the object to be actively transformed by him — action as well as sight has implications for the study of gender ideology. Not only pleasure but plot is derived from male fantasies which depend on the scopic and narrative exploitation of woman; she is the linchpin in the system whose losses propel the relay of looks and whose sins move the plot forward. In question, then, is the reliance of theatrical desire on the fetishized spectacle of woman and the narrative of her domination and punishment. Can we ever escape *The Taming of the Shrew?*

The join of feminism and cinema has clearly proved productive for the critique of traditional cinema and the construction of avant-garde films alike. Yet whereas cinema can challenge or deconstruct the symbolic by dissolving or dispersing the image, traditional theatre is necessarily more tied to the Symbolic — to the ego, the image, the unitary individual. Whereas theatre questions the validity of masks by virtue of their ability to be exchanged, it cannot dissolve or otherwise destroy them. As Shakespearean comedy reminds us, master and servant, husband and wife may exchange roles but never escape the tyranny of roles themselves—which is, after all, simply a function of the gaze, of being and so being seen in society. Theatrical narratives appear to promote the very ideology of difference they expose as arbitrary—insofar as their reliance on roles based on ego-identifications prevent it from moving outside of itself. If poetry exposes the limits of language, and cinema of the image, theatre exposes both along with the those of the ego at play in the gaze.

Traditional drama therefore mimes socialization, juxtaposing the deconstruction of the gaze against the inevitability of a theatre of representation, the Imaginary as alterity against the Symbolic of Oedipally inscribed inevitability. Its narrative form denies or contains the core theatrical impulse which displaces or fragments the ego (as in the middle of most Shakespearean comedies), offering stability in the form of provisional closure. Given traditional theatre superimposition of narrative inevitability, given its scopic regime of voyeurism and exhibitionism, and given its narrative regime of domination and mastery—all of which combine to expose traditional theatre as a taming of the gaze by the symbolic order, is a feminist deconstructive theatre possible?

Gallop would seem to be right about the fact that theatre works through polarities—as long as we replace the word "theatre" with the term "Western narrative drama." As Keir Elam reminds us, "theatre" is customarily associated with the performance aspects of a work, and "drama" with its traditional narrative form.[9] Classic drama generates identity and difference through the agon—the mirror image whereby person and persona, body and ego as supplement, confront one another and exchange places. Kate and Petruchio, Pentheus and Dionysus may fight for the same role, but difference is generated and complementary polar oppositions are reaffirmed as examples of "right relationship," whether of man to God (*Oedipus*), or man to woman (*Shrew*). The agon may confuse gender and social roles, or reveal their arbitrary basis, but it cannot let go of the masks—of ego, gender, or class—even as it points to the masquerade.

Given the reliance of theatrical narratives on the discovery of identity or place in relation to others, on various forms of the socialization process, the task of rethinking theatre may indeed require an Oedipus Wrecked. Yet a feminist theatre need not deny the limits of language, the place of images, the tyranny of gazes and roles, or the misrecognitions and displacements that attend them, as it goes about the work of reviewing them. A feminist theatre may well require that feminists share in the assumption of errors and misrecognitions associated by Lacan with the phallus alone (which explains why Lacan's attempts to subvert phallocentrism by reversing terms of value have failed). A feminist theatre may require, more precisely, that we reformulate the implications of the Lacanian gaze and the disruptive maternal gaze for feminist theory and practice in theatre and film.

This frame-up, then, is a challenge which means to expose the paradox that constitutes the theoretical standstill in feminism, psychoanalysis, and theatre studies

[9] Keir Elam, *The Semiotics of Drama and Theater* (London: Methuen, 1980).

alike. It is meant to expose the use of feminism by the avant-garde to stage itself, to invigorate its age-old rethinking of representation. It is meant to expose the way in which paradoxes and *en abyme* structures contain and entrap change, whether in *The Taming of the Shrew* or the taming of the gaze that is deconstructive philosophy. It is meant to ask what it means when Derrida writes, "it is not impossible that desire for a sexuality without number can still protect us, like a dream, from an implacable destiny which immures everything for life in the figure 2."[10] If self-reflexivity and theatricality are intermeshed in postmodern theory, this is not, I would argue, because theatre is the place of the *abyme*, but rather of the interruption of the *abyme* by a gaze within which explodes its container.

II

Both feminism and psychoanalysis face the central question of how to intervene in the cultural reproduction of sexual difference without always already being entangled in it—a problem posed not only by a play like *The Taming of the Shrew* but repeated in the writing on *Shrew*; not only by feminist and psychoanalytic theory but within the theories themselves. What feminism and psychoanalysis share is the goal of reconstructing subjectivity from the disruptive perspective of the unconscious and sexuality, language and ideology, so that it never rests stable or secure. Each discipline acknowledges the primacy of the signifying dependence of the subject on the Other, and is committed to developing ways of re-visioning the subject in relationship to the Other's gaze. Yet that very paradigm has also stymied productive feminist reformulations of subjectivity, insofar as "safe" descriptions of a phallocentric order have taken the place of prescriptions for change.

The play of the constitutive gaze in postmodern theory usually registers as a witty paradox rather than the trap of ideology containing and preventing change. The bind of the constitutive gaze has surfaced most notably in Julia Kristeva's descriptions of the problem of how to convey on the side of language and representation the experience outside of it.[11] Assuming that women have been excluded from the scene of representation—how to place that experience in representation? The constitutive gaze is characteristic of cinema in that it stages the desire to see oneself seeing oneself that never gets outside itself.

If psychoanalysis and feminism similarly expose the arbitrary and divisive construction of subject positions, both are similarly constrained precisely by that which they would change. Contemporary psychoanalytic theory offers an example, inasmuch as feminists who employ Lacanian methodology are in turn framed by a discourse of castration and phallic signifiers which they may well not seek to reproduce. Apropos here is Jane Gallop's assertion that if "the penis is what men have and women do not; the phallus is the attribute of power which neither men nor women have. But as long as the attribute of power is a phallus which refers to and

---

[10] Jacques Derrida, "Choreographies," *Diacritics* (Summer 1982): 76, from an interview with Christie V. McDonald.

[11] See Julia Kristeva, *Revolution in Poetic Language*, trans. Margaret Waller (New York: Columbia University Press, 1984).

can be confused . . . with a penis, this confusion will support a structure in which it seems reasonable that men have power and women do not. And as long as psychoanalysts maintain the separability of 'phallus' from 'penis,' they can hold on to their 'phallus' in the belief that their discourse has no relation to sexual inequality, no relation to politics."[12]

Those who read Lacan closely answer that his phallocentric discourse is intentionally reflective of the problems he sought to portray. Moreover, they remind us that the specific configurations of the Symbolic are indeed open to change in the Lacanian schema. As Ellie Ragland-Sullivan observes: "We must remember that the Symbolic here does not mean anything representative of a second hidden thing or essence. Rather it refers to that order whose principal function is to mediate between the Imaginary order and the Real. The Symbolic order interprets, symbolizes, articulates, and universalizes both the experiential and the concrete which, paradoxically, it has already shaped contextually."[13] Yet Lacan's Symbolic was developed in the context of a specific historical period of intellectual thought, one heavily influenced by structural anthropology. As Louis Althusser protests, "It is not enough to know that the Western family is patriarchic and exogamic . . . we must also work out the ideological formations that govern paternity, maternity, conjugality, and childhood."[14] Insofar as Lacan's writings ignore the material and historical nature of social organization and social change, they betray a disturbing complacency toward structuralist and phallocentric versions of a transcendent law, whether in the form of the phallic signifier, the law of the father, or the law of the symbolic order.

Lacan's Symbolic is heavily dependent upon Lévi-Strauss's account of the origin of our myth of difference in incest taboos, taboos which function to transform a state of "nature" into one of "culture": "The prime role of culture is to ensure the group's existence as a group, and consequently, in this domain as in all others, to replace chance by organization. The prohibition of incest is a certain form, and even highly varied forms, of intervention. But it is intervention over and above anything else; even more exactly it is *the* intervention."[15] As an exogamy rule, the incest taboo functions to establish a system of social relationships. It replaces the taboo of intrafamilial marriage with interfamilial marriage, and so sets up social roles and values. Of crucial interest here are the mythic and ideological aspects of Lacan's Symbolic Order, since it fails to explain the practice it describes, repeating the very difference it purports to explain. Observes Jacqueline Rose: "Lacan's use of the symbolic . . . is open to the same objections as Lévi-Strauss' account in that it presupposes the subordination which it is intended to explain. Thus while at first glance these remarks . . . seem most critical of the order described, they are in another sense complicit with that order."[16]

[12] Gallop, *The Daughter's Seduction*, 97.

[13] Ellie Ragland-Sullivan, *Jacques Lacan and the Philosophy of Psychoanalysis* (Chicago: University of Illinois Press, 1984), 268.

[14] Louis Althusser, *Lenin and Philosophy*, trans. Ben Brewster (London: Monthly Review Press, 1971), 211.

[15] Claude Lévi-Strauss, *The Elementary Structures of Kinship*, trans. James Harle Bell, John Richard von Sturmer, Rodney Needham (Boston: Beacon Press, 1969), 32.

[16] Rose, "Introduction," 45.

Lacan's symbolic must be understood both in the context of the structural anthropology upon which it drew and the object relations theory against which it defined itself. "Taking the experience of psychoanalysis in its development over sixty years," observes Lacan expansively, "it comes as no surprise to note that whereas the first outcome of its origins was a conception of the castration complex based on paternal repression, it has progressively directed its interests towards the frustrations coming from the mother, not that such a distortion has shed any light on the complex."[17] Lacan perceived the direction of object relations theory at the time as involved in a domestication of Freud's insights, in particular as involved in replacing the fundamental role of the unconscious, sexuality, and representation in psychoanalysis with the study of the quality of actual maternal care. To stress the importance of his intervention, Lacan introduced a third term, the name of the father, as an interruption of the asocial mother-infant dyad that brings to bear upon it the law of language and symbolic positions.

The context of Lacan's social role in this drama of psychoanalysis cannot be erased from the theory. Since the popularity of the project of rereading Freud is as much due to the Derridean reading of a Freud implicated in his own readings as to a Lacanian rereading of Freud's works, the reading of a Lacan implicated in his own theory of the gaze should not be surprising. We now acknowledge, for example, a Freud who represses the idea of repression, who wishes away threats to his theory of wish fulfillment, who refuses to give up the search for primal scenes which he elsewhere acknowledges exist only at the level of fantasied reconstruction, and who denies the bisexuality and gender instability he elsewhere theorizes with conviction. That Lacan could recognize gender ideology at work in his portrayal of the mothering function as asocial—whether in his narrative of maturation as dependent upon the Freudian male's resolution of the castration complex in the Oedipal phase, or in his equation of the (symbolic) phallus with that which alone ensures civilization—does not make his manipulation of that ideology more palatable. If the law of the father and the phallus is designed to expose place and position as fraudulent, rather than referring to any actual or fantasied father or phallus, the problem is that Lacan is in fact championing an equally irreversible place for his theory of displacement couched in the terms of a phallocentric discourse. And that very discourse reframes mother-infant relations as somehow always already outside language and representation. Lacan's dramatization of psychoanalytic history, in which the son figure (Lacan) rescues the dead father's authority (Freud) to intervene and save him from the mother's tyranny (object relations theory) is nonetheless open to reframing. Can we similarly reappropriate the gaze to take into account the way in which the mother's "no" functions as a displacing gaze and so displaces in advance the father as the privileged level of representation?

Like Petruchio, and like Freud, Lacan's work on gender is self-consciously paradoxical. At one level, he acknowledges the imposture of any cultural configuration of sexual difference posing as either natural or divine. At the same time, he regards

[17] Jacques Lacan, "Guiding Remarks for a Congress on Feminine Sexuality," in *Feminine Sexuality*, 86.

such imposture as inevitable, as the comic theatre of misrecognitions in which we necessarily exist. Like Petruchio, Lacan articulates the feminist dilemma in terms of the impossibility of breaking the mirror of ideology, yet exemplifies in his "corrected" misogyny the problem of being a part of the problem he would describe. He argues that woman does not exist except as a fantasy or theatrical construct, yet reifies a cultural myth of the exchange of women as the basis of civilization. Lacan equates a particular configuration of social power with the symbolic order, universalizes the Oedipal law, and identifies the paternal metaphor as the privileged level of representation itself, the inevitable third term that must intervene between mother and child, Oberon-like, to bring "nature" to a state of "culture."

Following Roy Schafer's analysis of psychoanalytic narratives, Teresa de Lauretis identifies the frame here: "while psychoanalysis recognizes the inherent bisexuality of the subject, for whom femininity and masculinity are not qualities or attributes but positions in the symbolic processes of (self)-representation, psychoanalysis is itself caught up in 'the ideological assignations of discourse,' the structures of representation, narrative, vision, and meaning it seeks to analyze, reveal, or bring to light."[18] If Lacan was the analyst most aware of this problem, by necessity he was also implicated by it. Juliet Flower MacCannell rightly warns us of "the tendency . . . to over-identify Lacan's analysis of the culture of the signifier . . . with his own stance *on* that culture," noting that "just as the physician may be said to be apart from the disease s/he discovers, even if s/he has been constrained by it, Lacan's analysis of the systems formed by the signifier, metaphor, the phallus, stand apart from his own 'system.' "[19] The paradox in reading Lacan derives from the play of playfulness in his style—for he as well as his most ardent supporters acknowledge his partiality and biases, but none can decisively fix the level at which they operate. Even Jacqueline Rose admits: "There is, therefore, no question of denying here that Lacan was implicated in the phallocentrism he described, just as his own utterance constantly rejoins the mastery which he sought to undermine."[20] We need to acknowledge both how Lacan played upon and with his own phallocentrism, and how that pleasure has its costs in a discourse which cannot be reproduced.

"In the psyche, there is nothing by which the subject may situate himself as a male or female being," asserts Lacan valiantly.[21] The very sentence is a marvelous example of what Lacan is talking about—how language directs biology, subverting the sexual drive into an identificatory one precisely by such maneuvers as interpellating the female reader as "he," "him," and "man." Yet insofar as we are not newly enlightened sexist males of the 1930s coyly pointing to the way in which our discourse places and displaces the subject, how can feminist theory support a vocabulary of phallic signifiers?

[18] Teresa de Lauretis. *Alice Doesn't: Feminism, Semiotics, Cinema* (Bloomington: Indiana University Press, 1984), 164; her quotation is from Ben Brewster, Stephen Heath, and Colin MacCabe, "Comment," *Screen* 16 (1975): 83–90.

[19] Juliet Flower MacCannell, *Figuring Lacan: Criticism and the Cultural Unconscious* (Lincoln: University of Nebraska Press, 1986), 19.

[20] Rose, "Introduction," 56.

[21] Jacques Lacan, "Alienation," *Four Fundamental Concepts of Psycho-Analysis* (New York: Norton, 1981), 204.

Teresa de Lauretis rightly critiques Lacanian theory for the way in which its descriptive features all too easily become prescriptive: "in opposing the truth of the unconscious to the illusion of an always already false consciousness, the general critical discourse based on Lacanian psychoanalysis subscribes too easily . . . to the territorial distinction between subjective and social modes of production and the cold war that is its issue."[22] More concerned with misrecognition as sites for change, de Lauretis suggests we redirect attention to the dialectical relationship between the means by which signs are produced and the codes themselves, so that we see meaning as a cultural production "not only susceptible of ideological transformation, but materially based in historical change."[23]

Feminist theory has itself been caught up in the double bind of the constitutive gaze. Given the increasing centralization of a group previously defined by exclusion from and oppression by the symbolic order, how is that group to redefine itself without destroying itself? Should it celebrate the scorned values with which it has been identified, abandon those values for those of the ruling class, or challenge the entire structure by which it has been defined, replacing it with a more inclusive sense of difference? As Ann Rosalind Jones reminds us, any celebration of the feminine is problematic in that it assumes an essential feminine to be celebrated, so that "theories of féminité remain fixated within the metaphysical and psychoanalytic frameworks they attempt to dislodge."[24] Luce Irigaray and Hélène Cixous would have us reverse the negative value assigned to woman, locating her specificity in multileveled libidinal energy, in a feminine unconscious shaped by female bodily drives which make their way in the style of feminist writings.[25] Yet Monique Wittig blames néoféminité's universalizing tendencies for making a fetish of the bar of difference, and so keeping us locked in an oppositional gender structure. Wittig demands that we "dissociate 'women' (the class within which we fight) and 'woman,' the myth. For 'woman' . . . is only an imaginary formation, while 'women' is the product of a social relationship,"[26] a group identity capable of effecting change. Yet even Wittig's political theatre, like much political theatre, is accused of various sins, among them denying a gaze that would disrupt its own. Can feminism be associated with action which effects change, assumes the image of woman and yet simultaneously disrupts any fixed image? The paradoxes of Kristeva's system, from which feminism cannot seem to escape, are very much at issue.

Could it be that feminism has (mis)appropriated the Lacanian gaze, offering readings of traditional drama and film that are incapable of interrogating their Oedipal

[22] de Lauretis, *Alice Doesn't*, 180–81.

[23] Ibid., 172.

[24] Ann Rosalind Jones, "Inscribing Femininity: French Theories of the Feminine," in *Making a Difference: Feminist Literary Criticism*, ed. Gayle Green and Coppélia Kahn (New York: Methuen, 1985), 106.

[25] See for example, Luce Irigaray, *Speculum of the Other Woman* (Ithaca: Cornell University Press, 1985); *This Sex Which Is Not One* (Ithaca: Cornell University Press, 1985); and Hélène Cixous, "The Laugh of the Medusa," trans. Keith Cohen and Paula Cohen, in *New French Feminisms*, ed. Elaine Marks and Isabelle de Courtivron (Amherst: University of Massachusetts Press, 1980), 245–64.

[26] Monique Wittig, "One Is Not Born a Woman," *Feminist Issues* 1, no. 2 (1981): 50–51.

basis, and the Oedipal basis of the symbolic? Could it be that feminism and psychoanalysis have been trapped by a constitutive gaze, by a paradox of the frame and the gaze which binds change in repetition and repression, in theories of *trompe l'oeil* and *dompte regarde*, in *mise en abyme* structures which ring hollow? Could it be that there is a radical aspect of theatre, what we might refer to as "theatricality" or "performance," as opposed to narrative drama, that is characterized by a disruptive gaze that never rests secure?

Against the *en abyme* paradoxes of cinema and deconstructive philosophy we may place the disruptive potential of the theatrical gaze, which is always ambivalent, always displacing one view and threatened by another in turn. The gaze disrupts *not* from the point of view of the paternal as representation, but from the point of view of a prior maternal gaze. The maternal gaze introduces the infant into the social order since it does not simply offer the infant a stable, cohesive image, but one that changes, that is not always as the infant would have it be, that reacts to the infant's gaze and reflects it differently. Like the mirror stage, the maternal gaze cannot logically be ascribed to a period prior to or outside of representation and the symbolic order. The idea of the contained breaking out of its container, of a deferred disruption always already contained within the mother-infant-dyad, yields a maternal disruptive gaze characteristic of theatre, a gaze capable not only of staging theory, but of shifting and displacing its sites of inquiry, its places of desire. Theatre provides a way of interrupting this self-contained and containing gaze from a point of view both within and outside it, much as the unconscious is the blind spot of our vision which in turn is constructed through and reflected by the gaze of the Other. Insofar as recent feminist performance art poses a challenge to traditional dramatic theatre by foregrounding a subversive force always already within it, and insofar as drama is itself always replaying the battle of presence and representation which occasions it, we must return theatre to its function as a disruptive and displacing gaze.

III

All of which returns us to the question with which we began: Is traditional theatre bound to certain representational models which prevent revisioning its construction of the subject? Since film theory has long ago addressed the limits of the avant-garde exploitation of feminism, a rehearsal of its debates may prove useful here. The problem of a feminist refiguring of representation has been nicely staged in the interaction between Constance Penley and Peter Gidal on feminism and the avant-garde as framed by Stephen Heath. First Penley: "If filmic practice, like the fetishistic ritual, is an inscription of the look on the body of the mother, we must now begin to consider the possibilities and consequences of the mother returning the look." Gidal replies: "The last words of your piece say it all. You search for the simple inversion, the *mother looking back*. I consider the possibilities of the not-mother, not-father (looking or not)." Heath joins Gidal: "To invert, the mother returning the look, is not radically to transform, is to return to the same economy (and cinema in the fiction film has always and exactly been concerned to consider the possibilities and consequences within the fetishistic ritual, including the *constitutive* threat of its endangerment, the play of eye and look, vision and lack): the difference inverted is also the difference maintained."[27]

The subtext in this game of two against one is a doubling of its content—the problem of woman. Since the cinematic look is read by these male theorists as constituted by a threat of the lack in woman (i.e., her castration), she had better not look back, nor, by implication, should Penley. Gidal's impulse is cinematic; he wants to dissolve, destroy images of women. (Is it not more avant-garde simply to delete women from films rather than to present her response to her reflection?) Penley's response is a looking back that looks forward. Her impulse is theatrical—she wants to reverse the look, which entails a rethinking of the limits of the cinematic apparatus, insofar as cinema posits the Absent One—the place of the camera—in the place of the Other as returned gaze in theatre.

Especially disturbing here is the argument that the cinematic look is constituted by a threat of its endangerment which is specifically associated with women's castration—a move which indicates how the Lacanian gaze has been reread through Freudian castration schemas to figure difference in film theory. The Freudian theory of castration explains how the human animal assumes its sexuality in a given social order: in a deferred reading of his (first?) sight of his mother's genitalia, the subject-as-little-boy interprets her "lack" in terms of the threat of the father's punitive, castrating "no" made good. In other words, he associates his mother's "actual" castration with his potential castration. That Lacan rereads this scenario symbolically does not, finally, save it for feminist theory. It harms in that it keeps this sexist construction alive and maintains an association of the look with a negative view of women and her sexuality. The theory is made no more palatable by the argument that, insofar as we are all lacking, woman is even more aware of her incomplete status.

In its stead we might consider the development of gender as identificatory and rooted in the problem of the gaze. The disruptive gaze would derive gender from an interruption of the male's primary feminism, developed in identification with the female as mothering person. Whereas the female subject resolves the mother's "no" by moving from *being* the mother's desire to *imitating* the mother's desire, the male in our society is not free to resolve the maternal "no" in this way. Given that the infant cannot always be what the mother wants, nor the mother what the infant wants, given that mothering involves helping the child come to trust in the return of a nurturing other who can leave and disappoint, the development of a way of coping with the mother's "no" is especially pressing for the male. Deprived of the shift toward mimetic desire left open to the female, the male's route can only be a rapid disidentification, resulting in ambivalence toward the nurturing object.

This stance has its precursors in feminist applications of object relations theory. Feminist psychoanalytic theory, in particular the work of Nancy Chodorow, interprets some male behavior as resulting from denied identification with the nurturing or

---

[27] Constance Penley's comment and Peter Gidal's reaction are taken from Stephen Heath's essay, "Difference," *Screen* 19 (1978): 97; Heath's comment is from the same essay, 97–98.

mothering figure.[28] Object relations theory has long suggested that the mothering function is not accomplished by simply drawing the child into an illusion of magical omnipotence but in helping the child accept separateness and disillusion through various "no's."[29] The disruptive maternal gaze is a gaze which reflects back to the child something other than what it wants to see, but which alone makes identity possible. This in turn suggests an interesting reversal; the greater repression is not of the mother's castration (what the child doesn't want to see), but of the subject's loss of face (what the mother doesn't want to see or can't see in the child). The reading which denies this argues that the father's intervention (and not the mother's "no") alone ensures the masculinity that the subject desired all along. The repression of the mother's crucial role in the socialization process is denied.

A more theatrical paradigm would enable women not only to reflect how they perceive they have been perceived, but to look back and forward, to see how their looking back is interpreted and disrupted by another gaze in a continuing theatre of interactive reflections. Lacanian theory has decisively and intentionally limited the potential of the mother's "no" in a variety of ways, then, and cinematic theory's use of the gaze has in turn been reduced to nothing short of male castration anxiety. However successful the application of a phallocentric theory for a reading of phallocentric films, such a model stymies the development of film theory and practice in new directions, resulting in such peculiar avant-garde stances as Gidal's refusal to portray women in his films *since* she is always already the castrated fetishized object.

The difference inverted is not always the difference maintained. To reframe Heath and Gidal via Penley is to point to her place and the mother's place both within and outside the system, and to observe that neither can be so neatly circumscribed. Since neither Heath nor Gidal proves capable of considering the "possibilities and consequences" of the mother returning the look, except as a reversal of the terms of the male look, which in itself is castrating, they project that threat onto Penley. Asks Heath: "What then of the look for the woman, of woman subjects in seeing? The reply given by psychoanalysis is from the phallus. If the woman looks, the spectacle provokes, castration is in the air, the Medusa's head is not far off; thus, she must not look, is absorbed herself on the side of the seen, seeing herself seeing herself, Lacan's femininity."[30] If Heath would distance himself here, his framing of Penley implies that castration is indeed in the air—that male fears of a reversal of their own system are being projected onto a rethinking of representation which begins on the other side of the screen.

The difference inverted is not always the difference maintained. The reply given by psychoanalysis is not always from the phallus. Penley asks about the possibilities of

---

[28] Nancy Chodorow, *The Reproduction of Mothering: Psychoanalysis and the Sociology of Gender* (Berkeley: University of California Press, 1978).

[29] See the survey by Jay R. Greenberg and Stephen A. Mitchell, *Object Relations in Psychoanalytic Theory*, (Cambridge: Harvard University Press, 1983), as well as the work of Margaret Mahler, *On Human Symbiosis and the Vicissitudes of Individuation* (London: Hogarth Press, 1969) and D. W. Winnicott, *Playing and Reality* (London: Tavistock, 1971).

[30] Heath, "Difference," *Screen* 19 (1978): 92.

returning the look because she realizes that no reversal of the look in the same terms is possible—except when the Woman as a construct of the male Imaginary is doing the looking, in which case she does not look from the point of view of *women*. Since Penley, following Laura Mulvey, is critiquing film practice as voyeuristic and fetishistic, her question asks for the development of new ways of looking—in essence the reconstruction of the woman's gaze. The mother's body is not simply a character in a film returning a look, but at once the material out of which a spectacle is constructed, the spectacle itself, and the means by which a spectator is constructed. To return the look in this context is to break up performance space, deconstruct the gaze, subvert the classical organization of showing and seeing, revision spectatorship, and restructure traditional canons, genres, and personal-political identities.

One argument that stalls this movement is summarized by Stephen Heath when he asks whether it is "possible for a woman to take place in a film without representing a male desire," since "any image of a woman in a film, by the fact of its engagement in a process of representation . . . inevitably re-encloses women in a structure of cultural oppression that functions precisely by the currency of 'images of woman.' "[31] He quotes Cixous, who observed: "One is always in representation, and when a woman is asked to take place in this representation, she is, of course, asked to represent man's desire." Yet Heath ignores the key word "asked"; when women are not asked by men to take place in a representation created by and for men, but occupy and share the sites of production and consumption, a different economy obtains. Women take place, and refigure that taking place, in ways that challenge traditional forms of representation and gratify, as they displace, the spectatorial gaze.

Penley cites the films of Yvonne Rainer, Chantal Ackerman, and Marguerite Duras, which "run counter to the Oedipal structuring of Western narrative form and the imaginary and fetishistic imperatives of the cinematic apparatus," effecting changes in "narrative organization, point of view and identification" which resituate "both the spectator and the narrator as 'outside' the scene . . . not caught up in or radically circumscribed by a masculine gaze or logic of desire."[32] Yet to what extent does this approach lead to a feminism that has so succumbed to its manipulation by an avant-garde as to be virtually indistinguishable from it, more concerned with revisioning representation than with exploring contemporary women's experiences?

One of the more challenging directions of avant-garde film has been its interest in fragmenting its representational space in the name of a feminist critique. As Jacqueline Rose observes:

> the impetus is clear: the attempt to place woman somewhere *else*, outside the forms of representation through which she is endlessly constituted as image. The problem is that this sets up notions of drive, rhythmic pulsing, eroticisation of energy pre-representation, a space of "open viewing," which then makes film process itself socially—and sexually—innocent. Film process is then conceived as something archaic, a lost or repressed content

---

[31] Ibid., 96–97.

[32] Constance Penley, " 'A Certain Refusal of Difference': Feminism and Film Theory," in *Art after Modernism: Rethinking Representation*, ed. Brian Wallis (New York: New Museum of Contemporary Art, 1984), 387.

("continent"), terms to which the feminine can so easily be assimilated, as it has been in classical forms of discourse on the feminine as outside language, rationality, and so on; arguments which are now being revived as part of the discussion of psychoanalysis and feminism, the search for a feminine discourse, specific, outside. The dangers are obvious. That such arguments overlook the archaic connotations of these notions of energy and rhythm for women, at the same time that they render innocent the objects and processes of representation which they introject onto the screen, seems again to be not by chance.[33]

In a critique of Lyotard's exploration of a nontheatrical representational space, Rose pointedly remarks: "We have to ask what, if the object itself is removed (the body or victim), is or could be such a space of open viewing (fetishisation of the look itself or of its panic and confusion)? And what does this do for feminism? Other than strictly nothing, dropping all images of women; or else an archaising of the feminine as panic and confusion, which is equally problematic, simply a re-intro-jection as feminine—the pre-mirror girl—of the visual disturbance against which the image of woman classically acts as a guarantee."[34] It would seem that theatre, via performance, is facing many of the same problems.

IV

Is it a coincidence that definitions of feminism, theatre, Lacanian psychoanalysis, and deconstruction are becoming practically indistinguishable? All define themselves as displacing activities designed to resist the suturing coherence of any fixed place. Julia Kristeva argues that "the very dichotomy man/woman as an opposition between two rival entities may be understood as belonging to metaphysics"[35] and offers instead a pulsion between the semiotic (pre-oedipal, prelinguistic energy and desire) and the symbolic (made possible by the semiotic which in turn is repressed for its es-tablishment). To work from the semiotic is to to adopt "a negative function; reject everything finite, definite, structured, loaded with meaning, in the existing state of society." It is to work "on the side of the explosion of social codes, with revolutionary movements."[36] Like Kristeva, Shoshana Felman defines femininity as a "real otherness . . . [which] is uncanny in that it is not the opposite of masculinity but that which subverts the very opposition of masculinity and femininity."[37] Avant-garde feminism's answer, then, is that woman, like theatre, does not take (a) place (Kristeva), but rather, revisions positionality itself.[38] In what sense does a feminism so defined differ from deconstruction? Or from theatre, which manages both to acknowledge the

[33] Jacqueline Rose, *Sexuality and the Field of Vision* (London: Verso, 1986), 209.

[34] Rose, *Sexuality and the Field of Vision*, 210.

[35] Julia Kristeva, "Women's Time," trans. Alice Jardine and Harry Blake, *Signs* 7 (1981): 33.

[36] Julia Kristeva, "Interview with Xavière Gauthier, *Tel Quel* 58 (1974), 98–102; reprinted in *New French Feminisms*, ed. Elaine Marks and Isabelle de Courtivron (Amherst: University of Massachusetts Press, 1980), 166.

[37] Shoshana Felman, "Rereading Femininity," *Yale French Studies* 62 (1981): 42.

[38] See Kristeva's "Modern Theater Does Not Take (a) Place," as well as her interview with Gauthier, noted above, where she identifies "the moment of rupture and negativity which conditions and underlies the novelty of any praxis 'feminine,' " and adds: "No 'I' is there to assume this 'femininity,' but it is no less operative, rejecting all that is finite and assuring in *(sexual) pleasure* the life of the concept" (167).

symbolic and disrupt it from within, to acknowledge and subvert positionality on a continuous basis?

Josette Féral, one of the few theoreticians to explore feminist deconstructive theatre, assumes both are possible—but only when theatre is not theatre *per se*.[39] For Féral, theatre is on the side of inscription in the symbolic, whereas performance is on the side of deconstruction in the semiotic (thus Féral's "theatre" corresponds to Elam's "drama," and her "performance" corresponds to Elam's "theatre").[40] Féral finds theatre and performance "mutually exclusive" "when it comes to the problem of the subject," since "in contrast to performance, theatre cannot keep from setting up, stating, constructing points of view" and depends on a unified subject which performance deconstructs into drives and energies, since theatre assumes and depends on the narrativity and models of representation which performance rejects in favor of discontinuity and spillage.[41] If performance highlights the "realities of the imaginary," "originates within the subject and allows his flow of desire to speak," the theatrical "inscribes the subject in the law and in theatrical codes, which is to say, in the symbolic."[42]

Yet finally Féral is describing a dialectic essential to theatre, not apart from it, which she herself acknowledges by arguing that "theatricality arises from the play between these two realities," and by describing performance as that within theatre which deconstructs it.[43] Féral observes that "in its stripped-down workings, its exploration of the body, and its joining of time and space, performance gives us a kind of theatricality in slow motion, the kind we find at work in today's theatre. Performance explores the under-side of that theatre."[44]

The relationship between performance art and traditional theatre is less a polar opposition than a continuum. We seek in theatre that moment when our looking is no longer a looking (as in film), but a being seen, a return of the look by the mirror image which denies the process. Whereas traditional drama achieves this by setting into motion a series of displacing gazes which succeeds when it disrupts our own gaze without showing us how, performance art puts theatrical construction itself onstage. In *Swan Lake, Minnesota* a stripper performs to a fascinated crowd of men by throwing down cardboard cutouts of her body in various states of undress; the last cutout is a mirror which reflects their gaze. In the performance piece *Waiting*, the author holds up sheets upon which are projected images of waitresses, and then inserts her body and voice in filmed images and narratives of restaurant life, simultaneously positioning herself as author, actor, screen, and the source of their mutual confusion and deconstruction.

Like much theatre theory and practice, Féral's thesis is itself symptomatic of the battle within theatre to differentiate presence from representation, reminding us that

[39] Josette Féral, "Performance and Theatricality," trans. Terese Lyons, *Modern Drama* 25 (1982): 170–84.

[40] See Keir Elam, *The Semiotics of Theatre and Drama* (London: Methuen, 1980), 2.

[41] Féral, "Performance and Theatricality," 177–78.

[42] Ibid., 178.

[43] Ibid., 178.

[44] Ibid., 176.

insofar as theatre stages presence it enacts the agon between being and representation implied in the concept of enactment, and so gives birth to itself by continually reposing that relationship. Féral highlights this fact by using "theatricality" to designate a class which encompasses both theatricality and performance, and by this doubling rightly tags theatre as a Strange or Tangled Loop. Criticized for assuming that performance reaches a presence outside of representation, she in fact merely observes that "performance seems to be attempting to reveal and to stage something that took place before the representation of the subject even if it does so by using an already constituted subject."[45] This is not, finally, at odds with, but rather an opposing approach to, Derrida's argument that: "Presence, in order to be presence and self-presence, has always already begun to represent itself, has always already been penetrated."[46] Thus the paradox of avant-garde theatre: in seeking to stage a moment outside of representation one cannot evade the play of gazes that constitutes representation.

Following Derrida, Herb Blau reminds us that theatre reveals "no *first* time, no origin, but only recurrence and reproduction."[47] Traditional mime has long exposed theatre as a machine of Difference which enacts the coding and decoding of the body, the place and displacement of presence, the construction and deconstruction of the gaze, the carving up and branding of presence (thus the ease with which tatoo art and various forms of bodily mutilation make their way into performance art). Theatre has always suggested a funhouse of mirrors we never escape, a precession of simulacra which remind us we can never reach a body outside of representation. Observes Baudrillard, "simulation is no longer that of a territory, a referential being or a substance. It is the generation by models of a real without origin or reality: a hyperreal."[48] Theatre doesn't hold the mirror up to nature, but is the quintessential simulation of simulations, a hyperreality.

Hélène Cixous offers, inadvertently, one of the best definitions of theatre: "men and women are caught up in a network of millenial cultural determinations of a complexity that is practically unanalyzable: we can no more talk about 'women' than about 'man' without getting caught up in an ideological theatre where the multiplication of representations, images, reflections, myths, identifications constantly transforms, deforms, alters each person's imaginary order and in advance, renders all conceptualization null and void."[49] Peggy Kamuf's "a woman writing like a woman writing like a woman"[50] is quintessentially theatrical, feminist, and deconstructive at once.

The performative side of theatre emerges here as a process of staging the disturbance and reversal of the gaze. Theatre is by definition not amenable to narratives

---

[45] Ibid., 178.

[46] Jacques Derrida, "The Theater of Cruelty and the Closure of Representation," *Writing and Difference*, trans. Alan Bass (Chicago: University of Chicago Press, 1978), 249.

[47] Herbert Blau, "Universals of Performance; or, Amortizing Play," *Sub-Stance* 37-38 (1983): 148.

[48] Jean Baudrillard, "The Precession of Simulacra," in *Art After Modernism*, ed. Brian Wallis (New York: New Museum of Contemporary Art, 1984), 253.

[49] Hélène Cixous, "Sorties," in *New French Feminisms*, 96.

[50] Peggy Kamuf, "Writing like a Woman," in *Women and Language in Literature and Society*, ed. S. McConnell-Ginet et al. (New York: Praeger, 1980), 298.

imported to contain its bent toward subversion. The multiple stages and plots of Renaissance and postmodern theatre alike better convey its function as a philosophical model, insofar as simultaneity of space and action is best suited to its ability to interrupt and stage itself. Observes Mària Minich Brewer: "Theatre allows a philosophical discourse to shift from thought as seeing and originating in the subject alone, to the many decentered processes of framing and staging that representation requires but dissimulates."[51] Theatre provides a theoretical model for postmodernism insofar as it is always setting into play the subversion of its insights.

A theatrical model is thus ideally suited to the project of decentering and subverting fields of representation that face postmodern theory. This explains why theatre is the source not only of much of the vocabulary of postmodern theory (framing, staging, mise en scène, rehearsal and repetition, reenactment), but also of many of its key strategies. A refusal of the observer's stable position, a fascination with re-presenting presence, an ability to stage its own staging, to rethink, reframe, switch identifications, undo frames, see freshly, and yet at the same time see how one's look is always already purloined—these are the benefits of theatre for theory.

Why is it that theatre alone has always staged identity as unstable, exposing gender and class as a masquerade? Why is it that theatre—so associated with self-reflexivity as to become a means of describing it—manages to avoid the *en abyme* structure, evade its own closure, and refuse its own frames? Could it be that, insofar as theatre cannot rest in the *abyme*, but stages the displacing gaze, the bursting of the container by its contents, theatre offers a way of dislodging the current critical standstill whereby we must use language to describe a place outside it?

The question of whether theatre can stage through representation a presence prior to it must be answered through the gaze, which is no less than a discovery of the splitting of subjectivity in its procuring. The gaze is a discovery that one is seen— that one's look is always already purloined by the Other. "It is not true that, when I am under the gaze, when I solicit a gaze, when I obtain it, I do not see it as a gaze. . . . Painters, above all, have grasped this gaze in the mask . . . . The gaze I encounter . . . is not a seen gaze, but a gaze imagined by me in the field of the Other" writes Lacan.[52] Theatre's disrupting gaze reflects any look as already taken; it stages presence as always already represented, and trapped by another's look.

Like the shield held up to view Medusa, theatre offers a perspective glass by means of which we see the object of our gaze as always already reflected. Whether in Sophocles' *Oedipus* or Duras's *India Song*, whether through the displacing gaze of the Medusoid Sphinx or the displaced or out of synch voices of staged characters in avant-garde feminist drama, theatre is always staging the desire to own the purloined place of one's look. Theatre tells the story of a rape which has always already occurred, thereby involving us in a series of gazes which splits and displaces our own. Whereas film is obsessed with seeing one's look, as in Hitchcock films which repeatedly distend

[51] Mària Minich Brewer, "Performing Theory," *Theatre Journal* 37 (1985): 16.

[52] Jacques Lacan, "Anamorphosis," *The Four Fundamental Concepts of Psycho-Analysis,* trans. Alan Sheridan (New York: Norton, 1981), 84.

and peer within the space of their own voyeurism, theatre is fascinated by the return of one's look as a displacing gaze that redefines as it undermines identity. Theatre calls the spectatorial gaze into play by exhibiting a purloined gaze, a gaze that announces it has always been presented to our eyes; is designed only to be taken up by them. The spectatorial gaze takes the bait and stakes its claim to a resting place in the field of vision which beckons it—only to have its gaze fractured, its look stared down by a series of gazes which challenge the place of its look and expose it as in turn defined by the other. The *larvatus prodeo,* or mask which points to itself, is the lure of theatre, a gaze which admits it belongs to the Other, only to become the Other of the spectator in turn.

If cinema appeals to the desire to see oneself seeing, theatre appeals to the desire to expose and displace the displaced gaze—that is, to entangle the other's gaze with one's always already purloined image, to reveal the play of one's look as inevitably, incessantly in motion—displaced and displacing in turn. The striptease is quintessential theatre, its stage the battle of the place of one's look. Will the stripper maintain the place of his look as always already purloined, so as to preserve the female spectator's look, or will he look back in a way that displaces her gaze? Theatre's masks announce that the "I" is always already another; its characters assure us of their displacement, announcing, "I am already taken," as in "this seat is taken," or as in, "That was no lady, that was my wife (mother)." Theatre is the place where a male ruling class has been able to play at being the excluded other, to reveal the sense that "I" is an other. If theatre has offered men a chance to identify with the place of a mother's look, to imitate the mother's desire, and to control the woman's looking back, theatre also offers the opportunity to reframe that moment from a point of view alien to it.

The paradox of the frame and the gaze, the problem of the constitutive gaze in relationship to key problems of change, needs to be worked out more fully both within the discourses of feminism, psychoanalysis, and theatre theory, and in the arguments with which they are involved. Feminism faces this problem in the Kristevan paradox of the semiotic and the symbolic; psychoanalysis faces this problem in the relationship of the Imaginary and the Symbolic; but theatre alone is capable of staging the paradox of the frame in a way that subverts it. Unlike feminism and psychoanalysis, theatre has no allegiance but to ambivalence, to a compulsion to subvert its own gaze, to split itself through a reflected image.

Theatre comfortably allies with feminism against psychoanalysis, with psychoanalysis against cinema, and with cinema against itself, without ever finding a resting point except as provisional and always already undermined. Whereas feminism and psychoanalysis seek to reflect the subject from a place where it can never see itself, be it gender, ideology, or the unconscious, theatre provides the tools—the stages, the mirrors, or reflecting gazes—through which perspectives are fragmented, shattered, and set into play against one another. A methodology necessarily tied to no master, theatre is quintessentially deconstructive, and poses a methodological challenge to feminism and psychoanalysis to escape its terms, its goals, its identity.

We close here with an open question, one posed at the end of Lacan's seminar, "The Split Between the Eye and the Gaze." "To what extent," asks X. Audouard, "is it necessary, in analysis, to let the subject know that one is looking at ⟨is⟩ is to say, that one is situated as the person who is observing in the subject t⟨h⟩ of looking at oneself?"[53] Freud prided himself on his particular position analytic setting—"seeing . . . but not seen myself."[54] But of course Freud ⟨v⟩ himself here, and it this delusion that Lacan would seem to have discovered. Yet Lacan answers defensively, belittling Audouard and almost purposefully misunderstanding him: "We do not say to the patient, at every end and turn, 'Now now! What a face you're making!,' or, 'The top button of your waistcoat is undone.' It is not, after all, for nothing that analysis is not carried out face to face."[55] Yet it is in the gaze that psychoanalysis, feminism, and theatre meet and revision one another. The mere presence of the analyst sets up the gaze; the patient knows she is being heard and watched, and so hears and watches herself differently; the second mirror is in play, mirroring the first, displacing and placing body, voice, and gaze.

The associations I have drawn here suggest that theatre opens up a constructive path for psychoanalytic theory and feminist theory to follow—if they are willing to fully accept the implications of their own displacing gazes. We need, that is, to reread Lacan against himself, to accept how feminism's gaze has been purloined, to interrogate the political implications of psychoanalysis. Theatrical reading is ambivalent reading, dedicated *not* to varying the look (which simply amounts to critical pluralism) but to disrupting it, (up)staging theories through one another. It requires that psychoanalysis read cinema and theatre read psychoanalysis, and —following the motto each would prescribe for the subject—that none of these disciplines ever rests secure in itself.

The question is not, therefore, whether a feminist or a deconstructive theatre is possible, but how separate, and how theatrical, these strategies really are. Can deconstruction stand outside of theatre as a technique to be used upon it, or is it always already within it? To theatricalize one must deconstruct, insert a difference in a term which splits it, mimics it, then displaces or usurps it. "A woman writing like a woman writing like a woman" is never the same woman. If neither feminism nor psychoanalysis can frame theatre, but only mine or mime it, the reason may be because their techniques have long been trapped inside it. The cost of exit is denial or repression—or perhaps another frame-up.

Can the contents explode the container? *Shrew* puns on the paradox of the enclosed enclosing and so nullifying its frame. Grumio jests that "the oats have eaten the horses" (III. ii. 201–3), and Tranio plots so that "A child shall get a sire" (III. i. 413). But can we reframe *The Taming of the Shrew*, and can we reframe its counterpart, *Oedipus?* The work has already begun. Listen—or rather, listen again: "Long afterward, Oedipus, old and blinded, walked the roads. He smelled a familiar smell. It was the Sphinx. Oedipus said, 'I want to ask one question. Why didn't I recognize

---

[53] X. Audouard, "Questions and Answers," following Lacan's "The Split Between the Eye and the Gaze," in *Four Fundamental Concepts*, 77.

[54] Freud, "An Autobiographical Study," trans. James Strachey (New York: Norton, 1952), 47.

[55] Lacan, "The Split Between the Eye and the Gaze," 78.

my mother?' 'You gave the wrong answer,' said the Sphinx. 'But that was what made everything possible,' said Oedipus. 'No,' she said. 'When I asked, What walks on four legs in the morning, two at noon, and three in the evening, you answered, Man. You didn't say anything about woman.' 'When you say Man,' said Oedipus, 'you include women too. Everyone knows that.' She said, 'That's what you think.' "[56]

[56] Muriel Rukeyser, "Myth," in *The Collected Poems* (New York: McGraw-Hill, 1978), 498.

Hélène Cixous's *Portrait de Dora:*
The Unseen and the Un-scene

Sharon Willis

With *Portrait de Dora*, Hélène Cixous re-opens Freud's Dora case. "Cracking" the case, breaking the frame of the portrait, this spectacle of circulating voices and images stages a particular theoretical encounter: that of feminism and psychoanalysis.

Dora: A Fragment of an Analysis of a Case of Hysteria is one of Freud's more compelling case histories. In its urgency to unravel the enigma of Dora's symptoms and to demonstrate in an unassailable theoretical formulation the sexual aetiology of hysterical neurosis, as well as neuroses in general, the case produces remarkable narrative effects. In some respects, the case reads like a detective novel, with Freud weaving ever more complex and startling interpretations around the clues he uncovers in the hysteric's symptoms and dreams. Freud repeatedly stresses the need for a narrative, which translates the symptoms into discourse. His anxiety to "get the story straight" is particularly intense because hysterics are marked by their inability to give complete and logical accounts; their narratives are full of gaps and blockages.

But this narrative strategy of recovery and disclosure — a full account — is linked in the Dora case to a certain blindness on Freud's part. By his own admission, as expressed in supplementary footnotes, Freud overlooked certain crucial features of the case. The principal among these was Dora's homosexual attraction for Frau K. It is this non-recognition of a feminine love object, as well as Freud's confining himself to an exploration of Dora's relationship with her father, thereby excluding the mother from his investigation, that has led feminist critics to re-read the case in a critical light. These re-readings, my own included, are marked by a particular intensity.[1] What is

Sharon Willis is an Assistant Professor of French at Miami University of Ohio. She has published on feminist theory and French literature, and has recently completed a book on the novels of Marguerite Duras.

[1] Feminist response to the case has been intense and wide-ranging. Much of this work has attempted to disclose contradictions that are at work in this case, and which seem to haunt Freud's psychoanalytic project when it deals with "the woman question." A special issue of *Diacritics*, 12, No. 4 (Fall 1983), devoted to the case of Dora includes articles that focus on Freud's counter-transference (his own desire as it

compelling about the case is its occlusion of feminine figures as objects of both desire and identification in a text that aims to eliminate a disturbance in sexuality, to make female sexual development run its proper Oedipal course, to tell the right story, to reach the proper conclusion. In so doing, the case contradicts psychoanalysis's own major currents, for it refuses the complexity and overdetermination of the family romance, just as it implicitly separates the analytic scene from the social world. And, in this case, the social world is one in which Dora finds herself to be an object of exchange between her father and his lover's husband, Herr K.

Feminist response to the case has focused on these features, coupled with the emblematic status of hysteria as the female disease par excellence of the nineteenth century. Hysteria, a disturbance of women's sexuality, constitutes a rupture in the social sexual economy. Moreover, the nature of hysterical attacks — a physical display where the body becomes a symptomatic map to be read by the clinical gaze — produces a site of condensation of major issues for feminist theory: woman as body-image-spectacle for a gaze historically construed as masculine.

In making a case of *Dora*, Cixous's text enters a peculiar bind: its efficacy depends on the spectator's knowledge of its pretext, and more generally, on some idea of the historical status of hysteria and its importance for the origins of psychoanalysis. Such a risk might be unreasonable were it not for the question that casts its shadow across Cixous's text: why should theatre be the arena in which such a meeting of theoretical discourses is staged, in which such an interpretive re-reading is enacted? Because *Portrait de Dora* reframes Freud's text in a way that puts into question the theatrical frame, and the body staged within it, it becomes exemplary of the critical operations of certain feminist performance practice, particularly in its steadfast refusal of the categories theory and practice.

Now, this text's relation to both psychoanalysis and theatre is highly ambivalent, if not contradictory. It is from psychoanalysis that we learn that interpretation is performance and performance interpretation. But psychoanalysis has also fallen in line with classical means of coding sexual difference and the gaze, by making a spectacle of the hysterical body. Although psychoanalysis has provided feminist theories with the groundwork for a theory of the construction of gendered subjects, and of sexual difference, the relationship between the two discourses remains uneasy precisely because psychoanalysis often codes the visible absence of a penis as lack. To play with visibility, with femininity as spectacle, allows feminist performance practice to uncover certain contradictions which inhabit psychoanalysis and the logic of the gaze. But to seize the apparatus of spectacle, to expose and to display a feminine body on stage demands

was invested in Dora and in the question of the outcome of the case), on the exclusion of the mother from his analytic interpretations, and on the question of the visual as the organizing metaphor of Freud's theory at this point. My essay in the collection, "A Symptomatic Narrative," concentrates on the question of visibility in the case, developing the summary I present above. More recently, *In Dora's Case* (New York: Columbia University Press, 1985), edited by Charles Bernheimer, is a collection of critiques of the case from sociological and historical perspectives as well as from within psychoanalytical discourse.

that this practice maintain a critical relation to its own discourse, a consciousness of the risk of reinstating these structures.[2]

But what of theatre, and its relation to the feminine spectacle — parade or fetish — and to the body? to desire? to fantasy? What can this scene that opens and closes before us, in its intermittancy, its shifting geometry, tell us about the body as spectacle? What can it tell us about the spectators, the gendered subjects who are addressed, however obliquely, and therefore set in place by the spectacle?

Portrait de Dora

The scene that opens before us is already split, divided; the stage contains a scrim on which images are projected: some filmed, some stills. These potential interference effects — the struggle between images and "real" bodies to capture our attention, the juxtaposition of moving images and immobile ones, the tension between speech and voice — contain all the contradictions this play asks us to work through, as well as the ones that underlie Freud's own case.

As the play opens, "Projected on the scrim is the 'incident by the lake.' . . . Freud's voice [in the French: *la voix de la pièce*], seated, from behind. '. . . these events project themselves like a shadow in dreams, they often become so clear that we feel we can grasp them, but yet they escape our final interpretation, and if we proceed without skill and special caution, we cannot know if they really took place.'"[3] The scrim is a screen which both conceals and makes visible.

Screens, in general, function both as barriers and as supports for projection, and this, not without *framing*, enclosing an image while excluding something else — as its outside. This citation also opens the question of reference, a question that haunted Freud's analytical research on the seduction theory (could there be a real referent, a real scene of seduction?), whose analysis eventually produced the theory of the

---

[2] It is all too easy to uncover certain apparent anti-feminist biases in the Dora case: Freud's discounting the importance of Dora's mother, or the libidinal force of her affection for Frau K., her father's lover. Because the case lends itself to a critique of Freud as narcissistically invested in perfecting his theory, and therefore blind to the issues, it allows construction of a "bad" Freud, who "blames the victim." This is coherent with the most simplistic versions of Freud in popular mythology. However, since feminist theory relies upon the tools of psychoanalysis in order to construct its own theories of subjectivity in language, which are necessary to account for feminine sexuality in its articulation in the social field where real women are oppressed, that very theory cannot leave psychoanalysis out of the picture, disowning its own generation. Such denial would be to retreat from and simultaneously to repeat the mistakes haunting the development of psychoanalytic theory, as it was generated in a confrontation with hysteria — a disturbance both *in* and *by* female sexuality.

[3] Hélène Cixous, *Portrait of Dora*, trans. Sarah Burd, *Diacritics* 13, No. 1 (Spring 1983), p. 3, henceforth cited as *Portrait* (also, *Portrait de Dora* [Paris: Éditions de femmes, 1976]). The founding reference of the play concerns screen memories, those sharply defined and coherently narrated childhood memories which are entirely innocuous and often *invented* to conceal the traumatic ones. Screen memories conceal but also produce the path of interpretation which leads to the significant memories, through resemblance and contiguity. See Sigmund Freud, "Screen Memories," *The Standard Edition*, ed. James Strachey (London: Hogarth Press, 1983), III: 320.

Oedipus complex.[4] Meanwhile, the problem of the referent was a source of constant struggle between Freud and Dora (she really was being sexually and emotionally manipulated by her father and his friends), and finally, in an oblique way, halted the progress of the analysis, since Freud insisted on too narrow a referential frame (by his own admission) for Dora's symptoms.[5] That is, he framed the case around the male principals, completely excluding Dora's mother, and failing to recognize Frau K. as a possible object of Dora's desire as well as her identification. Part of the play's project is thus to re-frame the case, shifting the structure of inclusion and exclusion and, in so doing, to call attention to the necessary consequences of any framing.

In another striking moment of citation, the play's Freud repeats a passage from the Dora case: "This first account may be compared to an unnavigable river whose stream is at one moment choked by masses of rock and at another divided and lost among shallows and sandbanks" (p. 4).[6] Here Freud refers to the hysteric's life story as told on entry into analysis: it is full of gaps and blockages, or amnesias, which the analysis sets about to restore.

[4] Much work and debate has recently appeared concerning the seduction theory, a theory which historically has been the source of controversy and splits, both within and outside the psychoanalytic movement. See, for example, Janet Malcolm, *In the Freud Archives* (New York: Knopf, 1984), for an account of Geoffrey Masson's recent assault on Freud's theory that infantile seduction, as recounted by analysands, refers to infantile sexual fantasies, rather than to historical sexual encounters with adults. The most consistent arguments advanced about the question of infantile seduction, however, do not insist upon refuting its fantasmatic character, but rather, attempt to show that admission of the possibility that some seductions are real does not undermine the theory of infantile sexuality. Freud insisted on *fantasized* seduction, where he had initially believed in a historical referent for the patients' discourse on paternal seduction. This insistence is related to a desire to preserve the integrity of the paternal figure, and correspondingly, to assure the coherence of his theory of the sexual aetiology of the neuroses by demonstrating infantile sexuality. While both impulses seem to be present in Freud's work, they do not undermine the theory. In the Dora case, the issue of the *referent* of the seduction scene is particularly intense, raised as it is by Dora's family and her analyst. The trauma of receiving Herr K.'s sexual advances, as described by Dora, is relegated to the level of fantasy by both Freud and her father. For the latter, this is convenient; it is a way of disposing of the consequences of a historical event that cannot be acknowledged. What is troubling to the feminist reader is the coherence of Freud's response, even though motivated by another interest, with the Victorian familial discourse.

[5] Dora suffered from a number of symptoms, the most prominent of which were aphonia, a sore throat, and a vaginal discharge. Freud's reading tends to situate them within a heterosexual framework, thereby leaving out possible homosexual references. He sees all of these symptoms as either displacements of sexual excitation produced by contact with Herr K., or as marks of identification with her father, who had a venereal disease. In so doing, however, he leaves out of consideration Dora's conversational — oral — exchanges with Frau K., as the desired love object and model with whom she identifies. For instance, when he interrogates the sources and extent of Dora's sexual knowledge upon discovering that she imagines the form sexual relations must take between Frau K. and her impotent father, Freud elaborately reconstructs her fantasy as a fantasy of fellatio, never considering a corresponding cunnilingus fantasy. In a distinctly un-Freudian manner, he thus reads her *oral* sexual knowledge, gained through exchange with Frau K., as purely literal, never seeing its possible figural signification — that of indicating a homosexual desire. In *Portrait*, Cixous sets in play these symptoms and the dream elements coherent with them. By distributing them differently, giving them different stress, this text throws into relief, brings to light, their overdetermined status, a status obscured by Freud's heterosexual interpretive frame, and by his decision to adhere to a strict referentiality of the symptom at certain points, while denying it at others.

[6] This passage appears in Sigmund Freud, *Dora: An Analysis of a Case of Hysteria*, ed. Philip Reiff (New York: Macmillan, 1979), p. 30. Also, *Standard Edition*, V.

What Freud strove to organize into a complete narrative account is reproduced in the play as fragmented, divided, a stream that is perpetually disrupted by obstacles or diverted in detours. The analysis, and the narrative coherence it aims for, are "pricked, pierced, stitched, unstitched. It's all women's work," as Dora comments (p. 16). "Women's work" here consists of fragmentation, juxtaposition, and interruption. In *Portrait*, Freud appears as both character and "voice of the play." The above citation adopts the ruse of a central controlling voice, a narrator, but this position is progressively undermined. The central voice's authority is undercut by the intervention of multiple, conflicting voices — another interference effect.

In the same vein, the texture of scenic coherence is fissured; the stage is quite literally split. As the Freud character speaks, the "incident by the lake," the moment of sexual trauma isolated in the Dora case — when Herr K. kisses Dora passionately — is represented on film. The analytic discourse here might be taken to explain the *referent*, the incident by the lake, just as the filmed scene might be taken as an illustration — the imagistic doubling of speech. But the staging of two representational modes here still leaves open the question of referentiality: how are we to read it, as memory or fantasy? While the spoken discourse throws into question the historical status of the events recounted by the hysteric, the filmed image might be taken to contradict speech, since the images necessarily attest to the existence of some *pro-filmic* event.

The split of the stage/scene — where performance works against narrative — is redoubled as the play produces a schism in its narrative pretext, the case history. Speaking as the "voice of the play," the Freud character *narrates* a new "take" on the incident by the lake.

> (Very cold and monotone, Freud's voice) during which time the incident by the lake is projected on the screen with several modifications.
> Doctor Freud could have dreamt this, at the end of December, 1899. Dora is an exuberant girl . . . She has something contradictory and strange about her which is attractive . . . Dr. Freud cannot take his eyes off her . . . Then, without any warning, she raises her dress in a purposely seductive gesture . . . (then, a chorus of voices, Herr B., Herr K., Frau K. and Freud speak in succession).
>
> [p. 19]

In this re-inscription of the traumatic incident by the lake, the speaking subject, the figure of Freud, who is already split into the voice of the play and the character, is again split — this time into narrator and narrated. The content of this fantasy scene reflects yet another split, one that conditioned the Dora case itself. "Freud," here, figures both the transference and the counter-transference. Such a narrative split works against any stable consolidation of a narrating instance as organizing authority that guarantees sense and legibility. The canon of voices splinters that central instance — multiplies and fragments it. Narration is continually diverted. The Freud figure is caught up in a hysterical relay of identifications, where filmed images and the staged scenes and a chorus of voices consistently set themselves *against* narrative. This split necessarily affects the position of the spectator, who is bound into narrative structure at its point of address, the subject for its meaning.

In a later effect of fragmentation, Dora tells a story which she simultaneously "acts out on a side stage" (p. 7). This performance becomes, in effect, the theatre within the analytic scene. It is a play on the technical term "acting out" — exactly what the analysand's discursive rendition is supposed to eliminate. The hysteric becomes an actress to make visible the scene she describes, thus sundering the analytic space and literalizing the figuration of the hysteric as an "actress," as a faker.

Cutting and segmentation are the crucial gestures of Cixous's text, on the structural and performative levels. *Portrait of Dora* is constructed like a collage — segments are ripped from the surrounding material of the case and juxtaposed with invented fragments. Speech and citations are lifted from the case, stolen from the characters to whom they are attributed in Freud's text and assigned/grafted onto other figures in *Portrait* in a montage effect.

Collage capitalizes on effects of interference, on a de-contextualizing and re-contextualizing that combines mutually exclusive or interfering discourses in such a way that both the selective and limiting functions of the *frame* are thrown into relief. At the same time, the re-framing necessarily stresses the division within the object (signifier-signified) even prior to its transposition.[7] In another kind of transference, a literal one, Cixous's text calls our attention to distinct, mutually interfering levels of reading, and to the reciprocal structuring effect between frame and field.

Not only does *Portrait of Dora* produce a fragmented ventriloquization of Freud's text, disseminating "citations" from it throughout, but it also choreographs a scene that is no longer the closed dialogue between analyst and analysand, or the third person structure of narration. Rather, the spectator is presented with an orchestration, a circulation of voices. Such a reversal of the implicit scenic space of the case (where "background" figures enter the scene) reflects the challenge that performance poses to narrative order and desire. Effects of circulation block "normal" narrative development from ignorance and concealment to knowledge and disclosure.

Such circulation is apparent on the level of discourse, signifiers, pronouns, and voices. For instance, on page 15 of *Portrait*, Dora cites Herr K.: "there was no reason to hope. Everything separates us. He told me: (Frau K.'s voice) 'Thus, nothing is different.'" Here the stroke of quotation marks, the citation, constitutes a radical detachment: the cited words are literally spoken by another voice, but *not* by the person to whom they are attributed. Partially or completely untethered from character, the ventriloquized voices, citations from the case, wander across the text. Voice takes on a life of its own, enters the scene as an agency. An exchange between Freud and Dora moves from vocal miming to complete autonomy of voice.

> Freud: No, it's a former patient; she has stayed in touch with my family since she was cured.

---

[7] See Gregory Ulmer, "The Object of Post-Criticism," in *The Anti-Aesthetic: Essays on Post-Modern Culture*, ed. Hal Foster (Port Townsend, Washington: Bay Press, 1983), p. 84. "The operation, which may be characterized as a kind of 'bricolage' (Levi-Strauss), includes four characteristics — *découpage* (or severing); preformed or extent messages or materials; assemblage (montage); discontinuity or heterogeneity. 'Collage' is the transfer of materials from one context to another, and 'montage' is the 'dissemination' of these borrowings through new settings." See as well, Benjamin Buloch, "Allegorical Procedures: Appropriation and Montage in Contemporary Art," *Artforum* (September 1982), 44.

Dora: In touch with my family.
Freud: Come on, don't be a baby. Believe me. Tell me your dream.
Dora: Don't be a baby.
(Frau K. is there, sitting not too far from Dora, who doesn't see her but who hears her. Frau K.'s voice reaches Dora from the back, goes right through her).

[p. 23]

Voice becomes an impossible element to stage. How could one represent it "going right through her"? An instrument that blocks exchange through ventriloquism, which produces an uncanny doubling, voice is split off from body. It is not clear whether the actress playing Frau K. *speaks* the words, or whether a mechanically reproduced voice is projected from another site on the set. In this detachment, Frau K.'s voice occupies the place of the analyst — who sits behind the analysand. She is heard, but not seen, by Dora. Voice overturns the privilege of sight and destabilizes the configuration of staged space through the non-coincidence of body and speech.

On another level, the circulation of voices disturbs relations among the characters, as criss-crossing identifications conflate identities — all of which turn on the reversibility or breakdown of subject-object relation. Following the lines of force of the original case, the drama is established around men's exchange and substitution of women. But identity is problematic on another level as well, for Dora's hysteria dramatizes a series of identifications: with Freud, with her mother, with Frau K. *and* Herr K. In the play Dora states this clearly: "She sometimes wondered if she weren't Herr K. herself. In his place, how she would have loved her" (p. 21). This utterance detaches gender from the body and from enunciative position.

A later dream of Dora's again displaces identity through identification:

> "I wanted to speak to Doctor K. I knew all the time that he wasn't a real doctor. I wanted to ask his advice. I ask for him on the phone. Finally I get him. It's not he, it's his wife. I feel her presence there, veiled, white, intriguing."
Frau K. (on the phone): "Who's calling?"
Dora: "She asks me. Frau K. speaking . . . I say."
Frau K. (on the phone): "That's going too far."

[p. 29]

Not only does Dora claim the place and the name of Frau K., whose voice *we* hear as telephonic as well, but she succeeds in superimposing three major figures: Frau K., Herr K., and Freud himself. Behind Frau K. is the veiled, unmentioned, intriguing figure of Freud, the doctor (whose status is in question), who is obsessed with anxiety around the charge that he is not a "real" or legitimate doctor. The moment of Dora's occupation of Frau K.'s place — mirroring her to herself, stealing her name — effects a vertiginous rotation of pronomial position, from "I" to "you" to "he/she." This gesture undermines all interlocutive situations, while foregrounding the imaginary and specular investments by which theatrical spectatorship is implicated here.

Toward the end of the text, this disruptive function reaches a heightened intensity in Freud's last words to Dora: "I'd like to hear from me. . . . Write to me" (p. 32). Within parentheses, the stage directions indicate, ironically, that "this slip of the tongue is not necessarily noticeable." This little disavowal naturally only heightens its effect: this is the culmination of the identificatory circuit, the utter collapse of the I-You opposition, as well as a playful turn on the phrase "slip of the tongue." Freud's Freudian slip here works to disclose the network of slips that are really slippages, displacements that dramatize not only Freud's final "hysterical" identification with Dora, but also a kind of hystericization of the entire stage through rampant identificatory exchanges among its characters. The instability of first and second persons necessarily rebounds upon the spectator position as well, since we are the invisible, unacknowledged, and also privileged "you" to whom the performance is addressed, whose desire it solicits.

The textual machine stages a complex and expanding fantasy structure, which may exceed the boundary of the stage. Fantasy structure is constituted as a "scenario with multiple entries," according to Laplanche and Pontalis. "Fantasy . . . is not the object of desire, but its setting. In fantasy the subject does not pursue the object or its representation, but is himself represented in the scene, although, in the earliest forms of fantasy, he cannot be assigned any fixed place in it."[8] The subject cannot occupy a fixed place; rather, it is "in the very syntax of the sequence in question." Desire is articulated in the fantasy, indissociable from the structure itself, which offers multiple entries and exits, since it is founded in the reversibility of the drives; they turn round into their opposites, a turning which is echoed in the syntactic shifts.

Where is *our* desire in all this? At what place do we, the spectators, arrive, take up our positions? At second person, at third? As spectators, we are bound into the performance structure through a form of identification as well. In this elaborate structure of multiple and fragmented address, offering multiple points of identification, the instability of the text's point of address is a means of insisting on performance *as* address. We can no longer establish our place as subjects outside the frame, subjects for whom the scene unfolds at a stable distance.

It is no accident that Freud is made to say "I'd like to hear from me," since certain readings of the Dora case uncover a narcissistic impulse that could be characterized, somewhat playfully, as the analyst's desire to hear from himself, to hear himself, across the analysand. The repercussions of such a disclosure are multiple. Freud's own desire is very much at stake in this case, and returns to him across the other, as if from another, both in his text and in *Portrait* — like a long-distance call. In a peculiar literalization of metaphor, when Dora calls Frau K. on the telephone and gives her name as "Frau K.," the latter receives a call from herself, hears from herself. Dora is a sort of switchboard across which sending and receiving become confused, and messages are re-routed. The stage is an hystericized body — a giant relay where identifications are acted out, but never consolidated in identities.

In this general slippage of pronouns and address, the notion of gender position as coincident with the body is disrupted. *Portrait of Dora* critically re-stages the bisexual pantomime of hysteria, which, for Freud, is related to an inability to separate desire and identification according to the proper Oedipal narrative scenario resolving itself in identification with the mother and desire for the father.

[8] Jean Laplanche and J.-B. Pontalis, "Fantasy and the Origin of Sexuality," *International Bulletin of Psychoanalysis*, 49 (1968), 17.

Most specifically, these issues arise around an *image* of a woman. Another sort of "portrait," the image of the Madonna, central to both the case and the play, becomes the site of intense contradiction here. Freud's most startling interpretive *tours de force* occur upon Dora's second dream, which is largely concerned with images: the Sistine Madonna she has recently seen and a landscape including a forest and nymphs. In Dora's fascination with this portrait, Freud finds a series of unconscious wishes and identifications. First, he sees an identification with the Madonna that reveals a maternal longing. Retrospectively, long after the analysis has ended, he remarks in a footnote upon the possible homosexual desire for Frau K. (Freud, *Dora*, p. 122), a desire whose significance he feels he has overlooked. Juxtaposed with the landscape in the dream thought, this image, according to Freud, also reveals an identification with a male suitor, and a fantasy of defloration — from the male point of view, penetrating the woods to reach the *nymphae* in the background. "'Nymphae,' as is known to physicians . . . is the name given to the labia minora, which lie in the background of the 'thick wood' of the pubic hair" (Freud, *Dora*, p. 120). (This interpretation was the screen that had concealed Frau K.'s importance in Dora's psychic drama.) The woman spectator, Dora, before a picture of a woman, occupies a position split between identification with the mother and with a desiring male subject.[9]

"A picture of a woman" is one of the critical moments in the play as well. When Freud asks Dora what it was that captured her in the painting, the following "scene" ensues.

> Dora: "The . . . Her . . ."
> Suddenly, the evidence, perhaps unnoticed by everyone: the infant Jesus held by the Madonna is none other than a baby Dora. Filmed sequence of three stills. The Sistine Madonna, substitution of the Madonna, and Frau K. Dora behind the Madonna, seen through a mirror.
> (The audience does not know who is speaking, Mary or Frau K.)
>
> [p. 11]

This remarkable sequence of substituting stills, which seems to enact the substitutability of women that underlies the social side of the Dora case, is also the only one where projected images are stills and not filmed. The motion of the pictures is then added on, a surplus — a cinematic effect that is produced right in the theatre. Such a technical decision marks out the segmentation; instead of a smooth flow of image into image, in effect, we *see* the frame, we see the cut. That is, we are aware of the operations of the enunciative apparatus.

But what is held in frame? First, the Madonna image of Freud's account. This is a materialization of the referent on stage, the coincidence of our view with Dora's. Next, the replacement-conflation of the Madonna and Frau K., which produces the coincidence on stage of a character and her photograph, the body and its image-in-frame.

[9] Freud reconstructs this fantasy around the following verbal figure: "because of what appears in the picture (the word, the nymphs), the 'bild' (picture) is turned into a 'Weibsbild' (literally, 'picture of a woman' — a derogatory expression for 'woman')" (*Dora*, p. 119, n. 11). Thus, he reads Dora's position unilaterally, as split in a binary opposition: as identifying with a woman who is a mother, or as a man desiring a woman. In this schema there is no place for a combination or conflation of desire and identification, for the coexistence of homosexual and heterosexual desire.

Finally, the image that destroys the coincidence of our visual fascination and Dora's — Dora herself — enters the frame. She is doubly framed, by the photograph and the mirror. Contemplating the Madonna, seeking an answer to the enigma of femininity through its image, Dora finds her own mirror image behind it. An allusion to the mirror stage — the imaginary plenitude of a totalized body is here complicated. The illusory plenitude of the body as image is overlaid in this figuration, as it is in the mirror stage itself, with the symbolic intervention constituted by the mother who holds the child before the mirror. What the subject here sees is not only the image of her own bodily integrity, but her separation both from the mother and from the image. This visual disclosure of the mother's autonomy is the first cut, the separation, in which language and desire arise. Thus, this sequence places the cut *in* the image as well as between images, refusing an uninterrupted plenitude.

The tensions articulated in the mirror stage, where the subject recognizes/ misrecognizes its image, are the initial mappings of the mechanisms of visual pleasure: voyeuristic and narcissistic. The imaginary plenitude of the mirrored image, over against the felt dispersion of the subject who views it, produces a sense of separation and lack, and an identificatory fascination simultaneously. These two impulses, routed through the castration complex, develop into voyeuristic scopophilia, which produces the subject's pleasure in separation from and mastery over an object, and the narcissistic pleasure of identifying with imaginary plenitude, figured in the fetish object.[10]

This opposition, voyeurism-narcissism, is clearly structured around a configuration of sexual difference, where "feminine" is read as object and lack, juxtaposed with "masculine" as subject and totality of presence. What is paradoxical and crucial about sexual difference is that, while it is the support of representation, its meanings are always produced and reproduced *through* representation.[11] The imaginary lining of representational practices, then, is distributed in figurations which are mapped in a social discursive field, itself always historical.

The body itself is coded in and through representation, just as the image and its spectator are constructed at the juncture of the imaginary with historical discursive structures which map the subject in discourse. On this view, if the lack-to-be of all subjectivity is figured in "woman" as image or spectacle to be held at a distance and contained within a frame assuring the spectator's restored imaginary plenitude, then this is a strategy that might be subject to displacement. Such a displacement might be effected through the production of a space of feminine spectatorship, based as it is in a split identification: with the gaze coded as the site of an active and coherent

[10] As Laura Mulvey puts it in "Visual Pleasure and Narrative Cinema," *Screen* 16, No. 3 (1975), 11: "desire, born with language, allows the possibility of transcending the instinctual and the imaginary, but its point of reference continually returns to the traumatic moment of its birth: the castration complex. Hence, the look, pleasurable in form, can be threatening in content, and it is women as representation/ image that crystallizes this paradox."

[11] For a very thorough treatment of this question, see Teresa De Lauretis, "Through the Looking Glass," in *The Cinematic Apparatus*, eds. Teresa De Lauretis and Stephen Heath (London: Macmillan, 1980), p. 189.

"masculine" subject, and with the image, as the site of passive "feminine" spectacle *for* that subject.

Cixous's text exposes and works on this split, a tactic that permits it to show the relation between spectator and image as one of reciprocal construction. That is, the spectator addressed by the spectacle is also mapped in place by it. Breaching the discursive frameworks that separate theatrical (and psychoanalytical) space, her text *performs* the "masquerade," the image of women as "the woman." [12] This is, in part, the significance of the choice of theatrical structure: what better site for intervention than that of hysteria, the original "object" of psychoanalysis, the spectacle of sexual disturbance mapped on the body in the bisexual pantomime of the attack. The hysteric is the spectacle of a "failure" to become fixed in the proper gender position. Femininity is revealed as a masquerade in the domain of masks: the theatre. But this hyperbolic performance of image construction calls into question the purity of the mask, source of theatrical pleasure. This performance refuses complete separation of mask from body, stage from social space, illusion from reference, by exposing the enunciative apparatus that maps our position as its point of address. Thus it is possible to conceive of the body, inscribed as it is in social space, as itself a mask, a masquerade.

The collision forced by the play provides the opportunity for feminist practice to work out of the confines of strict binary opposition: voyeurism-fetishism. It allows for examination of the contextual disposition of spectatorship, as social practice, within which we are *inscribed* and acted upon, but where we are also agents and producers of readings.

The image of Dora *behind* the Madonna and "unnoticed, perhaps, by everyone" as the baby Jesus, produces a split in the image that replicates the split of the stage. Its image inverts the dream image of the nymphs and woods, where Freud places Dora as viewing subject in a masculine position, seeing woods as pubic hair veiling labia and fantasizing about defloration. Instead, Dora is inside the image, looking out; she is both a picture of a woman and its spectator.

As spectators, we are invited to imagine that we see as Dora sees/saw the Madonna. But at the moment of Dora's insertion into the image as mirrored, the mirror turned outward then reflects her image and our absence from the image — a deviation of our perspective away from hers. The imaginary surplus disrupts our position, which is split between voyeurism and identification, and between the conventional constructions of "masculine" subject of the gaze and "feminine" object.

These still images are emblematic of the text's title, *Portrait of Dora*: the problem of woman immobilized in frame, as spectacle offered to view, is enacted in an overarching textual strategy. As interruptions in narrative flow, these images place us in

---

[12] See Stephen Heath, *Questions of Cinema* (Bloomington: Indiana University Press, 1981), p. 187. This is Heath's description of the psychoanalytic prolongation of a misrecognition involved in the presentation of woman as spectacle; the image offers an illusory presence, a plenitude that compensates the lack assigned to the feminine, just as women are totalized and homogenized under the category "woman." Both gestures also entail a conflation of sexuality with gender position.

the position of the fetishist who arrests his gaze, his narrative exploration of the woman's body *before* its conclusion, before the discovery of castration. As both veil and anticipated disclosure, the image of the woman threatens to reveal the truth of castration. Held in frame, a surface plenitude, it also reassures against it. But this is an image un-framed, perpetually re-framed, such that we as spectators cannot master it, contain it, or maintain a fixed distance from it.

Portrait of Dora constructs a space where immobility and flow are in contradiction; the fixed image disrupts the narrative flow, reveals the intermittancy, the perpetual loss in oscillation between presence and absence upon which narrative and performance structures are based, but which they also regulate. Completely unbroken by division into acts or scenes, *Portrait of Dora* nevertheless plays fixation against flow, rupture against continuity, illusory plenitude against anticipated loss. It continually stages effects of cutting like those performed in the montage of stills framed within the Madonna scene.

As Roland Barthes has it, representation rests upon the act of cutting, or *découpage*: the act of isolating and immobilizing a segment, an object.[13] Any act of *découpage* serves at once to assure the unity of a subject for whose gaze the segment is isolated, who assists the cut, and also to enframe something present to view, while excluding or holding off something outside the framed field. While *Portrait of Dora* plays with the various means of cutting out a segment, it also discloses and works with a more menacing form of cutting — amputation, separation, castration. The cut itself, then, is split into a menace to and a guarantee of the subject's consistency, coherence. *Découpage* is always linked to the suture effect, which intermittently discloses the subject's lacking in discourse in order to cover it over with a relay of signifiers that "stand in" for the subject, binding it into the signifying chain.

To figure segmentation is to promote the spectator's recognition of representation as an enunciative process that constructs not only the spectacle, but also the point of address it calls him to occupy. The spectator of *Portrait of Dora*, then, feels his own position as inscribed in the apparatus, through the system of cuts and relays of unstable identification it mobilizes. Without the desired consistency promised by a fixed point of address, the enunciative mechanism shows its operations, its processes of encoding. As such, this text disturbs the stability of the suture effect, not, of course, destroying it, but renegotiating it so that the spectator is forced to a theoretical recognition of its function and its bearing on sexual difference as construction.[14]

Portrait of Dora never ceases to play upon the term "cutting off," a term which retroactively conditions the whole Dora case, since Dora abruptly "cut off" the

---

[13] Roland Barthes, "Diderot, Brecht, Eisenstein," in *Image-Music-Text*, trans. Stephen Heath (New York: Hill and Wang, 1977), p. 70.

[14] As Kaja Silverman describes this representational operation, it is a "sleight-of-hand." "This sleight-of-hand involves attributing to a character within the fiction qualities which in fact belong to the machinery of enunciation: the ability to generate narrative, the omnipotent and coercive gaze, the castrating authority of the law." *The Subject of Semiotics* (Bloomington: Indiana University Press, 1983), p. 232.

analysis before Freud had finished. In the play, Dora frequently "cuts men off."[15] In the play's version of the second dream of the case, at the railroad station, "there's no train. The tracks are cut," which alludes to Dora's interrupting Herr K.'s seductive efforts, as well as Freud's interpretive ones — the interpretive dead ends (cut tracks) Freud runs into. An ironically re-constructed play on Freud's theories about women's castration, these cuts dramatize the anxiety and aggression that underlie the apprehension of an image or spectacle: re-enacting the projection of a totality and its loss. However, they also figure the possibility of resistance to suture into certain scenarios in order to open others.

In concentrating its focus on an image of an image, like the Madonna, or on the voice that really is heard through a phone, *Portrait of Dora* opens up the "theatrical illusion," literalizing figures, threatening to conflate sign and referent. The critical moment for theatrical illusion involves a gesture of disavowal. Through the theatrical illusion, the spectator's position, as mapped into theatrical space, is always split between two contradictory and interfering perceptions: what is perceived on stage is *real*, it does exist, but, at the same time, it is there in its present frame in order to refer to something else that is elsewhere, absent. As Anne Ubersfeld puts it: "the clivage/ split that introduces itself into the psychic mechanism of the spectator is between something that he accepts as real and something to which he refuses the judgement of truth, giving it only the status of an image, but the two 'things' are the same scenic sign."[16] The spectacle is a presence filling the scene, but already ruptured by reference to the absence its frame holds off. The containment and enframing by which the theatrical illusion produces a doubled perception (it's real but it's not true) provides me, the spectator, a certain pleasure, of not being a dupe. This is the pleasure articulated in the sentence, "I know very well, but all the same . . . ," the disavowal figured in the fetish.[17] Similarly, the theatrical illusion is *for* the subject whose position it fixes, thus passing the loss and absence that haunt it under the plenitude of a staged scene.

Portrait of Dora works out a particular interruption of scenic continuity and consolidation through noise. In a number of instances, the dialogic reference is doubled, tied to a noise which, rather than supporting diegetic movement, interferes with it, materializing reference in impossible ways, and representing the encroachment of a space "heard" but not seen, not presented to view. As such, noise constitutes a remainder and a *reminder* that there is a space absent from view, lost to view. As spectators who vacillate between seeing and hearing, we are not securely bound into coherent space.

[15] For example, Dora says of an encounter with Herr K.: "Herr K. had spoken to me sincerely, I think . . . But I didn't let him finish . . . . He told me: you know my wife means nothing to me. I immediately cut him off" (p. 27). Finally, in another literalization of a metaphor, Dora ends the phone conversation she has initiated with Herr K.: "He says: 'You know that . . .' But I don't let him finish. I hang up" (p. 30).

[16] Anne Ubersfeld, *L'École du spectateur* (Paris: Éditions sociales, 1981), p. 311. My translation.

[17] The classic disavowal, "I know very well, but nevertheless . . ." is a denial that implicitly acknowledges the very thing it denies. For a detailed examination of this sentence, see O. Mannoni, *Clefs pour l'imaginaire* (Paris: Éditions du Seuil, 1969), p. 12, in particular.

For example, in one exchange with Freud, Dora demands to know where his ciga-
rettes are, and we hear "sound of a lighter" (p. 19); we hear it, though neither character
speaks of it, and above all, we never see the expected flame which follows the only
sound a lighter emits.[18] The force of this interference between the "heard" and the
"seen" is elaborated in an exchange between Frau K. and Dora on the subject of
femininity:

> Frau K. "It takes practice. Patience, dear. It will come. With a bit of ruse too. Woman must
> learn her lesson. Close the curtains." (sound of curtains closing, then Dora's voice, mur-
> muring and growing more distant) . . . (Dora's voice in the distance) Sometimes full,
> sometimes empty . . . Time opens and shuts like hesitant eyes.
>
> [p. 12]

The secret scene of exchange between women, upon which Freud closed the curtain
in the case history, is a drama played behind the scenes, behind a closed curtain; it is
the *unseen*. But this is a complete de-stabilization of theatrical boundaries and illusion,
since the figures on stage remain before our eyes. The final theatrical cut, the lowering
of the curtain, is rehearsed and held off. The menace of closure, loss, of barred access,
however, persists. "Dora's voice grows distant." The scene opens and closes a
distance — between body and voice, eye and ear, speech and listener / spectator. As
spectators, we are torn between our capacities as viewers and as listeners; these are no
longer bound together in a stable instance of reception.

Such tension and interference arise in another moment of the voice's mobility. Con-
siderably before the end of the play, Dora threatens Freud with ending the analysis;
this she says "in a voice which comes to Freud from high up and far away" (p. 22). The
voice is untethered, disembodied; it comes to Freud from elsewhere. Such an effect of
scenic rupture produces the separation of and interference between body and voice.
The voice, which conventionally supports and coheres with the image, the body as
spectacle, becomes mobile here. It asserts the material and historical specificity of a
body. At the same time, as an indicator of the irreducible individuality of the speaker,
it here produces a non-coincidence of interior and exterior, a pure heterogeneity
within the body staged as sign. This is a portrait of a woman *voiced*, heard as well as
seen. The body cannot be entirely given over to spectacle when the voice resists consolidation within the frame.

This is a discontinuous scenic space, ruptured by effects of heterogeneity: the figures
materialized through noise, the multiple framings which split the gaze, and the voice
detached from body. Within such a space the body cannot be given as pure spectacle
for a spectator theorized as a consistent integrity, a fixed point of punctual reception
that is definitively separated from the scene before it. That spectator — a disembodied
one — gives way to a mobile position, intermittently occupying multiple points of address. Within this mobile positionality we are not without bodies. Rather, we find
ourselves inscribed in discontinuous theatrical space, at once within the scene and out-

---

[18] At another point, Herr B. speaks "I take the keys and I shoot" (p. 22), and we hear "a pistol shot."
Here it is precisely the literalization — sound that enters the stage, but that insists upon the "real" space as
well — that tears open scenic containment.

side it. The stage and the "house" are mapped as a social space of representations of and for gendered bodies.

We are "staged" by *Portrait of Dora,* as much as it is staged for us. This text calls our attention to its enunciative apparatus, the construction of a scenic frame, which is no longer a separated setting for our projective investment. This is a *mise en scène* that places us within the scene as well, forces us to find our position mapped there. Disjunction of body and voice, and body and its image, exposes the reciprocal construction of the body as sign on stage and the spectator as subject for that sign, as gendered subject to whom it is addressed.

Refusing the Romanticism of Identity: Narrative Interventions in Churchill, Benmussa, Duras

Elin Diamond

Questioned about the relationship between women and textual production, Julia Kristeva commented:

> . . . a woman cannot "be" . . . does not even belong to the order of *being*. It follows that a feminist practice can only be negative, at odds with what already exists. . . . In "woman" I see something that cannot be represented, something that is not said. . . . From this point of view, it seems that certain feminist demands revive a kind of naive romanticism, a belief in identity [which is] the reverse of phallocratism.[1]

Kristeva goes on to advocate an art that "dissolves identity, even sexual identities." These assertions with their implied prescriptions for feminist artists are worth considering in light of the contemporary practice of Caryl Churchill, Simone Benmussa, and Marguerite Duras. Arguably the representation of beings in action is the concern of the dramatist, but for these dramatists, female being is the problematical motive for play action. In fact Churchill, Benmussa, and Duras accede to Kristeva's insistence on the nonrepresentability of "woman," not by narrowing the field of representation, but by broadening it to include and encourage a feminist analysis of gender and history.

As Julia Kristeva's cultural perspectives are informed in part by Lacanian discourse, it might be helpful at the outset to consider her remarks with certain Lacanian principles in mind. The notion of identity or a coherent sense of "self" is explicitly denied in

---

Elin Diamond teaches in the English Department at Rutgers University, New Brunswick. The author of Pinter's Comic Play *(Bucknell 1985), she has published articles on drama and critical theory in* Modern Drama, Theatre Journal, The Drama Review, *and* Art and Cinema. *She is currently preparing a manuscript,* Feminist Stagings: Unmaking Mimesis, *to be published by Routledge.*

This article is based on a paper delivered at the Modern Language Association Convention in December 1984.

[1] From "La femme, ce n'est jamais ça" [Woman can never be defined], an interview by "psychoanalysis and politics" printed in *Tel quel*, Autumn 1974, later in *Polylogue*, 1977, here excerpted from Elaine Marks and Isabelle de Courtivron, eds., *New French Feminisms* (New York: Schocken Books, 1981), pp. 137–38.

Jacques Lacan's model of subjectivity and sexual difference. Not only do we suffer primordial loss when biologically sexed, we endure differentiation and "splitting" at every stage of infant development, culminating in the Oedipal phase with the entry into language — what Lacan calls the symbolic order. Entering language we are positioned in a system based on fixed hierarchies; we become not unique selves but speaking subjects, our individual expression shaped by a pre-existing field of social practices and meanings. This "we" is, of course, misleading; if the Oedipal conflict is based in language, the symbolic order (the order of law and culture) becomes the order of the Father, its principal symbol (according to Lacan) the phallus. To gain the privileges of the phallus, the little boy, under threat of castration, "mortgages" his penis. The little girl, lacking the penis, is refused symbolization in language. The symbolic order is by definition patriarchal; it does not represent her.[2]

Hence the blunt urgency of Kristeva's statements: from a Lacanian perspective, a woman cannot be, does not even belong to the order of being. Identity, then, becomes an ideologically corrupt notion because it mystifies or covers over the lack marked on the female psyche. It is obvious that Kristeva's missiles are directed at *écriture feminine*, a feminist discourse based on the idea of an irreducible female essence; for Kristeva this is just the flip-side of repressive male authority or phallocratism.[3] However, the Lacanian account of female subjectivity tends to disarm the very critique it invites; the position of the female in Lacan's model is as fixed as the linguistic system in which it is inscribed, as binary opposite (lack) to phallic fullness. Because she recognizes the tyranny of sexual difference, Kristeva prefers work that "dissolves identities, even sexual identities."[4]

But such work poses problems. A feminist artist firmly "at odds with what exists" may be unwilling to dissolve sexual identities since to do so would be to ignore the way sexual difference is inscribed not only in the female psyche but also in female experience. A feminist artist in theatre may want to give body to the historical and psychological conditions that support a phallocratic status quo. In fact she may want to attack identity from the point of view of "sex-gender" configurations which, Gayle

---

[2] This necessarily simplistic summary of Lacan is drawn from several sources: Kaja Silverman, *The Subject of Semiotics* (Oxford: Oxford University Press, 1983), pp. 149 ff; Juliet Mitchell and Jacqueline Rose, eds., *Feminine Sexuality: Jacques Lacan and the école freudienne* (New York: W. W. Norton, 1982), pp. 27–57; Jacques Lacan, *Speech and Language in Psychoanalysis*, trans. Anthony Wilden (Baltimore: Johns Hopkins University Press, 1968), pp. 159 ff.

[3] In another article, "Women's Time," in Keohane, Rosaldo, and Gelpi, eds., *Feminist Theory: A Critique of Ideology* (Chicago: University of Chicago Press, 1981), p. 43, Kristeva charges *écriture feminine* with "a more or less euphoric or depressed romanticism and always an explosion of an ego lacking narcissistic gratification."

[4] In "Women's Time," Kristeva explores the meaning of sexual difference for feminists and proposes for the "third generation" of feminists "now forming" a "demassification of the problematic of difference" (pp. 51–52). She wants feminists to stop viewing difference as an occasion for rivalry but as a condition inherent in the sociosymbolic contract which should be challenged and exposed from within. See my discussion of this article at the end of this essay. Opposing *écriture feminine* for what she sees as its essentialism, Kristeva cannot be placed within the materialist feminism of Monique Wittig. For an attempt to situate Kristeva see Alice Jardine, "Theories of the Feminine: Kristeva," *enclitic* 4, No. 2 (Fall 1980), 7–15.

Rubin reminds us, are not "ahistorical emanations of the human mind but products of historical human activity."[5]

It seems to me that Caryl Churchill's *Cloud 9*, Simone Benmussa's *The Singular Life of Albert Nobbs*, and Marguerite Duras's *India Song*, though vastly different texts, all meet the challenge of Kristeva's remarks: by dismantling the conventional representation of female character, all three refuse to romanticize female identity. But as feminists, these authors are also concerned with the historical human activity that confuses or conflates identity and gender. The issue for each dramatist is how to represent history without using the illusionistic apparatus of the stage to tell just another story in which female rather than male identity is valorized. To reinscribe a historical narrative in which woman is the signifier of power and authority would be to romanticize her, to remove her from history (which would be just the reverse of phallocratism). Their solution, perhaps most effectively staged in Benmussa's *Albert Nobbs*, is a radical representation of history itself — not as a backdrop or setting but as a narrative text which insistently shapes or interrupts the dramatic present and thus alters audience perspective on the event.

It is not surprising that feminist artists should turn to narrative as a means of incorporating and critiquing the problem of female identity and history. As Teresa de Lauretis has demonstrated, sexual identity is destiny in the major quest myths of Western culture: the female is positioned as static obstacle or as nondynamic space to be entered by the male and traversed. Along with other feminists, de Lauretis extends description to prescription, arguing that the subordination and exclusion of women is endemic to narrative, inherent in its very morphology.[6] Of vital concern here is the issue of narrativity: the process by which a spectator of any representational medium will construct a narrative, i.e., a causal chain of events moving toward a telos or completion.[7] If narrative art and, by extension, narrativity tend to reinforce the power relations created by sexual difference, then feminist revision of narrative texts means

---

[5] Gayle Rubin, "The Traffic in Women: Notes on the 'Political Economy' of Sex" in Rayna Reiter, *Toward an Anthropology of Women* (New York: Monthly Review Press, 1978), pp. 159 ff.

[6] See "Desire in Narrative" in Teresa de Lauretis, *Alice Doesn't: Feminism, Semiotics, Cinema* (Bloomington: Indiana University Press, 1981), pp. 103–57. Drawing on Freud, Greimas, Propp, and Lotman, de Lauretis explores the implications of Barthes's statement: "It may be significant that it is at the same moment (around the age of three) that the little human 'invents' at once sentence, narrative, and the Oedipus." De Lauretis does not advocate the abandonment of narrative but rather acknowledges that the most exciting work in feminist film is "narrative and Oedipal with a vengeance" insofar as it exposes the "duplicity" of the narrative form and the "specific contradiction" of the female subject who, as historical woman, must work "with and against Oedipus" (p. 157).

[7] The properties of narrative (the condition of narrativity in representation) are discussed in many of the articles in the *Critical Inquiry* issue "On Narrative" (Autumn 1980). Frank Kermode identifies "connexity, causality, and character" (p. 85); Nelson Goodman requires that the order of occurrence be inferable from the order of telling (p. 104). Implied in these and other statements is the suggestion that narrativity is a form of interpretation. Cf. Robert Scholes: "I employ the word 'narrativity' to refer to the process by which a perceiver actively constructs a story from the fictional data provided by any narrative medium [including drama]," in *Semiotics and Interpretation* (New Haven: Yale University Press, 1982), p. 60. See also Peter Brooks, *Reading for the Plot* (New York: Alfred Knopf, 1984), especially the chapters "Reading for the Plot," and "Narrative Desire."

not only exposing a representational form that delimits the female but also interrupting those processes of audience participation that collude in female subjugation.

Equally important for feminists is the often-discussed connection between history and narrative form. In Paul Ricoeur's argument, time enters human experience only through narrative so that history is inconceivable except as it takes on the attributes of narrative.[8] In Hayden White's discussion, modern historiography demands "that events be narrated . . . revealed as possessing a structure, an order of meaning, a beginning, middle, and end."[9] To understand history as narrative is a crucial move for feminists, not only because it demystifies the idea of disinterested authorship, but because the traditionally subordinate role of women in history can be seen as the legacy of narrative itself. With its relentless teleology, its ordering of meaning, narrative accrues to itself the power to define and legislate; it is, as Mária Minich Brewer puts it, the "discourse of authority and legitimation."[10] In her "typology of discourses," Kristeva stresses this coerciveness. Following Bakhtin she labels narrative (and the subset, history) "monological"—the discourse of prohibition which reinforces legal and social codes.[11] If we return now to one aspect of the Lacanian model—that within sexual difference the female is refused representation in culture—we might say that narrative history, in the way it structures and orders meaning for culture, both justifies and perpetuates that refusal.

Feminist artists in theatre are well placed to exploit the coercive structure of narrative, for though the theatre emphasizes one temporality—a series of "presents"—it assumes another—a story-line or narrative which is inferred by the spectator on viewing the dramatic representation. In fact theatre spectators probably conflate the two temporalities: while viewing action in the present, the spectator narrativizes the event, seeking its origins and telos as well as its causal relationship to other events. Keir Elam puts it this way:

> It is usually the prime object of the spectator's hypothesizing in witnessing the representation: he anticipates events, attempts to bridge incidents whose connection is not immediately clear and generally endeavors to infer the overall frame of action from the bits of information he is fed.[12]

In the perception of the spectator the inferred story (what Patrice Pavis calls the "metatext")[13] precedes and guides the enactment. This implicit causality between

[8] See "Time and Narrative: Threefold Mimesis" in Paul Ricoeur, *Time and Narrative* (Chicago: University of Chicago Press), pp. 52–57.

[9] Hayden White, "The Value of Narrativity," *Critical Inquiry* 7, No. 1 (Autumn 1980), 6, 9.

[10] Mária Minich Brewer, "A Loosening of Tongues: From Narrative Economy to Women Writing," *MLN* 19, No. 5 (December 1984), 1145.

[11] Julia Kristeva, *Desire in Language*, trans. T. Gora, A. Jardine, L. S. Roudiez (New York: Columbia University Press, 1980), pp. 76–77.

[12] Keir Elam, *The Semiotics of Theatre and Drama* (London: Methuen, 1980), p. 120. Elam relies on the Russian formalist distinction between *fabula* (story) and *sjuzet* (plot), in which the story (events in their logical order) is always inferred from the plot.

[13] "Spectators create a 'metatext' which arises from the reception of the theatre object as an artistic system," Patrice Pavis, *Languages of the Stage* (New York: Performing Arts Journal Publications, 1982), p. 150.

metatext and enactment is precisely what Churchill, Benmussa, and Duras make explicit. Narrative (and through it, history) invades their stages, interrupting the dramatic present with intimations of the past, forcing the audience to understand female identity as a historical and cultural construction whose causes and consequences constitute the drama being enacted.

Furthermore, this emphasis on two temporalities has its analogue in a doubling effect that is thematized both in the plays (female "identities" are doubled) and in the experience of the spectator. Listening, seeing, narrativizing — these nonsignifying practices of the spectator are made to signify; that is, audience response in the theatre (in conventional present time) is represented, through offstage voices in *Albert Nobbs* and *India Song* and, to a lesser extent, through the radical time shifts in *Cloud 9*. Since audience narrativizing enters into enactment, spectating requires a double awareness of one's own response and of the activity of responding. Thus spectatorship loses its ahistorical innocence and enters into the play of forces producing (and being produced by) the dramatic texts. The result — perhaps — is that the identity of the spectator (qua spectator) becomes as problematic as the identity of the female protagonists, not merely because the latter are refused whole coherent representation, but because the spectator's act of narrativizing them is itself put in crisis.

Crisis of identity, its causes and consequences, produces the comic critique in Caryl Churchill's *Cloud 9* (1979), her two-act play that follows a Victorian family into a twentieth-century setting. In the farcical sex tangles of Act I, an adult male actor plays a Victorian woman and an adult female plays a male child, making the point that sexual identity in the hallowed institution of the Victorian family is not "natural" but is constituted by prevailing gender codes. To problematize sexual identity in this way is of course to challenge the theatrical apparatus which dictates unitary representation of the individual. But Churchill makes cross-gender casting a result of sexual politics, as shown in the characters' first speeches, thumbnail autobiographies in comic doggeral. Betty's speech is particularly illustrative:

> I live for Clive. The whole aim of my life
> Is to be what he looks for in a wife.
> I am a man's creation as you see,
> And what men want is what I want to be.[14]

Betty is the perfect Lacanian female victim, a consequence of patriarchal structuring. However, Churchill is concerned to represent Betty's status concretely, for "what [we] can see" is a walking contradiction of the verbal and the iconic. When Betty utters the confused clichés of the oppressed Victorian wife, we laugh not only because they are consistent with the stereotypes we have of that figure ("What a long time they're taking, I always seem to be waiting for the men" [p. 15]) but because the stage image is radically disorienting. We see a man representing a woman, mouthing her inanities, making typically female fluttering gestures with distinctly male arms. There is no transvestism here — that is we are meant to see Betty included in the symbolic order

---

[14] Caryl Churchill, *Cloud 9* (London: Methuen, 1979), p. 4. Page references in my text are to this edition.

only insofar as she is male. The point is not that the male is feminized but that the female is absent. What remains is a dress, a palpitation, a scream, all encoded female behaviors adding up to a trace denoting absence. The *woman* Betty is not represented; *she* lacks symbolization in culture.

Worse, this man-made woman is contrasted with the sexually aggressive Mrs. Saunders, who humiliates her, and the frustrated lesbian Ellen, who adores her. The same actress plays both characters, the only example of double casting in Act I. Of course, ironic doublings abound in *Cloud 9*, but the particular instance of Mrs. Saunders/Ellen has special significance. Despite their obvious differences, they are two versions of female marginality, virtual doubles. Sharing the same body they must never meet — the theatrical convention (of double casting) abets the coercive narrative of female subjugation. Churchill's message is painfully clear: in patriarchy women are divided not only from other women (in this case the "woman" Betty) but from themselves.

A more radical critique of patriarchy comes with the time shift in Act II in which Churchill violates the theatrical convention that character time will be coterminous with the time frame of the text. In Act II time has advanced a hundred years but for the characters it is only twenty-five years later. By disturbing diachronic time Churchill lays bare the problematic of history and female identity. No longer the period setting for the zany actions of Act I, the Victorian era can now be read as a set of coded practices that continues to bear pressure on the contemporary characters of Act II. The radical feminist rhetoric by which Vicky tries to live cannot fully lift her out of the past when she was, we recall, a doll-child, separated from life. The lesbian Lin, confused about child care, gender markings, even jobs is as marginalized as Ellen, the governess and closet lesbian of the first act. Because of the time shift, the fears and indecisions we witness in Act II are lifted out of the causality of personal history and become evidence of the socio-sexual configurations we saw represented in Act I. Churchill thus succeeds in semiotizing, making readable, the narrative of history in which the parts for women are written by patriarchal law.

The time shifts in *Cloud 9* also challenge audience narrativity, our desire to construct a coherent narrative from events presented in sequence. Because conventional temporality is radically undermined in *Cloud 9*, audience narrativity necessarily proceeds from a sense of doubleness, so that events involving, say, Betty and Victoria in Act II will be perceived both as a near-realist representation of mother-daughter conflicts and as a historical scripting which places women in diminished relationship to men and in divisive relationships to each other. What is most effective in Churchill's conception is that the narrativizing desire of the audience of *Cloud 9* must do battle with the aggressive narrative constructed by the playwright. We are able to "read" Churchill's historical narrative because our conventional habits of reading a performance have been, at least to some extent, interrupted and refocused.

And yet the coerciveness of narrative history is also suggestively undermined in Act I: through the doll-Vicky, the man-Betty, history is metonymically represented as unreal and unnatural, thus susceptible to analysis or change. And in Act II change becomes Churchill's utopian theme. Having tampered with diachronicity, she now plays with synchronicity, bringing characters from Act I into Act II without motive or narrative logic. Curiously this estranging, deliberately theatrical gesture flattens her critique of gender and history. In Act II Churchill presents an image of reassembled female identity, no longer positioning her female protagonist as a victim of history but as a heroine in her own narrative of liberation. In a monologue near the end of the play Betty tells how she has learned to touch herself and in the final image of the play she embraces her Victorian male incarnation while rock music blares, "It'll be fine when you reach Cloud 9." The fact that the audience is happily consuming this moment of female transcendence makes it even more suspect. The signifiers put into play in Act I with the cross-gender casting are too neatly tied to the signified of self-acceptance, the unity of self. One might say that Churchill opts here for comic closure and narrative teleology rather than decentered play. Her historicist critique has become ahistorical romance.[15]

Simone Benmussa's *The Singular Life of Albert Nobbs* goes further than Churchill's play in refusing the romance of identity. For Benmussa's *Albert Nobbs* refers not only to the action and language of the character on stage but to another narrative, George Moore's "Albert Nobbs" published as part of his *Celibate Lives* in 1922. That is to say, the signifier "Albert Nobbs" cannot exist as identical with her embodied signified on stage but is dispersed over a textual field; Nobbs is not singular at all but plural, a gesture, a line of description, with no wholeness of identity to structure the field. This point is, of course, thematized in Benmussa's text, for the name Albert Nobbs is also a fictional signifier manipulated by a woman who, to obtain the powers of the phallus in Victorian culture, assumes the disguise of a male. Benmussa thus shows that gender is not natural but encoded and reproducible at will. But of course Albert pays a tremendous price for her relatively secure position in patriarchal culture: Albert as representation of non-Albert, the anonymous female body, lives at the limit of representation, knowing herself only as a "perhapser," a point cleverly made by the audience's first image of her as part of a *trompe l'oeil* setting, which implicates the spectator in Albert's misrecognition of her own sexuality.

Moreover, through the use of the disembodied voices of George Moore and his fictional interlocutor Alec, Benmussa brings narrative history into collision with dramatic representation. Benmussa preserves George Moore's own narrative frame — that of fictional autobiography into which Albert's story is inserted. But Benmussa alters the narrative premise in one crucial aspect. *Her* narrator claims that, unlike the stories he and Alec have previously exchanged, this story is "true." So it is the history of Albert Nobbs we are to hear (Benmussa being more concerned than Moore to expose the genesis of the story: a newspaper report of a male headwaiter at a Dublin

---

[15] In the preface to the Grove Press edition, Churchill herself expressed doubts about situating Betty's monologue at the end of the play — the choice was made by her director. However, I do not think that the actual position of the monologue — whether near the end or at the end — makes much difference. The Betty-Betty embrace translates into theatrical imagery what the monologue expresses.

The Singular Life of Albert Nobbs. Manhattan Theatre Club, New York, 1982.
Photo: Gerry Goodstein.

hotel who at the time of death was discovered to be a woman).[16] Benmussa is insistent about the authority of that history. While George Moore's narrator was the fictional anonymous "I," Benmussa nominates her narrator "Moore" and circulates his voice through the episodic events which constitute the life of Albert Nobbs. Moore, aggressively omniscient, is everywhere: he opens and closes Albert's story, speaks for Albert in the first scene with Mrs. Baker, articulates Albert's unconscious in the dream sequence, speaks contemptuously of Albert's appearance, just as though the Albert we see were absent from her own story, a mere diegetic description. And of course the woman concealed under the name "Albert" is representationally absent; her costume, says Benmussa, is not only her disguise but becomes her prison, then takes over her body.[17] Moore's voice which penetrates her mind, and which utters the narrative that contains her becomes identified with the shackles of the gender code.

Throughout *Albert Nobbs* the collision between the "here" of theatrical representation and the elsewhere of narration produces a play of signifiers that makes it impossible for the audience to consume a unified image of feminine identity. One is tempted to call the textual intersections in *Albert Nobbs* an instance of intertextuality, the transposition of one signifying practice into another. But this would be to misuse Kristeva's neologism. Intertextuality, by Kristeva's definition, means a "transposition" of signifying practices that opens up new possibilities of articulation.[18] What is crucial in Benmussa's text is that narrative is coercive; it will not be transposed. Moore's disembodied voice is the voice of phallic power for whose privileges, sanctioned and perpetuated by history, Albert sells her sexuality. She gains no new powers of enunciation, but merely assumes the gender markings appropriate to the status quo: that of a male. By refusing to grant Albert a status outside Moore's narrative, Benmussa semiotizes the patriarchal narrative that determines Albert's position. All characters are trapped, as Beckett's Hamm says, by the dialogue, but Albert Nobbs is trapped in a "true" history that refuses to symbolize her: in both stage and fictional narratives, Albert remains an old perhapser.

By foregrounding narrative, Benmussa exposes the audience's own narrativity — our desire for order and closure. The final stage image shows Albert in her death posture (which was also her life posture), seated holding her napkin and a pair of unshined shoes, tokens of her servitude while Hubert Page, her double and foil, muses on the impossibility of reversing her own gender change. (The doubling of Albert and Hubert is made thematically explicit when the latter announces that she, too, is female and when each, at different times, thinks of the other as a spouse.) Hubert decides that to resume her female identity would mean to cast herself once again into economic servitude. At this point Benmussa has Alec intervene, hungry for

---

[16] See Sue-Ellen Case, "Gender as Play: Simone Benmussa's *The Singular Life of Albert Nobbs*," *Women and Performance* 1, No. 2 (Winter 1984), 22. For more information on Benmussa, see Ruby Cohn, "Benmussa's Planes," *Theater* (Winter 1981–82), 51–54.

[17] Simone Benmussa, *Benmussa Directs* (London: John Calder Press, 1979), p. 22.

[18] Julia Kristeva, *Revolution in Poetic Language*, trans. Margaret Waller (New York: Columbia University Press, 1984), pp. 59–61.

The Singular Life of Albert Nobbs. Manhattan Theatre Club, New York, 1982.
Photo: Gerry Goodstein.

more details, and we spectators, because we partially share his stance, become im-plicated in his simple narrativity. Alec decides that Hubert could easily render her last years as a fairy tale because no one would believe that a woman could marry another woman and live happily with her for fifteen years. Such a woman is not "natural," says Alec, by which we infer that her story cannot be inscribed in a patriarchal sym-bolic that represents woman only as man's natural opposite.

Alec's dismissive treatment of Hubert's story illustrates the teleological and exclu-sionary pressure of the narrative form: Alec forecloses Hubert's story, insisting that it cannot be told. However, in Benmussa's stage directions, Hubert, in her man's clothes, sits "dreaming." After the closure of narrative, does the female subject dream of a discursive space accessible to female experience? Perhaps she dreams because this "space" is unknowable and resists knowing in the symbolic order as well as in nar-rative history. Benmussa's achievement in *Albert Nobbs* is to induce narrativity in the audience while insisting on the coercive effects of a male narrative that (inevitably) refuses or diminishes and distorts the experience of female subjects. Albert's story — or rather Moore and Alec's storytelling — indicts the practice of enacting or telling any woman's story, including those cultural myths and histories that women and men "naturally" consume, inhabit, and perpetuate.

To approach Duras's *India Song* with the ideas and strategies used so far seems at first incongruous. There is no overt reference to gender and female identity, no felt political urgency as in the other two texts. But Duras is crucial to my narrative for she lifts the veil of cultural history, of narrative and dramatic representation, to expose the desire underlying all representational acts. Anne-Marie Stretter is constituted not only by the near-moribund poses of the actress bearing that name but by the palpitating off-stage voices who at times comment on what they see and remember, at times assume the status of reading voices, activators of an unseen text, and at times most urgently speak to one another in the throes of their own desire. In this, Duras brings us back to Lacan and the subject's entry into language, a "point" which in-augurates the condition of desire. If language enables the subject to constitute a posi-tion in culture, access to culture also means permanent separation from instinctual drives; desire, then, persists "as an effect of primordial absence": regardless of the ob-ject chosen, desire refers to the impossibility of satisfaction, to the endless displacements impelled by an originary loss.[19]

Desire circulates ceaselessly in Duras's *India Song*. The four off-stage voices manage none of the authority or legitimating power of Benmussa's Moore because they can neither remember nor complete what they see, feel, or desire. Anne-Marie Stretter is the object, the magnet and occasion for desire, and for this reason the voices are unable to satisfy their longing to narrate her story. In other words, though the stage enactment seems to emerge from the memory of the voices, the voices are incapable of assuming a stable narrating position; rather they react fearfully, helplessly, anxiously, erotically, both to what they witness and to what they partially remember — of the

---

[19] Juliet Mitchell and Jacqueline Rose, eds., *Feminine Sexuality: Jacques Lacan and the école freudienne* (New York: Pantheon, 1982), p. 6.

party at S. Thala, of the beginning of the love affair between Anne-Marie Stretter and Michael Richardson, of the disgrace of the Vice-Consul, of the cries of the beggar woman. (Her seventeen-year wandering from Savannakhet to Calcutta and her constant proximity to Anne-Marie Stretter suggest that she is the protagonist's mad double. They are both, says Voice 2, "leper[s] of the heart").[20] Duras claims that she wrote *India Song* not because she wanted to deal with these narratives — already partially treated in *The Vice-Consul, The Ravishment of Lol V. Stein.* She wrote *India Song* because she had discovered a "new means of exploration," the voices "external to the narrative. . . . This discovery made it possible to let the narrative be forgotten and put at the disposal of memories other than that of the author . . . memories which might remember in the same way, any other love story. Memories that distort. That create" (p. 6).

Thus Duras inverts the conventional priorities of dramatic representation, or rather she reveals what representation must always be: a recovery of a past narrative replayed for, and narrativized by, spectators in the present. The enactment unfolds linearly: two days of intertwining love affairs ending with the death of Anne-Marie Stretter. But the stillness of the stage movements, the fact that voices almost never issue from the mouths of characters, belies the conventional view that "the passage of time in the drama is an absolute succession of 'presents.'"[21] Whatever feels present about the stage image derives from the offstage voices which have no presence but which hover "very close, enclosed like us in this place" (p. 12), discovering (or rediscovering) the story "at the same time we do" (p. 10). Duras's use of the communal "us" and "we" suggests that the voices are the spectators' doubles, their questions and reactions (the madness of Voice 1, the suffering of Voice 3) extreme versions of those of the embodied audience. And Duras permits her spectators no objectivity. Like the voices — *because* of the voices — the audience is trapped in a double awareness of image and sound in temporalities that are impossible to reconcile. The result is a growing sense of displacement: where is "this place" for the voices?[22]

As much as is conceivable, then, Duras's *India Song* dramatizes intertextuality, for the transposition of the reading voice into theatrical space, the simultaneous theatricalizing of faceless narrators, and the resulting disorientation of spectators create a plurality of discourses: the "place" of enunciation is not "single" nor is authority asserted (as in Benmussa's Moore).[23] On the other hand, intertextuality, with its suggestion of volatile free play, is restrained by the obsessive narrativizing of the voices, for only in telling the life of Anne-Marie Stretter can the voices activate their own passion; only by remembering (and inevitably distorting) her love story can they create (and recreate) their own.

[20] Marguerite Duras, *India Song* (New York: Grove Press, 1976), p. 29.

[21] Peter Szondi, *Theorie des modernen Dramas* (Frankfurt: Suhrkamp Verlag), p. 15. Cited in Keir Elam, *The Semiotics of Theatre and Drama*, p. 118.

[22] For the reader of *India Song*, Duras playfully confuses spatial reality: "All references to physical, human, or political geography are incorrect," p. 5.

[23] Kristeva, *Revolution in Poetic Language*, p. 60.

Duras leaves no doubt as to the cost of this passionate storytelling. Draped in black, silently weeping, entering and leaving her parties as though she were walking in her sleep, Anne-Marie Stretter is the fetishized object, dismembered and remembered by the voices circulating her name amongst themselves. At one point her undraped body is "offered" to the voices and they appropriate it: "(*The Voices are slow, stifled, a prey to desire, through this motionless body*)" (p. 27). Prey to desire, the voices prey on the naked body of the woman — and in this coercive voyeurism the audience is fully implicated. As the voices consume the body, the audience finds itself in the uncomfortable position of consuming her twice — by viewing her body and by listening to the passion her body excites. Linking her theatre spectators to her urgent off-stage voices, Duras insists on the link between spectating and narrating, and exposes the coercive desire underlying both activities. Furthermore with her plurality of narrators (in the audience as well as off-stage), with her mingling of various temporalities, Duras suggests that the narrativizing consumption of the female is a constant cultural activity, an aspect of human history. And though *India Song* does not thematize the issue of gender per se, it is worth noting that the women's voices are consumed in their own love story even as they consume Anne-Marie Stretter's, while the male voices have no relationship other than their shared fascination with the story. Significantly, the male Voice 4, who remembers most of the story (who asks no questions, only states "facts") also concludes it, narrating the final motions of Anne-Marie Stretter, which the stage figure then enacts.

Not surprisingly, the figure compelling so many narratives produces none of her own; in this way Anne-Marie Stretter, though embodied as a female on Duras's stage is as absent as Churchill's Betty in Act I of *Cloud 9* and as Benmussa's Albert in *The Singular Life of Albert Nobbs*. But for all three playwrights absence is strategic. Refusing their protagonists coherent identity, a recognizable selfhood, Churchill, Benmussa, and Duras both refuse the logic of social narratives in which women are inevitably constrained and refuse to perpetuate a romanticized female who transcends all contraints. They insist instead on acknowledging the exclusion or distortion of the female in cultural discourse. As feminists, all three dramatists politicize their cultural practice; using narrative as a metaphor for history, they implicate the operations of patriarchal history in the victimization of women. And all three writers disrupt the narrativity of the spectator — Benmussa and Duras most radically. In *Albert Nobbs* and *India Song* the narrative impulses of the audience are rerouted through offstage voices whose coercive treatment of the female provides a subtle critique on the activity of spectatorship.

The indictment of narrative history dramatized in *Cloud 9, Albert Nobbs*, and *India Song* is, ironically perhaps, corroborated in a work of narrative history — Julia Kristeva's "Women's Time," which identifies three "generations" or "phases" in modern Western feminism. In the first phase, women "aspired to gain a place in linear time,"[24] demanding social and political parity, equal pay, etc.; in the second phase, women concentrated on cyclical time, identifying mythical sources of female power outside of

---

[24] Kristeva, "Women's Time," p. 36.

male history and social-political institutions. Kristeva acknowledges the vital necessity of both orientations but critiques the first for tending to perpetuate the very power hierarchies that deny human liberation and the second for offering a utopian vision of a countersociety which would turn out to be a simulacrum of the society it opposes. Kristeva believes that contemporary feminists, her third generation, will eschew the excesses of the second phase and recognize the limitations of the first. The "sociosymbolic contract" (her term for the coercive social, legal, and linguistic systems in which we live, based on sexual difference and the repression of instinctual drives) must never be accepted and must never be ignored; it must be subverted from within. The contemporary practice of Churchill, Benmussa, and Duras, in the plays discussed here, seems to me to be congruent with Kristeva's vision of contemporary feminism. These writers refuse to define women by social roles (granting them "positive images") or to remove them from sociality into ahistorical communities of women, thereby permitting no analysis of coercive cultural practices.[25] What these playwrights offer is a provisional representation of the female subject in history. For it is in their narratives, which bear all too painfully the inscriptions of patriarchal history, that we find the female subject, not transcendent yet not erased, but rather carefully, subversively at odds with what exists.

[25] For just one description of these two kinds of feminist dramas, see Honor Moore, "Women Alone, Women Together," in *Women in American Theatre*, eds. Helen Krich Chinoy and Linda Walsh Jenkins (New York: Crown Publishers, 1981), pp. 184–90.

Part II

Centering Class and Ethnicity

The Cult of True Womanhood: Toward A Womanist Attitude in African-American Theatre

Glenda Dickerson

Whispering grass,
Don't tell the trees
Once you tell it to the trees
The trees will tell the birds and bees
Then everyone will know
Cause you told the blabbering trees.

Those are lyrics from an old Ink Spots song that my mother sang to me. "Today around the schools, they speak of cultural transmission. Back then, before I went to school, we called it 'Grandma say.' " Dr. Eleanor Traylor wrote those words in her wonderful essay on Toni Morrison's *Tar Baby*. In the essay Dr. Traylor talks about something that has always been central to my work as an adaptor/director. That something is folklore. She ends her essay with this original poem:

Sometimes at dusk of evening,
When lightning bugs would glow,
My grandma told me stories in the dark.

Now at dusk of evening,
When city lights burn bright,
I live the very stories that
She told.

Today, I want to talk about some of "Grandma's stories" that I find myself living, about the "miracle plays" I am trying to make out of these stories and about the journey I have taken from being a daughter of the patriarchy to being a "true woman." Now I don't want to talk too long because of something my friend told me. Her

Glenda Dickerson is an Associate Professor of Theatre Arts at the State University of New York, Stony Brook. She is also a writer, adaptor, folklorist, and award-winning director. She is a full-time PraiseSinger, residing in New York City with her daughter, Anitra Yalode.

It is our general policy not to publish papers. However, this oral style represents an alternative discourse central to the development of a woman-identified, ethnic language and outside of the white, upper-middle-class, gender-marked language of traditional scholarship.

dissertation was over a thousand pages long when she first submitted it and her advisers refused to read it for that reason. She said, "The problem is that women of color have been silenced for so long that when we finally get a forum, we can't shut up." So I'm not going to talk too long, but I am going to talk for a minute. And I want to talk today with and about the silenced voice of the woman of color. That voice has been silenced for centuries, breaking forth sporadically, choked, and gasping for air. It has been variously silenced by the obvious foot on the throat and the subtle whispering thought. It has been silenced as part and parcel of the corruption of the ancient matriarchy. The depiction and perception of African-American woman in this country through stereotypes has garbled her voice and distorted her image. The real tragedy is that the African-American woman herself has too frequently bought that distortion. For example, at the turn of the century a dangerous little idea took hold in this country. It was called "The Cult of True Womanhood." Some of the attributes necessary to gain admission to the "cult" were domesticity, submissiveness, piety, and purity. The ideals set up for "true women" were in actuality a fanatical method of sexual repression by white men to oppress and control women. But women were made to believe that unless they aspired to and, in fact, achieved these impossible ideals, they were less than moral, unnatural, unfeminine. The "cult" became virtually synonymous with the upper class because only they had the luxury of leisure. Women of color were triply locked out: by class, by race, and by history— they had been made the mule of the world in slavery, how could they now aspire to silk parasols and satin dresses. At one and the same time turn-of-the-century women of color found themselves abhoring the "cult" and aspiring to its tenents. This conflict spawned an ethos of contradictions which is with us today. African-American writers, feminists, and abolitionists found themselves railing against this notion of their inferiority by exhorting their sisters to "love virtue and abhor vice." Even until today, African-American women too often address themselves—though speaking or writing from the soul—to a white audience whose attitudes have been shaped by minstrel shows and plantation literature. "The fear of one's own inferiority in the face of a powerful racist white world, the inability to summon rage, the need to find a voice to maintain one's sanity and one's identity . . ." are part of the legacy left to me by my valiant foremothers (Mary Helen Washington, *Invented Lives*). In my work I have always tried to break down cultural stereotypes. My journey now leads me to redefine the nature of "true womanhood." Turn-of-the-century African-American writers were able to find artistic freedom in at least one way: the liberating, subversive weapon of their folklore. I take that weapon also as part of my inheritance.

Folklore has forever fascinated me. From animal stories I heard as a baby in Yoakum, Texas, Greek myths I read as a teenager in Tokyo, Japan, and African tales revealed to me at Howard, I have taken sweet pleasure. When I discovered Zora Neale Hurston in 1972, I discovered a kindred spirit, a soul mate. She is the first one who taught me to "love myself when I am laughing and then again when I am looking mean and impressive." She taught me to look for the real Negro theatre in the jukes and cabarets. The wonderful thing I have learned about drylongso (ordinary, plain, everyday) people of color who frequent the jukes, cabarets, and white folks' kitchens; who are symbolized by Aunt Hagar and Brer Rabbit, is that—while we may be like Atlas, holding up the earth and carrying history on our backs—we are also like Bessie

Smith who said, "I'll shoot you if you stand still and cut you if you run." Also like Aunt Jemima whose jolly accommodating laugh hides her fat hand as she sprinkles poison into the tasty stew. The image of the African-American woman has been sullied on the world stage. The trick for her now is to reclaim that image through self-definition, using Nommo, the magic power of the word; uncategorically rejecting the stereotypes which are not "my shame" (as Harriet Tubman said), they are the shame of the perpetuators. In my work I try to replace stereotypes such as mammies, coons, bucks, tragic mulattoes with the archetypes embodied and preserved in the myths, tales, folklore that document the Black experience in America; the stories that "Grandma say."

I have been creating theatre from various nondramatic sources for over fifteen years. Recently, I have started to call these events "miracle plays." I define a miracle play as a tapestry for the stage. It is at the other end of the spectrum from realism. It is, at once, more ancient and more futuristic than the traditional miracle play. It is rooted in and based upon myth, but it is not an enactment of a myth. Rather, these miracle plays recognize myth as the original mother tongue. My miracle plays embody history, culture, literature, symbols, dreams, and inspiration. They put the events of the extraordinary together in a meaningful way. They explore archetypes as they are revealed through the lives of drylongso people. They raise a joyful noise through music and shake a tail feather with dance. Their purpose is to help us remember, to enable us to climb and to delve: to count the stars, to know rivers.

My journey toward true womanhood began at Howard University. There I was influenced in a profound way by the patriarch Owen Dodson, a name which is going to be very familiar to a lot of people. The late Owen Dodson was for many years the head and guiding light of the Department of Drama at Howard, as well as an acclaimed poet, novelist, and playwright. He was my teacher and later my colleague when I taught at Howard. Later still, he became my inspiration for founding and directing the Owen Dodson Lyric Theatre, a theatrical event dedicated to becoming the Griot (storyteller, historian) of the people. Owen Dodson was well-acquainted with tragedy, both Greek and African-American; he communicated that familiarity to all of his students with a glint in his eye that made it impossible to forget Agamemnon, Oedipus, Clytemnestra, and all their children. I learned a powerful lesson from his epic poem "Powerful Long Ladder":

> It take a powerful long ladder to climb to the sky
> An catch the bird of freedom for the dark
> Yes, it take a long climb.

So I, the dutiful daughter, eager to please, set out climbing. I tried to stuff everything he had taught me into my work. Somehow the longing for liberation expressed in this poem made me realize that the language of oppression is the same the world over. In an early production of *The Trojan Women*, I discovered that the simple act of putting Euripides' words into the mouths of African-American women evoked the African slave atrocity eloquently and effortlessly:

> Hecuba: All kings we were and I must wed a king. And sons I brought my lord king, many sons; that was naught, but fine strong princes, in all Troy the best. Greece

nor Troy nor the gardened East held such a mother. And I saw them fall beneath Grecian spears. My hair I shore at the graves of the dead. And their father, gardener of my garden great, I did not learn from others that I must weep for him; these eyes beheld it. I my own self saw him when he fell, murdered on the alter and round him all his citadel was sacked. And my daughters, virgins of the fold, meet to be brides of mighty kings, Behold! it was for the Greek I bred them. All are gone and no hope left that I shall look upon their faces anymore nor they on mine. An old grey slave woman, I pass beneath my enemies' gates. And what task they know for this age, basest shall be mine, the door to shut and open, bowing low. I who bore Hector!

In the growing number of miracle plays I created throughout the 1970s, nothing that touched my life was excluded from my work. When "Black is Beautiful" became the slogan of choice, I embraced cultural nationalism and pop! that went into the tasty stew. I wanted to lay to rest the bugaboo that Black people had no history, no culture. I glorified the kings of Africa and the heroes of African-American folklore— mostly male. I dramatized tales from Sundiata, the Sun King to the Harlem Six. I conceived and directed a "reflection in black voices" which I called *The Unfinished Song*. In this "reflection," the actors sang the praises of Alain Locke's "new Negro" and concluded with a peacock feather-bedecked "king" leading them in this traditional African poem:

> Many days have passed
> They will wake and come again
> We are a master people
> A free people

These "free people," though genderless in the poem, were stealthily understood by all to be the "new Negro," the Black Panther, Black Power, Beautiful Black, New Black Man. But then two important things happened: I discovered Zora Neale Hurston and I gave birth. In adapting Ms. Hurston's *Their Eyes Were Watching God*, I lived Owen Dodson's line: "I have seen the dawn spring up like a miracle bird." The miracle revealed in *Eyes* was a dual one: sisterhood and self-definition. I closed the play, which I called *Jump at the Sun*, with these words from the novel:

> Janie: It's uh known fact, Pheoby, you got tuh *go* there tuh *know* there. Yo' papa and yo' mama and nobody else can't tell yuh and show yuh. Two things everybody's got tuh do fuh theyselves. They got tuh go tuh God, and they got tuh find out about livin' fuh theyselves.

In giving birth to my daughter, who is named for the Orisha (goddess) of the oceans and seas and for a Persian princess, I discovered the miracle of the blood rite that binds ancestors and heirs, mothers and daughters. I saw that every woman extends backwards into her mother and forward into her daughter. Through this miracle, I learned that liberation is not accomplished by the heroes who flash like lightning or the royalty who sit upon the throne. It is achieved by the drylongso folk, the ordinary people. Like Black feminists and abolitionists who struggled and triumphed in the nineteenth century though mired down by an ethos of contradictions: excluded from the "cult of true womanhood," exploited by racism, denied equality by their own husbands, yet determined to educate themselves and their children, take pride in themselves and their history and to "lift up the race." These drylongso women who struggled against the two-headed serpent—racism and sexism—were my foremothers. When told that the voice of the woman should not be heard in public debates, they decided (in the words of abolitionist and feminist Maria Stewart): "It is no use for us to wait any longer for a generation of well-educated men to arise." These were the so-called "race women" of Reconstruction. In a miracle play called *PraiseSinger, a soulstory for two voices*, I quoted the words of race woman Josephine St. Pierre Ruffin:

> We now issue this call to all the women's bodies throughout the country; the time is short but everything is ripe. And remember, earnest women can do anything. Let us unite under the name The National Association of Colored Women, under which name we have been working for 37 years; zealously guarding the interests of the race morally and socially with the significant and well chosen motto, "Lifting As We Climb." We have worked hard and long to prove what the Negro woman can do when the race is on trial. Future success commensurate with that of the past is ours if we hew to the line in teaching our sons and daughters to love virtue and that a good name is to be chosen rather than great riches.

White women were also victims of the cult of true womanhood, but they were mostly unwilling to align themselves with my foremothers in the mutual struggle for equality. At a women's rights meeting in Akron, Ohio in 1851, where Sojourner Truth delivered her now famous "Ain't I A Woman" speech, white feminists were at first reluctant to allow the legendary abolitionist to speak, fearing that their cause might be associated with "abolitionists and niggers." To underscore this unfortunate truth, I include here this poem by Lucille Clifton which I used in a miracle play for young women called "I Am A Black Woman."

To Ms. Anne

i will have to forget
your face
when you watched me breaking
in the fields,
missing my children.

i will have to forget
your face
when you watched me carry
your husband's
stagnant water

i will have to forget
your face
when you handed me
your house
to make a home,

and you never called me sister
then, you never called me sister
and it has only been forever and
i will have to forget your face.

If the "cult" caused Black women to prove they were ladies, it forced white ladies to prove they were women. When I read John Winston Gwaltney's superior book, *Drylongso, a Self-portrait of Black America,* which is a collection of fascinating, contemporary oral histories, I discovered that modern-day urban women of color still remember the "cult" and what they think about it. This quote, from Nancy White's oral history in *Drylongso,* I also used in *PraiseSinger*:

> When they have this Miss America mess on, I never pays any attention to it, and now that they have some brown or yalla fool up there showing everything she should hide, that make me even madder than before. In the country, that's just how they buys cows. Well, a woman ain't no cow and if she don't have no more sense than to think she is, then I don't personally give her one bit of credit! I don't know why they don't just bring in the auction block and just sell 'em altogether! But, you see, all that comes from this man out here telling these white women all that off-the-wall boogie-joogie about some women being angels and some other women being mules. White women believe all that stuff, so they don't want to see that that man is just patting them on the head and doing the same thing to them that he is doing to everybody else.

Well, I kept on climbing and in trying to lift as I climbed I did the miracle play I mentioned earlier "I Am A Black Woman." I wanted the young women who participated in that experience to learn what I had learned: that drylongso women are the culture bearers, the salt of the earth. This is another poem by Lucille Clifton from her collection "An Ordinary Woman":

> the thirty eighth year
> of my life,
> plain as bread
> round as a cake
> an ordinary woman.
>
> an ordinary woman.
>
> i had expected to be
> smaller than this,
> more beautiful,
> wiser in Afrikan ways,
> more confident,
> i had expected
> more than this
>
> i will be forty soon.
> my mother once was forty.
>
> in the thirty eighth
> year of my life,
> surrounded by life,
> a perfect picture of
> blackness blessed,
> i had not expected this
> loneliness.
>
> i had expected more than this.
> i had not expected to be
> an ordinary woman.

Well then, don't you know, like most of us, I went searching with Alice Walker for "our mothers' gardens." That's when I became a womanist. So naturally, I had to incorporate her salty definition into a miracle play:

> Womanist: from woman, a Black feminist or feminist of color; from the Black folk expression, "you acting womanish." Want to know more than is considered "good for one." Responsible, in charge, serious. Also, a woman who loves other women, sexually and/or nonsexually. Appreciates and prefers women's company, women's culture, women's emotional flexibility and women's strength. Traditionally capable as in, "Mama, I'm walking to Canada and I'm taking you and a bunch of other slaves with me." Loves music, loves dance, loves the movies, loves the spirit, loves love and food and roundness, loves struggle, loves the folk, loves herself—regardless!

> Womanist is to feminist as purple is to lavender.

When you start reading ancient myths and womanist literature and traveling to countries where the people look like you, you gain a so-called global perspective. Not only is the language of oppression the same the world over; the anguish of women is echoed around the world and resonates from continent to continent. The torture of mothers who lose their daughters to rape, war, drugs, poverty; the suffering of women who are tortured and die in Latin American prisons; the untimely death of young women who are killed by drunk drivers or yuppie lovers in New York's Central Park and then twice victimized by the courts and press: these women are sisters in suffering, fixed on the fangs of the two-headed serpent. Their silenced voices, their stilled tongues are symbolized for me in the illegal banning of South Africa's Nomzamo Winnie Mandela, whom the people call "Mother of the Nation." I dramatized her story in a miracle play called *Every Step I Take*. This is from one of her last public speeches before her voice was silenced by the ban:

> My African name "Nomzamo" means in Xhosa "trial," those who will go through many trials, including court trials. My life has been full of trials. They have treated me absolutely violently. I have been threatened with my life; I am completely at their mercy. But I am not going to move from here because this is my home. It was a criminal act on the part of the government to arrest me in the first place. Imagine the audacity of it. If anybody should leave, it's not me, it is the settler government. There is only one person who is oppressed in this country. That person is Black. Black people do not want their chains changed into gold and polished. We do not even want copper chains. We are fighting for our total liberation and the total hacking off of those chains. We are determined to fight to the bitter end for the liberation of our people.

I want you to understand that during all this time, the miracle plays I've been doing have been interspersed with so-called traditional plays. Into them I've been trying to bend and shove and tack on all this wealth of information I've accumulated as I climbed. Believe me, sometimes it worked and most times it didn't, because we are talking realistic plays here. Reading my reviews in the *New York Times* in those days was a gloomy undertaking. We won't dwell on that! But, finally, Aunt Jemima tapped my shoulder and told me that "well-made"—in my case—was a phrase which best modified beds. Looking back, I realize that I missed an important event in the 1960s, preoccupied as I was with male heroes. In that decade, the Apollo (or *sun*) mission landed the Eagle ship on the moon on the very eve of her movement out of Virgo—the celestial sign of the Virgin. It was *man* and not (hu)mankind who, in body and spirit, took us to the moon. Father culture had at last completely replaced Mother culture. The play from which I am about to quote is called *Magic and Lions*. I adapted it for the stage from the writings of Ernestine Walker. It is subtitled "an Egyptian myth steeped in the fire of the Dogon blacksmith." While it is not realistic in form and was well-met by the press, it now represents for me an ending. It was my last obeisance to a patriarchal world-view in a miracle play. The Egyptian tale of Isis and Osiris was the focal point around which I built *Magic and Lions*. The figure of Isis became the model for the archetypal mother-warrior-goddess in later civilizations. Elsewhere known as Demeter, Innanu, Nut, Ishtar, Au Set, Hathor, Yemaya, the Virgin Mary, she is the many sided Divine Ancestress. The hieroglyph for her name is the throne. Ruling kings take possession of the earth by mounting the throne. The true power of Isis as bisexual god, sorceress, and warrior has now been obscured. She is viewed as little more than an appendage of Osiris, searching the earth for his thirty-six scattered pieces. This trivialization of Isis's power reflects the trivialization of the matriarchy, of Mother culture, by modern man; the same modern man who is author of the "cult of true womanhood." What I know now, but didn't know when I did this play, is that Isis is more splendid than Ra the Sun God (symbol of the patriarchy). Even Norman Mailer in his gruesome *Ancient Nights* acknowledges this fact:

> Isis and Ra.
> Side by side
> They stood together and
> Isis was more splendid.

The tale of Isis and Osiris is ancient and archetypal. It resonates with countless other creation and resurrection myths. It predates the tales of Oedipus, Theseus and Jesus of Nazareth. This portion describes Osiris's restoration to life by Isis after he has been killed by his brother:

> Isis: So the richly decorated chest became the coffin of Osiris, from whom departed the breath of life. When the grievous tidings were borne to Isis, she let out a cry that became part of the shriek people utter when they behold their own wound. In her bitter grief, she called upon the sungod, Ra. Her voice ascended to high heaven thus: "The beautiful one of gold, the child of god, the maker of the heavens, the earth, and the underworld; the creator of the sky and sea, men and women, animals and birds, fish and creeping things, trees and plants, and the incorporeal beings who are the messengers who fulfill his wish and word, the beautiful child of gold is gone." Near to human was Isis in the depth of her unhappiness. In this sad time, her thoughts drew tears whose fall gave birth to rain. Ra, looking down from high heaven was moved to pity because of her sore distress and sent Isis a revelation. Whereby she set out toward Byblos in a ship, for it was there that the coffin of Osiris had been washed ashore. Claiming the coffin, Isis had it borne to her ship. The ship had hardly gone from sight of land before she began ministrations over the body in the coffin, for she was determined to repair the beauty of Osiris. She hovered over his body in the form of a hawk; she created light with her feathers and made air to come into being that was like unto the breath of life. And she uttered cries and lamentations, saying: "Come to me Osiris, for my speech hath power to heal. I am the lady of words of power and I know how to work with words and most mighty

are my words." By this time she so excited the seven scattered lights of Osiris that he came back from the swamps and harbors, mountains and seas of his death to the home of his body.

So anyway, now I've let my hair go back and reclaimed by sense of humor. This is the last poem I want to do for you. This poem I used in a miracle play, again for young women, called *Tar Baby, a paradigm for our time. Tar Baby* celebrated the emergence of the "colored girls" of the 1970s into the grown-up women of color of the 1980s. The young women who participated with me in this ritual glowed and fairly glittered when they performed. They wept and railed and reaffirmed themselves. They sang and laughed and performed dance that was reminiscent of flying. They stretched, they grew, they climbed, they delved. They loved themselves. The poem is called "Harlem Sweeties." Sterling Brown, a grand old patriarch from the Harlem Renaissance, wrote it. I can just see him standing on the corner, nudging his cronies as the "Harlem Sweeties" go by; but for me and the other participants, it became a celebration of ourselves, of our unstopped voices, our rapid tongues.

Have you dug the spill of Sugar Hill
Cast your gims on this sepia thrill
Brown sugar lassie, a caramel treat
Honey gold baby sweet enough to eat
Peach skin girly, coffee and cream
Chocolate darling out of a dream
Walnut tinted or cocoa brown
Pomengranate lipped, pride of the town
Rich cream colored to plum tinted black
Feminine sweetness in Harlem's no lack
Glow of the quince to blush of the rose
Persimmon bronze to cinnamon toes
Blackberry cordial, Virginia Dare wine
All those sweet colors flavor Harlem of mine.
Walnut or cocoa, let me repeat
Caramel brown sugar
A chocolate treat.
Molasses, taffy, coffee and cream
Licorice clove cinnamon to a honey brown dream
Ginger, wine-gold, persimmon, blackberry
All through the spectrum Harlem girls vary.
So if you want to know beauty's rainbow sweet thrill,
Stroll down luscious, delicious, *fine* Sugar Hill!

I have undergone the very rite of passsage—from child to adult—that fascinated me in my work. You can see that I'm grown up. I was about to say "Look at me, look at my arm. I have plowed and planted and gathered into barns and no man could head me. And ain't I a woman?" But then you might think that I think I'm Sojourner Truth, which I don't. I know that I am Topsy. By that I mean that I have sprung up from the earth. I carry my parents with me. I am a woman alone, a true woman. I am a woman not defined by or through men. In short, a virgin. The word "virgin" means belonging to no man, one-in-herself; not maiden inviolate, but maiden alone in herself. The celestial virgin acts according to her own nature; she may give herself to many lovers, but, like the moon, she can never be possessed. She is the goddess of childbirth and the womb opener, the goddess of fertility, but not of wedlock. All of this is to say what Grandma say: "If Caldonia don't want you, you are out of luck, because that thing between her legs is hers and hers alone!" Zora Neale Hurston is the celestial virgin who inspires me. I have learned at last that I am not Owen Dodson's child, I am Zora Neale's sister. I see clearly the vision of her real Negro theatre unfolding before me. And I know a miracle day is coming.

Today, I exhort you to join me in the new cult of true womanhood. Today, with you as my witnesses, I resign from the ranks of directors of plays and become instead a full time PraiseSinger. A true PraiseSinger is a guardian of the archetypes of her culture's collective unconscious. Her function is not to invent but to rediscover and to animate. From this day forth, I will be concerned not with acts, and scenes and curtains; but with redemption, retrieval, and reclamation. The chair in which I sit will no longer be called the director's chair, but the blood-bought mercy seat. From that seat, my work will be a mission, my goal will be a miracle. Oh I will still fight with Winnie Mandela to the bitter end for the liberation of our people. I will search like Isis to the ends of the earth to rediscover the hidden, lost, and suppressed mysteries of women. But the promise I bring to the altar today is the one to animate, to illuminate; to offer my life's work, energy, and blood to the exaltation and glorification of the ordinary African woman. For she is me and I am she. I am Isis, I am Sojourner Truth, I am Zora Neale, and I am Topsy. Now I want to tell you the secret that the whispering grass told the blabbering trees who told it to me. This is the secret: Persephone is restored to her mother; springtime shines upon the land. Unlike the Ink Spots, I want everyone to know. Hallelujah!

A Raisin in the Sun:
Anniversary of an American Classic

Margaret B. Wilkerson

Rarely, if ever, has a play by a Black-American been accorded the status of a classic. Parochialism and polemics, critics have claimed, render works based on Black experience unattractive and of limited or temporary appeal. Yet Lorraine Hansberry's *A Raisin in the Sun*, the first play by a Black woman to be produced on Broadway and to win the New York Drama Critics' Circle Award in 1959, has become an American classic within a quarter of a century. According to Samuel French, Inc., an estimated two hundred productions were mounted during the 1983–84 theatre season alone, including critical successes at the Goodman Theatre in Chicago, Yale Repertory Theatre, and the St. Louis Repertory Theatre. In a 1983 review in the *New York Times*, Mel Gussow called this play about a 1950s Black family in Chicago "an enduring work of contemporary theatre."[1] Lloyd Richards, director of the Yale Repertory and director of the original 1959 production, labeled *A Raisin in the Sun*, "An historic . . . and . . . a timeless piece."[2] Frank Rich, in his 1983 review of the Goodman Theatre revival, claimed that the play was dated only by "its dependence on plot mechanics."[3] The St. Louis Repertory Company's production attracted unprecedented sell-out crowds in 1984, while a 1986 production at the Roundabout Theatre drew the admiration of off-Broadway audiences. What accounts for the extraordinary appeal of *A Raisin in the Sun*? How has it transcended the racial parochialisms of American audiences?

A variety of factors have contributed to its enduring success: the finely crafted text; a brilliant cast in the original production and subsequent casts with talented performers; its historic reception on Broadway in the 1958–59 season and subsequent impact on a new generation of artists; and the events of the past quarter century that

Margaret B. Wilkerson is editor of Nine Plays by Black Women *published by New American Library, 1986. Professor Wilkerson, who has a Ph.D. in Dramatic Art and is an Associate Professor in the Department of Afro-American Studies at the University of California at Berkeley, is currently writing a literary biography on Lorraine Hansberry and has received Rockefeller and Ford Foundation Fellowships to support this work.*

[1] Mel Gussow, "Stage: *A Raisin in the Sun* at Yale," *New York Times*, 9 November 1983, p. C23.

[2] Samuel G. Freedman, "Yale Marking 25th Anniversary of *Raisin in Sun*," *New York Times*, 1 November 1983, p. C13.

[3] Frank Rich, "Theater: *Raisin in Sun*, Anniversary in Chicago," *New York Times*, 5 October 1983, p. C24.

confirmed Hansberry's prescience. However, textual additions and revisions since the original production, some as recent as 1984, have sharpened the major issues of the play, revitalizing the work for contemporary audiences. This essay will discuss the various social, historical, and artistic factors that have contributed to the play's contemporary relevance and popularity, with particular focus on recent script revisions published by Samuel French, Inc., in the 1984 Anniversary Edition of the play.

The history of that first production is the stuff of which theatre legend is made. "Housewife's Play Is a Hit," read one local headline,[4] indicating the sheer luck and nerve that allowed *A Raisin in the Sun* — a play written by an unknown Black woman, produced by inexperienced newcomers, and directed by an untried young Black man — to reach the professional New York stage. Although Sidney Poitier brought "star quality" to the show, the other performers (with the exception of Claudia McNeil) had yet to make their mark on the American theatre. Yet the talent of this first cast proved extraordinary and the chemistry perfect for a memorable show. Today the names of playwright Lorraine Hansberry, director Lloyd Richards, producers Phil Rose and David Cogan, actors Sidney Poitier, Claudia McNeil, Lou Gossett, Glynn Turman, Diana Sands, Ivan Dixon, Ruby Dee, Ossie Davis, understudies Douglas Turner Ward, Lonne Elder, Beah Richards, and others are widely known for their contributions to theatre.

Starting from a half empty house in New Haven, *A Raisin in the Sun* attracted larger audiences on its out-of-town trials through Chicago and other cities until a last minute rush for tickets in Philadelphia earned it a Broadway house. It had taken a year to raise the $100,000 needed for the show — the "smart money" would not take a risk on a serious play about a Black family. The tenuousness of its production life ended, however, with its New York opening. The show ran on Broadway for nineteen months and won the New York Drama Critics' Circle Award against such plays as Tennessee Williams' *Sweet Bird of Youth*, Archibald MacLeish's *J.B.*, and Eugene O'Neill's *A Touch of the Poet.*

The play's phenomenal reception can be attributed, in part, to its timeliness, for this drama reflects that moment in U.S. history when the country was poised on the brink of cataclysmic social and legal upheavals that would forever change its character. In his 1959 review of the show, Walter Kerr observed that Hansberry "reads the precise temperature of a race at that time in its history when it cannot retreat and cannot quite find the way to move forward. The mood is forty-nine parts anger and forty-nine parts control, with a very narrow escape hatch for the steam these abrasive contraries build up. Three generations stand poised, and crowded, on a detonating-cap."[5]

The tensions of the times that Kerr sensed in the play had been captured earlier in a short, provocative poem by Langston Hughes, a work that had given Hansberry the title and theme of her drama. "What happens to a dream deferred," asked the poet in his historical collection of poems on Harlem. "Does it dry up like a raisin in the

[4] Sidney Fields, "Housewife's Play Is A Hit," *New York Daily Mirror*, 16 March 1959.
[5] Walter Kerr, "No Clear Path and No Retreat," *New York Herald Tribune*, Lively Arts Section, 22 March 1959, pp. 1–2.

sun . . . or does it explode?"[6] Lorraine Hansberry answered by fashioning a play about the struggles and frustrations of a working-class Black family living in Chicago's South Side ghetto during the 1950s. Crowded into a cramped, roach-infested kitchenette, this family of laborers wages a constant battle to survive and to maintain hope for a better future. When Lena Younger (Mama), the elder of the household, receives a $10,000 widow's benefit, each family member sees the money as fulfillment of a private dream. The conflict is sharpest between the dual protagonists of the play, Mama and her thirty-five-year-old son, Walter Lee, who lives with his sister (Beneatha), his wife (Ruth), and son (Travis) in his mother's home. Walter, frustrated by his dead-end chauffeur's job, wants to invest in a liquor store as a way out of their economic and psychological trap. But Mama, seeking more physical space for the family and the psychological freedom it would bring, puts a down payment on a house that happens to be in Clybourne Park, a white neighborhood. Her decision decimates Walter who views the money as his last chance to gain some economic control over his life. When Mama realizes how deeply her decision has hurt her son, she entrusts him with the remaining money with a portion to be placed in a savings account for his sister's college education and the rest for Walter to do with as he wishes. His good fortune is short-lived, however, because he loses the money in a dubious business deal. A disillusioned man, Walter faces his mother and family in a highly emotional scene; when presented with the opportunity to recover his losses by selling out to the Clybourne Park Association (which is determined to keep the neighborhood white), he decides to take their offer despite its demeaning implications. However, Walter comes to realize that he cannot live with this denigration of his family's pride and consequently rejects the proposal. The play ends as the family begins to move to the new house.

The spirit and struggles of the Younger family symbolized the social progress and setbacks characteristic of the 1950s, and the Broadway audience of that time could not help but notice. In 1955, three years before the opening of *A Raisin in the Sun*, the Supreme Court had declared racial segregation in public schools illegal, marking a climax to decades of advocacy and legal challenges, but initiating a new level of resistance. The Montgomery bus boycott was staged the same year, marking the beginning of Martin Luther King's visible leadership in the Civil Rights Movement. Boycotts and sit-ins intensified as federal troops were called in to prevent interference with school integration in Little Rock, Arkansas. As the struggle continued in the United States, it was also raging in Africa as Ghana became an independent nation, signaling the imminent demise of European colonialism.

During the play's run and shortly thereafter, Black and white Freedom Riders headed South and were greeted by a wave of terrorism as Southern segregationists retaliated; lunch counters in over 100 Southern cities were integrated; sit-ins and protests accelerated; Martin Luther King was arrested and jailed repeatedly; Black children were murdered, and churches were burned by racists, while the President of

---

[6] The Langston Hughes poem, "Harlem," is reprinted as introduction to the text of *A Raisin in the Sun* in all editions. It was originally published in *Montage of A Dream Deferred*, now accessible in Langston Hughes, *Selected Poems* (New York: Alfred A. Knopf, 1971), p. 268.

the United States shattered precedent by declaring that segregation was morally wrong. The bloody years continued as public figures like Medgar Evers and President John F. Kennedy were assassinated.

"[Hansberry] saw history, whole," wrote Frank Rich in his 1983 review of the play, ". . . the present and the future in the light of the past."[7] The time was ripe for a play that could somehow bridge the gap between Blacks and whites in the U.S. while communicating the urgency and necessity of the civil rights struggle. Black militancy born of anger, frustration, and deferred dreams was captured in the explosive and desperate Walter Lee. Rosa Parks's sudden refusal to move to the back of the bus, which became the catalyst for the historic Montgomery Bus Boycott, was mirrored in Lena Younger's apolitical decision to live in Clybourne Park, and her unintentional challenge of the restrictive covenants of the day. The rise of independent African nations was reflected in the presence of Asagai, the African student, who brings home the reality of his people's struggle for liberation, while Beneatha's adulation of things Africaine anticipated a new wave of hair and dress styles that Black Americans would soon adopt. In an uncanny way, Hansberry sensed what was to come. Her prescience extended even a decade beyond to the assertion of women's rights and women's equality through the assertive Beneatha who aspires to be a doctor, and the loyal, loving Ruth who seriously contemplates an abortion. The play touched the vibrating nerve of a country on the verge of change and a people on the move.

The timeliness of the play was equalled only by the captivating characters with whom white audiences were willing to identify and of whom Black audiences could be proud. Lena Younger was a strong point of identification. She was everybody's Mama — strong, caring, determined — the glue that held the family together. The self-sacrificing love of wife and mother were recognizable in Ruth's quiet strength and giving nature. Although Walter Lee was a new kind of character for white audiences, intended as a "ghetto hero" by Hansberry, the generational conflict with his mother was very familiar. For Blacks, Walter was a welcome affirmation of the urgency and potency of the Black struggle, while his sister, the ebullient Beneatha, represented its intellectual potential. Each character was molded with skill, humor, and the best tools of realistic theatre. The human qualities of Hansberry's characters came through without negating their racial integrity, and the play was loudly acclaimed on that account.

Critics praised the play as much for what it did not do as for its achievements. It presented characters who were neither sentimentalized nor stereotyped. There was no special pleading. The play was honest and had integrity. It did not preach political dogma, reviewers claimed. Even the F.B.I. file on Hansberry confirmed that the play was not propagandistic, according to the agents' report. Apparently, it did not pose a danger to the Republic. Because the humanity of this family was so brillantly exposed, white audiences could see themselves reflected in those Black faces. Because the racial experience was so authentically portrayed, Blacks found a new voice and created a vital, provocative theatre movement in the next decade. However, during the 1960s,

---

[7] Rich, "Theater: *A Raisin in the Sun*," p. C24.

Black critic Harold Cruse labeled the play a "glorified soap opera,"[8] reflecting a few reviewers' growing impatience with realistic plot structures and disagreement with what they perceived to be the play's political views. Nevertheless, the vitality and sharp definition of characters, the wit and humor of its sparkling dialogue, and the continued affirmation of the play's "message" by Black and white audiences alike, have far outweighed that criticism, causing audiences to return year after year to relive the now well-known rituals of the Younger family. However, *A Raisin in the Sun* is also a play of ideas and functions on a deeper, philosophical level, which until recently has been obscured to some extent by the racial prism through which it was originally viewed.

Writing in her scrapbook of reviews, Hansberry agreed with a 1959 passage by Daniel Gottlieb of the *Hartford Times*: the playwright "manages to weave the threads of the Negro-white conflict, materialism vs. spiritualism, and the individual vs. his conscience into the play."[9] The seductiveness of material values is at issue in the play and the Youngers' struggle for a spiritual and economic future poses fundamental questions about the American dream of success. As Gregory Mosher, Director of the Goodman Theatre, asks, "Is Walter Lee right when he says money is all that matters? How important is economic success in securing rights for a minority group? Such goals give you power, but do they also corrupt you?"[10] In order to advance materially, must the Youngers also become materialistic? The contradiction between the profitable, economic values of acquisition, power, and status and the "unprofitable" values of integrity, justice, and freedom runs deep in the American psyche. Walter's desire to "make it" is as American as Mama's determination to retain the family's pride and honor.

Although the original production script contained ample confirmation of this theme, events of the last twenty-five years both offstage and on have helped audiences to perceive these fundamental issues more clearly. The re-insertion of some omitted lines has sharpened and clarified the philosophical content without altering the basic structure of the play. Some scenes were cut in the original production in order to minimize risk; the producers and director chose to keep the playing time as tight as possible without sacrificing the playwright's values. Among the scenes and lines that were eliminated were three portions of dialogue which have since been restored to more recent publications and were included in 1983–84 productions.[11] These sections offer important insights to the character of Walter Lee and Mama, the play's dual protagonists, and greatly strengthen the articulation of the fundamental theme.

---

[8] Harold Cruse, *The Crisis of the Negro Intellectual* (New York: William Morrow & Company, Inc., 1967), p. 278.

[9] Daniel W. Gottlieb, "*A Raisin in the Sun* Premieres at Schubert," *Hartford Times*, 24 January 1959.

[10] Tom Valeo, "Issues Raised by *Raisin* Haven't Begun to Dry Up," *Chicago Sunday Herald*, 2 October 1983, sec. 5, p. 4.

[11] In discussing these scenes, the following sources will be used: the original Samuel French acting edition and the Random House Edition, both published in 1959; the New American Library (N.A.L.) edition published in 1966; the 25th Anniversary Samuel French Acting Edition published in 1984; and the 1961 film version.

A Raisin in the Sun. Antoine Rosell as Travis, Brent Jennings as Walter Lee. Goodman Theatre, Chicago, 1983. Photo: Lascher.

The debate over materialism and integrity is framed by Walter Lee and Mama whose conflict drives the play. However, the full implications of Walter's desires must be grasped in order to perceive the deeper levels of the debate. The New American Library edition (1966) and the 25th Anniversary edition published in 1984 restored a scene which is key to this understanding. Inserted at the end of Act II, Scene 2, the scene shows a brief moment between Walter and his young son, Travis. Walter, who has just been entrusted with the remaining $6500 by his mother and who sees his dream of economic success within his grasp, speaks in a tender tone not heard before from him:

> You wouldn't understand yet, son, but your daddy's gonna make a transaction . . . a business transaction that's going to change our lives . . . That's how come one day when you 'bout seventeen years old I'll come home and I'll be pretty tired, you know what I mean, after a day of conferences and secretaries getting things wrong the way they

do . . . 'cause an executive's life is hell, man — . . . And I'll pull the car up on the driveway . . . just a plain black Chrysler, I think, with white walls — no — black tires. More elegant. Rich people don't have to be flashy . . . though I'll have to get something a little sportier for Ruth — maybe a Cadillac convertible to do her shopping in . . . And I'll come up the steps to the house and the gardener will be clipping away at the hedges and he'll say "Good evening, Mr. Younger." And I'll say, "Hello, Jefferson, how are you this evening?" And I'll go inside and Ruth will come downstairs and meet me at the door and we'll kiss each other and she'll take my arm and we'll go up to your room to see you sitting on the floor with the catalogues of all the great schools in America around you . . . All the great schools in the World! And — and I'll say, all right son — it's your seventeenth birthday, what is it you've decided? Just tell me where you want to go to school and you'll *go*. Just tell me, what it is you want to be — and you'll *be* it . . . Whatever you want to be — Yessir! You just name it, son . . . and I hand you the world! [12]

The placement of this speech is critical to its import for it catches Walter in a rare, reflective moment. Throughout the play, the audience has seen the restless side of Walter, constantly at odds with his family, desperately trying to convince his strong-willed mother of the importance of his plans. This speech is Walter's only chance in the play to explain his ideas fully, without interruption and criticism. While the speech verifies Walter's desire to shape a better future for his son, it also signals a shift in his value system — one which will make the outrageous offer from the white homeowners' association both attractive and logical. Walter is willing to buy into a system of roles and class stratification in order to realize his dream. His image is typical Americana — the independent male who controls the world and around whom the universe revolves. Wife, secretary, gardener, Cadillac, sports car — all are complements to his material universe. His manhood is at stake, he believes, and the women around him with their traditional values are holding him back.

Walter's speech was also deleted from the 1961 film version of the play. In its place was a brief exchange between Mama and Walter in which Walter equates his investment opportunity with his parents' move North out of the economic and spiritual traps of the Deep South. The money represents his chance to board his generation's train to the North. Without the Walter/Travis scene, however, the text lacks the subtle class and sexist implications of the American dream that Walter seeks.

To sharpen this fundamental debate, Lena Younger/Mama must be rescued from the persistent image of passivity, accommodation, and self-satisfaction associated with the Black Mammy stereotype. She must be revealed for what, in fact, she is, according to Hansberry: "The Black matriarch incarnate: The bulwark of the Negro family since slavery; the embodiment of the Negro will to transcendance. It is she who, in the mind of the Black poet, scrubs the floors of a nation in order to create Black diplomats and university professors. It is she who, while seeming to cling to traditional restraints, drives the young on into the fire hoses and one day simply refuses to move to the back of the bus in Montgomery." [13]

The original production script also included a scene in Act II, Scene 2, that clarified

[12] Lorraine Hansberry, *A Raisin in the Sun/The Sign in Sidney Brustein's Window* (New York: New American Library, 1966), pp. 88–89.

[13] Lorraine Hansberry, "The Origins of Character" (Address to the American Academy of Psychotherapists, New York, 5 October 1963).

A Raisin in the Sun. Roundabout Theatre, New York City, 1986. Photo: Martha Swope.

this image of Mama. However, the entire scene, along with the character of Mrs. Johnson, was eliminated in order to trim the show's playing time. It has now been published for the first time in the addendum of the 1984 Samuel French edition and has been included in several recent productions. The original producers may have sacrificed too much, underestimating the persistence of the Mammy stereotype in the American psyche. The perception of Lena Younger as a conservative, retarding force has been a difficult one to shed. Although the dialogue in this scene is carried by Mrs. Johnson, a nosy neighbor and somewhat humorous character, Mama's responses clearly place her in the militant forefront. Mrs. Johnson, always the happy bearer of

bad news, makes explicit the danger in the family's move and Mama's quiet determination to take the risk.

Johnson: I guess y'all seen the news whats all over the colored paper this week . . .
Mama: No—didn't get mine yet this week.
Johnson: You mean you ain't read 'bout them colored people that was bombed out their
place out there? . . . Ain't it something how bad these here white folks is getting
here in Chicago! Lord, getting so you think you right down in Mississippi! . . .
Course I thinks it's wonderful how our folks keeps on pushing out . . . Lord—I
bet this time next month y'all's names will have been in the papers plenty— . . .
"NEGROES INVADE CLYBOURNE PARK—BOMBED!"
Mama: We ain't exactly moving out there to get bombed.
Johnson: Oh, honey—you know I'm praying to God every day that don't nothing like
that happen! But you have to think of life like it is—and these here Chicago
peckerwoods is some baaaad peckerwoods.
Mama: We done thought about all that, Mis' Johnson.[14]

The conversation continues with Mrs. Johnson carrying most of the dialogue, while
Mama speaks briefly, but with quiet authority. Then Lena Younger makes a surprising philosophical connection.

Johnson: Sometimes . . . [Beneatha] act like she ain't got time to pass the time of day with
nobody ain't been to college. Oh—I ain't criticizing her none. It's just—you
know how some of our young people gets when they get a little education . . .
'Course I can understand how she must be proud and everything—being the
only one in the family to make something of herself! I know just being a chauffeur ain't never satisfied Brother none. He shouldn't feel like that, though. Ain't
nothing wrong with being a chauffeur.
Mama: There's plenty wrong with it.
Johnson: What?
Mama: Plenty. My husband always said being any kind of a servant wasn't a fit thing for
a man to have to be. He always said a man's hands was made to make things, or
to turn the earth with—not to drive nobody's car for em—or . . . carry they
slop jars. And my boy is just like him—
Johnson: Mmmmm mmmm. The Youngers is too much for me! . . . You sure one proud-
acting bunch of colored folks. Well—I always thinks like Booker T. Washington
said that time—"Education has spoiled many a good plow hand"—
Mama: Is that what old Booker T. said?
Johnson: He sure did.
Mama: Well, it sounds just like him. The fool.
Johnson: Well—he was one of our great men.
Mama: Who said so?[15]

The physical image of Mama (large, dark, dominant) suggests the Mammy
stereotype of countless American plays and films, but her criticism of Booker T.
Washington's ideas in this passage aligns her with Washington's intellectual opponent,

[14] Lorraine Hansberry, *A Raisin in the Sun*, 25th Anniversary Edition (New York: Samuel French, Inc.,
1984), pp. 137–39.
[15] Ibid., pp. 139–40.

W. E. B. DuBois. DuBois and other militant advocates for civil rights founded the National Association for the Advancement for Colored People (NAACP), the organization that provided much of the legal bases for protesting segregation. The Washington/DuBois debate framed the philosophical and political issues facing Black-Americans and the fight for human and civil rights early in this century. The stereotype of the Black Mammy suggests complicity with Washington's emphasis on accommodation and economic self-sufficiency. However, in an ironic twist, Hansberry equates Mama's determination with the militant spirit of DuBois's position and Walter's entrepreneurial interests with the materialism associated with Washington's philosophy. Lena Younger is not the accommodating Mammy who chooses the passive, safe path, but rather the folk figure, the courageous spirit that lends credence and power to the militant struggle. In her own determined way, she gives birth to revolutionaries and is herself a progressive force. The explicit reference to Washington in this scene illuminates the "revolutionary" aspect of Lena and sharply delineates the philosophical difference between Mama and Walter.

Hansberry's final and most definitive framing of the philosophical issues occurs at the beginning of Act III in the dialogue between Asagai and Beneatha. Abridged in early publications of the script, most of this exchange was cut from the film. As in the earlier Walter/Travis scene, the placement of this scene is important. It occurs just after the highly emotional moment when Walter and Mama discover that the money is gone. The audience, affected by the sheer magnitude of the loss, is now invited to reflect on the family's future. At a time when Mama's faith is being sorely tested and the materialistic underpinnings of Walter's faith have been destroyed, what values will shape the family's response? Here Hansberry places a key dialogue — the debate between Asagai and Beneatha. Some critics dismiss this section as a distracting, verbose passage, out of place in this realistic piece of theatre.[16] Yet a closer examination of the unabridged scene reveals its crucial role in the philosophical progression of the theme.

The question here is not whether the family should move or stay, but rather what they will learn from this tragedy. Will they act out of an affirmation of life or be paralyzed by despair? Asagai focuses on Beneatha, but Hansberry focuses her critique on Walter and all those who would base their future on the acquisition of things. As the money goes, so goes Beneatha's and Walter's faith in humankind. "Man is foul!" Beneatha says, "And the human race deserves its misery! . . . From now on, I worship truth — and the truth is that people are puny, small and selfish."[17] The logical extension of this "truth" is to ignore human values and to act, if one does at all, out of selfishness and the needs of the existential moment. This idea enables Walter later in Act III to consider any means to recover the lost money. But Asagai counters:

> Truth? Why is it that you despairing ones always think that only you have the truth? I never thought to see *you* like that. You! Your brother made a stupid, childish mistake — and you are grateful to him. So that now you can give up the ailing human race

---

[16] For example, see Max Lerner, "A Dream Deferred," *New York Post*, 8 April 1959, p. 2. The "theme of the African heritage and possible future of the Negro is marginal to the main theme of the play."

[17] Lorraine Hansberry, *A Raisin in the Sun/The Sign*, p. 114.

on account of it. You talk about what good is struggle; what good is anything? Where are we all going? And why are we bothering?[18]

Beneatha responds:

And you cannot answer it! All your talk and dreams about Africa and Independence. Independence and then what? What about all the crooks and petty thieves and just plain idiots who will come into power to steal and plunder the same as before — only now they will be black and do it in the name of the new Independence — You cannot answer that.[19]

Asagai shouts over her: "I live the answer!"[20] Asagai proposes his being, his life, his very existence — and the meaning that commitment creates — as the embodiment of his answer. Asagai acts out of a belief in the transcendent power of man and woman, a belief that cannot be shaken by the loss of money, material things, or even the devastation of human betrayal. This faith will be his armor when he returns to his troubled homeland to fight against terrible odds — poverty and ignorance, not to mention the British and the French — to achieve the full liberation of his people.

Asagai expresses in philosophical and political terms the affirmation that Lena Younger has lived. At this moment, he is her symbolic son — the long-desired reuniting of Africans and Afro-Americans through shared beliefs, not color alone. The debate anticipates the ambivalence of Walter's emotions as he is torn, up to the very end of the play, between an act of despair and an act of affirmation. Ironically, affirmation carries no assurances. For just as Asagai does not know whether he will be revered or murdered for his efforts on behalf of his people, so Walter and the Younger family will face an uncertain future in their new neighborhood. Although Asagai prevails in the debate, Walter must peer into the abyss of despair and lost pride before he can finally acknowledge the progressive, enlightened values of his forebears — the spirit of life which has allowed humankind to transcend its condition.

The play repudiates the kind of materialism that values money and acquisition over human dignity and life. The spirit of humankind, Hansberry insists, must affirm freedom, justice, integrity, caring — at the expense of comfort or even life itself. It is a courageous statement made in the face of the desperate economic needs of the Youngers of the nation. It is offered as a framework for the liberation struggles of the world, in defiance of traditional American notions of success. The uncut scene in Act III gives full expression to the debate and heightens the philosophical questions implicit in the Youngers' struggle. When this scene is cut, as in the film, or abridged, as in the early publications and the original production, the import of Hansberry's philosophical position is diminished and the intellectual dimensions of Beneatha and Asagai are trivialized. The Yale production used the full version of this scene with great success. One critic even claimed that this scene could well be the climax of the play.[21]

---

[18] Ibid.
[19] Ibid., pp. 114–15.
[20] Ibid., p. 115.
[21] Markland Taylor, "*Raisin, Jerusalem* a Case of Good vs. Poor Playwriting," *New Haven Register*, 13 November 1983, p. D9.

Hansberry's sensing of future trends was most evident in another casualty of the original production script: Beneatha adopts a natural hairstyle (long before the "Afro" became popular) and a bourgeois George Murchison is surprisingly appreciative of the look.[22] But the most dramatic change in the play occurred long before the show went into rehearsal. In an earlier version of the script, Hansberry wrote a more somber ending in which the family is shown sitting in the darkened living room of their new house, armed and awaiting an attack by their white neighbors. The accepted and ever popular upbeat ending, which shows a jubilant family moving to their new home, was no less true than the other ending. This more positive view did, however, emphasize the Younger's evolution and progress rather than the violent, retrogressive attitudes of the racists who awaited them.

Despite the loss of much of the play's philosophical dimension, *A Raisin in the Sun* was a smashing success in 1959 and has continued to attract audiences for a quarter of a century. The productions that recent audiences have applauded are for the most part based on an expanded text that includes portions of the scenes discussed in this essay and that provides greater definition of major characters and theme. The heavy financial risks associated with professional productions resulted in a necessarily conservative handling of the original production and robbed early audiences of the full import of Hansberry's achievement. It may have been asking too much of 1959 audiences to cope with the full vision of the play. Only the very naive would have expected them to accept the intellectual dimension emanating from the experiences of a working-class Black family and the pen of a Black woman writer during the heat and turmoil of those days. The timeliness of the play has not diminished. Its criticism of materialistic values is more poignant amidst the affluence and poverty of American society in the 1980s. At the same time, its depiction of the Black struggle against pernicious, persistent racism remains current as racial intolerance continues to pervade the country's institutions, albeit in more subtle forms. Perhaps because the idea of Black stage characters is not as exotic as it once was, the 1980s audience can perceive the full meaning of the play. Perhaps they are more capable of comprehending the theatre of Black experience, not only as literal portrayal, but as a metaphor for the American experience. Hansberry, however, did not wait for such enlightenment on the part of her audience; she insisted on restoring many of the deleted scenes as soon as possible. It is to her credit that she did so. Her literary executor, Robert Nemiroff, has continued in the same spirit, making other scenes available since the playwright's death. The expanded text has revitalized the play for this generation and has added a new dimension to the exploration of Black experience in the American theatre.

---

[22] The "Afro" was deleted because it was not attractive on actress Diana Sands.

The Female Subject in Chicano Theatre: Sexuality, "Race," and Class

Yvonne Yarbro-Bejarano

The Chicano theatre movement can only be understood in relation to the larger political and cultural movement of which it was a part.[1] It was an oppositional theatre, an arm of the Chicano movement to resist cultural and economic domination. The term Chicano designates people of Mexican ancestry living in the United States.[2] Since 1848, the historical experience of Chicanos has been one of economic exploitation, cultural domination, and social and racial discrimination.[3] As a female member of the social group of Chicanos, the Chicana bears the additional weight of gender oppression, in the dominant culture as well as in Chicano culture.

The initial goals of the Chicano theatre movement were those of the cultural project of the movement as a whole: to create an alternative to the dominant mode of production of mainsteam theatre, to make theatre accessible to a working-class Chicano audience, to validate forms of working-class Chicano culture, and to create accurate theatrical representations of Chicanos' historical and social experience. The term *teatro* refers to the theatre movement as well as the member groups. At its peak in the

---

Yvonne Yarbro-Bejarano is an Associate Professor of Romance Languages and Literature and Comparative Literature at the University of Washington. Her areas of research and publication include Spanish Golden Age theatre, political theatre, and Chicano literature. Currently she is working on a feminist analysis of the seventeenth-century honor play in Spain.

---

[1] For the politics of the Chicano Movement, see Renato Rosaldo et al., *Chicanos: The Beginnings of Brown Power* (New York: William Morrow, 1974).

[2] Originally applied to working-class Mexicans, especially migrant farmworkers, by upwardly mobile Mexican-Americans, the term Chicano became an ideological self-definition during the Chicano movement, designating political commitment and retaining the term's connotations of working-class Chicanos, their *mestizo* (mixed-blood) "race" and their popular Mexican culture. For discussion see Tino Villanueva's Introduction to *Chicanos: Antología histórica y literaria* (Mexico: Fondo de Cultura Económica, 1980); for summary in English see Shifra Goldman and Tomás Ybarra-Frausto, *Arte Chicano; A Comprehensive Annotated Bibliography of Chicano Art, 1965–1981* (Berkeley: Chicano Studies Library Publications Unit, University of California, 1985), pp. 12–13.

[3] For comprehensive histories of Mexicans in the United States see Rodolfo Acuña, *Occupied America: The Chicanos' Struggle towards Liberation* (San Francisco: Canfield Press, 1972); rev. ed. (New York: Harper & Row, 1981) and Carey McWilliams, *North from Mexico* (Philadelphia: Temple University, 1978); for literary application see Joseph Sommers, "From the Critical Premise to the Product: Critical Modes and Their Application to a Chicano Literary Text," *New Scholar* 6 (1977), 51–80.

mid-seventies, the Chicano theatre movement was a vigorous, grass-roots amateur theatre movement of national proportions.[4] The *teatros* played largely to "community" audiences in non-traditional venues: working-class Chicano communities in cultural centers in the *barrios* (Chicano/Latino neighborhoods), picket lines, political rallies, prisons, and schools. *Teatros* experimented with collective creation as well as the collective organization of the *teatros* themselves. In 1970, TENAZ (National Teatros of Aztlán) was founded. This national organization continues to sponsor annual theatre festivals and seminars with the regular participation of political theatre workers from the United States and Latin America.

The *teatros* were microcosms of the conflicts and contradictions of the larger movement. No homogeneous ideological platform unified the Chicano movement, although five or six areas of political activism can be identified.[5] Revolutionary rhetoric co-existed with reformist demands in the documents of the period. While some activists, writers, and theatre groups called for a materialist analysis of the economic exploitation of Chicanos as a class, the main tendency was that of cultural nationalism. Cultural nationalism located the oppositional relationship between Chicanos and the dominant society in the cultural arena rather than in class identity. Chicano culture as a whole was exalted in opposition to Anglo-American culture, which was perceived as materialistic and impersonal. Such an emphasis was important in creating a sense of cultural pride to counter the years of lived experience in a society permeated with degrading stereotypes of Mexicans. On the other hand, it led to a static view of culture, including the uncritical affirmation of the family and gender roles. Cultural nationalism fostered a mystification of racial identity and an ahistorical idealization of pre-Columbian cultures in a myth of origins.[6]

The prevalence of cultural nationalism also led to the reinscription of the heterosexual hierarchization of male/female relationships. In many organizations, male domination was the rule. Women were often excluded from the decision-making process. If their participation exceeded domestic tasks, they were often not credited for their ideas and labor. Chicanas' relationship to the leadership was at times in the form of sexual partners of the "heavies."[7] Since "women's lib" was labeled a white, bourgeois invention, Chicana feminists who recognized gender as well as racial, cultural, and class oppression ran the risk of marginalization. The response of women to the sexual politics of the movement covers a spectrum of positions: proving their loyalty by not dividing the movement over gender issues, remaining Chicana-

[4] For a history of the Chicano theatre movement, see Jorge Huerta, *Chicano Theater. Themes and Forms* (Ypsilanti: Bilingual Press, 1982). For bibliography on Chicano theatre, including unpublished dissertations, see *Literatura Chicana: Creative and Critical Writings through 1984*, comp. Roberto G. Trujillo and Andrés Rodríguez (Oakland: Floricanto Press, 1985).

[5] See Tomás Ybarra-Frausto, "The Chicano Movement and the Emergence of a Chicano Poetic Consciousness," *New Scholar* 6 (1977), 81–109.

[6] Henry Louis Gates warns against the pitfalls of appropriating "race" as a term for an essence in movements of color in his Introduction to "'Race,' Writing and the Difference It Makes," *Critical Inquiry* 12:1 (1985), 13.

[7] Adelaida del Castillo and Magdalena Mora, eds., *Mexican Women in the United States: Struggles Past and Present* (Los Angeles: Chicano Studies, U.C.L.A., 1980).

identified but critiquing sexism from a position within the culture, or working separately with the white women's movement.[8]

This article will review the history of Chicano theatre to examine the shift in the representation of the subject, from the early texts imbedded in cultural nationalism to the exploration of other alternatives in the eighties. Most texts constructed a male subject through notions of class, "racial," and cultural identity that reinscribed tacit cultural definitions of masculinity and femininity within the heterosexual structure of the family. In the eighties, texts have emerged that, while still concerned with class and cultural identity, attempt to focus on the female subject or address more directly questions of sexuality, including homosexuality.

Chicano theatre began as political theatre with the emergence of El Teatro Campesino (The Farmworkers' Theatre) in the grape strike of the United Farmworkers' Union at Delano, California in 1965. From 1965 to 1967 El Teatro Campesino developed short skits called *actos* to dramatize the issues of the strike and promote support for the union. *Las Dos Caras del Patroncito* (The Two Faces of the Little Boss) and *La Quinta Temporada* (The Fifth Season) date from this time.[9] From 1967 to approximately 1970, El Teatro Campesino withdrew from the immediate arena of the farmworkers' struggle to address the larger social, political, and cultural issues of the Chicano movement. *Los Vendidos* (The Sell-Outs) exposed the stereotypes of Mexicans in the dominant culture. *Vietnam Campesino* (Vietnam Peasant) and *Soldado Razo* (Foot Soldier) denounced the war in Vietnam. *No Saco Nada de la Escuela* (I Don't Get Anything Out of School) focused on the discrimination against Chicanos in the educational system.

The *acto* drew on working-class Mexican theatre traditions as well as Brechtian and agit-prop forms of European political theatre.[10] It consisted of an extremely broad gestural language, farcical visual and verbal humor, and stock characterization. One of its most revolutionary aspects was its representation of Chicano speech. The texts were bilingual, a mixture of Spanish and English called code-switching. They were trilingual as well, including Chicano working-class slang (*caló*). Performances incorporated contemporary Chicano/Latin-American protest songs and the *corridos* of the Mexican ballad tradition. The quality of *rascuachismo* opposed the refined finished product of bourgeois art with unpolished vitality. In the preface to *Actos*, published in

[8] For a bibliography on Chicana feminism see Elizabeth Ordóñez, "Sexual Politics and the Theme of Sexuality in Chicana Poetry," in *Women in Hispanic Literature*, ed. Beth Miller (Berkeley: University of California Press, 1983), p. 317, n. 2. For Chicanas' critique of the white women's movement and the sexism and homophobia of the Chicano movement, and the coalition project of women of color to define a feminism incorporating class, race, and cultural as well as gender oppression, see Cherríe Moraga and Gloria Anzaldúa, eds., *This Bridge Called My Back: Writings by Radical Women of Color* (Watertown: Persephone Press, 1981).

[9] Luis Valdez and El Teatro Campesino, *Actos* (San Juan Bautista: Cucaracha Press, 1971).

[10] For the popular Mexican theatre traditions in the Southwest during the late nineteenth and early twentieth centuries and their relationship to the Chicano theatre movement see *Mexican American Theatre Then and Now*, ed. Nicolás Kanellos (Houston: Arte Público Press, 1983) and Kanellos, *Hispanic Theatre in the United States* (Houston: Arte Público, 1984).

1971, founder Luis Valdez identified five guidelines to orient other *teatros* in the creation of *actos*: "Inspire the audience to social action. Illuminate specific points about social problems. Satirize the opposition. Show or hint at a solution. Express what people are feeling" (p. 6).

Around 1970, El Teatro Campesino moved away from the initial goals of the Chicano theatre movement. They settled in San Juan Bautista and started working with a new form to express a religious vision of reality combining Catholicism with aspects of Aztec and Mayan philosophy.[11] The *mitos* (myths) celebrated a mystical Indo-Hispanic identity.[12] Valdez now writes for commercial theatre and film, a process initiated in 1978 with the production of *Zoot Suit*.[13]

El Teatro Campesino exercised tremendous influence on the theatrical practice of other groups, ideologically as well as in the realm of style, form, language, and images. Founder Luis Valdez together with the poet Alurista were the primary spokesmen of cultural nationalism for the movement as a whole. The construction of the class, "racial," and cultural identity of the subject in the work of Valdez and El Teatro Campesino reproduced the heterosexual hierarchy reinforced by the cultural nationalism of the movement. Feminist critics have analyzed how the theatre perpetuates the power relations of sexual difference through the exclusive representation of the male subject and the relegation of women to the status of Other within the social construct of the gender "woman." The male appropriation of the subject role characterizes all phases of Valdez's theatrical production, including his first play (*The Shrunken Head of Pancho Villa*), the *actos*, the *mitos*, and the later commercial plays. The early *actos*, for example, created a male subject conscious of his economic oppression as a Mexican. They did not represent the female farmworker's additional responsibility for the "reproduction" of male workers and children and for the domestic economy of "making ends meet." While not unique to Chicano theatre, the representation of the male subject and of "woman" as Other was accomplished through discourses of class, sexual, "racial," and cultural difference that were culture-specific.

The myth of *La Malinche*

The myth of *La Malinche* is crucial in understanding the link between cultural nationalism and the exclusion of the female subject. *La Malinche*, as the site of representation of sexuality for a culture, illuminates cultural specificity in the construction of the gender of "woman."[14] *La Malinche*'s presence in the culture is as pervasive as that

---

[11] For a poetic exposition of the principles of Valdez's cultural nationalism, see *Pensamiento serpentino: A Chicano Approach to the Theatre of Reality* (San Juan Bautista: Cucaracha Press, 1973).

[12] Susan Bassnet-McGuire, "El Teatro Campesino: from *Actos* to *Mitos*," *Theatre Quarterly* 34 (1979), 18–21; Y. Yarbro-B., "From *acto* to *mito*: A Critical Appraisal of El Teatro Campesino," in *Modern Chicano Writers*, eds. J. Sommers and T. Ybarra (Englewood Cliffs: Prentice-Hall, 1979).

[13] R. G. Davis and Betty Diamond, "'Zoot Suit' on the Road," *Theatre Quarterly* 34 (1979), 21–25; Y. Yarbro-B. with T. Ybarra, "Un análisis crítico de *Zoot Suit* de Luis Valdez," *Conjunto* 42 (1979), 80–88.

[14] Cherríe Moraga, "A Long Line of Vendidas," in *Loving in the War Years* (Boston: South End Press, 1983); Norma Alarcón, "Chicana's Feminist Literature: A Re-vision through Malintzín, Or, Malintzín: Putting Flesh Back on the Object," in *This Bridge*, pp. 182–89; see also Marta Sánchez's analysis of Lucha Corpi's Doña Marina poems in *Contemporary Chicana Poetry: An Approach to an Emerging Literature* (Berkeley: University of California Press, 1985).

of her polar opposite, the redeeming virgin/mother, *La Virgen*. *La Malinche* is the Mexican/Chicano Eve; she too bears the blame for the "fall." During the conquest of Mexico, the noble Aztec woman Malintzín Tenepal (also known by her Spanish name, Doña Marina) acted as Cortes's mistress, translator, and tactical advisor. She becomes the mythical *La Malinche*, signifier of betrayal, through which the historical experience of domination is spoken in the language of sexuality. Her sexual union with the white conqueror made possible the defeat of a people and the destruction of their culture; she produced the "half-breed" or *mestizo* race. *La Malinche* represents *La Vendida* (slang for "sell-out" to the white race). She also represents *La Chingada* (the fucked one). Octavio Paz explicates the verb *chingar* as the verb that defines masculine and feminine roles as played out in the Mexican/Chicano male psyche: "*Chingar* then is to do violence to another, i.e., rape. The verb is masculine, active, cruel: it stings, wounds, gashes, stains . . . . The person who suffers this action is passive, inert, and open, in contrast to the active, aggressive, and closed person who inflicts it. The *chingón* is the macho, the male; he rips open the *chingada*, the female, who is pure passivity, defenseless against the exterior world."[15] *La Malinche* contributes to the construction of the gender "woman" as object, as other, reserving the active subject role for the masculine gender. Woman is viewed as sexually passive, therefore open at all times to use by men either through seduction or rape. Her lack of choice and "openness" also signal the possibility of sexual betrayal through use by white men. In *La Malinche*, female sexuality becomes the site of degradation and evil. *La Virgen* represents the redemption of her gender through self-abnegation and resignation. She is Mother, yet still miraculously intact. The equation of female sexuality with enslavement is translated through *La Virgen* into the cultural values of love/devotion, reinforcing women's subordinate position of servitude and obedience within a rigidly heterosexual hierarchy.[16]

Chicanas who question traditional gender roles and attempt to organize their desire independently run the risk of being labeled *malinchistas* (traitors). They are perceived as corrupted by "foreign" or "bourgeois" influences that threaten to destroy their people. Under the pressure of this conflation of class, racial, and sexual betrayal, the Chicana proves her fidelity to her people by means of a sexual commitment to the Chicano male, "putting the male first" within the heterosexual structures of the family and the culture.[17]

This in turn affects the ways in which Chicanas relate to each other. The cultural practice of putting the males first leads Chicanas to fear rejection and betrayal from other Chicanas. The daughter rejects the mother for her powerlessness and dependency; the mother's preference for the males reflects her own internalization of the culture's devaluation of female sexuality.[18] The deconstruction of the cultural signs of

---

[15] Octavio Paz, *The Labyrinth of Solitude: Life and Thought in Mexico*, trans. Lysander Kemp (New York: Grove Press, 1961); quoted in Moraga, "A Long Line of Vendidas," *Loving in the War Years*, pp. 118–19.

[16] Alarcón, "Chicana's Feminist Literature," p. 184.

[17] Moraga, "A Long Line," p. 101.

[18] For a discussion of the impact of the myth of La Malinche on mother/daughter relationships see Alarcón's discussion of Mexican writer Rosario Castellanos, "Chicana's Feminist Literature," p. 185.

La Malinche and *La Virgen* opens the possibility for Chicanas to replace self-hatred with self-love and fear of betrayal with solidarity.

El Teatro Campesino

The work of Luis Valdez and El Teatro Campesino replicated the gender roles codified in the myths of *La Malinche* and *La Virgen*. The creation of the active male subject was accompanied by the representation of woman in a position of servitude within heterosexual relationships. She appeared as *La Malinche*, the female as site of fallen sexuality, as well as *La Virgen*, the pure ideal of unswerving love/devotion.

Valdez wrote his first play, *The Shrunken Head of Pancho Villa*, in 1964 while he was still a student at San José State University; El Teatro Campesino produced the play in 1968.[19] According to the legend, after Pancho Villa was assassinated and buried, he was disinterred and decapitated, though the head was never found. Valdez used the head of Pancho Villa as a grotesque character in his play: the oldest son of a poverty-stricken Chicano family. The head was a multivalent sign. It signified the spirit of the Mexican Revolution, envisioned as a precursor of the Chicano Move-ment, which could "ride" again if only an appropriate "body" were found. One son became a kind of *barrio* Robin Hood, following the incitations of the head. At the end of the play he returned "brainwashed" from jail as a giant headless body. At the same time, the head signified the poverty and misery of the *barrio*, signalled by his steady diet of cockroaches. If the male subject was represented as a possible route out of poverty through the activism of the Chicano Movement, woman was represented as responsible for it, through her sexuality. The daughter, like the mother, played the passive, self-sacrificing role embodying love/devotion, serving the head and the other males in the family throughout the play. At the end, she exchanged the role of *La Virgen* for that of *La Malinche*. She became pregnant by her boyfriend and gave birth to another bodyless head, perpetuating the cycle of misery and poverty.

As discussed above, the absence of representation of the female farmworker's specific relationship to economic exploitation marked the earliest *actos* of El Teatro Campesino, produced in conjunction with the farmworkers' union. In *Las dos caras del patroncito*, woman appeared as "the blond in the bikini," the wife of the boss and the signifier of his power, appropriated by the male farmworker when the two "change places." In *La Quinta Temporada* women appeared only as allegorical figures: Spring, who encouraged the male farmworker protagonist to fight back and join the union, and the Church, who defended him and pressured the owner to sign a contract. In one of the later *actos*, *Los Vendidos*, woman was the ultimate "sell-out." It was Governor Reagan's secretary (pronouncing her name "Miss JIMenez") in search of the perfect brown-faced token for government programs who keyed "Honest Sancho's" selling of Chicano male stereotypes.

La Virgen as idealized representation of woman functioned most overtly in the *mitos* of El Teatro Campesino. She is revered in the company's annual dramatization of the appearance of the Virgin of Guadalupe to Juan Diego. In the myth *Bernabé* she

---

[19] In *West Coast Plays*, ed. R. Foster (California Theatre Council, Winter & Spring, 1982).

appeared in her aspect of Earth Mother, through her identification with Tonantzín, the Aztec fertility goddess.[20] In *Bernabé*, the male subject's mystical relationship to the land was allegorized through the hierarchical and heterosexual relationships of the family.[21] To marry *La Tierra* (the land), Bernabé had to first pass her brother, *La Luna* (the moon), who was jealous of her honor. He won the approval of her father, *El Sol* (the sun), who pronounced his daughter a virgin and blessed their multiplication.

Valdez's commercial plays continued to perpetuate the male in the subject position and the female in the role of *La Malinche* or *La Virgen*. In *Zoot Suit*, for example, Chicanas were represented as whores (the sexually open ex-girlfriend Berta) or virgins (new girlfriend Della), the mother once again exemplifying the ideal of love/devotion.[22] In *Corridos*, a musical review dramatizing popular ballads from the Mexican tradition, the ballads chosen for dramatization consistently represented women as victims of incest ("Delgadina"), murder ("Rosita Alvirez"), and males' exaggerated *machismo* ("Cornelio Vega").[23] Even the legendary figure of *"La Adelita"* of the Mexican Revolution was not represented as revolutionary subject, but as supporter and helpmate of male revolutionaries.

The appearance of a new male subject in Valdez's commercial works illustrated the rigid duality of gender construction along the *chingón/chingada* axis. The "white male savior" may have responded to the needs of the new audience of Valdez's commercial phase, white middle-class instead of working-class Chicano. He was the lawyer in *Zoot Suit* who convinced the Chicano youths to have faith in the American system of justice. In *Rose of the Rancho* (1981), an Anglo government official saved Rose's land from marauding opportunists after the Mexican-American war; in gratitude she married him instead of her Spanish suitor. In *Corridos*, the *"Adelita"* who had lost her man in a skirmish sought the protection of John Reed, with whom she spent one night of peace before taking up the next morning in the train of another male revolutionary. These liaisons between Mexican women and white men were not presented as sexual, historical, racial, and cultural betrayal as in the earlier plays of El Teatro Campesino. The contradiction may be explained by Valdez's new assimilationist goals, expressed in interviews around this time.[24] Besides limiting the representation of woman to passive pawn of male "use," *Corridos* also locked into the representation of the male Mexican/Chicano as *chingón*.

The dominance of narrative form in the work of Valdez and El Teatro Campesino reinforced the power relations already created by sexual difference in the representation of the active male subject and the passive female Other, bound in loving servitude through *La Virgen* or in fallen sexuality through *La Malinche*. Feminist critics such as

[20] In *Contemporary Chicano Theatre*, ed. R. J. Garza (Notre Dame: University of Notre Dame Press, 1976).

[21] For a discussion of male/female relationships in this play and other texts, see Margarita B. Melville, "Female and Male in Chicano Theatre," in *Hispanic Theatre in the United States*, pp. 71–79.

[22] For further discussion of female roles in *Zoot Suit* see my "Chicanas' Experience in Collective Theaters: Ideology and Form," *Women & Performance* 2:2 (1985).

[23] For reviews of *Corridos*, see Rodrigo Reyes, *Revista Literaria de El Tecolote* 3:3 (1982), 2–4 and Jeffrey D. Mason, *Theatre Journal* 37:3 (1985), 360–62.

[24] For example, in *Mother Jones* (June, 1979).

Teresa De Lauretis have argued that the Western quest narrative excludes women from the subject position and subordinates her as an object to be attained, an obstacle to be removed or a space to be conquered by the active male subject.[25] Elin Diamond has explored the connection between history and narrative form, building on Paul Ricoeur's argument that "history is inconceivable except as it takes on the attributes of narrative" and Hayden White's discussion of modern historiography demanding "that events be narrated . . . revealed as possessing a structure, an order of meaning, a beginning, middle, and end."[26] Valdez's *América*, a fusion of dramatic/poetic recitation and music,[27] narrativized history in three stages: the idealized representation of pre-conquest Mexico is followed by the rape of the Indian woman by the Spaniard. The oppression of the modern race of *mestizos* was related teleologically to this sexual and racial fall from Eden. *América* influenced the work of other *teatros*. For example, the Mexican theatre group Mascarones, closely allied to the Chicano theatre movement, performed a play modelled on *América*'s narrative history while on tour in the Southwest.[28] This narrative reinforced the tendency to represent women's subordination in terms of her fallen sexuality. In *The Shrunken Head of Pancho Villa*, for example, the conditions of poverty and economic exploitation were perpetuated through the daughter's offspring.

Chicanas' alternatives within the Chicano theatre movement

Chicanas working within the Chicano theatre movement attempted to counter male-domination in their representations as well as in the material conditions of theatre production. In production, the major achievement of Chicanas was the establishment in 1978 of a women's caucus called W.I.T. (Women in Teatro) within TENAZ, responding to the widespread perception that the national organization was not addressing itself effectively to the specific needs of female theatre workers. In February of 1980, W.I.T. singled out the following needs of Chicanas in *teatro*: "The need for women playwrights, producers and directors; the need for strong women's roles in the messages through which we educate our public; the needs of the individual woman, such as child care; and the need for support of all *Raza* for the development of women in *teatro*."[29] Through the years, W.I.T. has provided a much-needed communication network and support base for Chicanas in theatre organizations. In special workshops during the TENAZ seminars and festivals, W.I.T. has raised consciousness around women's issues and helped women just beginning to work in *teatro* to deal with their specific problems.

[25] Teresa De Lauretis, "Desire in Narrative," in *Alice Doesn't: Feminism, Semiotics, Cinema* (Bloomington: Indiana University Press, 1981), pp. 103–57.

[26] Elin Diamond, "Refusing the Romanticization of Identity: Narrative Interventions in Churchill, Benmussa, Duras," *Theatre Journal* 37:3 (1985), p. 276.

[27] A dramatic recitation of Valdez's *América* is included in the film *El Teatro Campesino* (1970); the text is performed by his brother Daniel Valdez on his record, *Mestizo*, on the A & M label (1974).

[28] Teatro Mascarones included a number on Teatro Chicano in their series *Cuadernos del pueblo* (Cuernavaca, Mexico: Ediciones Mascarones, 1976). This publication includes photographs, an interview with Luis and Daniel Valdez, a manifesto of the Chicano theatre movement and translations into Spanish of *Las dos caras del patroncito* and *Los vendidos*.

[29] See my "The Role of Women in Chicano Theater Organizations," *Revista Literaria de El Tecolote* 2:3, 4 (1981).

Another response to male-domination in the Chicano theatre movement was the formation of all-women *teatros*.[30] In form, these groups inherited a twin legacy: the narrative history of *América* and *teatropoesía*, a collage of poetry, prose, music, dance, and pantomine.[31] The lack of trained Chicano playwrights due to economic and social factors encouraged the incorporation of other genres. Other reasons for Chicanas' use of this form included the lack of time to develop a piece through collective creation, dissatisfaction with the subordinate roles for women in plays produced by other *teatros*, as well as the desire to recognize and disseminate poetic work by Chicanas. In 1974, Dorinda Moreno and a women's group called Las Cucarachas performed a *teatropoesía* piece called *Chicana*, first for a minifestival in San Francisco's Mission District and then in Mexico City during the Fifth Festival organized by TENAZ. Valentina Productions, a women's group based in San José, performed *Voz de la mujer* (Woman's Voice) for the Eleventh TENAZ Festival held in San Francisco in 1981. Although the *teatropoesía* form allowed for the representation of the female subject, the narrative history used to order the texts in these two pieces reinscribed the subordinate position of women inherent in cultural nationalism. *Chicana* began with a text about *la indígena* (the Native Indian woman of pre-Columbian Mexico), and progressed through the representation of *"La Adelita"* of the Mexican Revolution to *"la nueva Chicana"* (the new Chicana). *Voz de la mujer* began with an Aztec dance, progressing through the image of the poet/playwright Sor Juana Inés de la Cruz of Colonial Mexico and *"La Adelita"* to the modern Chicana. What is interesting in the women's narrative structuring of a beginning, middle, and end is that the "middle" no longer narrated the fall of *La Malinche*. Both texts passed over the Conquest in silence. Instead, *Chicana* placed the modern Chicana in relationship to the revolutionary "Adelita," while *Voz de la mujer* replaced her with the remarkable Mexican nun of the seventeenth century, Sor Juana, as a kind of intellectual precursor of modern Chicana feminism.[32] However, the narrative "beginning" in pre-Columbian times still placed the burden on the modern Chicana to redeem her gender through revolutionary and political struggle, while proving her loyalty to her people through motherhood and family in a context of love/devotion. Las Cucarachas made these goals explicit in the pamphlet they prepared for the Festival, stressing the perpetuation of family life as well as the recognition of India/Latina women who have passed into history for their participation in the liberation of their people. *Chicana* positioned representations of women as revolutionary subjects demanding equality with men in relationship to images of woman as Earth Mother/Tonantzín, symbol of fertility and mainstay of the strong, united family. Like *Chicana*, *Voz de la mujer* exalted motherhood. Although several poems and pantomimes dramatized the need for women to be independent, the group was careful to couch any critique of male/female relationships in a context of solidarity and support of men.

[30] Teatro Raíces, a women's group based in San Diego, did not use *teatropoesía* or explore specifically women's issues, working instead in the *acto* tradition. Cara Hill de Castañón developed a one-woman show consisting of texts by the Mexican nun Sor Juana, a strategy that avoided both the problems of group work as well as the "narrative history" form.

[31] For the history of the *teatropoesía* form in the Chicano theatre movement, see my "*Teatropoesía* by Chicanas in the Bay Area: *Tonges of Fire*," in *Mexican Theatre Then and Now*, pp. 78–94.

[32] See also Estela Portillo Trambley, *Sor Juana and Other Plays* (Ypsilanti, Mi.: Bilingual Press, 1983).

Yolanda Broyles has been carrying out extensive research on the women of El Teatro Campesino. Her research has revealed their lack of input and their growing dissatisfaction with subordinate roles and casting by Chicana "type." She has also called attention to their imaginative strategies for dealing with these limitations. Of particular interest is Socorro Valdez's creation of an "ungendered" role: *La Muerte* (Death). This role drew on the popular graphic tradition associated with the work of José Guadalupe Posada and the imagery surrounding the celebration of the Day of the Dead by Mexicans and Chicanos. Through Socorro Valdez's *tour de force* realization of this character, *La Muerte* became a major image of the Chicano theatre movement. *La Muerte* appeared in El Teatro Campesino's late *acto*, *Soldado Razo*, and gave rise to the death figures, or *calaveras* (skeletons), of *mitos* such as *El fin del mundo* (The End of the World). These *calaveras* used the make-up and costuming of *La Muerte* (black leotards with skull-face and bones painted on in white). While Socorro Valdez's creation of *La Muerte* effectively sidestepped the problematic construction of gender onstage, the *calavera* in the work of El Teatro Campesino became a neutral platform for rapid character changes that reproduced the traditional attributes of gender roles (adding the stole and mitre for the bishop, the apron for the wife/mother, etc.).

El Teatro de la Esperanza

The materialist analysis of El Teatro de la Esperanza (Theatre of Hope) stood in counterpoint to the cultural nationalism of the work of El Teatro Campesino and the groups influenced by them. Founded in 1971 and based until recently at the Casa de la Raza in Santa Barbara, California, the group has recently moved to the Mission Cultural Center in San Francisco. Their ideological orientation avoided the mystification of racial and cultural identity as well as the mythical narrative of history so prevalent in the work of El Teatro Campesino. Throughout their development they continued to define themselves as a political theatre, committed to the original goals of the Chicano theatre movement and working in close contact with the Latin-American "New Theatre" movement, especially with groups and organizations in Cuba, Colombia, and Nicaragua. The collective organization of this *teatro* also reflected their politics, as opposed to the hierarchical structure of El Teatro Campesino dominated by Luis Valdez. El Teatro de la Esperanza's efforts to distribute power within the group among both men and women involved not only decision-making, but also directing, collective creation, administration, and all aspects of production. They were sensitive to women's issues, being the only member group of TENAZ to institute child care as part of their policy. They were also aware of the even more difficult struggle to distribute ideological sophistication among the members of the group, recognizing that the kind of power which political analysis provides was often monopolized by males within the movement.

After early experiments with the *acto*, El Teatro de la Esperanza developed a form of docudrama that illustrated the difficulty of decentering the male subject of representation in narrative forms. Their first docudrama, *Guadalupe* (1974), used a collective protagonist, a group of parents of both sexes who organize to combat discrimination against their children in the educational system. Their next three plays were *La víctima* (The Victim, 1976), *Hijos* (Children), *Once a Family* (1979), and *El pulpo* (The

La muerta viene cantando. El Teatro de la Esperanza, Santa Barbara. Photo: Ira Mintz.

Octopus, 1980).[33] These docudramas concentrated on the weakness and contradictions of the male protagonist, placed in dialectical relation to active female characters who possessed a clearer vision of the economic and social forces composing the dramatic conflict. Samuel "sold-out" as U.S. immigration agent in *La víctima*. Manuel fantasized of maintaining the cultural values of his family intact in spite of economic exploitation and cultural domination in *Hijos*. Johnny Henry was blind to the Octopus's rapacious exploitation of the Third World in *El pulpo*. This technique permitted El Teatro de la Esperanza to represent women in the traditionally subordinate roles within the family structure as subjects in social struggles. For example, the sister in *La víctima* was the chief organizer of documented and undocumented workers alike at the factory where she worked. In *El pulpo* an old woman appeared as revolutionary subject, explaining the mechanism of corporate capitalism's exploitation of the Third World to Johnny Henry through a taco parable. In another scene, she pointed out the contradictions of male revolutionaries who attempt to relegate women to a subordinate position in the struggle through rigid gender division of labor. However, the

[33] For a discussion of these unpublished plays, see my "El Teatro de la Esperanza: Una experiencia del teatro chicano," *Conjunto* 49 (1981), 14–25, and "The Image of the Chicana in Teatro," in *Gathering Ground: New Writing and Art by Northwest Women of Color,* eds. Jo Cochran et al. (Seattle: Seal Press, 1984), pp. 90–96.

tyranny of narrative form limited the function of these female characters to that of catalyst in the development of the male protagonist. They succeeded in transforming his consciousness or bringing his contradictions to the point of maximum tension. In *La víctima*, it was the mother who confronted Samuel with his betrayal of culture and class. In *Hijos*, the wife/mother had contended on a daily basis with the realities of economic survival. At the end of the play she made Manuel realize that the family is not an island of security existing outside the pale of social conflict. In *El pulpo*, the old woman revolutionary opened Johnny Henry's eyes to the lies of the Octopus. Similarly, while El Teatro de la Esperanza provided a materialist analysis of the impact of economic and social forces on the Chicano family, the group did not offer a critique of the family structure itself.

El Teatro de la Esperanza's non-narrative muscial revue *La muerte viene cantando* (Death Comes Singing) drew on the *calavera* and *corrido* tradition of El Teatro Campesino. In this work they continued the practice of cross-gender casting begun in *El pulpo*, in which women played both the Octopus and the dictator La Rata (The Rat). In *La muerte viene cantando* the *calavera* of the old woman was played by a man, allowing for the humorous deconstruction of gender attributes. Their selection of *corridos* avoided the representation of women as passive victims of male violence and *machismo*. In the Mexican ballad tradition, women are also prepetrators of violence, both criminal and revolutionary. For *La muerte viene cantando*, El Teatro de la Esperanza chose a *corrido* that fused class struggle and sexuality. An army officer raped a peasant woman and shot her brother, actions that demonstrated his dominant position in both gender and class power relations. The woman's act of shooting him with his own gun appropriated for the female subject both familial revenge and revenge for sexual dishonor (a role usually reserved for men) as well as resistance to class oppression. Other songs involved the representation of armed women as revolutionary subjects, foregrounding their active role in the Mexican and Nicaraguan Revolutions. A highlight of the show was the dramatization of Domitila Barrios de Chungara's famous speech at the International Women's Conference held in Mexico City in 1975. In this speech the Bolivian mineworker rejected bourgeois Latin-American women's claim to sisterhood as long as they are implicated by class interests in the oppression of working-class men and women in Latin America.[34] The inclusion of such voices in *La muerte viene cantando* helped sketch the parameters of a Latina subjectivity inseparable from class identity.

Tongues of Fire

While the work of El Teatro de la Esperanza provided a materialist analysis of class in the construction of Chicano subjectivity, the predominance of narrative form continued to subordinate women to the male subject. The *teatropoesía* piece *Tongues of Fire* focused on the Chicana subject in relation to sexuality, "race," and class, yet avoided the coercive structure of narrative history that characterized the work of the other all-women groups discussed thus far. The play explored the relationship between the Chicana's subjectivity as a working-class woman of color and writing.

[34] For an English translation, see Domitila Barrios de Chungara with Moema Viezzer, *Let Me Speak*, trans. Victoria Ortiz (New York and London: Monthly Review Press, 1978).

Tongues of Fire, scripted by Barbara Brinson-Pineda with the collaboration of Antonio Curiel, was created for performance as part of the Cultural Heritage of Chicana Literature Conference held at Mills College in Oakland, California in October, 1981.[35] The texts were loosely grouped around various themes in five sections. The first section, "Collage in Brown," introduced the consciousness of the Chicana writer. A woman sat at a table, writing, an image maintained throughout the other sections of the show. As if reading from the pages before her, she recited fragments of poems that touched on the theme of writing. The other three actors positioned themselves around her in dialogue that included quotations from Gloria Anzaldúa's "Speaking in Tongues: A Letter to Third World Women Writers."[36] The passages from "Speaking in Tongues" focused the representation of the Chicana writer in terms of her triple oppression on the grounds of sex, race, and class. A long history of racial and economic oppression has relegated the Chicana to menial, back-breaking jobs and systematically denied her access to literacy. The Chicana's color exacerbates the feelings of inadequacy and self-hatred instilled in all women by patriarchal society and reinforced by her own culture. A key passage from "Speaking in Tongues" gave the show its title. In this quotation, Anzaldúa suggested that the Chicana writer turn the obstacles that have been placed in her path as a writer into strengths, the "deep core" from which she writes as a working-class woman of color: "The white man speaks: Perhaps if you scrape the dark off your face. Maybe if you bleach your bones. Stop speaking in tongues, stop writing left-handed. Don't cultivate your colored skins nor tongues of fire if you want to make it in a right-handed world" (p. 166). Through her writing the Chicana explores not only her personal identity, but a collective identity as well: her voice speaks for those who have been silenced.

By placing the individual subjectivity of the Chicana writer in a dialectic with collective identity, *Tongues of Fire* avoided the romanticization of a unified self. The "I" of the play was a decentered subject that could include both the writer and the voices of the recited texts. The writer herself was not presented as a unified subject, since all actors alternated in this role. At times the texts were spoken by individual actors or divided up among several actors, at other times they were recited in chorus. Some texts were fragmented and interrrupted by other texts. The accumulative effect of these devices was to create the impression of many different voices engaged in a dialogue about what it means to be female and Chicana.

Although the form of the work avoided the historicizing narrative of *América, Chicana*, and *Voz de la mujer*, the topic of history was crucial in the exploration of the Chicana's identity and task as a writer. "Visions of Mexico . . ." by Lorna Dee Cervantes expressed the need to dominate the written word in order to destroy stereotypes about Mexicans and rewrite history from the perspective of the oppressed class. The second section, "The Past within Us," explored the history of women's oppression, presenting two long poems as interlocking monologues. "María la O" by Brinson-Pineda told the intimate history of one woman's poverty and hardship in

---

[35] For a more detailed analysis of this play see my "*Teatropoesía* by Chicanas in the Bay Area: *Tongues of Fire*."

[36] In *This Bridge Called My Back: Writings by Radical Women of Color*, pp. 165–73.

Mexico and migration to work in the fields of the United States around the time of the Mexican Revolution. "Arriaga" by Shylda Alvarez captured a young girl's experience of the suffocating attitudes towards women and sexuality in Mexico in 1933. The fragmented presentation of the texts, as well as the inclusion of history as a process to be confronted critically rather than as a coercive narrative form, allowed a space in which to understand how "the past [works] within us," establishing both a sense of connection and continuity as well as the distance necessary for change.

The "tongues of fire" of the texts were double-edged, exposing oppression from without as well as within the culture. Some texts expressed the class consciousness of the Chicana subject in solidarity with her people as a whole. For example, a speech by María Moreno, farmworker mother of twelve, denounced the economic exploitation of farmworkers. The poem "Napa, California" by Ana Castillo, that interrupted this longer text, depicted backbreaking labor in the fields. Other texts spoke the Chicana's perception of the subordination of women within the culture through rigid gender roles and attitudes towards female sexuality. In a dialogue between father and daughter called "Amor y libertad" (Love and Liberty) by Rosa Carrillo, traditional family values clashed with the Chicana's changing self-image and desire for independence. Another play-within-the-play, "El diablo en forma de mujer" (The Devil in the Form of Woman) humorously deconstructed the misogynistic vision of female sexuality as instrument of the devil in Mexican folklore. In Lorna Dee Cervantes's "You Cramp My Style, Baby," the poetic voice addressed the Chicano Movement male whose enthusiastic embrace of "La Raza" and Chicano culture involved the perpetuation of the Chicana's role as servant and sex object. The poem fused the rhetorical discourse of the movement, including the emphasis on Mexican cuisine as part of cultural identity, with the language of sexuality: "You cramp my style, baby / when you roll on top of me / shouting, 'Viva La Raza' / at the top of your prick. / You want me como un taco (like a taco) / dripping grease, / or squeezing masa through my legs, / making tamales for you out of my daughters."

Other texts allowed the subjective musings of different female voices to be heard. Lyrical expressions of dreams and visions co-existed with poems pondering the complexity of self-naming and the relationships of women with other women. "Bloodline" by Alma Villanueva explored the positive connection between daughters and mothers. "When all the yous" by lesbian poet Veronica Cunningham articulated the difficulty of overcoming deep-seated inhibitions about writing for and about women. The poem affirmed the need for Chicanas to share the vision of their changing reality with other women, to create a spectrum of female solidarity that includes lesbian sexuality: "when all the yous / of my poetry / were really / she or her / and i could never / no / i would never write them / because / of some fears / i never even wanted / to see. / how could i have been frightened / of sharing / the being / and me."

Giving Up the Ghost

While *Tongues of Fire* created a collective female subject, the representation of sexuality was still fixed within the parameters of heterosexual relationships, with the exception of the short text by Cunningham. The homosexual subject first appeared in

Reunion by Edgar Poma. In 1981, members of two veteran Bay Area *teatros*, Teatro Latino and Teatro Gusto, came together provisionally as Teatro Yerbabuena to mount a production of *Reunion*. This play dramatized the conflicts surrounding the decision of a Chicano gay male to "come out" to his family by bringing his lover home for the holidays. The rejection of male homosexuality within Chicano culture is linked to the complex system of signs of which *La Malinche* is a part. The male homosexual is held in contempt because he voluntarily assumes the despised role of woman, the penetrated *chingada*.[37] The play provided a much-needed opportunity for dialogue around these questions.[38] While *Reunion* broke a fifteen-year silence on homosexuality within the Chicano theatre movement, its focus on gay males and its narrative form reinscribed the male subject.

Most recently, *Giving Up the Ghost* by Cherríe Moraga focuses on the lesbian as desiring subject: Marisa, a lesbian Chicana in her late twenties and Corky, her younger self at 12 and 17.[39] Marisa and Corky do not conform to the codified gender representation of "woman" on stage, neither in their appearance (hair cut short, clothes, etc.) nor in the way they move.[40] This is particularly clear in the young Corky, who appropriates the gestural language of the tough Chicano *cholo*. The third character is Amalia, a heterosexual Chicana in her late forties. The representation of female desiring subjects in *Giving Up the Ghost* is culture-, class-, and "race"-specific; their subjectivity as sexual beings is shaped in dialectical relationship to a collective way of imagining sexuality. The text explores the ways in which Chicanas, both lesbian and heterosexual, have internalized their culture's concepts of sexuality. While the sexuality of both Marisa and Amalia has been distorted and repressed through the myth of *La Malinche*, the text also affirms the Chicana's need to "untie the knot of her own desire" through her cultural identity.[41] For the lesbian subject, rejection of the

---

[37] Moraga, "A Long Line," p. 111.

[38] It was performed to large community audiences at the Cultural Center in the heart of San Francisco's Mission District. Performances were followed by lengthy, lively discussions. The exclusion of a performance of this play during the TENAZ Eleventh Festival in the Fall of 1981 revealed the depth of resistance to considering the Chicano theatre movement an appropriate vehicle for the exploration of questions of sexuality. This attitude was further demonstrated during the Festival by the virtual boycott of a workshop on *Reunion* and the heated arguments by Latin-Americans and Chicanos alike against a resolution condemning sexism and homophobia during the general assembly. Dialogue has recently been reopened within the Chicano community by a production of *Reunion* in June 1986 in Tucson, Arizona by Teatro Chicano, a member group of TENAZ headed by a woman, Silviana Wood.

[39] Cherríe Moraga, *Giving Up the Ghost* (Los Angeles: West End Press, 1986). For a review article of the play see my "Cherríe Moraga's *Giving Up The Ghost*: The Representation of Female Desire," forthcoming in *Third Woman* 3:1 (1986).

[40] For a discussion of the lesbian desiring subject, see Sue-Ellen Case and Jeanie Forte, "From Formalism to Feminism," *Theater* 16:2 (1985), 62–65. Readers interested in lesbian theories of gender construction onstage may consult Jill Dolan, "Gender Impersonation Onstage: Destroying or Maintaining the Mirror of Gender Roles," and Sande Zeig, "The Actor as Activator: Deconstructing Gender through Gesture," both in *Women & Performance: A Journal of Feminist Theory* 2:2 (1985). See also Monique Wittig, "The Point of View: Universal or Particular?" *Feminist Issues* 3:2 (1983), 63–69; Sue-Ellen Case, "Gender as Play: Simone Benmussa's *The Singular Life of Albert Nobbs*," *Women & Performance* 1:2 (1984), 21–24, "Classic Drag: The Greek Creation of Female Parts," *Theatre Journal* 37:3 (1985), 317–27.

[41] Moraga, "A Long Line," p. 130.

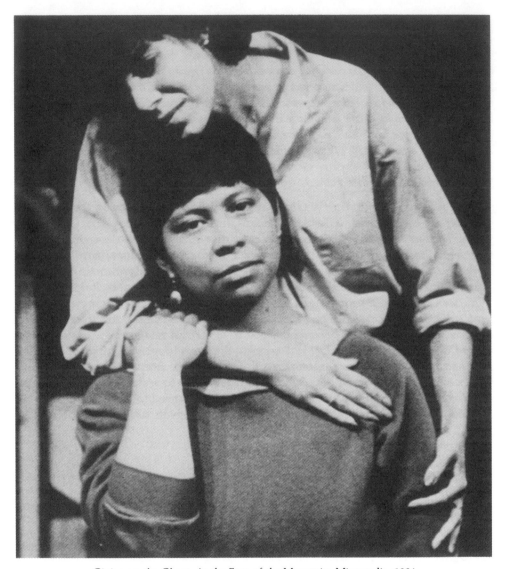

Giving up the Ghost. At the Foot of the Mountain, Minneaplis, 1984.

passive female role of *chingada* has led to identification with the active, but closed *chingón*. Marisa loves women, but her capacity to be loved by them is thwarted by her anger and fear of betrayal by women through the culture's mandate of putting the male first. The heterosexual female subject Amalia has been damaged emotionally by her sexual experiences with men. She has lost her capacity to feel and the desire to live. Her desire is expressed through her identification with Mexico, the land she seeks through men and finds in Marisa's *mestizo* features.

Like *Tongues of Fire, Giving Up the Ghost* eschews the ordering of meaning through narrative history. The monologues of Marisa, Corky, and Amalia cut through and across each other in time; the characters rarely interact, but can hear what the others say. The co-existence of Marisa and her younger selves in the play avoids the construction of a unified subject and allows for the deconstruction of the cultural forces that have shaped Marisa's choices and limitations as a sexual being in the present of the dramatic world. The juxtaposition of past and present in the text reveals the cultural construction of female identity, specifically through the restricted gender roles of masculine/feminine, active/passive, subject/object, penetrator/penetrated defined in Chicano-specific cultural terms through the myth of La Malinche and the chingón/chingada polarity. Corky exemplifies the limited choices available to girls who reject identification with the restricted gender roles of their culture. This is particularly true of ethnic cultures such as Chicano culture, given the exaggerated machismo of the males and the fewer alternative roles for women than in the dominant culture. Since Corky identifies with the males in her culture, both her appropriation of the subject role as well as her attraction to women are inscribed within the gender roles assigned in Chicano culture and the culture at large. Her erotic attraction to women is played out in contexts of violence and dominance, a dominance that includes seeing women as "Other." Corky's sense of the powerlessness of her sex that led to her male-identification is exacerbated by the realization of her mother's (and by extension her class and culture's) powerlessness vis-à-vis the dominant culture's intolerance of their difference. The only space left for her to be is the tough stance of the cholo.[42] Yet she is forced to confront her internal split between identification with the subjugating male and repressed self-knowledge as female. In a long, painful monologue Corky describes how she was raped. Up to the time of the rape, Corky had thought it could never happen to her because she had denied her femaleness, rejecting the role of chingada and identifying with the chingón, the active, aggressive, closed person who inflicts the wound. The rape brings home Corky's sex to her as an inescapable fact, confirming her culture's definition of female as being taken.

The text does present the possibility that Marisa and Amalia may free each other from "the prison of sex": Marisa may learn to accept the "opened" role of beloved and Amalia may learn to feel again by assuming the "active" role, expressed in the poetic imagery of the text as her dead husband being "born" inside her. But the non-chronological ordering of the monologues avoids the facile resolution of the contradictions and conflicts of the play. De Lauretis has stated that "all images are implicated with narrativity whether they appear in a narrative, non-narrative, or anti-narrative film," due to the hegemony of narrativity as a cultural mode.[43] Keir Elam has also commented on the spectator's tendency to narrativize the "present" events of the dramatic action, reinscribing the coercive structure of narrative in a search for origins, telos, and causal relationships between the events.[44] While it seems that no dramatic

[42] While Corky's identification with the male cholo involves the internalization of negative attitudes towards women and herself as female, it should also be pointed out that the cholo culture stands as a subculture in oppositional relationship to both the Chicano and the dominant culture. It represents a stance of resistance to cultural assimilation and the social, racial, and economic discrimination of the dominant culture as well as rebellion against the traditional values of the Mexican culture of the youths' parents.

[43] Teresa De Lauretis, "Oedipus Interruptus," Wide Angle 7:1, 2 (1985), 34–40.

[44] Keir Elam, The Semiotics of Theatre and Drama (London & New York: Methuen, 1980), p. 120.

representation can completely escape being narrativized by the spectator, texts such as *Giving Up the Ghost* make this process explicit. This is accomplished through the simultaneity of past (Corky) and present (Marisa) that causes the spectator to understand how Marisa's identity as desiring subject in the present is the result of historical and cultural experience. The inclusion of "the people" in the cast of characters foregrounds their participation in the construction of a possible narrative, or many narratives, sketched as possibilities in the events on stage. One such "story" is the possibility of Chicanas choosing to organize their sexuality independently; another is the vision of a Chicana feminism based on the love of Chicanas for themselves and each other as female, working-class, and *mestiza*.

The participation of the audience in the co-production of the play's meaning is affected by what Annette Kuhn calls the "social audience" in distinction to the individual subject/spectator.[45] While the psychoanalytic concept of the spectator as a gendered subject is essential in the discussion of representations of sexuality on stage with the female spectator in mind, the notion of audience as distinct from spectator brings into play social, gender, and economic factors that also determine the reception of the text. Most of the plays discussed here were performed for a specific social audience: the working-class Chicano community of the early theatre movement, the middle-class white audience of Luis Valdez's mainstream plays, or the mixture of working-class and "academic" Chicanos for *Tongues of Fire*. The composition of the audience affects both the production of representations (e.g., the appearance of the "white male savior"), as well as the reception and interpretation of the representations. In 1984, At The Foot of the Mountain, a white feminist theatre based in Minneapolis, performed *Giving Up the Ghost* as a staged reading.[46] "The people" designated in the cast of characters was in this case an all-women's audience, reinforcing the idea of women's community. Moraga has also read monologues from the play to all-Chicano audiences of both sexes at conferences and other gatherings in the Southwest, establishing a dialogue with this particular social audience.

In conclusion, the representations of female subjectivity and sexuality in Chicano theatre are related to the historical development of the Chicano movement. The phase that coincided with the heyday of cultural nationalism produced ordering narratives that tended to exclude the Chicana from the subject position and define her sexuality in terms of *La Malinche* or *La Virgen* within the heterosexual hierarchy of the family. Throughout the seventies, a materialist analysis countered the mystified racial and cultural identity of cultural nationalism with class identity, producing representations of revolutionary subjects, both male and female. The docudrama, however, reinscribed the male subject and the heterosexual structure of the family. Work in the eighties also produced non-narrative representations of the collective Chicana subject, exploring her identity in terms of her class and "race" identity and her sexuality in relationship to the heterosexual roles assigned in the culture. In the eighties the Chicano gay male subject was represented in a "coming-out" narrative. Most recently, the les-

[45] Annette Kuhn, "Women's Genres," *Screen* (Jan.-Feb. 1984), 18–28.
[46] The staged reading of *Giving Up the Ghost* by At the Food of the Mountain was directed by a black lesbian, with Marisa and Corky played by a Honduran lesbian and a Chicana lesbian respectively and Amalia by a heterosexual Puerto Rican woman.

bian Chicana emerged as desiring subject in a non-narrative form that showed the class and cultural construction of gender and sexuality. The representation of homosexual Chicano subjects co-exists with the dominant theatre practice of the Chicano/Latin-American political theatre movement, which privileges narrative form and the heterosexual subject. El Teatro de la Esperanza and other Chicano *teatros*, as well as Latin-American groups, will participate in the XIII TENAZ Festival hosted by Teatro Zero in Cuernavaca (Summer, 1986), providing fresh opportunities to study the representations of women in the Chicano/Latin-American theatre movement.

Beyond Brecht:
Britain's New Feminist Drama

Janelle Reinelt

Bertolt Brecht's theory and practice have had a strong influence on the British theatre, dating from the first visit of the Berliner Ensemble in 1956 and the English publication in 1964 of John Willett's compilation of the theoretical writings, *Brecht On Theatre*. Political theatre practice in England had benefited from the socialist movement as well as the impact of the Beveridge Report on the arts. Following Beveridge's mandated university grants, educated working-class men and women had found their theatrical voices in playwrights such as Shelagh Delaney, John Osborne, and Arnold Wesker. The continuing search for a political form and technique led to Brecht who, in shaping a dramaturgy specifically suited to social critique, provided a path beyond social realism to the epic theatre. Brechtian techniques provided a methodology for embedding a materialist critique within the theatrical medium. Political theatre requires the ability to isolate and manifest certain ideas and relationships that make ideology visible, in contrast with the styles of realism and naturalism, wherein ideology is hidden or covert. Brecht's theorization of the social gest, epic structure, and alienation effect provides the means to reveal material relations as the basis of social reality, to foreground and examine ideologically-determined beliefs and unconscious habitual perceptions, and to make visible those signs inscribed on the body which distinguish social behavior in relation to class, gender, and history. For feminists, Brechtian techniques offer a way to examine the material conditions of gender behavior (how they are internalized, opposed, and changed) and their interaction with other socio-political factors such as class.

The implied interchangeability of feminist and socialist concerns within this conception of political theatre glosses over the history of the relationship between socialism and feminism. In England, as elsewhere, this relationship has been characterized by theoretical and practical struggle. Michelene Wandor, Michele Barrett, Sheila Rowbotham, and others have written extensively about feminism in England and its relationship to the socialist movement.[1] In England, the feminist movement is at once

---

Janelle Reinelt is a Professor of Theatre Arts at California State University at Sacramento, currently writing a book on Brecht and Contemporary British Theatre.

---

[1] See Michele Barrett, *Woman's Oppression Today*; Sheila Rowbotham, Lynne Segal and Hilary Wainwright, eds., *Beyond the Fragments; Feminism and the Making of Socialism*; and Michelene Wandor, *Understudies; Theatre and Sexual Politics*.

largely working-class and heavily socialist, in contrast with America where feminism is strongly based in the middle class. The first national conference on Women's Liberation took place in 1970. During the next few years, socialist-feminist conferences were held in various locations. Several papers and journals began publication, including *Spare Rib, Women's Voice,* and *Red Rag,* and in 1974 women and men in the labor movement drew up the Working Women's Charter, proposing demands for material change. Contemporary with these events, the first Women's Theatre Conference encouraged the formation of a number of feminist theatre companies while also providing a new agenda for some of the socialist theatre groups which had previously ignored the "woman question." The attempt to develop an adequate theory of the relationship between socialism and feminism was carried on in artistic as well as political practice. Two of the central theoretical issues were and still are: the relationship of class oppression to sexual repression; and the ideological interpretation of production, reproduction, and procreation.

With regard to the first issue, socialist men criticized feminist women for being diverted from the "true" struggle (the class struggle) to what was essentially a bourgeois movement. The feminists replied that historically, women have been subject not only to the ruling class, but also to the patriarchy. They pointed out that the advantages to men resulting from the subordination of women are not restricted along class lines, and that even existing socialist practice still reveals structures of female oppression. Shulamith Firestone's early and influential work, *The Dialectic of Sex,* claims that the relations of procreation rather than production belong to the base and that other economic factors are actually part of the superstructure. She writes, "The sexual-reproductive organization of society always furnishes the real basis, starting from which we can alone work out the ultimate explanation of the whole superstructure of economic, juridical and political institutions as well as of the religious, philosophical and other ideas of a given historical period."[2]

Radical feminists had theorized a trans-historical subjection of women to men in the patriarchy as the central problem and fact of reality. This view encouraged socialist women to abandon alliances with men, even for purposes of class struggle; men were seen as the fundamental enemy, regardless of class affiliation. The socialist response was that the real oppression stems from capitalism and women must not abandon their historical place in the struggle against it through engaging in a bourgeois liberal movement. The question of men and their place in a feminist struggle caused deep disagreement among feminist groups and split the National Women's Liberation Conference in Birmingham in 1978, which was to be the last such conference. This issue continues to problematize socialist-feminism. In "The British Women's Movement," Angela Weir and Elizabeth Wilson argued that the current political climate is fostering retreat from class politics and dilution of the socialist edge through a splintering populism, especially in feminism.[3] Anne Phillips replied in "Class Warfare" that other

[2] Shulamith Firestone, *The Dialectic of Sex: The Case for Feminist Revolution* (New York: William Morrow, 1970), pp. 12–13.

[3] Angela Weir and Elizabeth Wilson, "The British Women's Movement," *New Left Review* 148 (November-December 1984).

oppressions such as gender and race are related to but not reducible to capitalism and that the whole concept of class must be reconstituted in more complex terms.[4]

In relation to the meaning of production, reproduction, and procreation, traditional Marxist analysis, following Engels, conceptualizes production as the conditions of labor in the workplace, locating issues of production in the public sphere. The domestic sphere is engaged in procreation and the reproduction of human labor power. The domestic sphere, therefore, is outside of the economic arena where the "real" material base lies. The home and family are part of the superstructure, determined by conditions of production in the public sphere. Socialist-feminists suggest a revaluation of domestic labor, or "women's work," as a productive form of labor having the same status as wage labor, mutually determining, along with traditional economic factors, the course of historical change. Issues of domestic labor focus on the reproduction of the laborer both through childbirth and through the material support the home offers the laborer.

The project of reconceptualizing production to include reproduction or the production of people is not without problems, and socialist-feminists do not all agree on the relation of the market to family relations, nor on all the differences between producing commodities and people. However, the exclusion of the domestic sphere from the conception of the economic base of society marginalizes women and the family leaving them in the unacceptable position of being incidental to and determined by the "real" economic base.[5]

These two theoretical issues focus the concern for socialist-feminism on the exploration of the relationship between social, economic, and sexual conditions in society. Alternative conceptions of these two issues are demonstrated or implied in playtexts, aided in many cases by Brechtian elements which have proven integral to the dramatization of these complex issues. The playscripts become working examples of possible ways of understanding the relationships between class, gender, labor, and capital.

Strike While the Iron is Hot affords an opportunity to perceive an evolving theoretical position actualized in theatrical practice. The Red Ladder Theatre which developed *Strike* began as an agit-prop group committed to the Labor Movement. They had looked to Brecht as a model for some time, and deliberately used *The Mother* as an early reference point for this script. In both plays, a central woman character has her consciousness raised and undertakes direct political action because of her experience of injustice. However, Brecht's play is male-biased and confirms traditional sex-role stereotyping while *Strike* challenges the distinctions between public and private spheres and the whole gender/class system.

The relationship between class and sex was actively debated in the group when the ideas for the play were forming. Some argued from the traditional Marxist position that class struggle is preeminent and sexual oppression subordinate to it. Others

---

[4] Anne Phillips, "Class Warfare," *New Socialist* 24 (February, 1985).
[5] For a full discussion of this problem, see Alison M. Jaggar, *Feminist Politics and Human Nature* (Totowa, N.J.: Rowman and Allanheld, 1983).

argued that sexual oppression was primary and must be dealt with independently. The play, while not resolving this issue neatly, dramatizes some of its complexities. Helen goes to work, joins a union, and becomes a fighter for economic justice, but she also struggles with her husband to change the conditions of the "labor" she performs at home. Thus the play focuses on the problem of the relationship between gender and class as well as the problem of the relationship of wage labor to household and family activity. *Strike* portrays the way in which class may sometimes subvert alliances based on sex. It also, however, shows how sexist behavior cuts across class. The female manager at the plant where Helen works will not allow the women time off when their children are ill. She is not sympathetic because she has an *au pair* girl to care for her children; class divides the experiences of women in the play. The men, on the other hand, when bargaining to settle a union wage dispute, cross over class lines to share sexist jokes, and the union men settle for a job evaluation scheme instead of equal pay for the women because they do not work for the women's interests as they had for their own. Thus the "old boy" network seems to transcend class, although the benefit, the play is quick to point out, falls to the management which evokes male fraternity to its own advantage. The play's final synthesis of the relationship between class struggle and feminist struggle is expressed on two banners raised at the end of the play, one saying, "Workers will never be free while women are in chains" and the other, "Women will never be free while workers are in chains."

The position on modes of production, developed through the dramatic action, is that the traditional division of labor in the home duplicates the oppressive exploitation of workers in the work place. Helen struggles to get her husband to help around the house when she goes to work. The connection between wage labor and home labor is explicit when Helen sings: "I'm not your little woman, your sweetheart, your dear. I'm a wage slave without wages. I'm a maintenance engineer." [6]

Red Ladder was persuaded at the time that women's work at home was a hidden wage-labor cost. In addition to profiting from the benefit of men's labor, owners also profit from women's domestic labor that maintains and services the worker so that he can maximize his output. This analysis produced agitation on two fronts: at the workplace for better wages, and at home for an end to the traditional division of labor. Helen's song makes this agenda and analysis explicit. "The truth began to dawn then / how I keep him fit and trim / so the boss can make a nice fat profit / out of me and him. And as a solid union man / he got in quite a rage / to think that we're both working hard / and getting one man's wage. / I said 'And what about the part-time packing job I do? / That's three men that I work for, love, / my boss, your boss, and you' / He looked a little sheepish / and said 'As from today, / the lads and me'll see what we / can do on equal pay. / Would you like a housewives' union, / do you think you should be paid / as a cook, and as a cleaner, / as a nurse and as a maid?' / I said 'Don't jump the gun, love, / If you did your share at home, / then I might have some time to fight / some battles of my own.'" [7] The song argues that

---

[6] Red Ladder Theatre, "Strike While the Iron is Hot," *Strike While the Iron is Hot; Three Plays on Sexual Politics*, Michelene Wandor, ed. (London/West Nyack: The Journeyman Press, 1980), p. 51.

[7] Ibid., pp. 52–53.

women's work is undervalued both in the workplace and at home, and that what is needed is not just better wages, but an end to the sexual division of labor.

The play also addresses the issues of equal pay and parity. In Brecht's *The Mother*, Vlassova learns about economic exploitation through comparing a table and a factory. This scene is directly adapted by Red Ladder, becoming a pub scene entitled "The Disputed Pint" in which Helen learns about the factory struggle for equal pay for similar work. Beer glasses provide the basic social gest of the scene. The shop foreman, impersonating Henry Ford, fills one man's pint glass half-full while he fills another's completely. Helen sees immediately that it is not fair to pay different wages for the same work, but she extends the argument to women's wages as well: "I'm still not getting as much as Mike and I'm doing the same work. . . . That means I should go on strike for parity with Mike." [8] The men had not anticipated this interpretation. Realizing that all the women at the table have half-pint glasses while the men have full, Helen decides that on the next round, she will have a full pint. Richard Seyd, who collaborated on the script development, cites this scene and its gestural technique with the beer glasses as Red Ladder's typical adaptation of Brecht. "We wouldn't talk about economic questions in the dialogue — we sought a more painterly approach where a physical element could communicate the idea. Then we wrote the scenes so that each would have a turning point, and gave them a title like *The Mother* had." [9]

The use of Brechtian techniques to provide a physical correlative of relations between genders appears in its clearest form in the play *Trafford Tanzi*. Brecht's gestural technique, the method for creating a central gesture or "gest," was employed by feminists to reveal the relations between the sexes. This technique is the central device in *Trafford Tanzi* where all the action takes place in a wrestling ring. Author Claire Luckham writes, "I also read a lot of Brecht's writing about the theatre and was particularly interested in his enthusiasm for boxing and the relationship between fighters and their audience, though then I thought, 'What is he on about' rather than, 'I want to write a play about a lady wrestler.'" [10] Brecht's 1926 essay, "Emphasis on Sport," lauds the sporting attitude which is missing in the theatre. People come to sporting events to have fun and to enjoy the skills they see presented. "A theatre which makes no contact with the public is a nonsense." [11]

Roland Barthes also perceived the appeal of wrestling and its fundamental possibilities for theatrical spectacle: "Wrestling is like a diacritic writing: above the fundamental meaning of his body, the wrestler arranges comments which are episodic but always opportune, and constantly help the reading of the fight by means of gestures, attitudes and mimicry which makes the intention utterly obvious." [12] Wrestling cannot be disinterested; watching it one takes sides. Because it provides clear

[8] Ibid., p. 42.

[9] Interview with Richard Seyd, San Francisco, 1 August 1984.

[10] Claire Luckham, *Trafford Tanzi, Her Hopes, Her Fears, Her Early Years* (London: Quartet Books, 1983), "Warmup."

[11] Bertolt Brecht, *Brecht on Theatre*, John Willett, ed. and trans. (New York: Hill and Wang, 1964), p. 7.

[12] Roland Barthes, "The World of Wrestling," *Mythologies*, trans. Annette Lavers (New York: Hill and Wang, 1972), p. 18.

distinctions between good and evil, it engages moral judgment. It is, in short, a perfect gest for feminist theatre.

Luckham wrote *Tanzi* for the Everyman Theatre Company to tour in pubs and clubs in and around Liverpool in 1978. The play was written for a working class audience and Luckham wanted something with direct appeal to active audience involvement. She decided to use wrestling to portray Tanzi's struggle to grow up, using wrestling as a metaphor for the struggle against gender-specific oppression and conditioning. The physical acting space and dominant action present a male-dominated world where the outcome is "fixed" because the outcome of each round is a foregone conclusion. Trafford Tanzi gradually becomes a successful wrestler and triumphs over the "beatings" given her by father, mother, and husband. Professional wrestling trainers coached the cast who actually performed the various holds and moves of wrestling. The referee comments on the action, announcing the rounds and their winners: "In Round Four, a submission to Dad by means of a Boston Crab." Various songs provide additional comment on the action and break up the narrative. Tanzi's mum sings, "I wanted a boy / And look what I got / Well I got a girl / All covered in snot." [13]

The songs, the referee, and the wrestling ring can all be perceived as Brechtian elements. The content of the play, however, seems to privilege a personal struggle for equality more than the specifically socialist issues outlined above. In fact, Michelene Wandor has argued that the play became a success in the commercial theatre because it did not pose a direct challenge to the prevailing socio-economic order. She writes, "In the end, the dynamic of the play remains most rooted in bourgeois feminism: in its positive aspect of celebrating women's equality with men, and in the negative aspect of taking the values of men as the norm." [14] Considering the audience for whom the play was originally conceived, Wandor's critique of the play as "bourgeois" seems a bit ironic. The play takes certain relationships for granted — all of the characters are working class, making it an in-house discussion. Actually, the co-option of women's work for capitalist profiteering is vividly portrayed when Tanzi's father attempts to become her manager and take a 50% cut of her wrestling profits. Tanzi gets him with a backhammer, and when he tries to plead his case, "But Tanzi . . . please. . . I'm your old dad. I'm family. And what about your mum? I've got to support her," Tanzi dropkicks him and says, "Tough bananas, Dad." [15] In addition, her arguments with husband Dean Rebel over the division of labor are framed in terms of the discussion of women's work as reproducing labor power mentioned above. "Dean: Look, I come home after a hard day's work, do I find a hot meal waiting for me? No, there's a note on the table. Well, that's not how champions is maintained y'know. Tanzi: Oh, that's what I'm s'posed to be, is it? A serving unit?" [16]

Within the context of a working class perspective already colored with socialist ideology, the debate about the relationship of work in the home to work in the public

[13] Claire Luckham, "Trafford Tanzi," *Plays By Women, Vol. 2,* Michelene Wandor, ed. (London: Methuen, 1983), p. 79.

[14] Michelene Wandor, "The Fifth Column: Feminism and Theatre," *Drama* (Summer, 1984), 7.

[15] Luckman, "Trafford Tanzi," p. 90.

[16] Ibid., p. 91.

sector is recognizable. But it is the wrestling match itself, that perfect Brechtian "gest" for the struggle of women to free themselves from male oppression both economic and sexual, which is the central feature of the play. This struggle must be conducted in the open, in the public arena, where the audience can participate in it and identify its political as well as its personal character. The transformation of traditionally private experience into public spectacle helps transform conceptions of individual problems into social ones. As Barthes points out, both wrestling and theatre give "intelligible representations of moral situations which are usually private." [17]

Both *Strike While the Iron is Hot* and *Trafford Tanzi* deal with contemporary experience. One of Brecht's major discoveries was that by historicizing the incidents of the narrative, a playwright can cause the audience to become conscious of certain habitual perceptions which have been established by the historical tradition and therefore partially determine the present. "Historicizing the incidents" may involve re-examining a concrete historical situation and its customary interpretation to see what is missing, or what new insights emerge if hidden aspects are thrown into relief. It may also involve making explicit the relationship between past and present, in order to show that human history is an open horizon, subject to constant change. Brecht writes, "Historical incidents are unique, transitory incidents associated with particular periods. The conduct of persons involved in them is not fixed and 'universally human'; it includes elements that have been or may be overtaken by the course of history, and is subject to criticism from the immediately following period's point of view." [18] Reconceptualizing women's place in history has been a fertile ground for feminist struggle. Not only have women discovered that they have systematically been excluded from the "great man" orthodoxy of most historical interpretation, they have also discovered that many traditional attitudes toward women have historical precedents. Exposing hidden aspects of the past and exploring their consequences for contemporary experience has provided a fruitful undertaking for feminist playwrights.

Caryl Churchill's play *Vinegar Tom* incorporates a socialist-feminist analysis in order to attack the problem of the relationship between gender and class. Using the notion of historicizing the narrative, it places sexuality within the history of witches and witchcraft, problematizing the traditional interpretation of that history and pointing to the vestigial remainder of such thinking in contemporary life. Written for the Monstrous Regiment, a theatre company formed in 1975 and committed to both feminism and socialism, *Vinegar Tom* was commissioned as part of the company's effort to "reclaim the history play from women's point of view." [19] In researching the play, Churchill recognized that received notions about witchcraft mystified concrete relations between outcast or marginal women (the old, the poor, the unconventional) and the religious and economic power structure. She writes, "One of the things that struck me in reading the detailed accounts of witch trials in Essex . . . was how petty and everyday the witches' offences were, and how different the atmosphere of actual English witchhunts seemed to be from my received idea, based on slight knowledge of the European witchhunts in films and fiction, of burnings, hysteria and sexual orgies. I

[17] Barthes, p. 18.

[18] Brecht, p. 140.

[19] Gillian Hanna, "Feminism and Theatre," *Theatre Papers*, 2nd Series, No. 8 (1978), pp. 10–11.

wanted to write a play about witches with no witches in it; a play not about evil, hysteria and possession by the devil but about poverty, humiliation and prejudice, and how the women accused of witchcraft saw themselves." [20]

The central action of the play involves the scapegoating of poor women by the farmer Jack and his wife Margery, a couple who are at high risk because of their attempts at economic expansion (they have sublet two new fields). Margery cannot bear the pressure of feeling incompetent and undeserving; Jack needs a target for his sexual and financial frustration. Not wanting to believe that God judges them "bad," they begin to interpret their misfortunes as acts of witchcraft committed by their poor neighbors, Joan and her daughter Alice. The Church provides the institutional mechanism for burning such witches; traditional prime targets are single women, economically marginal and sexually deviant from the puritan code. The accused include Ellen, the cunning woman or healer who earns her own living outside of the monetary system and works outside the sanctioned medical/male establishment; Alice, object of Jack's sexual desire, whom he accuses of making him impotent; and Susan, who has had an abortion for which she feels guilty. Internalizing the prevailing social and religious code, Susan feels that she must have been a witch without knowing it. In her conflation of economic and moral codes, Susan shows how women can remain unconscious of their oppression and can victimize themselves and others. The only escapee from punishments of torture and death is Betty, the land owner's daughter. However, while she escapes class oppression, she pays the price of sexual submission: she agrees to marry and become the thing she dreads, "a good wife." The play unfolds in 21 scenes and 7 songs. No one protagonist dominates the action. Churchill keeps the community and its socio-economic-sexual systems at the center of the play through several Brechtian devices. The songs, sung by modern women, break up the narrative and historicize the incidents, creating a critical distance from the historical events which allows comparisons to contemporary time and ruptures the flow of the narrative, emphasizing the possibilities for intervention and change.

Gillian Hanna of the Monstrous Regiment defends the songs against the objections of some who felt they were unnecessary: "We had a very real feeling that we didn't want to allow the audience to get off the hook by regarding it as a period piece, a piece of very interesting history. I believe that the simple telling of the historical story, say, is not enough. . . . You have to choose between what you keep in and what you leave out. It's at that point of choice where women on the whole find that they get left out. Our experience is that life is not the simple story, and that you have to find some way of recognizing that in dramatic form." [21] The songs determine a particular perception of the events of the narrative.

Churchill also employs Brecht's episodic play structure in which each scene is isolated and has a crucial turning point. Brecht writes, "The episodes must not succeed one another indistinguishably but must give us a chance to interpose our judgment. . . . The parts of the story have to be carefully set off one against another

[20] Caryl Churchill, "Vinegar Tom," *Plays By Women*, *Vol. 1*, Michelene Wandor, ed. (London: Methuen, 1982), p. 39.
[21] Hanna, pp. 10–11.

by giving each its own structure as a play within a play."[22] For example, in Scene Six, a doctor bleeds Betty, who is refusing to get married as her wealthy parents want her to do for their own economic gain. As she is visibly drained of her lifeblood, and symbolically drained of her strength to fight, the doctor tells her, "After bleeding you must be purged. Tonight you shall be blistered. You will soon be well enough to get married."[23] Thus the gest of bleeding contains the central action of the scene, and the scene itself is a potentially independent vignette in which a discrete situation portrays how middle-class women are controlled and socialized. The other scenes which deal with poor women are also discrete and yet are related across class through the collusion of the patriarchal church and state. In each case, intervention could have changed the particular instance, but the isolation of the women from one another because of class made such collective action impossible. The audience, however, viewing the situation in the present, is able to perceive how gender and class interrelate and hopefully, how to organize a coalition opposition.

The dramatization of sex and class systems is enhanced throughout the particular scenes by the Brechtian technique of finding a critical social gest which provides material focus. In Scene Four, Margery is churning butter without results throughout the scene. "Come butter come, come butter come. Johnny's standing at the gate waiting for a butter cake. Come butter . . . it's not coming, this butter. I'm sick of it."[24] The sexual and economic frustration captured in this gest explains Margery's cruelty to Joan, who comes begging for yeast, only to be abused. Margery's husband begins and ends the scene by abusing his wife, calling her a lazy woman, a "lazy slut" because the butter won't come.

The play specifies in concrete form the relationship between patriarchy and class society: they mutually support each other. Most oppressed are those who attempt to live outside the economic system like Ellen and Joan and the sexual system like Alice and Susan. The final song asks contemporary men if they are projecting evilness onto women in order to excuse their own inadequacies. "Evil women. Is that what you want to see in your movie dream?"[25] The historically-received notion of witches' evil power survives in contemporary mystifications of women as possessing dark, evil, secret power. The vestigial remainder of a false perception of the past, these ideas persist in determining aspects of contemporary ideology. *Vinegar Tom* dramatizes the dialectical relationship between history and consciousness.

All three of the plays discussed here achieve the breakdown of traditional distinctions between public and private spheres. The personal lives of individuals are seen to derive meaning from their social and political relations and, in turn, to shape the social whole. Such a feminist perspective, that the personal is political, demands the dramatization of personal, emotional life, drawing on, to some extent, the techniques of traditional bourgeois realism. Epic techniques, on the other hand, place the personal, individual experience of characters within their socio-political context, widen-

[22] Brecht, p. 201.
[23] Churchill, p. 24.
[24] Ibid., p. 38.
[25] Ibid., p. 38.

ing the focus to include the community and its social, economic and sexual relations. Out of the need to evolve a suitable dramatic form for socialist-feminist drama, a new theatrical style may be evolving which synthesizes older techniques. Of the Red Ladder experience, Richard Seyd writes, "As we were dealing with emotions on a personal level in the play . . . this necessitated strong, believable characters, because without that three-dimensionality the emotional content would appear shallow and false."[26]

Acting in the new feminist drama also seems to require a synthesis of techniques. Gillian Hanna of Monstrous Regiment talks about playing emotional elements: "My inclination and experience is all to do with a kind of Brechtian acting, which doesn't deny Stanislavsky but puts the emphasis elsewhere. . . . It doesn't work for me or for an audience, if I'm doing it just on the level of remembering some sort of pain that I've experienced. . . . Nor does it work on the level of 'I'm showing the audience something here.' The nights it seems to work best are when there is, and on a level that I've not experienced before, a meshing of those two."[27] Thus the feminist critique of the division between private and public concerns leads in the direction of both a new dramaturgy and a revised acting style.

Feminist transformation of Brechtian techniques illustrates Brecht's notion of the criticism of the received past from the standpoint of a concrete present. These plays and others from the British feminist theatre afford the opportunity to see revisions of theatrical technique in the context of the evolving formulations of a socialist-feminist analysis. Current feminist theatre practice thus contains vigorous interaction with progressive aspects of theatrical traditions such as Brecht's, while simultaneously engaging in the process of discovering appropriate and effective contemporary methods.

[26] Richard Seyd, "The Theatre of Red Ladder," *New Edinburgh Review* 30 (August 1975), 40–41.
[27] Hanna, pp. 6–7.

Feminism and the Jewish Subject in the Plays of Sachs, Atlan, and Schenkar

Vivian M. Patraka

> They say at the ends of time
> birds with madmen and children
> will have the gift of prophecy
> but I myself don't see
> understanding them
> Listening does not
> make me say
> they awaken
> a light
>
> Liliane Atlan, *The Carriage of Flames and Voices* (1971)[1]

In her article "A Manifesto for Cyborgs: Science, Technology, and Socialist Feminism in the 1980s," Donna Haraway includes the following critique of certain feminisms:

> Beyond either the difficulties or the contributions in the argument of any one author, neither Marxist nor radical feminist points of view have tended to embrace the status of a partial explanation; both were regularly constituted as totalities. Western explanation has demanded as much; how else could the 'Western' author incorporate its others? Each tried to annex other forms of domination by expanding its basic categories through analogy, simple listing, or addition. Embarrassed silence about race among white radical and socialist feminists was one major, devastating political consequence. History and

Vivian M. Patraka, Associate Professor of English at Bowling Green State University, has published in Theatre Journal, Modern Drama, Michigan Quarterly Review, Theatre Annual, Art & Cinema, Studies in American Drama, 1945 to Present, *and in the book* Making A Spectacle. *She is currently writing a book on representations of fascism in drama.*

I would like to thank Jill Dolan, University of Wisconsin, and Elin Diamond, Rutgers University, as well as my colleague at Bowling Green, Ellen Berry, and Margaret Lourie, University of Michigan, for their advice and editorial assistance. I also would like to thank Sallie Bingham and the Kentucky Foundation for Women for providing me with a month of uninterrupted time at Wolf Pen Women Writers Colony to work on my article.

[1]Liliane Atlan, *Theatre Pieces: an Anthology by Liliane Atlan*, trans. Marguerite Feitlowitz (Greenwood, Florida: Penkevill Publishing, 1985), 205.

polyvocality disappear into political taxonomies that try to establish genealogies. There was no structural room for race (or for much else) in theory claiming to reveal the construction of the category woman and social group women as unified or totalizable whole.[2]

I would like to suggest that the parenthetical "or for much else" contains the situation of "Jewishness" and Jewish women in relation to these totalizing feminisms, so that when "taxonomies of feminism produce epistemologies to police deviation from official women's experience" (74), and, implicitly, from the feminist theory that grows out of it, this includes Jewish women's experience as well as the relationship of that experience to feminist theory.

When I first began to think about writing this article on the plays of Nelly Sachs, Liliane Atlan, and Joan Schenkar, someone told me that what I should make visible in their work was the erasing of a gender discourse in representing the subject of the Holocaust. Although I am aware of the crucial work of feminist scholars and artists dedicated to the project of placing the gendered Holocaust experience of women in history, I was troubled by the idea that my purpose in writing about the pained attempts of these playwrights to reveal the landscape of the Holocaust, what Sidra DeKoven Ezrahi calls "the elusive and spiritually unedifying subject of large-scale physical suffering and submission to death,"[3] should be to focus on their lack, their flaw, their deviation from a notion of standard feminist theatrical treatments that foregrounds the analysis of sexism and gender. As both a feminist and a Jew, I refuse. Just as feminism resists being subsumed as an operation within a totalizing postmodernism, I want to resist subsuming the plays of Sachs, Atlan, and Schenkar on the Holocaust as an operation within a totalizing feminism. How can I, for example, simply mark Sachs's passionate response to atrocity—her mystery play reconstruction in *Eli: A Mystery Play of the Sufferings of Israel*[4] of a traditional Jewish community with its conservative gender relations—as a way of nostalgically naturalizing a virulent form of oppression in the face of a current focus on historical violation? In so doing I would be appropriating another perceptive analysis of Haraway's (91) wholesale without noticing that this context makes it trivializing and perhaps a little obscene. My own distress here, when I could comfortably critique nostalgic resurgencies of sex gender asymmetries in Lillian Hellman's anti-fascist play *Watch on the Rhine* in a recent article,[5] outlines the tensions between my own commitments as a feminist scholar and as a scholar of the Holocaust—tensions I have avoided previously by dealing with the two subjects more or less separately.

---

[2]Donna Haraway, "A Manifesto for Cyborgs: Science, Technology, and Socialist Feminism in the 1980s," *Socialist Review* 15 (1985): 78.

[3]Sidra DeKoven Ezrahi, *By Words Alone: The Holocaust in Literature* (Chicago and London: University of Chicago Press, 1980), 33.

[4]Nelly Sachs, *Eli: A Mystery Play of the Sufferings of Israel*, trans. Christopher Holme in *Plays of the Holocaust: An International Anthology*, ed. Elinor Fuchs (New York: Theatre Communications Group, 1987), 1–52.

[5]"Lillian Hellman's *Watch on the Rhine*: Realism, Gender and Historical Crisis," *Modern Drama* 32:1 (1989): 128–45.

In pursuing this argument, I am not insisting on some kind of "special case" status for my subject, nor justifying texts that erase women's experience in the Holocaust. I do agree with historian Joan Ringelheim that "even a cursory look at studies about the Holocaust would indicate that the experience and perceptions of Jewish women have been obscured or absorbed into descriptions of men's lives."[6] Nor am I ignoring the intersections of female or feminist and Jewish identities staged in these plays. I am asserting that the feminist critical strategies I have employed in other analyses must be seen through the prism of a Jewish critique in relation to this historical event of annihilation. The following short discussions present a gendered analysis of one of the three plays and then revises it in relation to the Holocaust as these playwrights represent it.

Drawing on a biological notion of female identity for *Eli*, Sachs privileges the site of the mother in her focus on the rebirth of an East European Jewish village. One dazed young woman with a child on her arm recounts how "in a hole in the earth I bore it, in a hole I suckled it—Death took its father, me he did not take, saw the milk in my breasts and did not take me." Although she "can't bear the light any more" but "mounds of earth I see dancing," her symbolic importance to the regeneration of the Jewish community is marked at the end of this scene when Sachs blots out the bodies of the dancers in "the glare of the evening sun"; "Only the Young Woman with her child stands out clearly in the light" (19–20). This biological emphasis on rebirth culminates in the transcendental text at the end of the play where in a circle above the dying murderer of the child Eli appears "The Embryo in its mother's womb." In response to this reduction of women to their biological and traditional roles, I must still consider how the mass murder of the Jewish population is the ground for Sachs's biological construction and resonates passionately with each of these images in the play.

A gendered analysis of Atlan's *Mister Fugue or Earth Sick*[7] would focus on the girlchild Raissa's central role in constructing a resistant discourse in response to the journey of four children toward Rotburg and death. The following example from the text foregrounds Raissa's metaphoric imagination, her insistence on infusing her fantasy with the material conditions that torment the four, and her own refusal to construct herself submissively even in relation to the other (male) children:

> *Raissa*: Look there's a big city with trains and lots of lights. Lots of noise. Iona, you're the train. Mister Fugue [a soldier caught trying to hide them and sentenced to death] you'll be the garbage can. Abracha, you're the sea, make sea sounds. . . . Tamar, you're the cat, go meow. Got it? Good. I need a rope. Well all right, Yossele, be the rope. Okay, so the cat and me, we're digging through the garbage, picking out things we can eat. I'm the owl, the bat, the hyena and god in heaven, it's all the same, I'm digging through the garbage. . . . You're not smart, Yossele.

[6]Joan Ringelheim, "Women and the Holocaust: A Reconsideration of Research," *Signs: Journal of Women in Culture and Society* 10:4 (1985): 741. For work in this area see also Sybil Milton, "Women and the Holocaust: The Case of German and German-Jewish Women" in *When Biology Became Destiny: Women in Weimar and Nazi German*, eds. Renate Bridenthal, Atina Grossman, and Marion Kaplan (New York: New Feminist Library/Monthly Review Press, 1985), 297–333.

[7]Liliane Atlan, *Mister Fugue or Earth Sick*, trans. Marguerite Feitlowitz, in *Plays of the Holocaust: An International Anthology*, ed. Elinor Fuchs (New York: Theatre Communications Group, 1987), 53–104.

Just a frayed rope. I'll put a match to it. That way, human beings, you won't be able to call me [god] by tugging on it. And if you do tug on it, you'll burn.

Yossele: What if you played becoming a little girl, a pretty little girl, Raissa, good and gentle.

Raissa: I spit on pretty little girls. I prowl around, I dig through garbage cans. I hear trains passing, I'd like to catch them. I hop one. The train wants no part of me. No use crying, this train's going to Rotburg. The whole earth is Rotburg.

[75–76]

Raissa's "blacker than night" awareness makes Mr. Fugue lose what he calls his stupidity as she initiates him into the horrors of this desolate Holocaust landscape. The Nazi Christopher's sadistic obsession with these children focuses especially on Raissa, who sings while being beaten and who refuses to bury Iona alive, so enraging Christopher that he shoots Iona and thus gives him a quick death. For Christopher, Raissa is "that Bitch" he identifies as leading their resistance "from the inside." Even when another child, Abracha, calls her "a bad woman" for not complying with a vision of future life the children are constructing, she responds by asserting her authority over the narrative: "The real article, you idiot, the real article. I'm the only one who's held up. Me, I saw the black and didn't build walls of fakery or music to hide it, and I still haven't fallen, and I can damn well betray you all at once if I want to, because that's how it is, I allow it" (100). Out of this material I can construct a narrative of struggle by Raissa against the verbal and physical incursions against her as a female by all the males in the play. But in doing so I am aware of foregrounding what, in the overall sense of the play, is backgrounded by Atlan's construction of the children as the last of the Jews of a ghetto engaged in a group strategy for endurance of terror and pain that eulogizes them and their culture, albeit in a fragmented or painfully satiric way.

Joan Schenkar's play does incorporate elements of a gender critique. Schenkar's depiction of fascist ideology in *The Last of Hitler*[8] links the dangerous, overweening imagination allowed to men under patriarchy and the destruction it wreaks to fascism. Dr. Reich, the male doctor figure in this play—a figure Schenkar associates with patriarchy in works such as *Signs of Life*[9]—tries to locate the emotional plague of anti-semitism through logic and scientific discourse and in so doing cannot apprehend either its sources or his own fascistic qualities. Those victimized by Reich's fascistic medical regimentation, the unseen but often referred to Dionne quintuplets, are females required to perform their victimization over radio and in public until they perish. Another female performer is victimized on the Mary Lee Taylor Cooking Show. While demonstrating how to cook a Kosher chicken, Mary Lee gets cooked in her own oven and eaten by the more violently anti-semitic John Cole. This suggests in a grotesquely comic way how women as "sympathizers" with other cultures become "chicken," i.e., oven food, along with the Jews. Here, although sexism is depicted, it is not foregrounded as it was in Schenkar's earlier play *Signs of Life. The Last of Hitler's* gender critique is imbedded in the staging of the anti-semitic discourse

[8]*The Last of Hitler* (1982) is in unpublished manuscript form.
[9]Joan Schenkar, *Signs of Life*, in *The Women's Project: Seven New Plays by Women*, ed. Julia Miles (New York: Performing Arts Publications and American Place Theatre, 1980), 307–62.

of the Other—its infiltration into mass culture and the complicitous response of its listeners—so it operates only marginally in the text.

What these examples illustrate is that the gender critique succeeds, in Haraway's terms, only to the degree to which it offers itself as a partial explanation. More generally, an analysis interweaving feminism and "Jewishness" is positioned within two sets of identity politics that resist two constructions of dominant discourse—one the discourse of sexism and the other the discourse of anti-semitism. Feminist theory has just begun to work out the specificities of the difference of Jewish women positioned in this way. For example, when Julie Greenberg, in her article "Seeking a Feminist Judaism" tries to interweave these subject positions, she asserts "There is a growing body of feminist Jews who care deeply and mutually about being both Jews and women. We are not willing to compromise on either identity and are equally committed to fighting anti-Semitism among feminists and sexism among Jews. . . . [T]here is not a Jewish self separate from a female self. Being a Jewish woman . . . is a totality and all experience is filtered through that integrated reality."[10] Consequently, in response to the difficulty of this project, Greenberg employs the same totalizing notion of identity for "being a Jewish woman" as that which I critiqued through Haraway, cancelling out the tension between the two identities she merges. Likewise, Judith Plaskow's solution to this conundrum also configures an essentialist identity: "The situation of the Jewish woman might well be compared to the situation of the Jew in non-Jewish culture. The Gentile projection of the Jew as Other—the stranger, the demon, the human non-quite-human—is repeated in . . . the Jewish understanding of the Jewish woman."[11] While I appreciate Plascow's labor in trying to work out this relationship, her formulation of "the Jewish Woman" equates two discourses on Otherness too simply. Moreover, the Holocaust is not about Otherness within Judaism but is about the Jew as Other: Jews were killed as Jews though they were victimized as women in the process.

In noting this I do not mean to refute the many provocative assertions of the marginalizing of Jewish women within Judaism found in such anthologies as *The Tribe of Dina: A Jewish Women's Anthology* or *On Being A Jewish Feminist*. But my studies of the treatment of the Holocaust convince me that Jewish feminist attempts directed at critique and re-vision need to take the Holocaust into account in their theorizing or risk being erased by the magnitude of this event. Or, at least, given my topic, I do.

The problem, then, is to locate "Jewishness" for women in regard to the Holocaust and the possibility of a collective identity that relates to that history. Cynthia Ozick's article "Notes toward Finding the Right Question" asserts that "The point is not that Jewish women want equality as women with men, but as *Jews with Jews*." Even if I

---

[10]Julie Greenberg, "Seeking a Feminist Judaism," in *The Tribe of Dina: A Jewish Women's Anthology*, eds. Melanie Kaye/Kantrowitz, Irena Klepfisz and, also, Esther F. Hyneman (Montpelier, Vermont: Sinister Wisdom Books, 1986), 180.

[11]Judith Plaskow, "The Right Question Is Theological," in *On Being A Jewish Feminist: A Reader*, ed. Susannah Heschel (New York: Schocken Books, 1983), 226.

disagree with her politics and believe many Jewish women want both and more, I have to note what she goes on to say:

> The point is the necessity—*having lost so much and so many*—to share Jewish history to the hilt. This lamentation—*having lost so much and so many*—produces not an analogy or a metaphor, but a lesson. . . . The nature of the excision [unnoticed by the vigilant Jewish mentality developed in the aftermath of group loss] is this: a great body of Jewish ethical thinkers, poets, juridicial consciences—not merely one generation but many; in short, an entire intellectual and cultural organism—has been deported out of the community of Jewish culture, away from the creative center. . . . And this isolation, this confinement, this shunting off, is one of the cruelest events in Jewish history.[12]

Based on the events of the Holocaust as they affected Jews, Ozick tries to create a feminist Jewish politics out of loss and of collectivity. However, despite her understanding of the loss, there is, in fact, no agreement on what is "the center of Jewish culture." At the same time, she risks essentializing "Jewishness" at the cost of nearly erasing gender difference. Finally, Ozick's formulation does not question the hierarchical aspects of insisting on an equality based on the most elite areas of a culture rather than the damaging effect of sexism on the lives of ordinary Jewish women. Thus, while Ozick does begin to suggest that grieving and critique are not mutually exclusive, she does not go far enough. Located, as it is, within the boundary of Jewish relations among Jews, her formulation would leave no room for the kind of outwardly-focused progressive Jewish feminist politics Melanie Kaye/Kantrowitz focuses on in her assertion in *Tikkun* that "some of the most hopeful developments in Black-Jewish relations have been among feminists."[13] Nor would there be room for the kind of activities that challenge the conservative Jewish establishment from the margins such as those described in the newsletter *Bridges* which recently focused on the efforts of Jewish Feminists, both American and Israeli, to organize to end the occupation.[14] Kaye's formulation of the question "Given [the] lack of agreement about even such basics as the nature of Jewish experience and identity, the parameters of anti-Semitism, how are Jews supposed to work politically *as Jews*?"[15] might begin to suggest a Jewish feminist politics of differences within Judaism that rests more on specificity and material history than on essentialism.

I do not presume I can come up with a formulation that encompasses the questions I am raising, but I am trying to outline some of the difficulties in answering them and suggest what such a project, this excursion into Haraway's parenthetical "much else," might be. One way of doing this is to look at the politics of Otherness as they apply to Jews in order to clarify why these playwrights foreground "Jewishness" over feminism in their Holocaust plays.

---

[12]Cynthia Ozick, "Notes toward Finding the Right Question," in *On Being A Jewish Feminist*, 136–37.

[13]Melanie Kaye/Kantrowitz, "Class, Women, and 'The Black-Jewish Question,' " *Tikkun: A Bimonthly Jewish Critique of Politics, Culture & Society* 4:4 (1989): 100.

[14]"Special Section: Jewish Feminists Organize to End the Occupation," in *Bridges, The Feminist Newsletter of New Jewish Agenda* 3:2 (1989): 10–19.

[15]Melanie Kaye/Kantrowitz, "To Be a Radical Jew in the Late 20th Century," in *The Tribe of Dina*, 275.

Even Haraway's statement that "Gender, race, or class consciousness is an achievement forced on us by the terrible historical experience of the contradictory social realities of patriarchy, colonialism, and capitalism" (72), (besides calling up accounts of anti-semitism in communist countries) reminds me that the category "Jewishness" is not perfectly analogous to the other three. On the one hand, it *is* a category created by oppression in which a grotesque, anti-semitic totalizing construction of "Jewishness" creates an awareness forced upon Jews by historical experience in opposition to the actual diversity of people within this category. Yet the three categories Haraway constructs are abstract constructions that aid in understanding how oppression works systematically; they don't correspond to specific peoples. On the other hand, Jews not only theorize Otherness under the terms of their oppression. They also theorize "Jewishness" based on a specific history and a range of ethnic, cultural and religious practices no matter how contested these are *within* Judaism. This is a theorizing not defined in terms of Otherness but in terms of its own multi-faceted particularity. Such a self-conscious communal history and web of traditions does not have to be essentialized in order to be asserted; nor is it defined by simply inverting the terms of the opposition of Otherness, reversing its valuations while staying within its binaries.

What is central (and different) is the threat of an alternate culture (not a subculture which can be appropriated over time by the dominant culture)—an historical collectivity resistant to the imposition of dominant discourse. It was this collectivity, this cultural body, translated by the Nazis into an implacable, biologically determined genetic opposition to make difference lethal, that was specifically being annihilated in the Holocaust. This paranoid rejection of difference is the very basis upon which Nazi ideology is constructed. Moreover, the irrationality of Nazi claims is inflected by the very fact that Jews are not visible ethnics, not a separate race, but can, so to speak, "pass"; Nazism translates these accommodations of Jews to the earlier and continuing religious and cultural anti-semitism into further proof of the threat of Jews and so further justification for death.

The Holocaust in this sense represents a definitional struggle where a subjectivity constructed within a different, already extant discourse is conceived as so threatening that not only must its discourse be annihilated and abused but so must all its speakers. Thus the huge radio speakers of Schenkar's play cancel out the individual Jewish speakers. For the Nazi Christopher of Atlan's play, even four Jewish children's voices threaten the stability of fascism. And Sachs culminates her play with the words of the Voice, inscribed with a capital "V," to counter the destruction with divine authorization. The works of Atlan, Sachs and Schenkar all locate themselves at the terminous of this murderous discourse of Otherness, privileging the loss of that Jewish collectivity in the Holocaust as well as the threat to it in contemporary anti-semitism. Sachs responds to loss by reconstructing a Jewish discourse in simultaneous communal and religious narratives. Atlan theatricalizes the construction in language of that collective Jewish subjectivity in response to a fascist discourse and a material landscape that objectifies and bestializes. Schenkar focuses on fascist discourse in order to exhaust its obsessions through repetition and to vulgarize it and domesticate it as a strategy to remove its power as a mesmerizing demonology against which the listener is powerless.

While these playwrights foreground this loss, none of the three chooses to do so within a documentary form. They do not assume the position of a memorializer faced with the imperative of transmission and its facticity, nor that of an investigative reporter. Nor do they become historians of these events, committed to a minimum of literary (in this case theatrical) intervention.[16] One way to account for this choice is to historicize the position of each playwright in relation to the Holocaust, as well as to the time in which each play was written.

None of the three is a survivor in the strict sense of the term. Sachs, originally "an assimilated young woman living in Berlin and writing neoromantic poetry" who refound Judaism in response to the slaughter, was forced to flee from Nazi Germany to Sweden in 1940. Thus writing *Eli: A Mystery Play of the Sufferings of Israel* in 1943, she had only partial knowledge of horrific extent of the destruction of European Jewry. In an impassioned response to what she did know, she dramatically recreated a community to which she might return and a village to rebuild when in actuality there would be fewer survivors to return and often nothing in Europe but wasteland awaiting her. She constructed her characters on a shifting ground midway between speaking spirits of the dead and rebuilding survivors. Many of their lamentation monologues focus on what happened in this Polish village before or as people were being taken away. Thus the play seizes this history as it was at its moment of disappearance. The time of the play's conception is also marked by Sachs's ability still to represent the murder of one child, Eli, as a symbolic event requiring holy retribution. By contrast her later poetry focuses on the deaths of children in the plural[17]—deaths too inconceivable in scope to be contained within a symbolic narrative. For *Eli*, Sachs chose a kind of ritual, invocative poetic theatre where, as Elinor Fuchs points out, "the very rhythms of her verse summon up the Hasidic world, full of motion and music."[18]

As children, Liliane Atlan and her sister Rachael were hidden away from their family (many of whom they knew had been deported) in a house in Lyon, France. Confined there, Atlan discovered an abandoned bathroom in the garden with a terrace and a window and there enacted theatre. Rachael was the audience and, in Atlan's words, "I was the stage: the actors, the author . . . Everything lived within me: I screamed, gesticulated, died. I would speak out my lamentations, my dirges, my psalms."[19] "The plays were always the same. There were many characters and they

---

[16]For an extended discussion of these categories of writing about the Holocaust, see Ezrahi's chapter "Documentation as Art," 24–48.

[17]For a selection in English of Sachs's poetry see Nelly Sachs, *O The Chimneys: Selected Poems, Including the Verse Play, Eli*, trans. Michael Hamburger, Christopher Holme, Ruth and Matthew Mead, and Michael Roloff (New York: Farrar, Straus & Giroux, 1967).

[18]Introduction to *Plays of the Holocaust*, xiii.

[19]Bettina L. Knapp, "Interview with Liliane Atlan," in *Off-Stage Voices* (New York: The Whitston Publishing Company, 1977), 200.

all died, one by one."[20] Her own experience of creating theatre pieces in an enclosed universe evokes her treatment, in the 1967 *Mister Fugue or Earth Sick,* of four children who stage theatre rituals in order to endure their ride in a huge wire cage at the back of a truck taking them from the ruins of a ghetto to be killed at Rotburg, the Valley of Bones. The techniques Atlan uses to portray the children's taking charge of their own chaotic, fragmented group narrative—a narrative they physically act out as they speak it—resemble the techniques of transformational theatre. Here, Atlan uses these techniques as strategies of the characters rather than simply of her own stage devices. According to the stage directions, "The children do not describe, *they see,* they live what they see. They do not search, *they find,* instantly" (56) and the loose narrative, shifting from one child to another, proceeds faster and faster the closer time presses. Atlan's description of the children as "no longer real children" places them and their excruciating experience, depicted in the text without a shred of sentimentality, outside the limits of conventional representations of childhood and children. That they are played by adult actors visually underscores the shifting space of their own self-identifications, especially as, out of a kind of ironic, blasphemous agony, they create and live out futures based on shards of the past. By using adults to play children, Atlan also marks the loss of those children: there will be no children to play those parts.

Schenkar, the youngest of the three playwrights, is positioned by the American distance Ezrahi identifies as marking a separation from direct knowledge of East European Jewish communities and from a grounding in the specifics of the horror, "anonymity and routine of mechanized mass death" (182). Writing *Last of Hitler* in the 1980s, Schenkar uses a kind of skewed historicizing technique, where she looks at the present through the prism of a reinvented past, incriminating both past and present in the process. Breaking a certain "Gentleman's Agreement," she places 1940s fascism in intimate relationship to 1940s America without ever abandoning the particularity of American references and discourse, especially as expressed in radio mass culture. Turning references to the ovens, soap, and showers of the concentration camps into obscene innuendo, the playwright marks a kind of pornographic fascination with the paraphernalia of death from the American distance which obscures both its material reality and those subjected to it. If Schenkar's work is a kind of circus of sliding metaphor, it is the mutating, flexible, recycling reproducability of fascist ideology and anti-semitism in language that her work is trying to capture and subvert. The radio show is organized around a group of escalating metaphors shifting from character to character in order to reveal the process of Othering that which is most feared, how that Other is identified as contagious, and how it is represented as victimizing the dominant group.

All three playwrights, then, have no direct knowledge of the Holocaust. They foreground the question of knowledge in their plays rather than offer Knowledge of the Holocaust. Eschewing realism, they do not present a story of the Holocaust as

[20]Kathleen Betsko and Rachel Koenig, "Liliane Atlan," *Interviews with Contemporary Women Playwrights* (New York: Beech Tree Books, 1987), 25.

if they were recapturing it or offering "the truth." Instead, they underline in the forms of their work, their own partial ability to represent it. Sachs, Atlan, and Schenkar reject realism's inscription of the subject as complete, coherent, and rational. There is for all three writers no disruption in the landscape of the Holocaust that is containable within the borders of realism and, in terms of form, no social order to which to return. There is no secret to be disclosed and exorcised or exiled, no enigma resolvable by logic and linear narrative. Yet they do not substitute a purely formalist analysis that celebrates a postmodern, decentered and dispersed subjectivity unattached to the circumstances of its construction, the material conditions that necessitates this kind of representation. Instead, all three write what could be called mystery plays, each presenting an enigma without a solution.

Yet, even their mysteries are marked by history. Sachs's narrative of divine revelation is, as her Postscript to *Eli* describes it, "designed to raise the unutterable to a transcendental level, so as to make it bearable" (52). This is fulfilled when the divinity shining through Michael, a shoemaker character described as "one of the thirty six Servants of God who, unaware of it themselves carry the invisible universe," makes the murderer of the child Eli crumble into dust. But even the transcendent, divine text is affected by history since "The new Pentateuch, I tell you, the new Pentateuch is written in mildew, the mildew of fear on the walls of the death cellars" (29). The mystery of representation in *Eli* is located in the theological inscription of unspeakable material events onto the invisible, transcendent world.

For Atlan, within the unimaginable universe of desolation, nature—birds, cliffs, the sea—constitutes an enigmatic and fragile space that Mister Fugue tries to create metaphorically with the children. But the children fracture a transcendent text based on nature, as when Yossele says "Now God, he went crazy, he knocked around in the sea like a fish, in the air like a bird, nothing but barbed wire, he doesn't dare anymore to sit or stand, he steals passes, but he doesn't leave" (66). Thus they appropriate Fugue's imagery to project their own history onto both the natural and the divine. The divine text Sachs conflates in the Voice and the Embryo has been ruptured permanently in Atlan's work; only children and madmen are left to prophecize but remain inscrutable or unheard. An enigma of representation circulates through the play: What or who are children whose material experiences render them unrepresentable as children? This enigma deconstructs the ideology of the "real" child, with its patriarchal genealogy, even as the play mourns the severed connections of the last four inhabitants of this particular ghetto. In fact, in all three works, children become a site of the problem of representation. One of the major nonrealistic devices of these plays is the way they mediate between the histories of these children and their theatrical representation. In Sachs one child is holy, dead, symbolic; another, daughter of the murderer of Eli, symbolically sinks into death after hearing Michael play Eli's pipe. In Atlan, in addition to the children enacted by adult actors, there is the mythically childlike Grol/Mr. Fugue and the deathdoll, Tamar, who, animated by the voices of the children to indirectly express their pain, stands in for a dead four-year-old-girl. In Schenkar, there is the speaking six-year-old skeleton Edmond and the much-referred-to but never seen or heard Dionne Quintuplets. Thus, children become a site of the impossibility of representation and these metaphoric, partial representations of them underscore this.

Schenkar, too, presents an enigma of representation in her play. The discourse of fascism and anti-semitism litters the stage with distorted and grotesque versions of "Jewishness." Taking Hitler's construction of the threat of the Jewish Other literally, Schenkar's characters are subject to contamination. They not only project "Jewishness" onto each other, they "catch it" like a disease that transforms them into burlesqued stereotypes which underscore the vulgarity of their conceptions. The pathology of cancer Nazism attached to Jews is countered by anti-semitism conceived as plague. Thus Schenkar's counter physicalization in disease refers to an earlier historical imagining of pathology and so suggests anti-semitism's long history. All the Jews in the play are "suppositious," leaving only a gap, an emptiness at the center of the play that combines the historical reality of annihilation with the absence in representation created by the discourse of the Jew as Other. Schenkar refuses to create an invented persona for this absence. The characters' occasional, incomplete lament "I will never understand" marks the way even the determination of what or who is erased by this discourse.

In reaching for this enigma, Sachs, Atlan and Schenkar attempt to put the site of the Othered into play, to inscribe the site of erasure when, in the words of Atlan's children, "Nothing lasts save erosion, this is the code" (102). The impossibility of a certain kind of visibility as, in the Atlan epigraph quoted earlier, "I myself don't see," becomes the lament of these plays. And the partial understanding they have and offer, formally never promising to "awaken a light" but, at most, in Sach's words, make the unutterable bearable, becomes the politics of their work. Sachs and Atlan counter this erasure of the Jewish subject in a cultural imagining of sociality that serves as a ground in language for its reconstruction. If the events of the Holocaust are in part about wiping out Jewish subjectivity, then an imagined sociality constructed in language functions as vestigal evidence of a continual subjectivity under grave threat of extermination. In opposition to the social that has been annihilated in material terms, they depict the creation of imagined socialities of "Jewishness" in resistance to a fascist discourse that erases and defiles. There is no linearity in this process; the texts and the characters slide backward and forward in time to recover a past that does not exist for a nonexistent future in a present that is an unspeakable absence.

Sachs renders sociality chorally through generic characters whose individual narratives make up a mosaic. The necessity for the divine text marks how threatened the sociality is; thus Sachs inscribes the provisional nature of what she does by using myth, insisting on a kind of eternal possibility of beginning. The bodies on stage create a sociality in themselves, but also outline the distance between those bodies and what has been lost historically. Sociality is also under excavation, marked in the text by characters piecing together fragments from the everyday life of a vanished world, pulled from the ground. This archaeological undertaking, combined with the images of the baby born in a hole and the old man rescued from a mass grave, create an unearthing, deliberately reversing one directional signal of death to create this new sociality in defiance of history.

Atlan's child characters, injured and ill, construct themselves in language in a situation where the material is out of their control, including their very lives. Near the end of the play, Iona, digging his own grave and beaten with a stick by Christopher, still intones "They were dying, the mountains, they were spitting blood, they fell like old people and still, Lord of the Worlds, they danced, and us too, we're dancing, for Yossele and Raissa, you see, are getting married. . . ." From the truck Raissas responds "In the commandos' faces, alleluia," and the others repeat "Alleluia" as they dance wildly (93). In portraying this, Atlan suggests the way that sociality is a collective, cultural construction in history, not just a static tradition, and is marked by its relation to the context in which it is being constructed. Thus instead of mourning the loss of a coherent, unified Jewish identity, Atlan, in revealing the very fragility of that provisional construction and the tenacity, nonetheless, of the children to this enterprise, makes the weight of what has been done by the Nazis that much worse.

Both Atlan and Schenkar place their notion of a Jewish sociality in history by emphasizing either the material terms in which it is created or, for Schenkar, the particularity of the contexts that threaten it. In a contradiction of representation, Schenkar visually stages the means by which the 1940s radio show of anti-semitism constructs its listeners. She explores the invasiveness of a simulated sociality created in mass culture that achieves its collectivity on the basis of bigotry and exclusion. If the text illustrates how the false, negating sociality of anti-semitism is always under construction, has to be obsessively reiterated, the emphasis is not on its fragility but on its tenacious ability to seep into the structure of everyday life by capturing its rhetoric. Investigating radio's potential to become "a vast circulatory system transmitting poisons to infected cells," Schenkar emphasizes the power of broadcasting, of the voice in the dark, to convey language undiluted by visual imagery penetrating within domestic spaces. Throughout the play, characters who obsessively listen to radio repeat the phrase "I heard it on the radio" as a validation of any popular sentiment they express—a direct transmission from the cultural brain to theirs. It is as if the voices on radio become a single, coherent, authoritative Voice: outside the Voice lurks the terrifying landscape of infectious difference, "the impure" of fascist ideology. At the end of the play, the figure of the Hasid, transformed into a devil figure as he was by Nazism, pulls the giant plug (which becomes a pitchfork) out of the radio, which becomes a crematorium. It is as if the grotesque formulations of the Other have become animated so as to annihilate the discourse that constructed them. The audience is left with the responsibility for imagining that absent sociality erased by fascism and its discourse of Otherness.

If, earlier in this article, I stated that Jewish feminist attempts directed at critique and re-vision need to take the Holocaust into account, I'd like to conclude by exploring the importance of a gender discourse in representing the Holocaust and the necessity for Holocaust scholars to use feminist strategies in identifying and analyzing their texts. To being with, if the work of Atlan, Sachs and Schenkar foreground the loss of a Jewish collectivity over specific gender concerns, it is also the case that for works that do gender this collectivity, feminist theory is a crucial frame for understanding them.

The degree to which the prevalent analysis of Holocaust work is not just partial but inadequate can be exemplified by what happens when Ezrahi, in an otherwise perceptive and eloquent book, groups a series of texts that concentrate on the experiences of women in the Holocaust. When she discusses what has been referred to as "survival literature," she notes that "Most of these novels have been written by women" (67) but cannot theorize as to why. She can identify works such as Ilona Karmel's *An Estate of Memory* or Zdena Berger's *Tell Me Another Morning* as a "significant trend" (68), but without a feminist analysis, she has trouble identifying exactly what that trend represents. Even though she is responsible for pioneering the inclusion of work by women in the Holocaust canon, without a discourse linking the feminist critique to the Holocaust available to her, she resorts to male thinkers on atrocity and the Holocaust to frame her inquiry. They foreground the "struggle to maintain integrity of self" and the resistance to "the debasement and disintegration of the individual" —both gender-neutral concepts (72). The effect of this is to subsume the focus in these novels on bonding among women within the topic of individual survival strategies. The tension between this frame, which rests on an idea of "universal human responses to concentrationary oppression" (72), and her topic becomes evident when Ezrahi suddenly switches her generic pronoun from he to she (77), while still negating the particularities of gender in the "mutually sustaining groups" (79) she describes.

One of the current projects of feminist historians of the Holocaust is to investigate these gendered strategies of maintenance among women, especially those of cooperation and the creation of "families" of support. There is, as yet, no Holocaust play I know of that focuses on the experience of Jewish women and how they configured themselves in response to oppression. There is, however, a play that portrays bonding among women political prisoners in Auschwitz. Charlotte Delbo's play, *Who Will Carry the Word?* (1972; English 1982),[21] concerns the determination of French women political prisoners in a death camp that one of them should survive to carry back to the world their history of atrocity and slow death. The metaphor of carrying extends to visual figuration since the women carry, support each other psychically, morally and physically as in the roll call scenes where whoever falls is killed. Again a play eschewing realism, *Who Will Carry the Word* explores, to quote Ringelheim, "the strength in women's friendships, . . . sharing, storytelling, and conversations" (756). And it does so without ever celebrating these traits and behaviors in such a way as to obscure the horrific circumstances that necessitated them or the reality that most of these women died. Delbo, who herself is a survivor of such a death camp, recreates this history using a choral structure of shifting voices, emphasizing in this way not only the cooperation among these women under extreme conditions, but their collective passion to have the narrative of their experience memorialized.

What is still needed is a play as eloquent as Delbo's that explores the experience of Jewish women and the intersection of female and Jewish identity in the Holocaust.

---

[21]Charlotte Delbo, *Who Will Carry the Word?*, trans. Cynthia Haft, in *The Theatre of the Holocaust: Four Plays*, ed. Robert Skloot (Madison: The University of Wisconsin Press, 1982), 267–325.

To use the title of Karmel's novel, the "estate of memory" of the Holocaust itself is incomplete without inclusion of what happened to women. In asserting this, Ringelheim asks:

> Why should ideas about the Holocaust as a whole exclude . . . women's experiences—exclude what is important to women—and thus make the judgment that women's experiences as women are trivial? These aspects of women's daily lives—vulnerability to rape, humiliation, sexual exchange, not to speak of pregnancy, abortion, and fear for one's children—cannot simply be universalized as true for all survivors.
>
> [745]

She also marks the way "maintenance strategies" among women were different and has focused in earlier work on how these strategies related to their survival.[22] Since the intersection of feminism and "Jewishness" is still being theorized, by the time of her 1985 article in *Signs*, Ringelheim is critiquing her own theoretical stance in earlier work for its totalizing "cultural feminist" approach. She asserts that "such uncritical valorization" of women's behavior in the Holocaust, including reclaiming the "values, ways of life, and skills" of women "as if they have not arisen within an oppressive situation" have the effect of "valorizing oppression" and "blunt[ing] or negating its effects" (756). "What," she asks, "does the transformation of female gender roles really mean in the face of the oppression and genocidal murder perpetrated during the Holocaust," especially in the face of how few women and men actually survived? (760).

Her own statement in the *Newsletter* of the Holocaust Project, a project by artist Judy Chicago who is "committed to emphasizing (though not isolating) women's experience in this project" for her murals, traces one answer to Ringelheim's question:

> During the Holocaust women were victimized as women and not only as Jews; Jewish women were the targets of the Nazis *because* they were Jews. But they were attacked and used as women—as mothers, as objects of sexual derision and exploitation, as persons even less valuable than Jewish men because of the curious and damaging sexual division of labor. My own research shows that more Jewish women may have been deported and killed than Jewish men. Thus it is absolutely clear that there is a serious and deadly relationship between anti-semitism and sexism. It can no longer be ignored if we want to understand the lives and deaths of women during the Holocaust. It is time to refocus and rearrange the politics of the Holocaust.[23]

I would add that it can be no longer ignored in order to understand the lives and deaths of Jews during the Holocaust since women make up half its population. In line with her assertion that there is a politics in how the Holocaust is conceived and represented, it seems to me that the particularity of the differences within Judaism

---

[22]This was the subject of a grant she directed for a conference in 1983 entitled "Women Surviving the Holocaust." See *Proceedings of the Conference on Women Surviving the Holocaust*, eds. Esther Katz and Joan Miriam Ringelheim (New York: Institute for Research in History, 1983). In later work, Ringelheim would replace the term survival, with its celebratory connotations, with that of maintenance, thereby distinguishing the support systems women constructed to endure deprivation, from the omnipresent threat of death in the camps that made survival a matter of luck.

[23]*Newsletter* for *The Holocaust Project* 2 (October 1988).

are where the strength of any critique of the Holocaust lies; a material approach, one which tries to understand specific conditions and specific histories, including women's, will help in the formulation of a contemporary discourse on the Holocaust. That Ringelheim identifies as crucial to this project that not-as-yet theorized intersection of the "deadly relationship between anti-semitism and sexism" in the Holocaust suggests a fruitful direction for a theory interweaving feminism and "Jewishness" in order to navigate the two sets of identity politics and the two discourses of Otherness within which a Jewish feminism is positioned.

Part III

Reconfiguring the Fathers

Unbodied Figures of Desire

Carol Cook

In the scene in *Troilus and Cressida* which brings the lovers together, just prior to the consummation of their union, Troilus articulates a radical asymmetry at the heart of desire. This skewed relation between desire and its objects infects both the masculine enterprises which drive the play — his own quest for satisfaction in "Cressid's love," and the Greeks' and Trojans' competition for the "inestimable" prize of Helen:

> This is the monstruosity in love, lady, that the will is
> infinite and the execution confined; that the desire is
> boundless and the act a slave to limit.
>
> [III. ii. 82–85][1]

Troilus' description of the disproportion between aspiration and achievement has been anticipated earlier in Agamemnon's observation on his army's failure, after seven years, to topple Troy:

> The ample proposition that hope makes
> In all designs begun on earth below
> Fails in the promised largeness.
>
> [I. iii, 3–5]

The passages, similar in their resignation to a certain impossibility in the nature of things, reinforce the close parallel between the war plot and the love plot. But their differences are also important. For Agamemnon, disappointment follows from "checks and disasters," obstacles and interruptions which "Grow in the veins of actions highest reared," and would therefore seem interior to, inherent in, the action and designs they defeat; yet he displaces them onto an exterior agency — "the protractive

---

Carol Cook is an Assistant Professor of English at Princeton University. She has published essays on Shakespeare in PMLA *as well as* Theatre Journal, *and will have essays appearing in two anthologies now in production. She is currently completing a book on gender and subjectivity in Shakespeare.*

---

[1] Quotations from the play are taken from the Signet Classic edition of *Troilus and Cressida*, ed. Daniel Seltzer (New York: New American Library, 1963).

trials of Great Jove" (I. iii. 20). Troilus, on the other hand, describes not a circumstantial defeat, but a "monstruosity," a paradox or outrageous enigma that doesn't "check" desire, but constitutes it. The monstrosity of love, I would suggest, is more than an issue which the play thematizes;[2] the play reveals a deeply problematic relation between desire and representation in which the play itself is entangled, a relation which is revealed particularly in the problematic status of women as objects of desire.

As a description of the operations of desire, Troilus' speech contains a notable absence: the drive has an aim — the execution of "the act" — but no object. This desire goes forth from its subject as a boundless energy and returns unspent in slavish acts. It repeatedly affirms the magnitude of the lover's subjective experience while negating the world of "acts" and effectively scotomizing the object, her with whom the lover must "coact." (Troilus bitterly uses this verb of Diomed and Cressida — V. ii. 116 — uses it intransitively, as though to *co*act anything were degrading.) Furthermore, Troilus' reflection on the insufficiency of "the act" comes oddly just prior to a moment he has long anticipated in imagination, a moment he had described at the beginning of this scene as the tasting "indeed" of "Love's thrice repurèd nectar," an experience perhaps "tuned too sharp in sweetness" to be sustained by the senses. Between that anticipated insufficiency of his own body, and his resignation to the insufficiency of "the act," both in the same scene, comes his first face to face encounter with Cressida.

In a discussion of Marlowe, Steven Greenblatt has written that the problematic elusiveness of objects of desire "is one of the major preoccupations of Renaissance thinkers from the most moderate to the most radical . . . ." As an example, Greenblatt cites in a note this passage from Giordano Bruno's *The Heroic Frenzies*:

> Whatever species is represented to the intellect and comprehended by the will, the intellect concludes there is another species above it, a greater and still greater one, and consequently it is always impelled toward new motion and abstraction in a certain fashion. For it ever realizes that everything it possesses is a limited thing which for that reason cannot be sufficient in itself . . . because the limited thing is not the universe and is not the absolute entity, but is contracted to . . . this form represented to the intellect. . . . As a result, from that beautiful which is comprehended, and therefore limited, and consequently beautiful by participation, the intellect progresses toward that which is truly beautiful without limit or circumspection whatsoever.[3]

Bruno resolves the monstrosity of desire by directing desire toward "the absolute entity," or God — a resolution not available (or certainly not explicitly) in the world of

---

[2] The failures of desire and aspiration in the play have been treated thematically by D. A. Traversi, *An Approach to Shakespeare* (Garden City, N.Y.: Doubleday and Co. Inc., 3rd Edition, 1969), pp. 324–40; Robert Ornstein, *The Moral Vision of Jacobean Tragedy* (Madison: University of Wisconsin Press, 1960), pp. 240–49; and Willard Farnham, "Troilus in Shapes of Infinite Desire," *Shakespeare Quarterly* 15:2 (1964), 257–64. Each of these critics discusses the problem as an ethical one (Troilus fails to establish "an adequate conception of value" — Traversi, p. 340) or as a comment on human limitation; in so doing, I would suggest, they tend to reduce the "monstrosity" called to our attention by Troilus' language to rather commonplace thematic formulations which do not account for the peculiar relation of desire to its objects in the play.

[3] Steven Greenblatt, *Renaissance Self-Fashioning* (Chicago: University of Chicago Press, 1980), pp. 218, 296.

Troilus and Cressida. Bruno translates the restlessness of infinite desire into a desire of the infinite where, in Troilus' formulation, the possibility of an object commensurate with desire does not arise. Nonetheless Bruno's description of the restlessness itself seems very close to what we see in the play. For Bruno, the insufficiency of objects is discovered in their "limited" forms, in the fact of their being representable. The allure of what can be "represented to the intellect" is quickly exhausted, the intellect "impelled toward new motion and abstraction" in an attempt to escape the confines of representation.

The enigma of desire in *Troilus and Cressida* has much to do with an ambivalence toward representation. The desires and aspirations which drive the play — Troilus' passion, the enterprise of the Trojan war — are directed toward women, toward Cressida and Helen. Yet the play consistently reveals the operations by which women — or, insofar as Helen is the legendary paragon of feminine allure, *woman* — are *produced* as objects. Masculine desire puts woman in the place of "that unbodied figure of the thought / That gave't surmisèd shape" (I. iii. 16–17). The woman's body becomes the means by which masculine desire represents itself to itself, but the insufficiency of the image provokes at moments violent impulses, a rage articulated in images of a fragmentation of the woman's body. While the play does insistently expose the element of narcissistic fantasy in this economy of desire, the monstrosity in love tends to appear as the monstrosity of women. The repetition of desire described by Bruno, which leads the desirer from object to object, is displaced onto Cressida in the scene of betrayal (though she seems able to experience desire only as its object), a displacement which assures Troilus of his authority as "truth's authentic author" (III. ii. 182). The only scene in which Helen appears, the center of the play in more ways than one (III. i), is fetid with a stupefying verbal repetition which seemingly emanates from her. Helen and Cressida can be enjoyed in fantasy as disbursed and fetishized signs, flickering images, unbodied figures of the thought, but as bodies they threaten a monstrous entrapment in finitude, repetition, representation.[4]

"Th'Imaginary Relish"

The play opens with the excruciating desire of Troilus, who experiences passion as that which tears him from within — "my heart, / As wedgèd with a sigh, would rive in twain . . ." (I. i. 36–37). He is "mad in Cressid's love," beside himself, *not* himself as Pandarus tells Cressida in the next scene; his heart is an "open ulcer" and love a "knife" that "gashes." This first appearance of Troilus reveals some of the peculiarities which mark his love throughout the play. His desire is presented as radically fragmenting, threatening his reason, his identity, his very life. His enunciation of his desire also reveals its paradoxical relation to its object. His desire is intensely, excruciatingly physical and is directed at Cressida's body, but as it rends his body so it fragments hers. She figures in his speech as a Petrarchan *blazon* of parts and attributes — "Her

---

[4] Though I do not discuss Cassandra in this essay — she doesn't figure significantly in the play as an object of desire — it may be relevant to consider her in this connection. A story which is not told in the play but borders on it tells how Cassandra comes by her gift and curse of prophecy: she is the object of Apollo's desire who, for her refusal to satisfy him, is doomed to the repetitious prophecy of Troy's destruction which no one heeds.

eyes, her hair, her cheek, her gait, her voice" (I. i. 55) — a body savored sequentially in imagination. At the same time, this body, which represents to Troilus the very essence of woman's beauty, becomes almost *pure* essence as his language gestures beyond the reaches of the visual imagination, a rarefied distillation of the physical. Troilus objects to Pandarus' "handling in his discourse"

> O that her hand
> In whose comparison all whites are ink
> Writing their own reproach; to whose soft seizure
> The cygnet's down is harsh, and spirit of sense
> Hard as the palm of a plowman.

(I. i. 57–61]

This ambivalent relation of desire to the body produces a dread which dominates Troilus' anticipation of union with Cressida. The prospect of the metaphorical "death" of sexual consummation carries some literal force in his imagination such that he perceives himself upon the threshold of extinction, stalking about Cressid's door "Like a strange soul upon the Stygian banks / Staying for waftage" (III. ii. 8–9). As Pandarus goes to fetch Cressida, Troilus contemplates the effects of translating his "imaginary relish" into experience:

> I am giddy; expectation whirls me round,
> Th'imaginary relish is so sweet
> That it enchants my sense. What will it be
> When that the wat'ry palates taste indeed
> Love's thrice-repurèd nectar? Death, I fear me,
> Sounding destruction, or some joy too fine,
> Too subtle, potent, tuned too sharp in sweetness
> For the capacity of my ruder powers.
> I fear it much; and I do fear besides
> That I shall lose distinction in my joys,
> As doth a battle, when they charge on heaps
> The enemy flying.

[III. ii. 17–28]

Troilus is intently engaged with the body here. He has longed to "wallow in the lily beds / Proposed for the deserver" (11–12), but now his enchanted "sense" appears to him possibly inadequate to the demands of "Love's thrice-repurèd nectar." He anticipates love as an intense and highly refined sensation received by the "sense," by the "palates," yet imagines it also as rarefied beyond the "capacity" of the body, of his "ruder powers," so that it threatens to overwhelm him completely, destroying all "distinction," all boundaries, all difference, and consuming him with a violence that registers in the incoherence of the image which describes it.[5] Significantly Cressida

---

[5] In "'This Is and Is Not Cressid': The Characterization of Cressida," in *The (M)other Tongue*, ed. Shirley Nelson Garner, Claire Kehane, and Madelon Sprengnether (Ithaca: Cornell University Press, 1985), pp. 119–41, Janet Adelman treats at length the fantasy of maternal engulfment evident in the orality of Troilus' imagery. Adelman argues that Cressida is initially presented by the play as a fully realized character but comes to be subsumed by Troilus' ambivalent fantasy of union with the mother. In focusing on the problematic characterization of Cressida rather than on her character — recognizing that Cressida

does not appear as a body here at all, but only as a disembodied experience which nearly defies representation. If the terrifying object of Troilus' desire is an experience beyond the capacity of his "ruder" bodily powers, how could that object *be* a body? Yet it is only in relation to Cressida's body, to her "eyes, her hair, her cheek," that Troilus' desire assumes any shape at all.

The question of Troilus' desire opens up the larger problem of the relation of desire to bodies in the play. Just as Troilus' desire for Cressida structures the love plot through its consummation in III. ii, so the desire of the Greeks for Helen (and the Trojans' desire to keep her) structures the containing action of the Trojan war. The play addresses itself explicitly to the operations of an economy of masculine desire and to the way it produces its objects. The economic nature of this system reveals itself not only through the insistent language of commerce in which desire is articulated in the play, but also in the use of women as objects of exchange mediating the relations among men. Troilus, while on the one hand imagining Cressida in terms which exceed any kind of coherent representation in the body, also conceives of her as a commodity: "Her bed is India; there she lies, a pearl," and of himself as "the merchant, and this sailing Pandar / Our doubtful hope, our convoy and our bark" (I. i. 104, 107–108). In the course of the play, Troilus will obtain his "pearl" only to lose it to another transaction, as Cressida is "changed for Antenor."

Helen, of course, serves as the prototypical object of desire for whom "Every tithe soul, 'mongst many thousand dismes" had died. Like Cressida, Helen is referred to as "a pearl," a commodity within the circuit of exchange, stolen in recompense for "an old aunt whom the Greeks held captive" (II. ii. 77). The theft of Helen for Hesione suggests that the forcible "exchange" of women between Greeks and Trojans might have become an endless cycle of repetition; but Helen is given a peculiar status within this structure of violently competing desires which breaks the repetition. She functions at once as an object of exchange within this economy and also as the transcendent term governing the entire system. She is the pearl "Whose price hath launched above a thousand ships / And turned crowned kings to merchants" (II. ii. 82–83). Though her value is questioned by Hector, and treated as an obscene delusion by Thersites and Diomedes, none of them deserts the struggle for her — even Thersites remains engaged, if only in his voyeuristic fascination with "those that war for a placket" (II. iii. 21). The desire for Helen is the energy that drives the vast enterprise of the war, and to a large extent, therefore, the play. Helen functions as the source of all value because she herself is "inestimable" (II. ii. 88), not to be weighed "in a scale / Of common ounces" (II. ii. 27–28). The Trojans have nothing of comparable value for the Greeks to steal in return; the Greeks can only strive to retrieve what they have lost.

That Helen's value is produced by the economy which she also activates is repeatedly suggested by the play: it is in men's estimations that Helen is "inestimable." In the urgency of his desire for Cressida, Troilus impatiently berates the "fools on both sides"

---

is not quite a character — Adelman illuminates some of the problems of representation in the play in a way that more psychologizing feminist readings of Cressida have not (see note 25 below). Though I have not followed Adelman's own psychological treatment of Troilus' maternal fantasies, my understanding of the play's structure owes a debt to her incisive argument.

with the remark that "Helen must needs be fair, / When with your blood you daily paint her thus" (I. i. 94–95). But though he recognizes Helen's value as a fiction created out of men's willingness to die asserting it, Troilus argues vigorously for keeping Helen. The war is "a quarrel / Which hath our several honors all engaged / To *make* it gracious" (II. ii. 123–125, my emphasis). He sees her value in the effects she produces: "She is a theme of honor and renown, / A spur to valiant and magnanimous deeds . . ." (II. ii. 199–200). Helen's worth is inestimable, absolute, unlimited, but has no basis outside of men's desire for such an object. She becomes the measure (in Troilus' view at least) of the Trojans' capacity to imagine, create, and desire the infinite.

Helen functions purely as a cipher in the world of *Troilus and Cressida,* and it is only as such that she produces her powerful charge. Her absence from Menelaus' bed is the nothing or lack which generates both desire and violence, and which makes possible all value and identity. Her appropriation by the Trojans provides the occasion for the war, essentially a masculine ritual to establish difference: the difference between those who possess and those who lack Helen, the difference between Trojan and Greek, victor and vanquished.

Helen's mystique depends on her equivocal position, simultaneously outside of representation, of what can be "estimated," weighed in "a scale / Of common ounces," and within it, as what can be seen. She is "love's invisible soul," yet enjoyment of her is primarily visual. It is specifically as a sexual object, as a woman "whose youth and freshness / Wrinkles Apollo's and makes pale the morning," that she is prized. In arguing for keeping Helen, Troilus chooses a telling analogy to illustrate the problem of "election" and honor:

> I take today a wife, and my election
> Is led on in the conduct of my will —
> My will enkindled by mine eyes and ears,
> Two traded pilots 'twixt the dangerous shores
> Of will and judgment. How may I avoid,
> Although my will distaste what it elected,
> The wife I chose?

> [II. ii. 61–67]

The analogy, with its insistence on the erratically stimulated "will," suggests that the "election" to steal Helen was similarly a matter of "enkindled" senses. Paris insists that he is not alone in enjoying "The pleasure such a beauty brings with it" (II. ii. 148).

Helen thus becomes the site of a contradiction similar to that which governs Troilus' conception of Cressida. The impossibility of representing what so provokes desire lies partly in the problematic relation of desire to the body. Helen is inestimable in her physical beauty, yet the discourse of desire obsessively reaches beyond literal corporeality. The most corporeal references to Helen describe her not as an object of desire, but as an object of loathing, disgust, and horror. As the empty marker of value in the economy of masculine desire, she is also the black hole which draws all things to it. She is thus conflated at certain moments with the devouring lust and violence which engulf the play, with "the hot digestion of this cormorant war" which "consumes" all "honor, loss of time, travail, expense / Wounds, friends, and what else dear . . ." (II. ii. 3–4). Diomedes describes the "hell of pain and world of charge" Helen has cost:

> For every false drop in her bawdy veins
> A Grecian's life hath sunk; for every scruple
> Of her contaminated carrion weight
> A Trojan hath been slain.
>
> [IV. i. 69–72]

Conceived as a body, as "a flat, taméd piece" (IV. i. 62), Helen can be weighed in the common scale, "estimated" to the last scruple.

The rhetoric of *Troilus and Cressida*, both verbal and theatrical, effects a demystification of the object at its center. This Helen is not Marlowe's "face that launched a thousand ships, / And burnt the topless towers of Ilium," but "a pearl, / Whose price hath launched above a thousand ships, / And turned crowned kings to merchants"; the deflating allusion prevents our participation in Troilus' enthrallment with what he describes. Though Helen is a subject of discussion from the beginning, she is withheld from the audience until Act III, scene i, nearly the middle of the play. When she does appear, she appears precisely as an empty center, a vacuous "Nell" who draws those around her into flirtatious imbecility. This scene — Helen's only appearance in the play — breathes a stale air of insipidity and boredom, its language reduced to fatuous repetition in the ingratiating babble Pandarus speaks to Helen ("Sweet queen, sweet queen, that's a sweet queen, i'faith . . . What says my sweet queen, my very, very sweet queen?") and in her own bathetic effusions: "Let thy song be love. This love will undo us all. O Cupid, Cupid, Cupid!" (III. i. 72–73, 81–82, 111–112).

Through the war for Helen's possession, the play represents the powerful effects she produces as the object of masculine desire. But it also represents her as the vacancy at its center. As long as she is withheld from the stage, the *idea* of Helen ("the mortal Venus, the heartblood of beauty, love's invisible soul") serves, notwithstanding its attendant ironies, to rationalize the play of drives.[6] Her presentation on the stage, however, confronts the spectator with the disparity between the idea and its embodiment in the flesh. This scene has often been treated as a moment of satiric unmasking. S. L. Bethell, for example, sees in it "the theme of 'fair without and foul within,' . . . a remorseless Shakespearean 'debunking'" in which "the real Helen is revealed, the inadequate object of so much misplaced idealism."[7] Such an argument implicitly treats the disparity as an ethical problem, a matter of duplicity, as Bethell's tone of moral censure suggests (he characterizes Helen as "a worthless strumpet"). His "without / within" metaphor and the emphasis on revelation suggest the exposure of an imposture: the "real Helen" (worthless strumpet that she is) is not the *real* Helen.

Could any object be "adequate" to the desires which aggregate around Helen and Cressida? The play reaches toward a more fundamental questioning of the relation

---

[6] Pandarus' confusion over whether these "attributes" belong to Helen or to Cressida (III. i. 35–37) suggests the interchangeability of women as signifiers for the idealized object of desire.

[7] S. L. Bethell, *Shakespeare and the Popular Dramatic Tradition* (London: Staples Press, 1944), rpt. in The Signet Classic edition of *Troilus and Cressida*, p. 233.

between desire and its objects than discussions of the women's "inadequacy" have been able to address. In explicitly portraying the production of objects of desire through "estimation," fantasy, "th'imaginary relish," the play locates desire not in the realm of satiable need, but in the register of the symbolic. Lacan's distinction between *need* (the internal tension which achieves satisfaction in its appropriate object, as for example, the infant's hunger is satisfied with its mother's milk), *demand* (the attempt to articulate and address the need), and *desire*, which resides in the gap between need and demand, between the biological and its symbolic formulation, points to the inherently "excentric and insatiable"[8] nature of desire which is the monstrosity in love:

> [D]esire is situated in dependence on demand — which, by being articulated in signifiers, leaves a metonymic remainder that runs under it, an element that is not indeterminate, which is a condition both absolute and unapprehensible, an element necessarily lacking, unsatisfied, impossible, misconstrued (méconnu), an element that is called desire.[9]

Desire is the drive's mediation through signs, fantasy, "hallucinations," and is maintained in the subject's relation not to bodies — objects — but to signs.[10] The very impossibility of satisfaction through objects, however, makes possible another kind of satisfaction through fantasy: the pleasure of omnipotence in relation to the object. In the absence of an other who might intrude upon the subject's pleasure with other demands, other desires, the subject fantasizes without obstacle. What presents itself as obstacle to the subject's access to the object removes any obstacle to the subject's gratification in fantasy. Instead of being that in which desire is satisfied, the object, subsumed as fantasy, becomes that in which desire is kindled, its signs serving a fetishistic function.[11] In the absence of Cressida's body, Troilus savors in imagination "her eyes, her hair, her cheek . . . ." The conventions of courtly love, represented in *Troilus and Cressida* by the chivalric Trojans, establish the conditions for this fetishization of woman. As Cressida knows, "Men prize the thing ungained more than it is" (I. ii. 301).

"Some obstacle is necessary," writes Freud, "to swell the tide of libido to its height; at all periods of history, wherever natural barriers in the way of satisfaction have not sufficed, mankind has erected conventional ones in order to be able to enjoy love."[12] The lover worships from afar: the inaccessibility of the lady guarantees his enjoyment of her as fantasy object, his enjoyment of his desire, of himself as desirer. Troilus, in

---

[8] Alan Sheridan, "Translator's Note," in Lacan, *Four Fundamental Concepts of Psychoanalysis* (New York: W. W. Norton & Company, 1978), p. 278.

[9] Lacan, *Four Fundamental Concepts*, p. 154.

[10] Freud describes wish fulfillment as a re-cathexis of a "mnemic image" or hallucination of an original "experience of satisfaction" which was biological but is available thereafter only through the mediation of signs. See *The Interpretation of Dreams*, trans. James Strachey (New York: Avon Books, 1965), pp. 604–5.

[11] Sheridan, p. 279, suggests this: "Desire (fundamentally in the singular) is a perpetual effect of symbolic articulation. It is not an appetite: it is essentially excentric and insatiable. That is why Lacan coordinates it not with the object that would seem to satisfy it, but with the object that causes it (one is reminded of fetishism)."

[12] Sigmund Freud, "The Most Prevalent Form of Degradation in Erotic Life" (1912), in *Sexuality and the Psychology of Love*, ed. Philip Rieff (New York: Collier Books, 1963), p. 67.

his longing, invokes a mythic prototype of his desire and a topographical image of his relation to Cressida:

> Tell me, Apollo, for thy Daphne's love,
> What Cressid is, what Pandar, and what we.
> Her bed is India; there she lies, a pearl.
> Between our Ilium and where she resides
> Let it be called the wild and wand'ring flood,
> Ourself the merchant, and this sailing Pandar
> Our doubtful hope, our convoy, and our bark.

(I. i. 103–108]

The "wild and wand'ring flood" suggests both the obstacle barring access to Cressida and the swollen tide of Troilus' passion, a desire that is its own obstacle, an obstacle that swells what it restrains; and it intersects a symbolic landscape mapped out in the language of mercantile venture. Cressida is the rare commodity for which Troilus negotiates, a pearl, a self-enclosed, luminous, petrified sphere. Is Daphne, the petrified woman, the ideal object — forever unavailable as woman, forever available as sign?

Hom(m)o-sexuality: The Circuit of Exchange

This heterosexual economy in which women are pearly commodities intersects another economy in the play, a set of relations for which Luce Irigaray has coined a useful neologism. "The use of and commerce in women subtend and uphold the reign of hom(m)o-sexuality," she writes, "while maintaining it in speculations, mirror games, identifications, appropriations more or less rivalrous, which defer its real practice."[13] The heterosexuality founded on a traffic in women is a mediated homosexuality. While Troilus "cannot come to Cressid but by Pandar" (I. i. 99), Pandar cannot come to Troilus but by Cressid. Pandarus' investment in the transaction complicates the circuit of desire. He reveals his desire in his first scene with Cressida. Cressida's display of indifference to Troilus provokes Pandarus to remark, "Well, Troilus, well, I would my heart were in her body" (I. ii. 80–81). Cressida's body is the means of Pandar's access to Troilus, but the wish that his own heart were in her body suggests a desire for a less mediated relation. He relishes the signs of Troilus' manhood as feverishly as Troilus does Cressida's eyes and hair and cheek: "Mark him, note him. O brave Troilus! Look well upon him niece. Look you how his sword is bloodied, and his helm more hacked than Hector's — and how he looks, and how he goes. O admirable youth!" (I. ii. 239–243). Pandarus prides himself on his knowledge of all the "flowers of Troy," and in providing a running commentary on the military procession, repeatedly asserts his privileged relation to Troilus: "*I'll* show you Troilus anon" (200–201, my emphasis). His exultation bespeaks a vicarious participation in Troilus' glory, a desire to identify and be identified with him: "If he see me, you shall see him nod at me. . . . I could live and die in the eyes of Troilus" (201–202, 251–252). Pandarus' desire is to found his identity in this look, this moment of mutual recognition.

---

[13] Luce Irigaray, "Le marché des femmes," in *Ce sexe qui n'en est pas un* (Paris: Les Éditions de Minuit, 1977), p. 186, translation mine.

This structure of homosexual desire is repeated at the level of the war. The Greeks and Trojans require the mediation of a woman to "come by" one another. Helen serves as the pretext for the war as a whole, establishing the pattern for chivalric encounters which is repeated on a smaller scale. When Hector, angry at Ajax's scornful treatment of him in battle, wishes to meet him in single combat, he gratuitously formulates his challenge as a quarrel over a lady:

> kings, princes, lords,
> If there be one among the fair'st of Greece
> That holds his honor higher than his ease,
> That seeks his praise more than he fears his peril,
> That knows his valor and knows not his fear,
> That loves his mistress more than in confession
> With truant vows to her own lips he loves,
> And dare avow her beauty and her worth
> In other arms than hers — to him this challenge;
> Hector in view of Trojans and of Greeks,
> Shall make it good, or do his best to do it;
> He hath a lady wiser, fairer, truer,
> Than ever Greek did compass in his arms . . .

[I. iii. 264–276]

The pun on "arms" (272) suggests the eroticization of combat: the "other arms" are not only weapons but also the combatants' own arms as they grapple in violent embrace. The challenge thus becomes something of a proposition, a seduction.

Though the amatory pretext for the tournament is never mentioned again, the contest remains charged with a certain eroticism, as it engages both combatants and spectators in a more intimate encounter than is possible on the field of battle. Achilles, titillated at the prospect of full visual access to his Trojan counterpart, sends

> T'invite the Troyan lords after the combat
> To see us here unarmed. I have a woman's longing,
> An appetite that I am sick withal,
> To see great Hector in his weeds of peace,
> To talk with him and to behold his visage,
> Even to my full of view.

[III. iii. 236–241]

In Act IV, scene v, the ritual combat is suggestively anticipated by the ritual kissing of Cressida. The fanfare meant to summon the Trojan challenger to the Greek camp is answered not by the appearance of Hector, but by Diomedes' entrance with Cressida. Ulysses then proposes that Cressida be "kissed in general" and a series of highly formalized encounters ensues, each man prefacing his kiss with a ceremonious or witty comment. Though Cressida is the focus of this moment, she is silent until well into the scene; rather than participating actively in the kissing game, she becomes another feminine pretext for exchanges between men. Patroclus makes her an occasion for insulting Menelaus by usurping "his" kiss with Cressida and, in effect, duplicating the cuckolding of Menelaus by Paris ("for thus popped Paris in his hardiment, / And parted thus you and your argument"). Achilles, in kissing Cressida, takes Nestor's kiss from her lips (IV. v. 24). The titillation of the ritual arises from transactions among men as much as from their encounters with Cressida, an excitement expressed aggressively and competitively. The aggression is finally discharged back onto Cressida in Ulysses' scathing remarks on her wantonness (IV. v. 54–63), of which more shortly.

The men's ritualized kissing of Cressida preludes the ritual exchange of embraces among the men themselves. The long awaited contest between Hector and Ajax is thoroughly anti-climactic, occupying a mere seven lines of text; though its duration on stage may vary in production, its brevity is consistent with the repeated use of anti-climax in the play. The fighting simply provides an occasion for mutual admiration, exchanges of courteous compliments, and embracing. Hector embraces Ajax, Agamemnon embraces Hector, Nestor embraces Hector, Hector embraces Nestor. Like Pandarus, they could all live and die in the eyes of one another. The exchange of recognition and admiration among men narcissistically reinforces their idealized images of themselves as heroes and soldiers "worthy of all arms" (IV. v. 162).

Speculation

It is in the image of their desire that the men in *Troilus and Cressida* constitute their subjectivity, their identity — an image reflected in the object as mirror. The play repeatedly points to a mediation of identity by representation, and particularly by mirroring. In Act III, scene iii Ulysses leads Achilles through an object lesson on reputation, of which the point is that a man "Cannot make boast to have that which he hath, / Nor feels not what he owes but by reflection" (98–99). "How dearly ever parted" a man may be, his disparate "virtues" do not acheive the status of identity "Till he communicates his parts to others" (96, 117). Achilles concurs with this argument:

> This is not strange, Ulysses.
> The beauty that is borne here in the face
> The bearer knows not, but commends itself
> To others' eyes; nor doth the eye itself,
> That most pure spirit of sense, behold itself,
> Not going from itself; but eye to eye opposed
> Salutes each other with each other's form;
> For speculation turns not to itself
> Till it hath traveled and is married there
> Where it may see itself. This is not strange at all.
>
> [III. iii. 103–111]

The recognition by the eye (or "I") of its reflection has been described by Jacques Lacan as "the mirror stage," the "jubilant assumption of his specular image by the child at the infans stage." [14] The story that Lacan tells and the story that Achilles tells are interestingly resonant with one another. Lacan's child, who is "still sunk in his motor incapacity and nursling dependence," experiencing its body only as the fragmented site of heterogeneous sensations, receives from the mirror a gratifyingly unified image of itself with which it then identifies, in effect "misrecognizing" itself in the reflected totality. It is in this mediation of subjective experience by an exterior agency that the

---

[14] Jacques Lacan, "The Mirror Stage," from *Écrits*, trans. Alan Sheridan (New York: W. W. Norton & Company, 1977), p. 2.

"I," the ego, is conceived. The specular moment produces a spectral self, a mirage of wholeness eluding direct experience and accessible only in reflections.

The double-entendre of "speculation" in Achilles' speech reminds us that the apparition of the self materializes within a symbolic matrix.[15] "Speculation" links the act of looking with that of conjecture or evaluation.[16] The self is constituted, according to Ulysses, in the mirror of opinion: one is as one is valued. Ulysses' speculation on speculation is not innocent, of course. He hopes to manipulate Achilles back into battle by persuading him that his price has fallen in the market of men's eyes, that he can become a valued commodity only by emerging from his tent and offering himself to the speculators' gaze, for "The present eye praises the present object" (III. iii. 179). Thus the constitution of the "specular I" in the "drama" of the mirror stage, as Lacan calls it, prefigures the constitution of the "social I" within a particular economy of values.

Not only women, then, but also men are objects produced by "speculation," by "estimation," fragmented "parts" brought into relation by mediating mirrors. Troilus is offered to Cressida through "the glass of Pandar's praise":

> Pandarus. Is not birth, beauty, good shape, discourse, manhood, learning, gentleness, virtue, youth, liberality, and such like, the spice and salt that season a man?
> Cressida. Ay, a minced man . . .
>
> [I. ii. 263–266]

The characters' "parts" or qualities are also textual fragments. Ajax is described by Alexander as a man that "hath robbed many beasts of their particular additions," which he inventories at length, concluding that Ajax "hath the joints of everything, but everything . . . out of joint . . . (I. ii. 19–30). Ajax's disjointedness is partly a matter of his being composed of the "additions" of two literary precursors, the Ajax Telemon and Ajax Oïleus of Homer, additions which are further disseminated through the many medieval retellings of the Troy story.[17] Ulysses "translates" Troilus' virtues to Agamemnon as they have been "translated" to him by Aeneas (IV. v. 96–112), and translated to Shakespeare through Lydgate's *Hystore Sege and Dystruction of Troye*, an English account of the Troy story working primarily from Guido delle Colonne's *Historia Troiana*, which was itself a Latin prose rendering of the French verse of Benoit de Saint-Maure's *Roman de Troie*.[18] The metaphor of the mirroring eye organizes the multiplicity of textual refraction into a more stable specular opposition, though it retains the idea of a mediating representation of the self.

The trope of the eye reflected in the eye is conventional in Renaissance poetry. "It is familiar," as Ulysses says (III. iii. 112), though primarily in a context where the gaze is

---

[15] Ibid.

[16] The *OED* records no specifically commercial use of "speculation" earlier than the eighteenth century, though in the context of this play the word's more general sense of "assessment" takes a commercial form.

[17] See Geoffrey Bullough, *Narrative and Dramatic Sources of Shakespeare* (London: Routledge and Kegan Paul, 1966), VI, 85, 88–89.

[18] Bullough, pp. 83–111, suggests that Ulysses' account of Troilus derives from Lydgate and traces the diverse literary heritage of the *Troilus* material in the whole of his introduction to the sources.

erotic, where lovers "make babies" by reproducing their images in miniature in one another's eyes (as, for example, in Donne's "The Extasie," 11–12). Achilles retains some of the erotic force of the figure in his evocation of marriage in line 110: the moment of self-recognition consummates the union of the self with itself in the mirror of the other. Sexuality and sexual difference come to hold a special place in the narcissistic genesis of identity in the play, for part of what the men desire of women is a stable reflection of themselves.

The integrity of the self is always tenuous in this play, a fiction created by mirrors and easily shattered. The specular I is subject to another effect of the mirror stage, according to Lacan: a retroactive fantasy of the body-in-pieces which appears as a correlation of the alienating ego, an aggressivity arising from that alienation.[19] This impulse is most persistently voiced in the play by Thersites — himself described as a "fragment" (V. i. 8) — in his obsessive anatomizing of the Greek commanders whom he reduces to their constitutive diseases. But this vengeful impulse to fragment comes increasingly in the play to be directed at the women. We see it in Diomedes' verbal dissection of "every scruple" of Helen's "contaminated carrion weight" and in the dissolution of Troilus' vision of Cressida into "fragments, scraps [and] bits" in Act V, scene ii. The instability and fictionality of identity is finally located and exorcized in Cressida.

As the play opens, Troilus experiences his desire for Cressida as lacerating, something which mutilates and emasculates him. He suffers a "cruel battle here within," which "rives his heart in twain," "gashes" him, leaves him "weaker than a woman's tear . . . , / Less valiant than the virgin in the night," "womanish" in his absence from the field (I. i. 9–11, 111). He yearns after Cressida as the object he lacks and needs to complete himself. A "pearl," she exists for him as a luminous opacity, a spherical self-sufficiency, perfectly whole: the image both of what he wishes to possess and of what he wants to become. Paradoxically, though, this fragmenting experience of desire allows for a consolidation of the self in a singleness of aim and an intensity of experience not otherwise available.[20] Troilus luxuriates in his frustration, enumerating the sensations of desire in an infinite expansion and replication of his subjectivity. Cressida is the distant mirror before which he creates himself as lover.

Ticklish Readings

If Cressida represents for Troilus that which he needs to complete him, she comes to be also that against which he defines himself as whole. Once the lovers meet face to face, he speaks no more of a disintegrating passion, no longer seems to fear destruction from the tasting of love's nectar. Instead his constant theme becomes his own "truth" in love. His references to his "truth," "constancy," "integrity," "simplicity," "purity," "plainness," all point to a vision of the self as whole and perfect in its wholeness,

---

[19] "The Mirror Stage," p. 4. I have here used Donald Nicholson-Smith's translation of Lacan's phrase "le corps morcelé" in Laplanche and Pontalis's *The Language of Psychoanalysis* (New York: W. W. Norton & Company, 1973), pp. 251–52.

[20] "*Desidero* is the Freudian *cogito*," writes Lacan, *Four Fundamental Concepts*, p. 154.

untainted by "addition": "Few words to fair faith" (III. ii. 161, 166, 168, 170; IV. iv. 24, 106; III. ii. 97–98). Indeed Troilus sees himself not merely as true, but as *truth*:

> True swains in love shall in the world to come
> Approve their truth by Troilus. When their rhymes,
> Full of protest, of oath and big compare,
> Wants similes, truth tired with iteration,
> "As true as steel, as plantage to the moon,
> As sun to day, as turtle to her mate,
> As iron to adamant, as earth to center,"
> Yet, after all comparisons of truth,
> As truth's authentic author to be cited,
> "As true as Troilus," shall crown up the verse
> And sanctify the numbers.
>
> [III. ii. 173–184]

As "truth's authentic author," Troilus represents himself as a kind of transcendent term toward which language strives, only to exhaust itself in "iteration." He thus seems to place himself outside of any signifying matrix, prior to difference. Yet the speech may also be taken to reveal the dependence of Troilus' "truth" on "simile," on "big compare" — that is, on something less than truth, some difference against which to take shape. In his famous defense of "degree," Ulysses illustrates the dependence of authority on a vast hierarchy of difference without whose "endless jar" right and wrong "should lose their names" (I. iii. 118). Troilus' "truth" must attain its authority and its name in a jarring or play of difference. He finds that difference in Cressida and grafts the opposition of truth and falseness onto sexual difference:

> O that I thought it could be in woman —
> As, if it can, I will presume in you —
> To feed for aye her lamp and flame of love
> . . . .
> Or that persuasion could but thus convince me
> That my integrity and truth to you
> Might be affronted with a match and weight
> Of such a winnowed purity in love:
> How were I then uplifted! But, alas,
> I am as true as truth's simplicity,
> And simpler than the infancy of truth.
>
> [III. ii. 159–171]

Though Troilus makes the hesitant gesture of "presuming" that a woman might transcend her sex to match him in truth, his last three lines here seem to reject the possibility. Rather than serving as the mirror which duplicates him, Cressida now functions as the negative to his positive. Hence the irony that in their vows of fidelity Troilus projects himself in time as the type of truth and Cressida is left to project herself as the pattern of falseness:

> If I be false or swerve a hair from truth,
> When time is old and hath forgot itself,
> When waterdrops have worn the stones of Troy,
> And blind oblivion swallowed cities up,
> And mighty states characterless are grated

To dusty nothing, yet let memory
From false to false among false maids in love,
Upbraid my falsehood! When they've said, "As false
As air, as water, wind or sandy earth,
As fox to lamb, as wolf to heifer's calf,
Pard to the hind, or stepdame to her son,"
Yet let them say, to stick the heart of falsehood,
"As false as Cressid."

[III. ii. 185–197]

This moment requires a certain wrenching of our perspective to accommodate Cressida's speech, which rings oddly in context as the utterance of a woman vowing fidelity to her lover, but fits instead another pattern: the pattern of the story as it is already written. Suddenly the moment of theatrical presence, the eternal now in which drama always occurs, reveals itself scored with the pressure of a narrative tradition in which Cressida's betrayal is always an accomplished fact. Her vision of time as a vast forgetting, a blind oblivion that razes the characters of history — some of the most powerful poetry in the play — arrests our engagement with the movement of events and raises the question "who is speaking?" Though Cressida's "if" nominally locates her within the fiction of a temporal unfolding, the force of the speech lies in the knowledge it shares with the audience: that we are seeing etymology staged.[21] Cressid's voice, like Cassandra's, seems to come from an impossible place, both inside and outside the play. It is the voice of a woman who has read her own story and who recognizes the textuality of her existence: she exists to be the term which puts closure on a literary declension of woman's falseness.[22]

The love plot hinges upon Troilus' betrayal by false Cressida, a moment which not only structures the narrative movement of the play but also provides its crucial reference point. Coleridge was correct, if somewhat obtuse, in writing that the "faithful" and "fervent" love of Troilus and the "sudden and shameless inconstancy" of Cressida provide "the golden thread on which the scenes are strung."[23] Similarly, the war plot is structured by the struggle for false Helen; Thersites describes it as the contest of "those who war for a placket" (II. iii. 19–20). Thersites' obscene metonymic reference to Helen identifies woman as an opening, a gap (a placket is, literally, the opening of a petticoat). What the play intermittently reveals and masks is the dependency of its parallel fables of masculine enterprise on this textual aperture — the feminine absence upon which masculine desire and truth are erected.

Cressida threatens to betray not only Troilus, but *Troilus*. In revealing herself as the creation of a literary tradition, the effect of a textual operation, Cressida discloses the

---

[21] I borrow this phrase from Norman Rabkin, *Shakespeare and the Common Understanding* (New York: The Free Press, 1967), p. 53.

[22] Bullough, p. 97, illustrates the accuracy of Cressida's prophecy, in recording Turbervile's reference to his faithless mistress as "faire Cressid's heire" and this passage from George Whetstone's *Rock of Regard* (1576): "The inconstancie of Cressid is so readie in every mans mouth, as it is a needlesse labour to blase at full her abuse towards yong Troilus, her frowning on Syr Diomede, her wanton lures and love."

[23] S. T. Coleridge, "Strength and Pregnancy of the Gothic Mind," in *Troilus and Cressida: A Casebook*, ed. Priscilla Martin (London: The Macmillan Press Ltd., 1976), p. 41.

ideological tendentiousness of literary codes. Her sexual immodesty is also textual immodesty; she talks too much, she shows and tells. Arnold Stein accuses her of "a kind of gross directness barely disguised."[24] A. P. Rossiter calls her "a chatty, vulgar little piece."[25] Cressid herself recognizes that her value as an object of masculine fantasy requires that she keep herself veiled in mystery, unattainable and unreadable:

> more in Troilus thousandfold I see
> Than in the glass of Pandar's praise may be.
> Yet hold I off. Women are angels, wooing;
> Things won are done, joy's soul lies in the doing.
> That she knows naught that knows not this:
> Men prize the thing ungained more than it is
> . . . .
> Then, though my heart's content firm love doth bear,
> Nothing of that shall from mine eyes appear.
>
> [I. ii. 196–207]

Cressida's desire is to sustain Troilus' desire, but his desire depends upon her masking her own. When Pandarus literally unveils her before Troilus ("Come, draw this curtain, and let's see your picture" [III. ii. 44–45]), she panics at the exposure. She berates herself for speaking her own desire: "See we fools! / Why have I blabbed?" (III. ii. 122–123). She knows that "blabbing" threatens the whole fabric of fantasy upon which idealizing desire depends.

Cressida is not mistaken in her assumption that legibility breeds contempt. The legible woman becomes a degraded object, though an object still for male fantasy, as Ulysses' pronouncement on Cressida demonstrates:

> Fie, fie upon her!
> There's language in her eye, her cheek, her lip;
> Nay, her foot speaks. Her wanton spirits look out
> At every joint and motive of her body.
> O, these encounters, so glib of tongue,
> That give a coasting welcome ere it comes,
> And wide unclasp the tables of their thoughts
> To every ticklish reader, set them down
> For sluttish spoils of opportunity
> And daughters of the game.
>
> [IV. v. 54–63]

This textualization of Cressida's body coincides with an aggressively fragmenting reading of it. Ulysses is repelled by what he sees as her bodily *openness*, the speaking flesh that actively exhibits "spirits" and renders legible "thoughts" — at least to such ticklish readers as himself. Ulysses' contemptuous explication of Cressida's "eye, her cheek, her lip . . . her foot," in obliquely echoing Troilus' ecstatic Petrarchan catalogue of "her eyes, her hair, her cheek, her gait, her voice," underscores the conjunction of titillation and aggression here. The tone of revulsion in this speech coincides with a pruriently detailed *handling* of Cressida's parts (as Pandarus had "handled" her

---

[24] Arnold Stein, "The Disjunctive Imagination," in the *Casebook*, p. 187.
[25] A. P. Rossiter, "*Troilus* as 'Inquisition,'" in the *Casebook*, p. 102.

in his "discourse"), suggesting that Cressida exercises for Ulysses the disturbing fascination of a pornographic text. He is caught by what he sees as a brazen exhibitionism, the spirits *looking* out, soliciting welcome, the tables wide unclasped, awaiting the reader's gaze. A recent analysis of the "direct address" of the pornographic image offers an interesting gloss on Ulysses' experience:

> The very arrangement of the figure in the image re-enforces their [sic] status as designed for "my" look. . . . In porn, there is no way the viewer can fade into the diegesis or, alternatively, shove the responsibility of the discourse onto the author. The viewer is left squarely facing the image without even the semblance of an alibi justifying his or her presence at the other end of that look.[26]

Ulysses' dismissal of Cressida as "sluttish spoils of opportunity" betrays, in its vitriolic excess, a violent dissociation of himself from that which would implicate him as a "ticklish reader."

Feminist critics have attempted to vindicate Cressida from the misogyny of ticklish writers of critical commentary in terms of a psychology of character — an exploration of her motives, an attempt to explain or reconcile her inconstancy and inconsistency by examining her position in a world where women are as they are valued.[27] It is striking, however, how resistant Cressida is to a consistent psychologizing, how frequently she seems to expose the mechanisms of "psychological illusionism."[28] A kind of bizarre textual psychosis seems to voice itself through her; she is a creature of intertextuality, of Chaucer, Lydgate, Caxton, Henryson, and others ("the wanton of tradition," L. C. Knights has called her[29]), endowed with self-consciousness and wondering what makes her do the things she does. She stands in the same relation of exteriority to herself that the critics do, and, like them, speculates on her motives:

> Perchance, my lord, I show more craft than love,
> And fell so roundly to a large confession
> To angle for your thoughts.
>
> [III. ii. 154–156]

She feels she has "a kind of self" that baffles and betrays her, "But an unkind self, that itself will leave / To be another's fool" (III. ii. 149–151). In Act V, scene ii she acts out the scene of betrayal at the center of a concentric structure of voyeurism, Thersites watching Ulysses and Troilus watching Cressida. Their commentaries on her behavior suggest an echo of those narratives in which Cressida has acted out the scene before:

[26] Paul Willemen, "Letter to John," *Screen* 21:2 (1980), 59. Willemen's article is an epistolary reply to John Ellis's "Photography / Pornography / Art / Pornography," *Screen* 21:1 (1980), 81–108.

[27] See Gayle Greene, "Shakespeare's Cressida: 'A kind of self,'" in *The Woman's Part: Feminist Criticism of Shakespeare*, ed. Carolyn Ruth Swift Lenz, Gayle Greene, and Carol Thomas Neely (Urbana: University of Illinois Press, 1980), pp. 133–49. See also Carolyn Asp, "In Defense of Cressida," *Studies in Philology* 74 (1977), 406–17, Grant L. Voth and Oliver H. Evans, "Cressida and the World of the Play," *Shakespeare Studies* 8 (1975), 231–39, and R. A. Yoder, "Sons and Daughters of the Game: An Essay on Shakespeare's *Troilus and Cressida*," *Shakespeare Survey* 25 (1972), 11–25.

[28] Rosalie L. Colie, *Shakespeare's Living Art* (Princeton: Princeton University Press, 1974), p. 326.

[29] L. C. Knights, "The Theme of Appearance and Reality in *Troilus and Cressida*," *Some Shakespearean Themes* (Stanford: Stanford University Press, 1959), p. 69.

Troilus' tragic sense of betrayal echoing Chaucer's sadness, Thersites' scathing misogynist satire recalling Henryson's vindictiveness. Before she leaves the stage for the last time, Cressida becomes a watcher of herself (echoing the pun on eye/I), and in what sounds like an effect of ventriloquism, offers a moralizing comment on "her sex":

> Troilus farewell. One eye yet looks on thee.
> But with my heart the other eye doth see.
> Ah, poor our sex! This fault in us I find,
> The error of our eye directs our mind.
> What error leads must err. O, then conclude,
> Minds swayed by eyes are full of turpitude.
>
> [V. ii. 104–109]

The vertigo produced by this character who is no character, this phantom who is no woman but represents one, is partly voiced by Troilus:

> If there be rule in unity itself,
> This was not she. O madness of discourse
> That cause sets up with and against itself:
> Bifold authority, where reason can revolt
> Without perdition, and loss assume all reason
> Without revolt. This is and is not Cressid.
>
> [V. ii. 138–143]

Troilus' paradox, that the woman he sees "is and is not," suggests the logic of fetishism. The fetish, the visible sign, arises from a moment of traumatic seeing — the boy's glimpse of the woman's body, of what appears to him as her castration and implies the threat of his own. The fetish denies castration by signifying the woman's penis; it allows the fetishist to disavow reality in a partial imitation of psychosis, and retain a fantasy to which the woman is reappropriated as object. But the fetish, by virtue of its being a sign, also signifies what it disavows: it is a representation and not the thing itself. The paradigm of fetishism might usefully be extended here to the play's "madness of discourse," the perceptual oscillation Cressida induces by alternately engaging us in the hallucinations of representation and revealing herself as a trick of signs. Cressida's duplicity is the duplicity of the play itself — "A juggling trick," as Thersites puts it, "to be secretly open" (V. ii. 23).

Troilus, in his initial shock at what he sees, attempts to preserve his illusion, to retain "his" Cressida:

> Sith yet there is a credence in my heart,
> An esperance so obstinately strong,
> That doth invert th'attest of eyes and ears . . .
>
> [V. ii. 117–119]

But the attempt fails. The double vision of Cressida cannot be sustained: it disintegrates into "fractions," "fragments, scraps," and "bits" (V. ii. 155–156).[30] Her final

---

[30] J. Hillis Miller, "Ariachne's Broken Woof," *Georgia Review* 31:1 (1977), 44–60, discusses Troilus' questioning of "the rule in unity itself" as a challenge to "monological metaphysics." He argues that Cressida is the meeting place of two competing systems of signification which cannot be reconciled, exposing as a fiction "the reasonable discourse of Western metaphysics."

appearance in the play, if we can call it that, is as a letter — a complete reduction of woman to text — which Troilus tears and scatters: "Words, words, mere words. . . . Go, wind to wind, there turn and change together" (V. iii. 108, 110).

Cressid's monstrous infidelity provides a rationalizing revision of the disturbing idea of a monstrosity in love, sustaining a fantasy that the monstrous disproportion between desire and its limited realizations can be laid to the insufficiencies of women as objects. The self-idealizing idealism of masculine desire requires that the woman either betray her lover, revealing her inadequacy in her corruption, or die — as Desdemona does — to preserve the lover from enslavement to limit. Troilus wishes to keep his Cressida by separating her from "Diomed's Cressida," the bodily Cressida who can be seen, watched, read. Othello wishfully says to the sleeping Desdemona "I will kill thee, / And love thee after" (V. i. 18–19). The disembodied object, the lost object, cannot obtrude a limiting presence on the fantasy "impelled toward new motion and abstraction," to return to Bruno's words; that object alone can be "truly beautiful without limit or circumspection whatsoever."

Playing The Woman's Part: Feminist Criticism And Shakespearean Performance

Lorraine Helms

Feminist film theorists have revealed ways cinematic representation constructs the female as the object of the male spectator's gaze.[1] Their analyses have raised parallel questions for theatrical and specifically Shakespearean representation: to what extent and through what strategies does Shakespearean performance also construct female characters for the spectator's eye, and, since Shakespearean theatre is as verbal as it is visual, for the auditor's ear? Kathleen McLuskie argues that the representational strategies of the playwright she calls "the patriarchal bard," like cinematic cues, "resist feminist manipulation by denying an autonomous position for the female viewer of the action." Shakespearean texts, bearing the traces of their history in a theatrical enterprise which completely excluded women, construct gender from a relentlessly androcentric perspective. Yet, as McLuskie also remarks, "the gap between textual meaning and social meaning can never be completely filled for meaning is constructed every time the text is reproduced in the changing ideological dynamic between text and audience."[2]

I do not intend to press this analogy between theatre and film, but I draw it in order to underscore my concern with Shakespearean performance. The feminist critique of Shakespearean texts has transformed literary critical interpretation of "the woman's part," but few feminist Shakespeareans have considered the sexual politics

Lorraine Helms, who teaches English and Theatre at Simmons College, is the author of several articles on English Renaissance Drama. She is currently working on The Politics of Shakespearean Feminism: Criticism, Performance, Pedagogy, and Social Change *with Dympna Callaghan and Jyotsna Singh.*

[1]See especially Laura Mulvey's influential essay, "Visual Pleasure and Narrative Cinema," *Screen* 16:3 (1975): 6–18. I find Mary Ann Doane, "Film and the Masquerade: Theorising the Female Spectator," *Screen* 23:3–4 (1982): 74–87, and Annette Kuhn, *The Power of the Image: Essays on Representation and Sexuality* (London: Routlege and Kegan Paul, 1985), particularly suggestive for questions of theatrical representation.

[2]Kathleen McLuskie, "The patriarchal bard: feminist criticism and Shakespeare—*King Lear* and *Measure for Measure*" (93), in *Political Shakespeare: New Essays in Cultural Materialism*, eds. Jonathan Dollimore and Alan Sinfield (Ithaca: Cornell University Press, 1985), 88–108.

of playing that part. My allusion to the anthology *The Woman's Part* will, I hope, further underscore my immediate concern: to extend the feminist critique of Shakespeare to contemporary theatrical practice.[3]

A feminist critique for Shakespearean performance must, as McLuskie argues, acknowledge Shakespeare's androcentric playhouse as the originating context for his representation of gender before seeking a feminist potential within twentieth-century theatre conditions. Yet the convention of the boy actor vexes critical speculation.[4] Cross-casting marks the nexus of character and performer in subtle and shifting ways which historical inquiry cannot recover. The performance of the boy actor could have been eroticized for some spectators, aesthetically distanced for others. It could have been illusionistic at one moment, only to be broken by self-reflexive theatricality at another, as the textual references to the boy actor playing the woman's part in *Antony and Cleopatra* and *As You Like It* suggest. Its ideological valence is ambiguous. It could foreground the social construction of gender by imposing femininity on male bodies and at the same time trivialize women's social roles in puerile caricatures. It could celebrate female heroism while it excluded women from the economic and expressive opportunities of theatrical activity. Certainly the theatrical convention resonates with the cultural practices of a patriarchal society in which women shared their children's disenfranchisement. The boy actor playing Rosalind obliquely comments on this disenfranchisement when he remarks that "Boys and women are for the most part cattle of this color."[5] Yet the theatrical effect of his having said it remains elusive.

But in the social contexts and physical settings of twentieth-century Shakespeare productions, women play "the woman's part." To what extent does this re–casting transform the cultural resonances of Shakespeare's construction of gender? Elaine Showalter argues optimistically that "when Shakespeare's heroines began to be played by women instead of boys, the presence of the female body and female voice, quite apart from details of interpretation, created new meanings and subversive tensions in these roles."[6] Less optimistic (or more radical) critics of the dramatic canon have argued that female roles originally written by men for male performers—the Medeas and Antigones of the Greek theatre as well as the Rosalinds and Cleopatras

---

[3]*The Women's Part: Feminist Criticism of Shakespeare*, eds. Carolyn Ruth Swift Lenz, Gayle Greene, and Carol Thomas Neely (Urbana: University of Illinois Press, 1980).

[4]Discussions of the boy actor include Juliet Dusinberre, *Shakespeare and the Nature of Women* (London: Macmillan, 1975); Lisa Jardine, *Still Harping on Daughters* (Brighton: Harvester, 1983); Phyllis Rackin, "Androgyny, Mimesis, and the Marriage of the Boy Heroine on the English Renaissance Stage," *PMLA* 102:1 (1987), 29–41; and Sue-Ellen Case, *Feminism and Theatre* (New York: Methuen, 1988). See also my "Roaring girls and silent women: the politics of androgyny on the Jacobean stage," in *Women in Theatre*, ed. James Redmond (London: Cambridge University Press, 1989) and " 'Marina thus the Brothel 'Scapes': The Senecan Rhetoric of Rape in Shakespeare's *Pericles*" (forthcoming).

[5]*As You Like It*, III, iii. 414–415. Quotations from Shakespeare are from *The Riverside Shakespeare* (Boston: Houghton Mifflin, 1974). Subsequent references to this edition will be cited in the text.

[6]Elaine Showalter, "Representing Ophelia: women, madness, and the responsibilities of feminist criticism" (80), in *Shakespeare and the Question of Theory*, eds. Patricia Parker and Geoffrey Hartman (New York: Metheun, 1985), 77–94.

of Shakespeare's—are caricatures, and that they should again be played by men to emphasize the fact that the classic roles are, in Sue-Ellen Case's phrase, "classic drag."[7]

Now for a feminist who wishes to make her living in the theatre, Showalter's view has certain obvious attractions. Yet the feminization of the boy actor is the theatrical strategy through which the Shakespearean representation of gender was structured; a feminist critique must confront its residual effects. Theatre historians regularly attribute the paucity and brevity of Shakespearean women's roles to the inadequacy (or the expense) of the apprenticed boy players. They have not as often remarked that female characters rarely appear unaccompanied by males. Stage practice does not in this simply mime social restrictions on women's freedom of movement, but reveals its dependence on the narrowed range of difference at its disposal. The all-male acting company contrasts the boy and the mature male to create the illusion of female presence. To leave a boy actor alone on stage is to relinquish the difference on which his feminization partly depends. At such moments, poetic, rhetorical, and narrative strategies must accomplish what the presence of the adult actor does in other scenes: they must maintain the female persona by dominating the impersonator.

Such textual strategies, originally designed to feminize the boy actor, may infantilize or eroticize the woman who now plays the woman's part. Showalter's promise of feminist re-interpretation will not automatically be fulfilled. To create "new meanings and subversive tensions" in Shakespearean roles demands specific strategies for intervention. These strategies must interrogate the ideological continuity between apparently antithetical theatrical practices. The twentieth century, like the seventeenth, still divides humanity into men on the one hand and women and children on the other. The patriarchal structures which hierarchize physical and social distinctions between male and non-male characterize contemporary cultures as well as Shakespeare's. The actor who wants to play Shakespeare's female characters without playing parts scripted by a "patriarchal bard" must confront the linguistic recalcitrance of the Shakespearean construction of gender.

The Gendered Subjects Of Shakespearean Soliloquy

Shakespearean verse, as John Barton remarks, gives the actor "stage directions in shorthand." He offers examples throughout *Playing Shakespeare:* monosyllables demand more rapid delivery; shared lines tell the actor to pick up the cue.[8] Such stage directions create individuated patterns of speech and structure representation of the social categories of class and gender. They are perhaps most subtly directorial in soliloquies. Soliloquy, by convention, allows an actor to establish a privileged relation to the audience, either to tell the character's side of the story by creating the illusion

---

[7]Sue-Ellen Case, "Classic Drag: The Greek Creation of Female Parts," *Theatre Journal* 37 (1985): 317–27. See also the opening chapter of her *Feminism and Theatre*.

[8]John Barton, *Playing Shakespeare* (London: Metheun, 1984). The book is based on a series of videotaped workshop programs which the Royal Shakespeare Company made in 1982 for London Weekend Television.

of interiority or to restructure the theatrical event by breaking through the dramatic fiction. But Shakespeare's female characters are rarely alone on stage and even more rarely do they address the audience directly. When they do, the conventions of the soliloquy are regularly adapted to the female character, revealing the extent to which the Shakespearean soliloquy is ordinarily gendered as male.[9]

In *Hamlet* and *Macbeth*, the protagonist's soliloquies provide an internal analogue to the unfolding of the plot. They not only focus audience response on the speaker, but direct it toward his interpretation of events. But throughout Ophelia's soliloquy after the nunnery scene, Hamlet remains before the audience: "O, what a noble mind is here o'erthrown!" (III. i. 150). When Lady Macbeth is alone on stage, Macbeth remains before the audience, as she reads a letter from him and then turns to apostrophe: "Glamis thou art, and Cawdor, and shalt be / What thou art promis'd" (I. v. 15–16). The subjectivity of the female characters, even in soliloquy, is, for the audience, mediated through their shared concentration on the male protagonist. The text insistently interposes a male presence between the female speaker and the auditor.

Comic soliloquies deploy quite different strategies and seem to offer greater possibilities for feminist intervention. In *A Midsummer Night's Dream*, Helena addresses the audience directly:

> How happy some o'er other some can be!
> Through Athens I am thought as fair as she.
> But what of that? Demetrius thinks not so.
> He will not know what all but he do know;
> And as he errs, doting on Hermia's eyes,
> So I, admiring of his qualities.
>
> [I. i. 226–231]

End-stopped couplets replace the normal blank verse of the Shakespearean soliloquy. Their self-conscious artifice, through which Helena analyzes her situation so shrewdly and articulates it so cleverly, can, in performance, effect her transformation from a greensick girl into a commentator who interrogates the vagaries of erotic experience. This transformation plays on the soliloquy's power to privilege Helena's relation to the audience and yet distances the actor from the character. It creates an opportunity for the "gestic feminist criticism" which Elin Diamond calls for, a Brechtian practice which would "foreground those moments in a playtext in which social attitudes could be made visible."[10]

A similar prosodic device appears in *Troilus and Cressida*. Like Helena, Cressida addresses the audience on the subject of the ephemeral nature of male desire. But

---

[9]The most recent full-length study of the Shakespearean soliloquy, Wolfgang Clemen, *Shakespeare's Soliloquies* (London: Metheun, 1987), does not employ gender as a category of analysis.

[10]Elin Diamond, "Brechtian Theory/Feminist Theory: Toward a Gestic Feminist Criticism" (91), *The Drama Review: A Journal of Performance Studies* 32:1 (1988), 82–94. In conjunction with Margot Heinemann, "How Brecht read Shakespeare" (*Political Shakespeare*, 202–30), Diamond's "gestic feminist

when Cressida articulates her love and her despair in rhymed couplets, prosodic and syntactical strategies simultaneously construct, delimit, and subvert the subjectivity of the female speaker:

> Words, vows, gifts, tears, and love's full sacrifice,
> He offers in another's enterprise,
> But more in Troilus thousandfold I see
> Than in the glass of Pandar's praise may be.

[I. ii. 282–285]

Why, in this speech, do rhymed couplets, sometimes in feminine rhyme, replace blank verse? Does their calculated artificiality serve mimetically to represent the coquetry which patriarchal criticism attributes to Cressida? Do they heighten a pleasure which the actor is to offer by playing Cressida in the posture of a whore? Shakespeare's versified stage directions, it would then appear, undermine the rhetorical force of the character's argument. They provide a sort of linguistic analogue to cosmetics; they warn the audience that this is not an honest woman. Thus the Shakespearean script exploits Cressida's speech to tell Troilus's tale of feminine treachery rather than her own story of male violence. Discursive strategies recuperate the subversive potential of the speech, turning Cressida's analysis of male desire into a source of eroticized aesthetic pleasure for the male auditor. Even in soliloquy, Cressida remains an object of desire and disdain.

The syntax of the speech as well as its rhyme contains stage directions which further diminish the performer's opportunity to communicate directly to the audience. The formal structure of Cressida's speech, like Helena's in its prosody, differs strikingly in its syntax. Helena's soliloquy parodies a scholastic Petrarchism in its analysis of desire:

> Things base and vile, holding no quantity,
> Love can transpose to form and dignity.
> Love looks not with the eyes but with the mind;
> And therefore is wing'd Cupid painted blind.
> Nor hath Love's mind of any judgement taste;
> Wings, and no eyes, figure unheedy haste;
> And therefore is Love said to be a child,
> Because in choice he is so oft beguil'd.
> As waggish boys themselves in games forswear,
> So the boy Love is perjur'd everywhere.

[I. i. 232–241]

Helena's argument is articulated with comically pedantic clarity. But Cressida's argument against male hegemony, which is equally knotty and more profoundly subversive, is aphoristic and obscured by ellipses:

criticism" suggests a range of possibilities for feminist Shakespearean performance that I hope to explore more fully in the future. See also Griselda Pollack, "Screening the seventies: sexuality and representation in feminist practice—a Brechtian perspective," 155–99 in her *Vision and Difference: Femininity, Feminism, and the Histories of Art* (London: Routledge, 1988).

> Women are angels, wooing:
> Things won are done, joy's soul lies in the doing.
> That she belov'd knows naught that knows not this:
> Men prize the thing ungain'd more that it is.
> That she was never yet that ever knew
> Love got so sweet as when desire did sue.
> Therefore this maxim out of love I teach:
> Achievement is command; ungain'd, beseech.

[I. ii. 286–293]

While the artificiality of rhymed couplets works against the actor who tries to motivate a character who can tell her own story, the obscurity of this elliptical syntax works against the actor who tries to use the speech to comment on the dramatic fiction. Shakespeare's stage directions impede feminist revision in both naturalistic and gestic modes.

If a feminist re-interpretation of *Troilus and Cressida* is to succeed theatrically, the performer must find ways to re-interpret these stage directions. Patriarchal literary criticism has assumed Cressida's vanity and duplicity, while feminist re-readings have argued for her intelligence and vulnerability.[11] Although literary analysis of Cressida's soliloquy can work through the androcentric text toward a feminist reading, it leaves theatrical practice with as patriarchal a bard as ever. Vanity and duplicity at least offer a theatrically viable motive for action. A feminist re-interpretation must discover performance choices which offer as much scope for motivated activity as showing off. The actor must transpose the mimetic foundation of Cressida's language into another key.

Yet what could Cressida's motivation be when the ellipses occlude the female subject: It is the soul of male joy that lies in the doing; it is male achievement and male command to which Cressida refers, while she herself is one of the "things" to be won and done. Cressida is already speaking from the androcentric perspective which she will more fully internalize at the end of the play. In her last speech, her alienation is complete, and with it, the actor's options for consciously motivated action are further narrowed.

This second speech, again in rhymed couplets, occurs after the eavesdropping scene, in which Thersites spies on Troilus and Ulysses as they watch Diomedes force Cressida, through symbolic and perhaps physical violence, into sexual submission:

> Troilus, farewell! One eye yet looks on thee,
> But with my heart the other eye doth see.
> Ah, poor our sex! this fault in us I find,
> The error of our eye directs our mind.
> What error leads must err; O then conclude,
> Minds sway'd by eyes are full of turpitude.

[V. ii. 107–112]

---

[11]Feminist defenses of Cressida include R. A. Yoder, " 'Sons and Daughters of the Game': An Essay on Shakespeare's *Troilus and Cressida*," *Shakespeare Survey* 25 (1972): 11–25; Gayle Greene, "Shakespeare's Cressida: 'A kind of self' " in *The Woman's Part*, 133–49; and Arlene N. Okerlund,

These lines make sense from Troilus's perspective, from Ulysses' or Thersites', but not from Cressida's. Such de-centering renders this speech among the most difficult to perform in the Shakespearean canon; it also presents perhaps the greatest challenge to a feminist performance. Janet Adelman argues that, during the eavesdropping scene, the text has moved suddenly and inexplicably "into opacity . . . at exactly the moment at which we most need to understand what Cressida is doing, we are not only given no enlightenment but are forced to acknowledge our distance from Cressida by the structure of the scene itself." An actor will, she concludes, have to speculate on Cressida's motives "in order to play the part at all," but such speculation cannot be grounded in the text.[12]

What are Shakespeare's versified stage directions? Although the speech is delivered at a moment of intense emotion, that emotion is mediated by rhymed couplets which echo those of the earlier speech. This formal repetition implies a continuity of character that may undermine Troilus's interpretation of Cressida's inconstancy: "This is, and is not, Cressid" (V. ii. 146). Yet Cressida's words renew and deepen the alienation of the "Women are angels" soliloquy. They announce her collusion with the ideology Thersites offers as commentary on her speech: "A proof of strength she could not publish more, / Unless she said, 'My mind is now turn'd whore' " (V. ii. 113–114). Can the contradiction between the violence Cressida suffers and the blame she accepts create a space for a feminist performance as it has for a feminist literary criticism? What are the performance choices? Is there a motive which would subvert the androcentric perspective of the speech? Or a gest which would foreground the social contexts from which the character's alienation arises?

Cressida's soliloquies illustrate the technical and theoretical problems which a feminist theatrical practice encounters in re-interpreting "the patriarchal bard." Can one suit the action to the word if the word subverts the speaker? The 1987 Stratford, Ontario production resolved the dilemma in favor of the action. In the eavesdropping scene, in which the audience sees Thersites watch Troilus and Ulysses spy on Diomedes and Cressida, Diomedes subjected Cressida to relentless symbolic violence, intermittently underscored by physical menace. He left Cressida so near hysteria that when she came to her soliloquy, the words were virtually unintelligible. The text of Cressida's collusion gave way before an image which represented the terror of rape as forcefully as Gloucester's on-stage blinding represents the horror of mutilation.

"In defense of Cressida: character as metaphor," *Women's Studies* 7 (1980): 1–17. See also my " 'Still Wars and Lechery': Shakespeare and the Last Trojan Woman," in *Arms and the Woman: Feminist Essays on War, Gender, and Literary Representation*, eds. Helen Cooper, Adrienne Munich, and Susan Squier (Greensboro: University of North Carolina Press, 1989).

[12]Janet Adelman, " 'This Is and Is Not Cressida': The Characterization of Cressida" (128), in *The (M)other Tongue: Essays in Feminist Psychoanalytic Interpretation*, eds. Shirley Nelson Garner, Claire Kahane, and Madelon Sprengnether (Ithaca: Cornell University Press, 1985), 119–41. See also Linda Berning Labranche, *The Theatrical Dimension of* Troilus and Cressida. Diss. Northwestern University, 1984. Ann Arbor: UMI, 1984 (8502394). In " 'Still Wars and Lechery': Shakespeare and the Last Trojan Woman," I argued that the language of Cressida's submission reveals a subtext of resistance; my concern here is with performance choices that will make such a subtext theatrically effective.

The Ontario production exposed Cressida's victimization at the price of her silence. her inarticulate hysteria deconstructed the patriarchal representation of a vain and shallow coquette, but did not in itself foreground the social attitudes and circumstances which structure sexual victimization. Troilus's response to the scene, however, in some measure completed Cressida's gest. His self-indulgent grieving for what he willfully interpreted as Cressida's faithlessness went extravagantly over the top. The audience had just seen a rape scene; they now saw patriarchal ideology at work as Troilus bustled about blaming the victim: "The fractions of her faith, orts of her love, / The fragments, scraps, the bits and greasy relics / Of her o'er-eaten faith, are given to Diomed" (V. ii. 158–160). Such theatrical moments may move spectators from empathy to anger.

Having praised the Ontario staging of the eavesdropping scene, I must also remark that the program notes do not affirm the interpretation for which I praised it: "No sooner has Troilus won Cressida than they are parted and, despite her desperate protests, she is sent to join her father in the Greek camp. There, confused and susceptible in her new womanhood, she is quickly seduced by Diomedes."[13] A similar gap between program notes and theatrical performance characterizes another recent Shakespearean production in which, again, soliloquy focuses the tension between an androcentric playtext and a performable feminist critique.

How The Jailer's Daughter Escaped

Fletcher and Shakespeare's *The Two Noble Kinsmen* represents or evokes fourteen female characters. The three principals are Hippolyta, the Amazon queen who Theseus has conquered in a single combat; her sister Emilia, whose love for women underscores her suffering when Theseus orders her to marry the survivor of Palamon and Arcite's duel; and the nameless Jailer's Daughter, who fulfills her dramatic function in the main plot when she releases Palamon from her Father's prison and fulfills her function in the sub plot when, mad for unrequited love of the knight whom she has freed, she is seduced and thereby cured by a suitor who sleeps with her pretending to be Palamon. The text, like other texts of "the patriarchal bard," constructs these characters from a masculinist perspective which celebrates Hippolyta's defeat in her combat with Theseus, which validates Emilia's brutally forced marriage, and which mocks the sexuality of the Jailer's Daughter. Yet in contemporary performance, the female characters of *The Two Noble Kinsmen* may challenge the patriarchal perspectives of the text.

The Two Noble Kinsmen has only recently been rescued from long oblivion in Beaumont and Fletcher's *Collected Works*. In 1980, Glynne Wickham set the play in the homoerotic context of the Jacobean court, remarking that Theseus's love for Pirithous had "an all-too-evident counterpart" in James's relation to his favorite, Robert Carr, Earl of Somerset.[14] In 1985, Richard Abrams further questioned the play's sexual

---

[13]In this production, directed by David William, Cressida was played by Peggy Coffey, Diomedes by Lorne Kennedy, and Troilus by Jerry Etienne. The program notes are unsigned.

[14]Glynne Wickham, "The Two Noble Kinsmen or *A Midsummer Night's Dream*, Part II?" (183), in *Elizabethan Theatre* VII, ed. George Hibbard (Hamden: Archon Books, 1980), 167–96.

politics, noting that it is "with each other's fantasies, rather than Emilia's, that Palamon and Arcite, [who call themselves] 'one another's wife,' obviously interlock" and that Emilia's own "stated sexual preference is for other women."[15] In 1986, Barry Kyle's production at the Swan in Stratford and then at the Mermaid in London gave *The Two Noble Kinsmen* a place in the repertory of the Royal Shakespeare Company, extending these questions of the play's sexual politics to their significance for twentieth-century audiences. As *The Two Noble Kinsmen* enters the academic and theatrical arenas where the contemporary meanings of Shakespeare are contested, it offers new perspectives on the relation between the scope of feminist criticism and the tasks of theatrical representation.

The elite cultural contexts of *The Two Noble Kinsmen* focus literary critical interpretation on the setting of Theseus' court. The duel between Palamon and Arcite for possession of Emilia and her torment thereby become the play's most significant representation of the physical and symbolic violence which underlie the exchange of women. A feminist critique of this exchange can recognize, with Richard Abrams, that "the play's deepest conflict is not between the kinsmen, but between Theseus, as patriarchal ruler of Athens, and Emilia as representative of 'the powers of all women' " (Abrams, 74 [III. vi. 194]). Yet the narrative resolution of Emilia's story reveals its significance most fully when it resonates theatrically with the representation of the Jailer's Daughter, for this character, a crazed and nameless victim in the text, can command an extraordinary presence on stage—a presence which undermines both androcentric and elitist interpretations of the playtext. In resisting heterosexuality, Emilia exposes the symbolic violence of dynastic marital rites; in contesting the barriers to the marriage she desires, the Jailer's Daughter illuminates the intersecting hierarchies of class and gender.

The plot demands the sexual humiliation of the Jailer's Daughter, and it is this aspect of her role that the Royal Shakespeare Company program notes chose to underscore: they place the Jailer's Daughter among Shakespeare's "wanton wenches from the lower orders who give rein to their sexual appetites" and who are "contrasted with high-born ladies who put a proper price on their own virginity." She "is less a mad sister to Ophelia than a tragi-comic version of the all-too available Jaquenetta in *Love's Labour's Lost*—or perhaps a sort of siamese twin from *As You Like It*, combining the honest earthiness of Audrey with the pretensions of poor Phebe, likewise fobbed-off with an inferior substitute for daring to fall in love beyond her social station."[16]

Like the Ontario production of *Troilus and Cressida*, the Royal Shakespeare Company production of *The Two Noble Kinsmen* belied the sexism and elitism that the commentary attributed to the playtext, for Imogen Stubbs, as the Jailer's Daughter, created a heroic figure who was at once socially marginal and theatrically central. The text invites this conflict between the social structures it seems to reinforce and its own

---

[15]Richard Abrams, "Gender confusion and sexual politics in *The Two Noble Kinsmen*" (71 and 69), in *Drama, Sex, and Politics*, ed. James Redmond (London: Cambridge University Press, 1985), 69–76.

[16]*The Two Noble Kinsmen by William Shakespeare and John Fletcher: A programme/text with commentary by Simon Trussler* (London: Methuen, 1987), xvii.

theatrical strategies, for Fletcher and Shakespeare give the Jailer's Daughter four soliloquies. The first, in II. iii, opens with an analysis of the barriers she faces in her quest for Palamon's love:

> Why should I love this gentleman? 'Tis odds
> He never will affect me; I am base,
> My father the mean keeper of his prison,
> And he a prince. To marry him is hopeless;
> To be his whore it witless. Out upon't!
> What pushes are we wenches driven to
> When fifteen once has found us!
>
> [II. iv. 1–7]

To combat the disadvantages of class and gender, she must challenge both political and domestic order:

> What should I do to make him know I love him,
> For I would fain enjoy him? Say I ventur'd
> To set him free? what says the law then?
> Thus much for law or kindred! I will do it,
> And this night, or to-morrow, he shall love me.
>
> [II. iv. 29–33]

She frees Palamon and sends him, still in chains, to hide in a nearby wood until she comes to bring him files and food. The second soliloquy begins with a cry of triumph:

> Let all the Dukes and all the devils roar,
> He is at liberty! I have ventur'd for him.
> . . . .
>   If the law
> Find me, and then condemn me for't, some wenches,
> Some honest-hearted maids, will sing my dirge,
> And tell to memory my death was noble,
> Dying almost a martyr.
>
> [II. vi. 1–2, 13–17]

In the third soliloquy, she realizes that Palamon will not keep their meeting in the wood. Fearful that he has fallen prey to the wolves she hears howling nearby, her struggle for her sanity begins:

> My father's to be hang'd for his escape,
> Myself to beg, if I priz'd life so much
> As to deny my act, but that I would not,
> Should I try death by dozens. I am mop'd:
> Food took I none these two days—
> Sipp'd some water. I have not clos'd mine eyes
> Save when my lids scoured off their [brine]. Alas,
> Dissolve, my life, let not my sense unsettle
> Lest I should drown, or stab, or hang myself.
>
> [III. ii. 22–30]

Her last soliloquy is delivered after she has gone mad:

> I am very cold, and all the stars are out too,
> The little stars and all, that look like aglets.

> The sun has seen my folly. Palamon!
> Alas, no; he's in heaven. Where am I now?

[III. iv. 1–4]

In Cressida's speeches, versified stage directions contain the representation of female subjectivity to recuperate patriarchal ideology; in these four soliloquies, as in Hamlet's and Macbeth's, they create an internal analogue to the action of the plot. Interrogative sentences, resolutions, and narrative speculations all reinforce a mode of direct address; and direct address offers an opportunity either to communicate a character's interiority or to comment on the scene.

Shakespeare more often extends this opportunity to his Hamlets than his Ophelias, and indeed, textual scholarship often attributes these soliloquies to Fletcher rather than to Shakespeare.[17] If this is true, then Fletcher, having been the collaborator of "the patriarchal bard," can now become the collaborator of feminist Shakespeareans. When the actor who plays the Jailer's Daughter truly seizes her opportunity, the audience cannot easily dismiss her character as "a wanton wench from the lower orders" punished for failing to know her place or control her sexual appetites.

In the Royal Shakespeare Company production, Imogen Stubbs's performance fully realized the desperate heroism of the Jailer's Daughter. The actor's intelligence granted dignity to the character's erotic energy and her vulnerability made that dignity poignant. Perhaps most importantly, Stubbs is also an athlete. During her mad scenes, her skill enabled her to climb a flagpole and to cross downstage walking on her hands while singing. Such explicitly theatrical actions charge the nexus of performer and character with an extraordinary vitality. They compel spectators to acknowledge that the physical presence of the performer constitutes the fictional character on stage; they insist that a character in a play is, as Michael Goldman argues, "something an actor *does*."[18] When the Jailer's Daughter was realized as the enactment of Imogen Stubbs, the performer's skill and strength turned the madness of the Jailer's Daughter, not, like Ophelia's, to prettiness, but to power.

This power can refract the ideology of the Shakespearean playtext, expanding the strategies through which a feminist critique of Shakespeare can intervene in theatrical practice. This feminist critique may explore alternatives to the performance choices, tasks, and motivations by which masculinist productions have trivialized or demonized female characters; it may investigate more radical revisions through alienation effects, applying Diamond's gestic feminist criticism to the Shakespearean playtext. And it may also applaud the performer whose special skills can destabilize power relations in both the dramatic fiction and the theatrical space. Through such explorations and affirmations, feminist Shakespeareans may begin to create a theatre where patriarchal representations of femininity can be transformed into roles for living women.

---

[17]Paul Bertram argues for Shakespeare's authorship in *Shakespeare and* The Two Noble Kinsmen (New Brunswick, New Jersey: Rutgers University Press, 1965), but the scenes in which the soliloquies of the Jailer's Daughter occur are more commonly attributed to Fletcher. For a concise summary of the debate, see Hallett Smith's introduction to the play in the Riverside edition.

[18]Michael Goldman, *Acting and Action in Shakespearean Tragedy* (Princeton: Princeton University Press, 1985), 149.

Anti-Historians:
Women's Roles in Shakespeare's Histories

Phyllis Rackin

Historiography is a major concern in Shakespeare's history plays. Characters repeatedly allude to history, past and future, and define their actions as attempts to inscribe their names in the historical record. Like their playwright, these characters show an obsessive concern with the work of the historian — the writing, reading, and preservation of historical texts.

No woman is the protagonist in a Shakespearean history play. Renaissance gender role definitions prescribed silence as a feminine virtue, and Renaissance sexual mythology associated the feminine with body and matter as opposed to masculine intellect and spirit. Renaissance historiography constituted a masculine tradition, written by men, devoted to the deeds of men, glorifying the masculine virtues of courage, honor, and patriotism, and dedicated to preserving the names of past heroes and recording their patriarchal genealogies. Within that historical record, women had no voice.

The protagonists of Shakespeare's history plays, conceived both as subjects and as writers of history, were inevitably male. The women who do appear are typically defined as opponents and subverters of the historical and historiographic enterprise — in short, as anti-historians. But Shakespeare does give them a voice — a voice that challenges the logocentric, masculine historical record.[1] For the most part, and especially in his early histories, Shakespeare depicts male protagonists defending

Phyllis Rackin teaches English at the University of Pennsylvania. Her publications include Shakespeare's Tragedies *(New York: Ungar, 1978) and numerous essays on Shakespeare and literary theory. This essay grows out of her long-standing interests in Renaissance historiography and in gender construction in early modern England. An expanded version will appear in her new book on Shakespeare's English history plays to be published by Cornell University Press in 1990.*

[1] See Linda Woodbridge, *Women and the English Renaissance: Literature and the Nature of Womankind, 1540–1620* (Urbana: University of Illinois Press, 1984), p. 208: "Women's tongues are instruments of aggression or self-defense; men's are the tools of authority. In either case speech is an expression of authority; but male speech represents legitimate authority, while female speech attempts to usurp authority or rebel against it."

masculine historical projects against both female characters who threaten to obstruct those projects and feminine appeals to the audience that threaten to discredit them. In Shakespeare's later history plays those feminine voices become more insistent. They both threaten to invalidate the great, inherited historical myths that Shakespeare found in his historiographic sources and imply that before the masculine voice of history can be accepted as valid, it must come to terms with women and the subversive forces they represent. However, as soon as Shakespeare attempts to incorporate those feminine forces, marrying words and things, spirit and matter, historiography itself becomes problematic, no longer speaking with the clear, univocal voice of unquestioned tradition but re-presented as a dubious construct, always provisional, always subject to erasure and reconstruction, and never adequate to recover the past in full presence.

In this paper I will focus on the roles of women in two plays, beginning with *1 Henry VI*, the first of Shakespeare's English history plays, where the pattern of masculine history-writing and feminine subversion can be seen in its simplest terms. Here Shakespeare contrives his action to subvert the subversive female voices and ratify the masculine version of the past. Then I want to look at a curious episode in *King John*, a play in which Shakespeare exposes the historical record as a fragile and dubious construct, as mortal as the king it describes, a "scribbled form, drawn with a pen upon a parchment," shrinking up against the fires of mutability (V. vii. 32–35).[2] In this play, women's roles are more various and prominent than in any of Shakespeare's other English histories, and their subversive power to undermine the masculine historical project is most fully revealed.

The pattern of masculine history-writing and feminine subversion is probably clearest in *1 Henry VI.* Here Shakespeare defines the project of writing English history as an effort to preserve the legacy of English glory left by Henry V and associates it with the masculine, military struggle to secure English power in France. Michel Foucault's observation that the Greek epic "was intended to perpetuate the immortality of the hero" aptly characterizes Shakespeare's conception of history at this point in his career. In Foucault's view, the hero's death represents a kind of trade-off between the hero and his story: "if he was willing to die young, it was so that his life, consecrated and magnified by death, might pass into immortality."[3]

The process by which human mortality is translated into textual immortality was a frequent theme for Renaissance theorists of historiography as well as for Shakespearean sonnets. However, a problem arises — as it did for historians during Shakespeare's own lifetime — when history, the second party to this trade, comes to be seen as itself subject to mutability. Various forces were conspiring in Shakespeare's time to compel a recognition that the historical past was not necessarily identical with the historiographic text. Faced with a growing sense of alienation from the past, a

[2] William Shakespeare, *King John*, ed. E. A. J. Honigmann, Arden edition (London: Methuen, 1967). All subsequent citations will be from this edition and will be noted in the text.

[3] Michel Foucault, "What is an Author," in *Textual Strategies: Perspectives in Post-Structuralist Criticism*, ed. Josué V. Harari (Ithaca: Cornell University Press, 1979), p. 142.

newly critical attitude toward texts, and an increasing reliance on physical remains to verify or refute verbal reports, the medieval union of history and myth was breaking down.[4] Written accounts of the past were no longer accepted as authentic simply because they existed. Like the Bible itself, historical writing no longer had a direct, unequivocal relation to truth. Translated into the vernacular, subjected to different interpretations from rival Christian sects, the Bible had become a problematic document in which alternative words contended to translate the meaning of the original text and alternative interpretations contended to explicate it. In a similar way, alternative accounts of historical events and opposed interpretations of their causes and significance now threatened to disrupt each other's authority. Thus undermined, history loses its power to make the hero immortal. In such a case, the hero's death becomes meaningless, and heroism itself becomes impossible.

This is the problem dramatized in *1 Henry VI*. The play begins as history itself begins, with (or immediately following) the death of the hero. The opening scene depicts the funeral of Henry V, the legendary warrior-king who was, we are told, "too famous to live long" (I. i. 6);[5] and the entire play can be seen as a series of attempts on the part of the English to write a history that will preserve Henry's fame. That conflict begins in the opening scene when the audience (along with their countrymen on stage) are confronted with reports of French victories that threaten to erase Henry's name from the historical record as surely as death has destroyed his body. Bedford's heroic invocation of Henry's ghost, implying that the dead king will occupy a place in history even more glorious than Julius Caesar's, is interrupted mid-sentence by a messenger bringing news that eight French cities have been lost.

The French action — to erase the English record — operates at two levels. Within the represented action, the French fight to drive the English from their country. At the rhetorical level, they attack both the English version of history and the values it expresses with an earthy iconoclasm that subverts the inherited notions of chivalric glory invoked by the English. Talbot, the English champion, and Joan, his French antagonist, speak alternative languages.[6] His language reifies glory, while hers is the language of physical objects; and the play defines their conflict as a contest between English words and French things, between the historical record that Talbot wishes to preserve and the physical reality that Joan invokes to discredit it. Shakespeare departs from his sources in having Talbot bury Salisbury, one of the last English heroes of the former age, in France. The real Salisbury was buried in England, but Shakespeare's Talbot announces that he will erect Salisbury's tomb in the "chiefest temple" of the

[4] Gabrielle M. Spiegel, "Genealogy: Form and Function in Medieval Historical Narrative," *History and Theory: Studies in the Philosophy of History* 22 (1983), 43–53. See also Peter Burke, *The Renaissance Sense of the Past* (London: Edward Arnold Ltd., 1969) and F. J. Levy, *Tudor Historical Thought* (San Marino: The Huntington Library, 1967).

[5] William Shakespeare, *The First Part of King Henry VI*, ed. Andrew S. Cairncross, Arden edition (London: Methuen, 1962). All subsequent citations will be from this edition and will be noted in the text.

[6] In *Henry V* the women will literally speak an alternative language. There Shakespeare departs from theatrical convention to write the women's lines in French, excluding them from the linguistic community that includes virtually all of the male characters — French as well as English — along with his English-speaking audience.

French "upon the which, that every one may read, shall be engrav'd the sack of Orleans, the treacherous manner of his mournful death, and what a terror he had been to France" (II. ii. 13–27). Talbot's effort here, as in his military campaign to secure Henry's French conquests, is a struggle to leave an English historical record in France.[7]

Shakespeare repeatedly calls attention to the fact that the French champion is a woman, thereby defining the conflict between England and France as a conflict between masculine and feminine values — chivalric virtue vs. pragmatic craft, historical fame vs. physical reality, patriarchal age vs. subversive youth, high social rank vs. low, self vs. other. "English Talbot" is a venerable gentleman who fights according to the chivalric code. Joan is a youthful peasant whose forces resort to craft, subterfuge, and modern weapons (a French boy sniper shoots the great Salisbury, and Joan recaptures Rouen by sneaking in, disguised as the peasant she really is, to admit the French army).

In addition to Joan, *1 Henry VI* includes two other female characters — the Countess of Auvergne and Margaret of Anjou. All three are French, and all three represent threats to the English protagonists and to the heroic values associated with history as the preserver of masculine fame and glory.[8] Like Joan, the Countess attacks Talbot; like Joan, she resorts to craft and stratagem; and like Joan she places her faith in physical reality over verbal report. The Countess says she wants to verify the reports of Talbot's glory by seeing his person: "Fain would mine eyes be witness with mine ears / To give their censure of these rare reports." What she sees — "a child, a silly dwarf . . . a weak and writhled shrimp," in short, Talbot's physical appearance — convinces her that "report is fabulous and false" (II. iii. 9–22).

The Countess's preference for physical evidence over historical report associates her with the French and female forces in the play as a threat to the project of writing English history. We see this conflict in its purest form after Talbot's death when Sir William Lucy calls for him in heroic language:

> But where's the great Alcides of the field,
> Valiant Lord Talbot, Earl of Shrewsbury,
> Created for his rare success in arms
> Great Earl of Washford, Waterford, and Valence,
> Lord Talbot of Goodrig and Urchinfield,
> Lord Strange of Blackmere, Lord Verdun of Alton
> Cromwell of Wingfield, Furnival of Sheffield,
> The thrice victorious Lord of Falconbridge,
> Knight of the noble order of Saint George,

[7] David Riggs, *Shakespeare's Heroical Histories: Henry VI and Its Literary Tradition* (Cambridge: Harvard University Press, 1971), pp. 22–23; 100–113, shows how the conventions of the funeral oration are used to characterize Talbot as well as Salisbury and Henry V. Riggs argues convincingly that Talbot exemplifies "the aristocratic ideal of military service and gentle blood" that was disappearing at the very time when *Henry VI* was written and that Joan "epitomizes the external forces that threaten[ed] that ideal."

[8] See David Bevington, "The Domineering Female in *2 Henry VI*," *Shakespeare Studies* 2 (1966), 51–58; and Sigurd Burckhardt, "'I am But Shadow of Myself': Ceremony and Design in *1 Henry VI*," in *Shakespearean Meanings* (Princeton: Princeton University Press, 1968), pp. 47–77.

Worthy Saint Michael, and the Golden Fleece,
Great Marshal to Henry the Sixth
Of all his wars within the realm of France?

[IV. vii. 60–71]

Rejecting the grandiose pretentions in the string of titles Lucy bestows on Talbot and relying on material fact to debunk the titles and attack Lucy's language, Joan replies:

Here is a silly-stately style indeed!
The Turk, that two and fifty kingdoms hath,
Writes not so tedious a style as this.
Him that thou magnifiest with all these titles,
Stinking and fly-blown lies here at our feet.

[IV. vii. 72–76]

Lucy describes Talbot as history was to describe him, decked in the titles that designate his patriarchal lineage and heroic military achievements. Joan, like the Countess, insists on physical fact, rejecting the masculine historical ideals and significance that Lucy's glorious names invoke.

Joan's reductive, nominalistic attack has an obvious appeal for an audience: her vigorous language, tied to the material facts of earth, threatens to topple the imposing formal edifice Lucy has constructed with his tower of names. But in this, the first of Shakespeare's English history plays, the subversive female voice is never allowed to prevail for more than a moment, and it is tempting to speculate that at least some in Shakespeare's audience may have realized that the glorious words of Lucy, unlike Joan's fictitious speech, take their authority from an enduring historical monument, Talbot's tomb at Rouen, where they were inscribed.[9]

In the case of the Countess, no such speculation is required. Shakespeare contrives Talbot's encounter with the Countess so that she, and the audience along with her, will be clearly instructed in the superiority of report over physical fact. Just before Talbot summons the hidden soldiers who will free him from her trap, he announces, "I am but shadow of myself: You are deceived, my substance is not here" (II. iii. 49–50); and a minute later the Countess acknowledges that the verbal reports she doubted were really true. For the audience, Talbot's lines were doubly significant: a "shadow" was a common term for an actor, and in that sense the man who spoke those lines was quite literally "but a shadow" of the elusive Talbot, the emblem of a lost historical presence, celebrated by historiographer and playwright, but never present in substance even to the Countess who thinks she has him captured in her castle. Relying as it does on physical presence, the reductive, French, female version of Talbot is always vulnerable to metadramatic attack, which invokes the ultimate fact of

---

[9] Although Lucy is not mentioned in Shakespeare's chronicle sources, there was a historical Sir William Lucy who lived near Shakespeare's home and was three times Sheriff of Warwickshire in the time of Henry VI. It has been suggested that Shakespeare knew of him from local oral tradition. Perhaps there is a connection between the fact that Lucy was historical — although not historiographic — authority and the fact that he recites the words that really were inscribed on Talbot's tomb at Rouen even though they, like Lucy himself, were not recorded in Shakespeare's chronicle sources.

theatrical occasion to remind the audience that no actual physical presence is involved.

This reminder is important because the whole issue of physical presence vs. historical record, dramatized in *1 Henry VI* as a conflict between English men and French women, is central, not only to this particular play, but to the history play genre itself. Urging the value of English history plays, Thomas Nashe used Talbot as an example when he wrote that in these productions,

> our forefathers valiant acts (that have line long buried in rustie brass and worme-eaten books) are revived, and they themselves raised from the Grave of Oblivion. . . . How would it have joyed brave Talbot (the terror of the French) to think that after he had lyne two hundred years in his tomb, he should triumph again on the stage, and have his bones new embalmed with the tears of ten thousand spectators who . . . imagine they behold him fresh bleeding.[10]

The audience, as Nashe reminds us, went to the play hoping to see those historical records brought to life and to make direct contact with the living reality that was celebrated but also obscured by the "worme-eaten" books of history.

For Shakespeare's audience, as for the characters in the play, Talbot's "glory [still] fill[ed] the world with loud report" (II. ii. 43). His mere name, like the name of God, is sufficient to rout the French soldiers (I. iv. 49; II. i. 79–81). Although Talbot is finally killed, his glory survives his physical death. Like the Countess, Shakespeare's audience wanted to *see* the renowned Talbot, and like her, they were likely to be disappointed. Exploiting its own inadequacies to validate the historical record, the play instructs its audience along with the Countess that the sight they see on stage is only a "shadow" of Talbot — that history and renown portrayed him more truly than physical presence ever could. The masculine authority of history is thus sustained against the feminine challenge of physical presence as the play is revealed as a representation. Presence remains ineluctably absent — the elusive Other, that, like the feminine principle itself, must be suppressed in order to sustain the masculine historiographic narrative. The nominalist challenge posed by the women's appeals to physical fact is discredited by reminders that the drama contains no physical facts, and so the verbal construction of Talbot's glory survives.

In this context the scene of Talbot's death is instructive. A long contention between Talbot and his son — a son repeatedly addressed by his father as "Talbot," the father's own name — in which each urges the other to save his life by fleeing from battle and in which neither, of course, will flee ends with the death of both. Talbot's paternal solicitude and his son's filial devotion, along with their mutual devotion to honor, have insured that there will be no survivor to carry their name into the future. And yet the name will still survive, recorded in history books, alive in sixteenth-century memory and celebrated on Shakespeare's stage — stripped now of any living human referent but still potent and significant.

---

[10] Thomas Nashe, *Pierce Penilesse his Supplication to the Diuell* (1592), reprinted in E. K. Chambers, *The Elizabethan Stage*, Vol. IV (Oxford: The Clarendon Press, 1923), pp. 238–39.

The argument that finally convinces Talbot to allow his son to stay with him and die in battle is the boy's claim that if he runs away, he will lose his patriarchal English title and become "like . . . the peasant boys of France": "If I fly, I am not Talbot's son. . . . If son to Talbot, die at Talbot's foot" (IV.vi.47–53). Talbot and his son both make the heroic choice described by Foucault, sacrificing their lives to preserve their heroic titles. In direct contrast, Shakespeare contrives Joan's final interview with her father to show her placing life above historical glory. We see her rejecting her father, revealed as a bastard, and finally claiming to be pregnant with yet another bastard, all in a futile effort to save her life (V. iv).

This final schematic contrast between the strong bond that unites the male Talbots and Joan's denial of her peasant father completes Shakespeare's picture of Talbot and Joan as opposites and connects the various terms in which their opposition has been defined – historian vs. anti-historian, noble man vs. peasant woman, realist vs. nominalist. As Kenneth Burke has pointed out, the medieval realist conception of language had strong affinities with the medieval feudal conception of the family, for both realism and feudalism treat "individuals as members of a group" or "tribe." In direct contrast, nominalism, the subversive movement in medieval philosophy, is "linguistically individualistic or atomistic," because it treats "groups as aggregates of individuals." Realism and feudalism both imply history because both involve what Burke calls "an *ancestral* notion." A realist conception of language holds that universals precede things and "give birth" to them.[11] Nominalism, like Joan, denies history because it denies the diachronic links that unite meaning and word like the successive generations of a great feudal family (the kind of family whose name the Talbots die to preserve). Drawing the same kind of connections, R. Howard Bloch associates the story of Abelard's castration with the fact of Abelard's nominalism: just as Abelard's intellectual position disrupted the "intellectual genealogy" of words, so too is his own physical genealogy represented as disrupted.[12] And, although Bloch does not mention it, the castration, like the nominalism, also associates Abelard with the feminine.

Joan's sexual promiscuity, hinted from the first, is less obviously connected than her nominalism to her role as anti-historian, but it is connected nonetheless. Just as her nominalism associates her with the Countess of Auvergne, so her sexual promiscuity associates her with the third French woman in the play, Margaret of Anjou, soon to become the adulterous queen of Henry VI. Immediately linked to Joan in the audience's eyes, Margaret is introduced by being led captive onto the stage at the same time that Joan is led off it after her final capture. Moreover, we quickly learn in 2 *Henry VI* that the marriage between Margaret and Henry threatens to erase history itself:

---

[11] Kenneth Burke, "Realist Family and Nominalist Aggregate" and "Familiar Definition," both in *A Grammar of Motives* (Cleveland: Meridian Books, 1962), pp. 247–52 and 26–27.

[12] R. Howard Bloch, *Etymologies and Genealogies: A Literary Anthropology of the French Middle Ages* (Chicago: University of Chicago Press, 1983), p. 149. Bloch also cites a fourteenth-century Provencal author who developed an elaborate system of analogies between modes of paternity and modes of lexical derivation (p. 42).

Fatal this marriage, cancelling your fame,
Blotting your names from books of memory,
Razing the characters of your renown
Defacing monuments of conquer'd France,
Undoing all as all had never been!

[I. i. 98–102]

Besides Joan, Margaret is the only woman who plays a major part in the *Henry VI* plays and the only character of either sex who appears in all four plays of the first tetralogy. Margaret's disruptive role becomes increasingly prominent as the story progresses and the world of the plays sinks into chaos. A virago who defies her husband, leads armies into battle, and gloats at the murder of an innocent child, Shakespeare's Margaret has a "tiger's heart wrapped in a woman's hide." Shakespeare follows Hall in making her "a manly woman, usyng to rule and not to be ruled," but he departs from his historiographic source in making her an adulteress.[13]

Like Joan's sexual promiscuity, Margaret's adultery has no real impact on the action of the *Henry VI* plays. In both cases, the women's sexual transgressions seem almost irrelevant — dramatically unnecessary attributes, at best added to underscore their characterization as threats to masculine honor, at worst gratuitous slanders, like the slander by which a Renaissance woman who transgressed in any way, even by excessive gossip and railing, was commonly characterized as a whore.

In the first tetralogy, Shakespeare fails to elaborate the relationship between sexual transgression and historical subversion, but there is a very important sense in which sexual transgression is central to women's characterization as subverters of history. To describe it, I will turn to *King John*, the most troubling and deeply subversive of all Shakespeare's English histories. As Gabrielle Spiegel has pointed out, history is not simply a record of heroic names and glorious deeds or an aggregate of individual biographies: it is also a connected story, tracing the passing down of land and titles from one man to another and validating the legitimacy of their current apportionment. Genealogy lies at the base of the chronicle structure which constitutes a narrative of patriarchal succession designed to legitimate the social order at the time in

---

[13] Edward Hall, *The Union of the Two Noble and Illustre Famelies of Lancastre and Yorke* (London, 1548–50), rpt. (London: J. Johnson *et al.*, 1809), p. 249. Robert Greene's famous attack on Shakespeare as a *"Tygers hart wrapt in a Players hyde"* (*Greens Groats-worth of Wit*, 1596, reprinted in Chambers, IV, 241) offers a tantalizing suggestion of identity between the gentle playwright described in Ben Jonson's *Discoveries* ("honest, and of an open, and free nature") and the wicked queen. Stephen Orgel, in a recent article ("Prospero's Wife," *representations* 8 [Fall 1984]) suggests that Prospero (who is generally recognized as a Shakespearean self-representation), in his claim to have raised the dead, "has incorporated Ovid's witch, the wicked mother." Nowhere is Shakespeare/Prospero's claim more applicable than in the English history plays, and nowhere is Orgel's observation more suggestive. In those plays, Shakespeare incorporates the women and raises the dead in order to confute the historical record. And he does so with women's own weapons — lies (fictitious characters, dialogues, events) and materiality (stage spectacle), both of which he uses to oppose the written historiographic text.

which the history is written and read.[14] An adulterous woman at any point can make a mockery of the entire story, and for that reason women are inevitably threatening to the historiographic enterprise.

The verbal historiographic narrative suppresses women because it must suppress the knowledge that all men and women have of the physical impossibility of ever discovering a sure biological basis for patriarchal succession. Hence the association of women with nominalism and their characterization as subverters of the historiographic record.[15] In a very important sense, chronicle history was not simply written without women: it was also written *against* them. Patriarchal history is designed to construct a verbal substitute for the visible physical connection between a mother and her children, to authenticate the relationships between fathers and sons and to suppress and supplant the role of the mother.

This is the story told by Renaissance historians, and this is the story Shakespeare told in most of his English history plays. Even such historically significant and consequential events as royal marriages are typically ignored (as in the case of Henry IV) or presented as disasters (as in the case of Henry VI or Edward IV). Only at the ends of the two tetralogies and in *Henry VIII*, the last of all his English history plays, does Shakespeare attempt to incorporate and transvalue the feminine. In *Richard III*, Margaret is transformed from a destructive French interloper whose marriage to the English king threatens to "cancel" English fame and "blot" English "names from books of memory" to the voice of Divine vengeance, descending upon the guilty Yorkists to purge England and make it ready for the glorious Tudor accession. At the end of that play, it is the marriage of Richmond and Elizabeth that finally resolves the problems of the past and enables the prosperity of the future. Similarly, *Henry V*, the last play in the second tetralogy, culminates in the arrangements for the marriage of Henry to the French princess, and *Henry VIII*, the last play of all, culminates in the birth of the Princess Elizabeth. In all these cases, however, the incorporation of the feminine represents the end of the historical process, a movement beyond the limits of the

[14] Spiegel, "Genealogy: Form and Function," p. 47. Spiegel is writing about late medieval French historiography, but, as scholars have long recognized, the Tudor sponsorship of historiography was clearly motivated by Tudor genealogical anxiety. The Tudor historiographers constructed a fable of ancient descent and Providential purpose to authenticate the new dynasty in its claim to the English throne. David Riggs's observations about Elizabethan nostalgia for the fast-vanishing ideal of the hereditary feudal aristocrat are also relevant here, as is the fact that Queen Elizabeth, whose refusal to marry had always provoked anxiety about the succession, was now well past the age of marriage and child-bearing.

[15] Gayle Rubin, in "The Traffic in Women: Notes on the 'Political Economy' of Sex," in *Toward an Anthropology of Women*, ed. R. Reiter (New York: Monthly Review Press, 1975), p. 188, quotes Lacan discussing Levi-Strauss's observation that the structures of language are implicated "with that part of the social laws which regulate marriage and kinship," i.e. with legitimacy and patriarchal succession, mythologies that serve male interests. Jacques Derrida, in *Of Grammatology*, trans. Gayatri Spivak (Baltimore: The Johns Hopkins University Press, 1974), pp. 124–25, also cites Levi-Strauss, concluding, "It is now known, thanks to unquestionable and abundant information that the birth of writing (in the colloquial sense) was nearly everywhere and most often linked to genealogical anxiety" and "The genealogical relation and social classification are the stitched seam of arche-writing." Also see Bloch, especially chapters 1 and 2.

historiographic narrative. The marriages are announced, but they will not take place until after the plays have ended; and their announcements, like the announcement of Elizabeth's birth, are accompanied by prayers for future prosperity that go beyond the known facts of history, looking forward to the present time of the audience and even beyond it to an unknown future. The incorporation of the feminine can only take place at the point where history stops.[16] A world which truly includes the feminine is a world in which history cannot be written.

Shakespeare's only attempt to depict such a world is *King John*. Female characters, for the first time, are sharply individualized, and they play more important and more varied roles than in any of Shakespeare's other English histories. In the first tetralogy, the female characters fall neatly into groups, and their generic gender characteristics always transcend and subsume their individual identities. In *1 Henry VI*, although Joan is a peasant and the Countess of Auvergne and Margaret of Anjou are noblewomen, all three are united in nationality and in their roles as enemies to the English, male protagonists' struggle to preserve the legacy of Henry V. In *Richard III*, Margaret is a vengeful Lancastrian widow and Elizabeth a Yorkist Queen. But before the play ends they too will be united with each other and the Duchess of York in a chorus of distinctively female lamentation — all victimized and bereaved, all gifted with the power to prophesy and curse and articulate the will of Providence.

In *King John*, by contrast, there is no way to reduce the female characters to a single class or category. The *Henry VI* plays depict a world where male right is threatened by female wrong; in the wicked world ruled by Richard III, the women line up on the side of heaven and the Earl of Richmond; but no such simple moral equations are possible in *King John*. Like the ambiguous ethos of the play itself, the female characters here are deeply divided, as is the feminine spirit. Eleanor is a soldier queen, a tough, Machiavellian dowager, while Blanche is a helpless victim and Constance an outraged, lamenting mother. The natural bonds that unite mother and child serve to divide Eleanor and Constance, who back rival claimants for the English throne and wrangle openly on stage, accusing each other of adultery and adroitly subverting each other's claims and arguments (II. i. 120–194). Blanche and Constance are both depicted as suffering victims, but neither can be consoled without wronging the other, and when they kneel together before the Dauphin (III. i. 233–238), they do so to plead for opposite decisions.

In the world of *King John*, women no longer serve their traditional functions as creators of male bonds and validators of male identity. The marriage of John's niece

---

[16] Although a number of the history plays offer positive images of women, none of them attempts to represent female authority, even though all but the last were written during the reign of Queen Elizabeth. Shakespeare does not bring Elizabeth onto the stage until *Henry VIII*, written during the reign of her successor; and she comes in only at the end and only as a newborn baby, the object of the characters' hopes for the future, the audience's nostalgia for the past. Female authority is always absent in Shakespeare's histories, a dream of ultimate validation, an object of yearning as well as fear, which inevitably escapes the historiographic narrative.

Blanche to the French Dauphin, which momentarily promises to unite the rival forces after their inconclusive battle for Algiers, is immediately contravened by the intervention of the papal legate Pandulph, a spokesman for a religious power as ambiguous as every other source of authority in this play.[17] Blanche, the conventional compliant woman, allows herself to be used, like the inert material of masculine history-making, as an instrument of kinship arrangements, political alliance, and patriarchal succession. But in this play the material also includes the recalcitrant Eleanor and Constance. Constance's immediate, outraged rejection of the news of the marriage as a "tale" "misspoke, misheard" and her hyperbolic demand to have the day on which it took place removed from the calendar (II. ii. 4–5; III. i. 10–25) remind an audience that the political alliance the marriage is designed to effect would still leave Constance and Arthur and the hereditary rights they urge upon us unincorporated and unappeased and that the marriage will have no impact upon history. Denying the men's story and demanding the literal erasure of the date, Constance speaks for the anti-historical forces that dominate this play.

The passivity of Blanche's character and her role in the plot make her a kind of feminine archetype. Imported into the plot (as John, apparently, imports her to France) only for her ill-fated marriage to the Dauphin, Blanche is cast in the familiar female role of a medium of exchange between men, designed to effect a relationship between them. But instead of becoming a medium to unite the warring factions, Blanche becomes the embodiment of their divisions. Niece to the English King, wife to the French Dauphin, she pleads desperately for the peace her marriage was designed to secure. Having failed in her plea, she cries,

> Which is the side that I must go withal?
> I am with both; each army hath a hand,
> And in their rage, I having hold of both,
> They whirl asunder and dismember me.
>
> [III. i. 253–256]

This image of dismemberment makes Blanche the human embodiment of the many divisions that characterize this play — of the divisions among the female characters, of the division of the English throne between John's possession and Arthur's right, and especially of the divided allegiances that perplex the audience as they struggle with the

---

[17] Sigurd Burckhardt argues in "*King John*: The Ordering of This Present Time," *Shakespearean Meanings*, pp. 116–43, that every source of authority fails in *King John* except the ties of blood and the simple human decency that prevents Hubert from murdering Arthur. Burckhardt's demonstration of the ways the play subverts religious and political authority is thoroughly convincing, but I find it difficult to accept his claims about Hubert. In the world of this play, no actions are conclusive, neither marriages nor battles, nor the human kindness that finally persuades Hubert to spare Arthur. In the chronicles, the reports of Arthur's death were ambiguous, and although Shakespeare provides his audience with eyewitness knowledge of the scene that no one but Arthur ever saw, he also shows the false reports that kept even Arthur's contemporaries from true knowledge of the circumstances of his death, and he shows the political and military effects of their ignorance in the nobles' defection from John. The truth of Hubert's mercy has no impact upon the plot of the play or the course of history.

ethical and political ambivalences that make *King John* the most disturbing of all Shakespeare's English histories.[18]

Like *1 Henry VI, King John* looks back to a dead, heroic king, but while the legacy of Henry V was opposed and endangered in the world his infant son inherited but could not rule, it remained an intact and clearly defined, if increasingly remote, ideal. In *King John*, the legacy of the great Coeur-de-lion is called into question when we learn in the same scene that his "honour-giving hand" knighted Robert Faulconbridge (I. i. 53) and that he also dishonored Faulconbridge by seducing his wife. Coeur-de-lion has left no clear successor. His only biological son is a bastard. His heir by law of primogeniture is his nephew Arthur. The Bastard has "a trick of Coeur-de-lion's face" and "the accent of his tongue" (I. i. 85–86). Arthur, a dispossessed and defenseless child, has his lineal right to the throne. And John, who has neither, sits upon that throne.

The dispersion of Coeur-de-lion's legacy among three defective heirs makes it impossible even to know who is the rightful king of England, and it gives rise to the crucial issue in *King John* — the problem of legitimacy. If the central problem in *1 Henry VI* is the disjunction between words and things, the central problem in *King John* is the closely related issue of the disjunction between fathers and sons. The entire action hangs on the unanswerable question: "who is the legitimate heir of Coeur-de-lion?"; and the presiding spirit of this play is not the king who gives it its name but the Bastard, the most powerful and dramatically compelling of the characters, the one to whom John assigns "the ordering of this present time" (V. i. 77) and Shakespeare allows the last word in the play. The Bastard's literal illegitimacy characterizes the status of the king (who relies on "strong possession" rather than "right" for his throne), the problems the play explores, and the curious nature of Shakespeare's creation.[19] The Bastard has no real place in history, neither in the chain of patriarchal succession,

---

[18] In *King John*, Shakespeare exposes the inadequacy of all explanatory schemes — law, *realpolitik*, Providential order, natural-humanistic right — and leaves his audience, like the Bastard, "amazed" and "lost" "among the thorns and dangers" of its incomprehensible world (IV. iii. 140–141). Constance reminds the audience that "when law can do no right / Let it be lawful that law bar no wrong! / For he that holds his kingdom holds the law; / Therefore . . . law itself is perfect wrong" (III. i. 111–115). John reminds sixteenth-century Englishmen that the Pope's authority is "usurped" (III. i. 86), and he trades charges of usurpation with the King of France (II. i. 118–120). Eleanor reads the Bastard's face aright to find him Coeur-de-lion's son, but Pembroke and Salisbury (IV. ii. 70–81) and John (IV. ii. 221–222) all misread Hubert's face to mistake him as Arthur's murderer.

[19] Failures of authority — problems of legitimacy — take a variety of forms in and around *King John*. For the characters within the play, these range from specific, literal accusations of bastardy (brought against Arthur and John as well as Philip Faulconbridge) to the general absence of any clear royal authority. For the audience watching the play, there is no unblemished cause and no unquestioned authority to claim their allegiance. For scholarly editors, the play has a problematic text and a clouded authorial genealogy. Not only does it include an abundance of fictional material not found in the historiographic sources, but there is also no way to know whether Shakespeare is the original author of that fictional material, since much of it is also found in a roughly contemporary play, *The Troublesome Raigne of Iohn King of England* (London, 1591). Nor has anyone been able to determine which play was written first (although, of course, many arguments have been advanced on both sides of the question). Estimates of the date of Shakespeare's composition range from 1591 to 1598. For a detailed account of the problems concerning the sources, the text, and the dating, see E. A. J. Honigmann's Introduction to the Arden edition.

where he can never inherit his father's throne, nor in the historical record Shakespeare found in Holinshed. He dominates a play which is unique among Shakespeare's English histories for its own separation from the temporal and genealogical chain that unites the two tetralogies and its own lack of historical authority. *King John* has the flimsiest of relationships to its historiographic sources, ignoring Holinshed's account of the historically significant Magna Carta and centered instead on a historically insignificant character invented for the sixteenth-century stage.[20]

A curious episode, which serves to introduce the Bastard, takes up most of the first act in *King John* and exposes, like nothing else in any of Shakespeare's histories, the arbitrary and conjectural nature of patriarchal succession and the suppressed centrality of women to it. The Bastard — here called Philip Faulconbridge — and his younger brother Robert come before the king to dispute the Faulconbridge legacy, Robert claiming that his older brother is not really their father's son and should not inherit the Faulconbridge lands and title. Their quarrel, like the quarrel between Arthur and John over the English throne, hinges on ambiguities and ruptures in the relationship between legal and biological inheritance. Both disputes involve the mothers — but not the fathers — of the contending heirs. John's mother, Eleanor, and Arthur's mother, Constance, play important roles in the historical contest between their sons, but neither is the chief actor. The fictional Faulconbridge quarrel, on the other hand, centers on a woman, for Lady Faulconbridge's infidelity has created the nightmare situation that haunts the patriarchal imagination — a son not of her husband's getting destined to inherit her husband's lands and title. Like Shakespeare's ubiquitous cuckold jokes, the Faulconbridge episode bespeaks the anxiety that motivates the stridency of patriarchal claims and repressions — the repressed knowledge of women's subversive power.

John's attempt to arbitrate the Faulconbridge quarrel exposes a deep contradiction in patriarchal law. "Sirrah," he says to Robert, "your brother is legitimate":

> Your father's wife did after wedlock bear him,
> And if she did play false, the fault was hers;
> Which fault lies on the hazards of all husbands
> That marry wives. Tell me, how if my brother,
> Who, as you say, took pains to get this son,
> Had of your father claim'd this son for his?
> In sooth, good friend, your father might have kept
> This calf, bred from his cow, from all the world;
> In sooth he might; then if he were my brother's
> My brother might not claim him; nor your father,
> Being none of his, refuse him: this concludes;
> My mother's son did get your father's heir;
> Your father's heir must have your father's land.

> [I. i. 116–129]

[20] Honigmann writes (Arden, p. xxxi), "*John* has been called his most unhistorical play." If the *Troublesome Raigne* was a source for Shakespeare's play, the Bastard has a dramatic source there, but the historical basis for the Bastard is confined to one sentence in Holinshed on "Philip bastard sonne to king Richard, to whom his father had given the castell and honor of Coinacke, [who] killed the vicount of Limoges, in revenge of his fathers death" (Raphael Holinshed, *Chronicles of England, Scotland and Ireland*, 2nd ed., 1586 [London: J. Johnson *et al.*, 1807], II, 278).

According to the laws of patriarchy as expounded by John (and according to good English law in Shakespeare's time), the woman, like a cow, is mere chattel, possession of the man. All her actions, even an act so radical as betrayal of the marriage bond, are totally irrelevant, powerless to affect her son's name, possession, legal status, or identity. Only the man's entitlement has significance under law. She is his possession, and any child she bears is his, even if he is not the biological father. Thus, the very absoluteness of patriarchal right provides for its own subversion.

By admitting that the relationship between father and son is finally no more than a legal fiction, John attacks the very basis of history. Relying on "strong possession" rather than "right" for his throne (I. i. 40), John opposes the patriarchal authority that would legitimate Arthur. Having himself crowned a second time, he denies the permanence and efficacy of the ritual that made him king (IV. ii. 1–34). Everything, even the supreme ritual by which patriarchal authority is passed down in temporal succession from one hand to another, is now endlessly repeatable and reversible. In this play, it is not John but the King of France who values history and wants to write it. The French king supports Arthur's lineal right to the English throne, and he describes Arthur as a "little abstract" of what "died in" Arthur's father, which "the hand of time shall draw . . . into as huge a volume" (II. i. 101–103). With this description of father and son as "volume" and "abstract," the French king grounds the historical record in nature. But John's verdict on the Faulconbridge controversy demythologizes that record, depriving it of the natural status implied by the French king's metaphor of man as volume and boy as abstract and exposing it as a social construct designed to shore up the flimsy and always necessarily putative connections between fathers and sons.

Eleanor is the first to guess the Bastard's true paternity, for she can read the wordless text of his physical nature:

> He hath a trick of Coeur-de-lion's face;
> The accent of his tongue affecteth him.
> Do you not read some tokens of my son
> In the large composition of this man?
>
> [I. i. 85–88]

But without Lady Faulconbridge's testimony, the Bastard's paternity would remain conjectural, and his name and title would belie the biological truth of the paternity they purported to represent. It takes one woman to guess the truth and another to verify it. In Holinshed, Coeur-de-lion recognizes his bastard son, giving him "the castell and honor of Coinacke." In the *Troublesome Raigne*, the Bastard guesses his true paternity even before he asks his mother.[21] Only in Shakespeare is he required to receive his paternity from the hands of women.

Lady Faulconbridge is an unhistorical character, but she is the only one who knows the truth about the Bastard's paternity. The Bastard's words are significant: "But for

---

[21] In *The Troublesome Raigne*, Philip gets the news from Nature herself: "Methinks I hear a hollow echo sound," he says, "That *Philip* is the son unto a King: / The whistling leaves upon the trembling trees, / Whistle in concert I am *Richard's* son; / The bubbling murmur of the water's fall, / Records *Phillipus Regis filius*; / Birds in their flight make music with their wings, / Filling the air with glory of my birth; / Birds, bubbles, leaves and mountains, echo, all / Ring in mine ears, that I am *Richard's* son" (i. 242–251).

the certain knowledge of that truth / I put you o'er to heaven and to my mother" (I. i. 61–62). The Bastard's ironic coupling of his adulterous mother with heaven as the only sources of the elusive truth that no man can know on earth suggests a deep affinity between them as keepers of the unwritten and unknowable truth never directly accessible to the knowledge of men, the Others who delineate the boundaries of the male Self's kingdom of knowledge and control. To incorporate women in the story, as Shakespeare does in *King John*, is to go beyond the patriarchal historical narrative into the realm of the unwritten and the conjectural, the inaccessible domain (the no-man's land) of the true paternity of a child and the actual life that can never be fully represented in the words of the historical text.

Renaissance historiography constructed a patriarchal mythology, delineating a chain of inheritance passed down from father to son. Like the strings of "begats" in the Old Testament, it suppressed the role of women. The son's name and entitlement and legitimacy all derived from the father, and only the father was included in the historiographic text. But only the mother could guarantee that legitimacy. As bearers of the life that names, titles, and historical records could never fully represent, the women were keepers of the unspoken and unspeakable reality that always threatened to belie the words that pretended to describe it.

The Bastard's mother is a fictitious English lady, and Joan is a historical French peasant, but both perform analogous acts of subversion. Like Joan's nominalism, Lady Faulconbridge's adultery belies the men's words and subverts their claims to authority. The women in Shakespeare's English history plays differ in virtue, strength, nationality, and social rank; and they speak with a variety of voices. But despite their many roles, they are never the central actors, and they differ only as the masculine project of writing history is conceived differently. In the world of history, women are inevitably alien, representatives of the unarticulated residue that eludes the men's historiographic texts and threatens their historical myths.

We can explain the subversive roles of women in Shakespeare's history plays in various ways. We can postulate that Shakespeare derived them from observation of real women. Joan Kelly has pointed out that early feminist writers, opposing their own experience to masculine texts, were "unremittingly critical of the authors — ancient, modern, even scriptural — at a time when the *auctores* were still *auctoritates* to many."[22] We can explain the subversive roles of Shakespeare's women as projection. Shakespeare, as a male writer of history that denied the feminine, may have expressed his anxiety about that denial by projecting it onto his female characters. We can say that Shakespeare's gift for imaginative sympathy or the logic of his structure

[22] Joan Kelly, "Early Feminist Theory and the *Querelle des Femmes*, 1400–1789," *Signs* (Autumn 1982), 4–28. Kelly cites Christine de Pisan's *City of Women*, 1404 (translated into English, 1521, as *The Boke of the Cyte of Ladies*) as an example of this opposition of women's experience to men's texts: "Although you have seen such things in writing, you have not seen them with your eyes," says one of Christine's female speakers, addressing her in what Kelly calls "tones of modern empiricism, urging her to accept as true only what conformed to her (and other women's) experience." And, as Maureen Quilligan has reminded me, the problematic union of patriarchal authority and female sex embodied in Queen Elizabeth — who had herself been declared a bastard — provides a crucial contemporary context for Shakespeare's practice in his English history plays, and especially in *King John*.

forced him to cast his women as anti-historians, necessarily opposed to a masculine script designed to suppress their roles and silence their voices. But whatever explanation we choose to adopt, we come to the same conclusion: the women were anti-historians because they had to be. It was the only part they could play in the story the men had written.[23]

[23] This paper was originally prepared for the University of Pennsylvania's Mellon Seminar on the Diversity of Language and the Structure of Power. I am indebted to the members of that seminar — especially to Lucienne Frappier-Mazur, Gwynne Kennedy, Maureen Quilligan, and Carroll Smith-Rosenberg — for their stimulating questions and suggestions.

Painting Women:
Images of Femininity in Jacobean Tragedy

Laurie A. Finke

In a scene that both repeats and parodies the Renaissance's idealizations of women, *The Revenger's Tragedy* opens with Vendice addressing — and fondling — the skull of his murdered beloved.

> Thou sallow picture of my poisoned love,
> My studies' ornament, thou shell of death,
> Once the bright face of my betrothed lady,
> When life and beauty naturally fill'd out
> These ragged imperfections,
> When two heaven-pointed diamonds were set
> In those unsightly rings — then 'twas a face
> So far beyond the artificial shine
> Of any woman's bought complexion.
>
> [I. i. 14–22][1]

Gloriana's skull functions here and throughout the play as a grisly emblem uniting two dialectical notions of femininity: woman as ideal, as an object of adoration, and woman as death's head, as a figure which evokes fear and hostility. Both of these images are, in effect, reflections of Vendice's mind, masculine perceptions of woman that transform her into extreme projections of man's own fears of mortality. Gloriana's skull is, for Vendice, a kind of fetish, a "sallow picture," or "studies' ornament." It has become a fragment of a once whole, living woman. Yet, as it plays a past

---

Laurie Finke is Associate Professor of English at Lewis & Clark College. She has published articles on Chaucer, Langland, Shakespeare, Wollstonecraft, and Kierkegaard; she is also coeditor of two collections of essays: From Renaissance to Restoration: Metamorphoses of the Drama *and* Medieval Texts and Contemporary Readers.

---

[1] Cyril Tourneur, *The Revenger's Tragedy*, ed. Lawrence J. Ross (Lincoln: University of Nebraska Press, 1966). All subsequent citations will be from this edition and will be noted in the text. For a discussion of the *memento mori* in Shakespeare's plays that bears on my discussion of *The Revenger's Tragedy*, see Marjorie Garber, "Remember Me: Memento Mori Figures in Shakespeare's Plays," *Renaissance Drama*, 12 (1981), 3–25.

ideal off against a present horror, Vendice's opening soliloquy implies that Gloriana in life was, for him, neither whole nor vital. The imagery throughout is life-denying and fragmenting. Words like "picture," "ornament," and "shell" reduce Gloriana to the status of an *objet d'art* — a painted woman — even as they attempt to contrast past beauty with present devastation. The Petrarchan image, "heaven-pointed diamonds," suggests a kind of crystalline and lifeless perfection that is the essence of the ideal that Vendice creates. In life, as in death, we see only Gloriana's head; she is silent and decapitated. Vendice's descriptive strategy fragments his lover's body by making its parts, here the head, into signs — ciphers — of his own morbid imagination, his obsession with corruption and death.

When the skull reappears in Act III, it has been transformed from a *memento mori*, the death's head Vendice keeps on his desk to fuel his hatred, into the instrument of his revenge. He has painted and dressed his skull to represent "a country lady, a little bashful at first" (III. v. 132), counting on the Duke not to see the skull beneath the "skin," and to perceive the superficial painting as a tantalizing form of "innocence," "a sin rob'd in holiness" (III. v. 138). Here the Petrarchan image of the living Gloriana merges with its inverted mirror image, woman as death's head. Gloriana's painted — and poisoned — lips literally amount to death for the Duke. Idealized beauty, as a strategy to shield man from the actuality of death, is exposed as a transitory delusion by the poet/revenger who wallows in his realization. He asks of the skull:

Does the silkworm expend her yellow labors
For thee? for thee does she undo herself? . . .
Does every proud and self-affecting dame
Camphire her face for this? . . .
    See ladies, with false forms
You deceive men, but cannot deceive worms.

[III. v. 71–72, 83–84, 96–97]

For Vendice, woman's attempts to preserve, through the artifice of cosmetics, the ideal of beauty inherent in his Petrarchan evocation of the living Gloriana, reveal, behind the fictions of idealization, the horrors of the grave. But if the ideal and death imply each other, then Vendice finds himself caught in a double bind: his idealized "painting" of woman (like her cosmetics), in its attempts to deny death, becomes little more than an ironic affirmation of the decay of the flesh.

I

Vendice's painted skull is a particularly appropriate image with which to begin a study of femininity in Jacobean tragedy because it suggests a fundamental equivalence between the beloved as an idealized object and motivation for revenge, on the one hand, and as an object of terror and instrument of revenge, on the other. Vendice's painted skull emphasizes the double sense of "painting": as art — a changeless, timeless ideal designed to transcend death — and as cosmetics — a form of disguise and a futile attempt to cheat death. In this respect, painting conflates the dialectical images of women — as ideal and as *memento mori* — that structure a common, if often unspoken, perception of women in Jacobean tragedy. As Gloriana's skull suggests, the two images of the feminine, at once inviolate and irrevocably corrupt, stem from the same source: a fear of and hostility toward women that results from man's awareness of his own carnality and the "contingency of the flesh." As Simone de Beauvoir has argued,

> The slimy embryo begins the cycle that is completed in the putrefaction of death. Because he is horrified by needlessness and death, man feels horror at having been engendered; he would fain deny his animal ties.[2]

In *The Revenger's Tragedy*, Vendice circumvents his own "animal ties" both by emphasizing woman's unique carnality, her bestial sexuality, and by denying her flesh, transforming her into a disembodied art object. He sees all women either as morbidly sexual, like the Duchess "that will do with the devil" (I. i. 4), or as bloodless virgins, like Castiza, garnering "crystal plaudites" (II. i. 240).

Jacobean tragedy, particularly when it is most lurid, as in Tourneur's *Revenger's Tragedy*, exploits these male fears that link the feminine with death. These tragedies enact, usually with deadly results for the heroine, the life-denying tendencies inherent in "painting" women. Recent feminist readings of Shakespearean tragedy have begun calling attention to the violence and "male fear of contamination" that underlie his heroes' expressions of both love and hatred for women in the plays. In particular, Madelon Gohlke and Harry Berger have argued that his heroes "strive to avoid an awareness of their vulnerability in relation to women." Because they regard such vulnerability as "feminine," they become obsessed with their own "manliness," displacing their powerlessness onto women. "It is," Gohlke argues, "the so-called masculine consciousness, therefore, that defines femininity as weakness and institutes structures of male dominance designed to defend against . . . an awareness" of masculine vulnerability.[3]

In the tragedies of the early seventeenth century, these strategies are most often violent, and include rape, prostitution, and murder. The debauchery that runs rampant throughout *The Revenger's Tragedy* reduces the women in the play to mere objects whose femininity is exclusively defined by their sexuality: "The woman is all male, whom none can enter" (II. i. 111). Even when they are virtuous, like Lord Antonio's ravished and dead wife or Gloriana, they are "fair monuments" ripe for the plundering; virginity "is a paradise lock'd up . . . And 'twas decreed that man should keep the key" (II. i. 153–155). But, if all women are objects, defined solely by their sexuality, they are also all potentially sexual threats because they are all potentially false lovers. This masculine fear of betrayal is the source of much of the play's hostility toward female sexuality, its reduction of all women to whores or potential whores. Even the most chaste and virtuous women, whether those locked up in the "crystal tower" of honor or those safely dead, might humiliate or dishonor a man. This fear drives Vendice to play the pimp to test a sister whose virtue he cannot doubt (indeed

[2] Simone de Beauvoir, *The Second Sex*, trans. and ed. H. M. Parshley (New York: Vintage Books, 1974), p. 165.

[3] Madelon Gohlke, "'I wooed thee with my sword': Shakespeare's Tragic Paradigm," in *Representing Shakespeare: New Psychoanalytic Essays*, eds. Murray M. Schwartz and Coppélia Kahn (Baltimore: Johns Hopkins University Press, 1980), pp. 170–84; see especially p. 180. Harry Berger, Jr., "Text Against Performance in Shakespeare: The Example of *Macbeth*," *Genre*, 15 (1982), 64–78.

whose virtue is inscribed in her name — Castiza) and to exploit the skull of his dead lover as the instrument of his revenge against the Duke who, in his turn, had tried to exploit her sexually in life. Lurking behind these fears of sexual betrayal at the hands of women, and contributing to this play's particularly lurid atmosphere, is the obsession with woman as a *memento mori* masked by a beautiful facade. Vendice's hostility in Act III, scene v — "See ladies, with false forms / You deceive men but cannot deceive worms" — reveals his preoccupation with woman as a powerful agent of death who deceives man and betrays him through her beauty and sexuality.

This sense of betrayal underlies and informs the sexual hostility that pervades both Webster's *Duchess of Malfi* and John Ford's *'Tis Pity She's a Whore* as well. The fictions about femininity shared by Shakespeare's and Tourneur's heroes also form the backdrop against which Webster's and Ford's tragedies are played. Indeed, *The Revenger's Tragedy*, *The Duchess of Malfi*, and *'Tis Pity She's a Whore* assume the forms they do because their authors simultaneously participate in, and call into question, the Renaissance's cultural repression of the feminine and its concomitant assertion of masculine power. The tragic playwright's role is paradoxical: the closer his attention to the dynamics of feminine idealization and desecration, the stronger become the repressive mechanisms that reinforce cultural perceptions of women as either saints or whores.[4] Misogyny is not — in and of itself — simply a theme in any of these works; it inheres in what Berger calls the "institutional 'deep structure'" of Renaissance patriarchy.[5] The playwrights' rhetoric participates in a collective mystification of the feminine even as it probes the dark underside of a rhetorical strategy for neutralizing the twin threats of betrayal and death laid out earlier by the sonneteers and lyricists. For this reason, before exploring the "deconstruction" of this rhetorical pose more fully in *The Duchess of Malfi* and *'Tis Pity She's a Whore*, it is worth a brief backward glance at the Renaissance lyricists' "painting" of women — and at the Renaissance moralists' perception of woman's attempts to "paint" herself.

II

A male poet of the Renaissance could and did acknowledge, and even wallow in, his fears of mortality by emphasizing death's essential contiguity with the feminine, as Tichborne does in "I sought my death and found it in my womb" or Drayton in "There's nothing grieves me but that Age should haste."[6] But much more frequently he

---

[4] For a discussion of this problem in relation to *Macbeth* see Berger, "Text Against Performance," pp. 64–78. Such a reading is not intended to condemn Jacobean playwrights ahistorically by twentieth-century standards, but to call attention to the ways in which a feminist perspective may enhance our understanding of Jacobean tragedy.

[5] Berger, "Text Against Performance," p. 64.

[6] Drayton's sonnet employs the same counterpointing of beauty and decay that structures Vendice's opening soliloquy in *The Revenger's Tragedy*: "That there where two clear sparkling Eyes are placed / Onely two loope-holes, then might I behold. / That lovely, arched, yvoried, pollish'd brow, / Defac'd with Wrinkles, that I might but see." The poet's meditation on his beloved contrasts present beauty with future devastation, and, like Vendice, plays on the Petrarchan strategy of "scattering" the woman's body into a series of objects — ivory, pearl, roses, moss — to emphasize the inevitability of the decay of the flesh. *The Works of Michael Drayton*, ed. J. William Hebel (Oxford: Basil Blackwell, rpt., 1961), II, 314.

attempts to deny mortality and neutralize the threat posed by woman's carnality by transforming her, through his lyric, through art, into an ideal, eternally changeless because essentially lifeless. This strategy is brilliantly illustrated in the "absent" subject of Robert Browning's poem, "My Last Duchess" (a Victorian redaction of the Renaissance heroine). She is "painted on the wall / Looking *as if* she were alive. . . . Fra Pandolph's hand worked busily a day and there she stands" (italics mine). The poem enacts a strategy for "killing" a woman into art (to use Sandra Gilbert and Susan Gubar's phrase from *Madwoman in the Attic*),[7] as frequent in the Renaissance lyric as it is natural for a man of Ferrara's megalomania. Through the agency of the *male* artist, Browning's villain makes his Duchess a static and two-dimensional painting, reducing her to an appearance, an illusion. He denies her physical being by painting her into lifeless immortality.

The Petrarchan lady of the Renaissance, no less than the Duchess of Ferrara, must be killed into art so that she may remain forever present and forever beautiful. Sonnet after sonnet in the Renaissance contrasts the decay that is the fate of all "fleshly" women with the "eternal summer" promised by the lyricist. Drayton spells out this opposition in the following sonnet from *Ideas* (1619) through the tension between the "painted" women of the first line and the woman addressed in the sonnet, the poet's "thou":

> How many paltry, foolish, painted things,
> That now in Coaches trouble ev'ry street,
> Shall be forgotten, whom no Poet sings,
> Ere they be well wrap'd in their winding Sheets?
> Where I to thee Eternity shall give.[8]

The painted women, distanced from the poet as "things," stand metonymically for the death he wishes to avoid. Through art, that is through the sonnet, the lover avoids their "winding sheets."

> So shalt thou flye above the vulgar Throng,
> Still to survive in my immortal Song.

The poet, assuming the godlike power to grant immortality, momentarily suspends time and circumvents his own death as well as that of his lover. But what the sonnet can only imply in the tension between the two "types" of women is that, like the Duke of Ferrara, the poet purchases immortality — his own and his lover's — at the price of her vitality. "Words assassinate and they immortalize," writes Sharon Cameron in *Lyric Time*, "and they do both as a consequence of the death of presence."[9] This paradox is the essence of the sonnet's oppositions. While affirming the eternal presence of woman, the poem reduces her to a sign, to "flesh made words," and, in so doing,

---

[7] Sandra Gilbert and Susan Gubar, *Madwoman in the Attic: The Woman Writer and the Nineteenth Century Literary Imagination* (New Haven: Yale University Press, 1979), pp. 14–17.

[8] *Works*, II, 313.

[9] Sharon Cameron, *Lyric Time: Emily Dickinson and the Limits of Genre* (Baltimore: Johns Hopkins University Press, 1979), p. 246.

proclaims woman's absence.[10] "Painting" in the Renaissance lyric is a form of idealization that allows the painter to escape mutability and death. The Duke of Ferrara can have the ideal Duchess — constant and unchanging. The lyricist can create an ideal lover, one who will never grow old and die and who, therefore, will never remind him of his own aging and death. But idealizations have their price. The "painted woman" cannot die because she cannot live. As Wolfgang Lederer has pointed out about cosmetics, that is precisely the point: "where nothing is lifelike, nothing speaks of death."[11]

One of the consequences of "painting" a woman, of killing her into art, is already implicit in her transformation from body to text: she is dispersed into words, her body fragmented into a series of lifeless objects. Nancy J. Vickers, in a recent study of Petrarch's *Rime sparse*, argues that Petrarch's descriptive strategies, which set the standard for portraying feminine beauty in the Renaissance, neutralize the threat of death posed by women (or in *Rime sparse 52*, of dismemberment, since the poet/narrator plays Actaeon to Laura's Diana) by scattering her body. She becomes "a collection of exquisitely beautiful, dissociated objects," which fail to add up to any coherent or human whole.[12] Her textures may be those of metal or stones — the face of Chaucer's Rosamound, for instance, shines "as the cristal," while her cheeks are "lyke ruby" — or, like Shakespeare's Juliet, she may be disembodied, a light given off by the sun or stars. She may also be vegetative, like Thomas Campion's idealized lover in "There is a Garden in Her Face," but she remains no more human than Petrarch's Laura or Chaucer's Rosamound:

> There is a Garden in her face,
> Where Roses and white Lillies grow!
> A heav'nly paradise is that place,
> Wherein all pleasant fruits doe flow.
> There Cherries grow, which none may buy
> Till Cherry ripe themselves doe cry.[13]

The poet's imagery, while loosely held together by its garden *topos*, suggests none of the humanity of the lover's face; he has fragmented it into a series of discrete, non-human objects — lillies, roses, cherries, pearls, angels, and bows. Shakespeare's sonnet

---

[10] Murray Krieger explores this contradiction between the absence and presence of the beloved in the Renaissance love lyric in terms of the poet's desire to give bodily presence to language's representational nature: "Words are empty and belated counters because it is their nature to seek to refer to what is elsewhere and has occurred earlier. Any pretension by them to present reality is frustrated by the *re*, which requires that what they would represent — what has already presented itself in person — has had its presence, its presentness, elsewhere and earlier." The poet "would make language more than properly representational . . . [he] would make it nothing less than presentational," but is constantly frustrated by language's deferred nature. Woman dispersed into words is at once necessarily absent and present. "Presentation and Representation in the Renaissance Lyric: The Net of Words and the Escape of the Gods," in *Mimesis: From Mirror to Method, Augustine to Descartes*, eds. John D. Lyons and Stephen G. Nichols, Jr. (Hanover: University Press of New England, 1982), p. 118.

[11] Wolfgang Lederer, *The Fear of Women* (New York: Harcourt Brace Jovanovich, 1968), p. 42.

[12] Nancy J. Vickers, "Diana Described: Scattered Woman and Scattered Rhyme," *Critical Inquiry*, 8 (1981), 266.

[13] *The Works of Thomas Campion*, ed. Walter R. Davis (New York: Doubleday and Co., 1967), p. 174.

130 — "My mistress' eyes are nothing like the sun" — both parodies this "scattering" of the beloved into text and testifies to its popularity among lyric poets of the Renaissance.

My mistress' eyes are nothing like the sun;
Coral is far more red than her lips' red;
If snow be white, why then her breasts are dun;
If hairs be wires, black wires grow on her head.
I have seen roses damasked, red and white,
But no such roses see I in her cheeks.[14]

Unlike Fra Pandolph's portrait of Ferrara's Duchess, the descriptive strategy illustrated by Campion's poem and parodied by Shakespeare's sonnet rejects "realistic" representation altogether. Instead it transforms her, creating fetishes, forerunners of Gloriana's skull, from her dismembered body. The result, as Vickers suggests, is "the development of a code of beauty that causes us to view the fetishized body as a norm and encourages [women] . . . to seek to be 'ideal types, beautiful monsters composed of every individual perfection.'"[15] Idealized woman must become painted woman.

As Vickers suggests, woman must attempt to live up to the lyricists' idealizations of her. She must kill *herself* into art through "careful coiffure, through adornment and make-up"[16] that stress the "eternal type" over the mortal individual. But still she cannot win. The "painted woman" for the Renaissance moralist is also the death's head. "That picture," writes St. Ambrose [of painted women], "is of corruption and not comely, that painting is deceitful."[17] In *The Duchess of Malfi*, Bosola remarks, "I would sooner eat a dead pigeon taken from the soles of the feet of one sick of the plague, than kiss one of you [painted women] fasting" (II. i. 41–43).[18] Addressing Yorick's skull, Hamlet commands, "get you to my lady's chamber and tell her, let her paint an inch thick, to this favor she must come" (V. i. 212–214).[19] Indeed, this connection between woman's vanity and death, evoked also by Vendice's Act III soliloquy to Gloriana's painted skull, is not entirely gratuitous since the effects of mercury based cosmetics available to Renaissance women included gradual decomposition. In a treatise against painting, Thomas Tuke notes that

the excellency of this mercury sublimate is such, that the women, who often paint themselves with it, though they be very young, they presently turn old with withered and wrinkled faces like an ape, and before age comes upon them, they tremble (poor wretches) as if they were sick of the staggers, reeling, and full of quicksilver, for so they are . . . it eats out the spots and stains of the face, but so, that with all, it dries up, and consumes the flesh that is underneath, so that of force the poor skin shrinks . . . The harm and incon-

---

[14] William Shakespeare, *Sonnets*, ed. Barbara Herrnstein Smith (New York: Avon Books, 1969).

[15] Vickers, "Diana Described," 277.

[16] Lederer, *Fear of Women*, p. 42.

[17] Quoted in Thomas Tuke's "A Treatise Against Painting" (1616), in *Blood and Knavery: A Collection of English Renaissance Pamphlets and Ballads of Crime and Sin*, Joseph H. Marshburn and Alan R. Velie, eds. (Rutherford: Fairleigh Dickinson University Press, 1973), p. 186.

[18] John Webster, *The Duchess of Malfi*, ed. Elizabeth Brennan (London: Ernest Benn, 1964). All subsequent citations are from this edition and will be noted in the text.

[19] *The Complete Plays and Poems of William Shakespeare*, eds. William Allan Neilson and Charles Jarvis Nell (Cambridge: Houghton Mifflin, 1942).

venience (although it be great), yet it might well be dissembled, if other greater than this did not accompany it; such as are, a stinking breath, the blackness and corruption of the teeth which this soliman engenders.[20]

This description of mercury poisoning works on two levels: as a medical warning and a metaphorical image. It vividly evokes all the horrors, both visual and olfactory, of the putrefying corpse. By attempting to kill herself into art, to realize in her own flesh the idealizations of the lyricists, Tuke's painted woman literally kills herself. Like Gloriana's painted and poisoned skull, with which this essay began, she has become an instrument of death as well as a powerful *memento mori*.

III

The heroine in Jacobean tragedy is frequently a victim of the two activities of painting I have been describing: man painting woman as a lifeless, dismembered object (both an ideal and the corruption of that ideal) and woman painting herself to conform — pathetically — to the tragically double image men have of her. *The Revenger's Tragedy, The Duchess of Malfi,* and *'Tis Pity She's a Whore* work out, with disastrous results, the destructive potential of feminine idealization that in the lyric remains only symbolic. These plays "fix" women dialectically. Their heroines are caught between male fantasies of idealization and exploitation. Like the dead Gloriana, Webster's Duchess and Ford's Annabella are forced into silence and their "eternal presence" is assured only by their deaths; they are *literally* killed into art, *literally* dismembered. Like *The Revenger's Tragedy, The Duchess of Malfi* and *'Tis Pity She's a Whore* demonstrate that the lyric's idealization is, at best, a highly unstable poetic moment, a male fantasy of power which, when acted upon by the male characters, ultimately turns against them and exposes their tragic delusions.

Webster's *Duchess of Malfi* demonstrates — tragically — that the most serious consequence of painting for women lies in the power which man coopts for himself to impose upon her and the world his fictions about femininity. These fictions, like his desires, are contradictory. Malfi is a place in which all women have become "signifiers" which must be "interpreted," often in unflattering ways, to accord with men's desires. Yet, as Susan McCloskey has recently argued, the play's central "sign," the Duchess of Malfi, remains an unreadable cipher for all the play's male characters.[21] To Antonio, her husband, she is a saint whose

> days are practis'd in such noble virtues
> That sure her nights — nay more her very sleeps —
> Are more in heaven than other ladies' shrifts.

[I. ii. 123–125]

To Ferdinand, she becomes a whore who "likes that part which, like the lamprey / Hath ne'er a bone in't" (I. ii. 255–256). To the "common rabble" she is a strumpet. To Bosola she is now "a box of worm seed," "a salvatory of green mummy," a "little

---

[20] Tuke, "A Treatise Against Painting," p. 183.
[21] Susan McCloskey, "The Price of Misinterpretation in *The Duchess of Malfi*," in *From Renaissance to Restoration: Metamorphoses of the Drama,* eds. Robert Markley and Laurie Finke (Cleveland: Bellflower Press).

crudded milk" (IV. ii. 123–125), now a woman who displays a "behavior so noble / As to give majesty to adversity" (IV. i. 5–6). Modern critics' readings of the Duchess have often been as divided as the characters'. One critic, in the same breath, sees her as a "great lady in command of her household," and a "mere voluptuary." [22] Clifford Leech condemns her for "overturning a social code" and defying "the responsibilities of degree both as a woman in speaking first and as a Duchess in marrying beneath her." He insists on the parallels between the Duchess and the whore Julia: "It is difficult to resist the idea that Julia is meant to provide a comment on the behavior of the Duchess; they are sisters, Webster hints, in their passions and in their consequent actions." [23] Harriett Hawkins, on the other hand, notes that Webster's "'noble' Duchess of Malfi is radiant, intelligent, brave, witty, warm, and loving. . . . throughout her tragedy, Webster insists that she acts in accordance with a finer and fairer morality than the one which persecutes and condemns her." [24]

These contradictory "readings" of the Duchess are more than merely the kind of critical "one-up-man-ship" Richard Levin criticizes in *New Readings vs. Old Plays,* [25] yet they cannot be easily reconciled. They illustrate the ways in which patriarchal ideologies, the "masculine consciousness" Gohlke discusses, both create and ultimately judge the Duchess even for modern readers. Antonio's high praise of her virtue results from his perception of her as a potentially dutiful wife. Yet, by the very same standards, she can be condemned for overstepping the bounds of a dutiful sister (a dilemma shared, to some extent, by the heroines of both *The Revenger's Tragedy* and *'Tis Pity She's a Whore*). The virulence of Ferdinand's condemnation of women who wed twice, "whores by that rule are precious," suggests a fear of sexual betrayal similar to that which prompts Vendice to test his sister Castiza in Tourneur's play. His reaction reflects an attitude best articulated, as Gohlke notes, by the player queen in *Hamlet*: "A second time I kill my husband dead / When second husband kisses me in bed" (III. ii. 188–189). [26] Ferdinand perceives female sexuality, even when condoned by lawful marriage, as a form of violence and reacts to it violently.

Webster suggests, however, that the Duchess's dilemma is inevitable. At the height of her suffering, the Duchess asks Cariola, her maid, "Who do I look like now?" The answer confirms what one imagines are her worst fears: that she is condemned by a body that speaks more eloquently than she:

> Like to your picture in a gallery,
> A deal of life in show, but none in practice;
> Or rather like some reverent monument
> Whose ruins are even pitied.
>
> [IV. ii. 31–34]

[22] Gunnar Boklund, *The Duchess of Malfi: Sources, Themes, and Characters* (Cambridge: Harvard University Press, 1962), p. 91.

[23] Clifford Leech, *John Webster: A Critical Study* (London: Hogarth Press, 1951), pp. 69, 75; for the comparison between the Duchess and Julia, see also Boklund, *The Duchess of Malfi,* p. 90.

[24] Harriett Hawkins, *Poetic Freedom and Poetic Truth,* (Oxford: Clarendon Press, 1976), p. 28.

[25] Richard Levin, *New Readings vs. Old Plays: Recent Trends in the Reinterpretation of English Renaissance Drama* (Chicago: University of Chicago Press, 1979).

[26] Gohlke, "Shakespeare's Tragic Paradigm," 173.

The question is a strange one (she asks not "what do I look like?" but "who do I look like?"); the answer is even stranger. Both women seem to realize that the Duchess of Malfi is as much a "painted woman" as the "Old Lady" Bosola reacts to with such disgust in Act II. She has become her own portrait, literally a "sign" of her former — idealized — self. Like the Duchess of Ferrara in Browning's poem, she has been "killed into art," transfixed and imprisoned by the images — saint and whore — those around her have created and imposed upon her, images that reflect the painters' own fears and obsessions, rather than her own subjectivity.

In this respect, the Duchess's tragedy is the archetypical tragedy of the Renaissance heroine. While the men around her "paint" her to conform to their own perceptions of the feminine "Other," she is silent. She can talk, but she cannot speak; she can make noise, but can have nothing to say. Ferdinand's pun, "women like that part, which, / like the lamprey / Hath ne'er a bone in't," is significant, in this regard, because it may refer either to the tongue or the phallus. Susan McCloskey notes that *The Duchess of Malfi* abounds in images and scenes which emphasize the Duchess's entrapment in a world in which she can talk eloquently, but cannot speak.[27] Early in the play, Antonio praises her "discourse," but only by evoking, in the same breath, her silence:

> For her discourse, it is so full of rapture,
> You only will begin then to be sorry
> When she doth end her speech; and wish, in wonder,
> She held it less vainglory to talk much
> Than your penance, to hear her.
>
> [I. ii. 112–116]

It is not her speech so much as her "sweet countenance" that "speaketh so divine a continence, / As cuts off all lascivious and vain hope" (I. ii. 121–122). With her brothers, the Duchess hardly utters a word. In fifty lines of Act I, scene i she speaks four times, never more than two lines, and is interrupted twice. In Act III, after exchanging trivialities with Antonio and Cariola, she is confronted by Ferdinand and told "Do not speak" and "cut out thine tongue" (III. ii. 75, 108). He refuses to let her speak her innocence. Finally, during her torture, Bosola notes that "her silence . . . expresseth more than if she spake" (IV. i. 9–10).

These images of talking and silence remind us that, although a woman's weapon is supposed to be her tongue, women always remain outside language, which, as Jacques Lacan argues, is essentially phallocentric. If this is true, the effects on women's consciousness are psychologically profound: Hélène Cixous notes that "If man operates under the threat of castration, if masculinity is culturally ordered by the castration complex, it might be said that the backlash, the return on women of this castration anxiety is its displacement as decapitation, execution of women, as loss of her head."[28] The Duchess's death by strangulation is a metaphorical working out of this anxiety. During her lifetime the Duchess remains outside language and powerless precisely because she is silent. In death she is silenced, her tongue literally "cut off" from her

[27] McCloskey, "Price of Misinterpretation," pp. 36–37.
[28] Hélène Cixous, "Castration or Decapitation," *Signs*, 7 (1981), 43.

body. This image recurs throughout Renaissance tragedy and seems to be a literary enactment of the lyrics' symbolic "scattering" of the female body to neutralize its threat. Sexual hostility most frequently results in the silencing "decapitation" of the tragic heroine: Lavinia raped, her tongue cut out (and her hands cut off so she cannot write) in *Titus Andronicus*, Desdemona strangled in *Othello*, Gloriana reduced to a grinning skull in *The Revenger's Tragedy*.

If the heroine of John Ford's play, *'Tis Pity She's a Whore*, suffers a dismemberment, a "scattering," of a different sort, her fate reminds us, no less than the Duchess's, that idealizations in tragedy stand metonymically for the permanence of death. For Annabella to be literally painted into a lifeless immortality, or to be made into a mirror that reflects the painter's virtues (as well as his fears), necessarily produces disastrous results. Forced by Giovanni's love to juggle several ideals, to fulfill the conflicting demands of a faithful sister and lover and a dutiful wife and daughter, the living Annabella can finally be none of these. Therefore, Giovanni logically concludes, she must die so she cannot betray him, so that she might remain faithful to the ideal: "Love me or kill me," brother and sister echo one another (I. ii. 252, 255). Like the Duchess of Malfi, Annabella is the play's central cipher, unknown and unknowable, as Thomas Ellice's ambivalent commendatory verses suggest.

> With admiration I beheld this Whore
> Adorn'd with beauty such as might restore
> (If ever being as thy muse hath fam'd)
> Her Giovanni, in his love unblam'd.
> The ready Graces lent their willing aid,
> Pallas herself now play'd the chambermaid,
> And help'd to put her dressings on. Secure
> Rest thou that thy name shall herein endure
> To th'end of age; and Annabella be
> Gloriously fair, even in her infamy.[29]

Ellice's uncertainty as to whether to praise her as a tragic heroine or censure her as a whore is representative of the reaction Annabella seems designed to generate. While N. W. Bawcutt praises her as "a more thoughtful and sensitive person than her brother," and one who "loves deeply," T. S. Eliot regards her as "pliant, vacillating, and negative . . . virtually a moral defective."[30] Finally, like the Duchess of Malfi, she can be only the silent image of what others — onstage and in the audience — paint her to be — angel and whore, goddess and monster — securing through her death, both her immortality (and immortal beauty) and that of her "painter," John Ford.

Although at first glance "crudely sensationalist,"[31] Ford's choice of incest as his central romantic entanglement underscores the narcissistic root of Giovanni's idealization of Annabella and of all such idealizations. Through incest, Giovanni quite self-

---

[29] John Ford, *'Tis Pity She's A Whore*, ed. N. W. Bawcutt (Lincoln: University of Nebraska Press, 1966), p. 2. All citations are from this edition and will be noted in the text.

[30] Bawcutt, Introduction to *'Tis Pity She's a Whore*, p. xx; T. S. Eliot, *Selected Essays* (London, 1932), p. 198.

[31] Bawcutt, "Introduction," p. xiv.

consciously attempts to achieve a union with himself by "annihilating the otherness — the autonomy" of his sister.[32]

> Say that we had one father, say one womb
> (Curse to my joys) gave both us life and birth;
> . . . to be ever one,
> One soul, one flesh, one love, one heart, one all?
>
> [I. i. 28–29, 33–34]

That Giovanni sees his own reflection in Annabella seems clear from the prominence of mirror imagery associated with their union: "Look in your glass and there behold your own [beauty]" (I. ii. 201). By making his sister his reflection, he can eliminate her difference from himself. Annabella becomes a passive and silent mirror of her brother and, like a mirror, she can only be a physical, and hence unthreatening, reflection. All of the play's characters, and particularly Giovanni, praise only her physical beauty. Even the passive feminine virtues of chastity and submissiveness are hardly mentioned. Annabella seems to be virtuous only because she is beautiful.

> Where the body's furniture is beauty
> The mind's must needs be virtue . . .
> My sister's beauty being rarely fair
> Is rarely virtuous.
>
> [II. v. 18–23]

Her nullity in all else but beauty places in relief Giovanni's masculinity, those virtues and flaws which define him as a man. These the Friar outlines in Act I:

> Art thou, my son, that miracle of wit
> Who once, within these three months, wert esteem'd
> A wonder of thine age, throughout Bolonia?
> How did the University applaud
> Thy government, behavior, learning, speech,
> Sweetness, and all that could make up a man!
>
> [I. i. 47–52]

Even his tragic flaws are masculine: a kind of Faustian belief in his own power and knowledge and his desire "to make our love a god and worship it" (I. ii. 146). Giovanni's masculinity contains and allows him to assume the godlike role of Annabella's creator. Because Annabella looks like him, and because her virtue is validated only by her beauty and not by her actions, Giovanni can create himself as a god and worship the reflection of his own beauty in Annabella without any threat to his own masculinity or identity.

Like the lyricists, Giovanni attempts to neutralize any threat of change and ensure Annabella's constancy by verbally scattering her body into signs, which seem changeless because they are lifeless.

---

[32] Gilbert and Gubar, *Madwoman in the Attic,* p. 208. They continue, "To the extent that the desire to violate the incest taboo is a desire to be self-sufficient — self-begetting — it is a divinely interdicted wish to be 'as Gods.'"

View well her face, and in that little round
You may observe a world of variety:
For color, lips; for sweet perfume, her breath;
For jewels, eyes; for threads of purest gold,
Hair, for delicious choice of flowers, cheeks;
Wonder in every portion of that throne:
Hear but her speak, and you will swear the spheres
Make music to the citizens in Heaven.

[II. iv. 49–56]

The jewels, threads of purest gold, and the music of the spheres function as images to fix Annabella, paint her frozen, if only for a moment, into a changeless immortality. Giovanni briefly creates in Annabella the rhetorical ideal of the Petrarchan lyricist, and for a moment he is allowed to enjoy it. But, as with the Petrarchan lyric, such a suspension of time and mutability can only be a poetic moment, highly unstable. Taken out of "lyric time," the ideal begins to self-destruct, virtually at the moment of its creation. Its contradictions are revealed in the tension created by the "scattering" of Annabella's body, particularly the constant dismemberment of her heart. "Owning her heart," her father tells her intended husband, "what need you doubt her ear?" (I. ii. 54). Annabella herself refers to her "captive heart" (I. ii. 242) and Giovanni to their "one heart" (I. i. 34), as if hers were already detached from her body. Even in jest, her male suitors reveal a tendency to disembowl her: "I almost burst her belly with laughing" remarks Bergetto (I. iii. 54).

No doubt much of this imagery is conventional, even clichéd. But when Annabella cannot live up to the ideal created by her brother and her husband, their language of verbal dismemberment becomes more and more violent and the insistent repetition of these conventional images becomes more disturbing. When her husband, Soranzo, discovers Annabella's advanced state of pregnancy, he offers to "rip up [her] heart," and "hew [her] flesh to shreds" (IV. iii. 53, 58). Like Vendice, he associates her all too apparent sexual betrayal with his fear of death and loss of immortality: "How thou hast mock'd my hopes and with the shame / Of lewd womb even buried me alive" (IV. iii. 113–114). Her obvious femininity has made him vulnerable to the processes of time.

Like Soranzo, Giovanni reacts to his sense of betrayal at the hands of a "faithless sister" with a desperate and failed attempt to control the forces of life and death by controlling the feminine: "For in my fists I bear the twists of life [Annabella's heart]" (V. vi. 72). The pattern of verbal dismemberment culminates in Annabella's literal dismemberment. To "save [her] fame" Giovanni must "fix" her through death. In performance, his entrance in Act V, scene i with Annabella's heart impaled on his dagger must seem melodramatic and sensational; the heart, nevertheless, serves as a powerful representation of the masculine attempt to control life and death, to thwart or coopt the feminine power of reproduction ("this dagger's point plough'd up / Her fruitful womb" (V. vi. 32–33)) — when necessary, by violence, by dismembering, impaling, fixing:

> The hapless fruit
> That in her womb receiv'd its life from me
> Hath had from me a cradle and a grave.

[V. v. 94–96]

If Gloriana's skull is an apt image with which to begin a study of femininity in Jacobean tragedy because it powerfully represents the pun in my title on "painting," Annabella's heart seems an appropriate place to end. Like the skull, it stands as both cipher and fetish. Like Annabella, indeed like all women, it is a sign of ambivalence, of alienation of body and spirit; it is the object of both admiration and scorn. The heart reveals the male fantasy of power beneath the surface of the "painting" and aptly stands for the failure of all three plays' heroes — Giovanni, as well as Vendice, Ferdinand, and even Bosola — their inability to actualize the fictions of lyric representation, or perhaps their tendency to actualize those fictions all too well.

Beatrice-Joanna and the Rhetoric of Love in *The Changeling*

Sara Eaton

> Forsooth, if we are to hear of no wickedness,
> history must be done away with. So those comedies
> should be prized which condemn the vices which they
> bring to our ears, especially when the life of impure
> women ends in an unhappy death.
> — Scaliger

Scaliger's prized deaths of "impure women" suggest the seriousness of Renaissance attitudes toward femininity. Conventionalized in Courtly Love literature and under scrutiny in Puritan sermons and the popular press, femininity was considered especially in terms of modes of appearance, whether physical or theatrical. As Tuke explained in his *A Treatise against Painting*, "It is not enough to be good, but she that is good, must seem good: she that is chast, must seem chast."[1] This distinction between feminine being and seeming pervaded dominant Renaissance ideologies concerning and defining the wickedness of women. Implicit in the Courtly Love and edenic ideologies, for instance, is the assumption that women may be what they are, but that their gender does not allow them to seem so. Such logic allowed for a woman who failed to seem pure to be thought impure.

Complicating these Renaissance notions of feminine "seeming" is the fact that their source was male. Edenic and Courtly Love representations of women focus on female figures whose apparent purity is undercut by their failure to fulfill male expectations of their behavior. These notions of femininity subjected woman to a double-bind of either being pure but not seeming so or seeming so but not according to male conventions. Middleton and Rowley, I will suggest, locate the "frightful pleasure" of *The Changeling* in this double-bind. By linking the male problem of knowing women, the

---

Sara Eaton teaches in the Department of English at the University of Minnesota.

---

[1] T. Tuke, *A Treatise Against Painting* (London, 1616), p. 10, as quoted by Sandra Clark, *The English Pamphleteers* (East Brunswick, N.J.: Farleigh Dickinson Press, 1983), p. 178.

confusion of being and seeming, to the rhetoric of Courtly Love and edenic longing, the play displays its linguistic exchanges as a drama of sexual revenge leaving the deaths of impure women to be "prized."

Throughout *The Changeling*, Beatrice-Joanna succeeds all too well in her attempts to be as she is perceived. On one side of Courtly Love's polarities, she portrays Alsemero's idealization of her. On the other side, she personifies DeFlores's view of self-degradation. Her rhetoric merely reproducing theirs, Beatrice-Joanna becomes an apparently harmonious representation of their conflicting desires. As a woman capable of seeming to be as they perceive her, she comes to perceive herself as an image of both idealized and degraded femininity — as a fallen Eve. Not autonomous in her actions, Beatrice-Joanna internalizes and reflects the inherent contradictions in male perceptions of women, especially as couched in the rhetoric of Courtly Love. Through Beatrice-Joanna's representation of the effects of Courtly Love, *The Changeling* indicts courtly rhetoric in its historical personification as unhappy death.

If it is not surprising that Middleton and Rowley use Courtly Love rhetoric to expose its contradictions, it is surprising how many critics, like Scaliger, argue that Beatrice-Joanna is morally culpable in how she is perceived.[2] Such critical arguments repeat the characters' expectations for feminine behavior, that women should be as they seem. From this point of view, Alsemero or DeFlores is seen as the hero of the play, and Beatrice-Joanna, who has concealed her ethical vacuity and fooled the male characters into believing romantic notions about women, gets exactly what she deserves. This perspective does not account for the play's action, which forms in reaction to Beatrice-Joanna's attempts to be equal to the male characters' perceptions. If the critical endeavor accepts the notion that female characters should be merely the vehicles for other characters' moral and aesthetic "pleasures," Beatrice-Joanna's fate is trivialized, the male characters' views are valorized, and the main thrust of Middleton and Rowley's drama is lost.

The question the play asks, then, is what kind of pleasures women can offer. It shifts attention from the revenge tragedy motifs, heroic concerns, to psychological and linguistic ones that can reflect the mechanics of sexual revenge. Although one of *The Changeling*'s most obvious dramatic constructs is a tragic exploration of "the lunatic, the lover, and the poet," contemporary expectations for Senecan conventions are distinctive in this play's dramatic structure primarily because they matter so little. For example, Alonzo's ghost, instead of either terrorizing the guilty DeFlores and Beatrice-Joanna or urging his brother toward revenge, becomes "some ill thing that haunts the house."[3] His brother, the justified avenger, is frustrated; DeFlores enacts a

[2] Fredson Bowers, *Elizabethan Revenge Tragedy, 1587–1642* (Gloucester, Mass.: Princeton University Press, 1959), p. 204; Christopher Ricks's important study, "The Moral and Poetic Structure of *The Changeling*," *Essays in Criticism*, 10 (1960), 295; Roger Stilling, *Love and Death in Renaissance Tragedy* (Baton Rouge: Louisiana State University Press, 1976), p. 250–56; Lenora Leet Brodwin, *Elizabethan Love Tragedy* (New York: New York University Press, 1971); and Robert Jordan, "Myth and Psychology in *The Changeling*," *Renaissance Drama*, NS 3 (1970), p. 165.

[3] Thomas Middleton and William Rowley, *The Changeling*, in *Drama of the English Renaissance*, Vol. II, ed. Russell A. Fraser and Norman Rabkin (New York: Macmillan, 1976), V. i. 62. All subsequent references from this edition are included in the text.

sexual revenge. Traditional Senecan conventions are trivialized so that the audience must focus on characters who appear in a tragic "moonlight madness," slowly turning into a nightmare that explores the possession of women through the language of Courtly Love.

The dialogue in the first four acts presents polite, courtier-like statements, full of the customary wit and neoplatonic conceits common to wooing in Renaissance drama. But the characters puncture these dialogues with frequent asides that reveal to what extent the public, idealized language masks the characters' other assessments of situations. For example, in Act II, scene i, approximately two-thirds of the first ninety lines are spoken in either soliloquies or asides. Regardless of how this display of "private" language is staged, the audience is aware of these shifts in the play's language. Indeed, most of the dialogue between Beatrice-Joanna and DeFlores is directed toward the audience through asides:

> Bea. [Aside] Again!
> — This ominous ill-faced fellow more disturbs me
> Than all my other passions.
>
> DeF. [Aside] Now't begins again;
> I'll stand this storm of hail though the stones
>   pelt me.
>
> [II. i. 52–54]

Her passionate revulsion and his physical determination are forcefully articulated — to the audience. The content and tone of the asides in themselves introduce a second level of signification in addition to that of the play's public language.[4]

The public and private languages demonstrate both sides of the rhetoric of Courtly Love, the idealized language appropriate to wooing, and the private language reflecting physical corruption. Beatrice-Joanna lives in a world where expectations of "transformations" in love are expressed in one version of Courtly Love rhetoric while the characters' private assessments of their world and each other are expressed in another. In a sense, then, the public dialogues, both in the plot and subplot, are merely a veneer covering other meanings in the play. By Act V, moreover, the asides of the first four acts disappear, as their reflections on the nature of love's transformations prevail and become the primary language. Although *The Changeling* here moves toward a rhetorical unity, I will suggest that this unity is essentially repressive: both the public and private languages hinge on the possession of females. In fact, Beatrice-Joanna's death at the end of the play means the end of her attempts to be rhetorically effective in her own world. The rhetorical unity of the play, then, amounts to the silencing of Beatrice-Joanna.[5]

---

[4] M. C. Bradbrook, *Themes and Conventions of Elizabethan Tragedy* (Cambridge: Cambridge University Press, 1952), p. 124.

[5] The *OED* sheds light on both the title of the play and what I have been describing. Contemporary usages of "changeling" suggest: 1) One given to change, fickle or inconsistent person (the most cited explanation of the title); and 2) A person or thing (surreptitiously) put in exchange for another. Besides referring to the bed-switch and nearly every characters' shift in position in the play, the second meaning also would apply to a rhetorical exchange. The *OED* refers, moreover, to Puttenham's description of the rhetorical figure, hypallage, as a "changeling." Etymology suggests, then, that the meanings of the word are variations on exchanges or what one might call metonymic transfers.

Beatrice-Joanna's body is the referent of the play's rhetoric; the male characters discuss her as an object to be claimed and possessed. Alsemero views her as the ideal lady in a Courtly Love scheme in which he wants to believe; his language is the most obvious example of *The Changeling*'s public discourse. His talk of magic potions and his constant observations of omens reflect his doubts about love while reinforcing his idealized perceptions of Beatrice-Joanna as the perfect woman. His opening declaration, "With man's first creation, the place blest, / And is his right home back, if he achieve it" (I. i. 8–9), closes off Beatrice-Joanna's actual sexual identity by linking it to Eden and the temple where he first sees her. His perception of her sacred sexuality is verified and, from his point of view, realized, in his physician's closet. There he keeps his "Book of Experiments Call'd Secrets in Nature" (IV. i. 24–25), the "key that will lead to a pretty secret" (IV. ii. 111) — the secrets of chastity and feminine sexuality. Declaiming that she is "Chaste as the breath of heaven, or morning's womb, / That brings the day forth, thus my love encloses thee" (IV. ii. 149–150), he perceives Beatrice-Joanna as a way back to a sacred and enclosed world through his possession of her. His exalted perception is ironically revealed as an obsessive possessiveness when, in the last act, he forces her into the closet with the macabre threat, "enter my closet; / I'll be your keeper yet" (V. iii. 86–87).

But from the beginning of the play, when Alsemero tells her that "there is scarce a thing but is loved and loathed" (I. i. 126), we are aware that his view includes the underside of the Courtly Love tradition: the woman-as-monster, the Duessa. Alsemero "cannot be too sure" (IV. ii. 126) as he tests her virginity; he is disturbed and uncertain about his role as a courtly lover and distrusts his own judgment (an attitude that Jasperino, his man, aids and abets). Beatrice-Joanna argues that Alsemero is as implicated as she is in the murders, because she has become a "cruel murd'ress" (V. iii. 65) to insure their marriage. He is not affected by this reiteration of the argument used so successfully with Beatrice-Joanna by DeFlores. He ignores any logic or psychological truth in her argument, and instead pronounces his sense of her static, inherently flawed sexuality. Saying "Twas in my fears at first, 'twill have it now: / Oh, thou art all deformed" (V. iii. 76–77), he thinks of the marriage-bed in a crypt, "itself's a charnel, the sheets shrouds" (V. iii. 83), even though the marriage has not been consummated. Conflating sex and death, ignorant of how Beatrice-Joanna, DeFlores, and even Diaphanta have allied to insure his marriage, "this dangerous bridge of blood" (V. iii. 81), Alsemero expects Beatrice-Joanna to be a chimerical representation of female sexuality. She functions as a vaginal pathway back to an edenic world that he would also test in this one.

Alsemero begins the play as a frustrated revenger, and manages to continue in that role as he constantly suspects the "murderer" of his illusions to be one of the characters around him. Beatrice-Joanna becomes the vehicle for his return to a perfect world at the same time that she represents that impossibility. This dream requires a passive Beatrice-Joanna who does not murder, who will remain in the closet of "sweet secrets" as an imagined but frustrated version of female sexuality. When Alsemero forces her into the closet in Act V, his language again stresses love's dual nature: "I'll be your pander now; rehearse again / Your scene of lust, that you may be perfect" (V. iii. 114–115).

Alsemero's actions after this reveal the extent to which he has strengthened his allegiance to Vermandero, Beatrice-Joanna's father, in reaction to his own perceptions of love. His consolation to Vermandero as they view the bodies — "Sir, you have yet a son's duty living" (V. iii. 216) — suggests that "his right home back," the edenic world he has searched for since the opening of the play, is organized around a father who is still living. Alsemero sees himself as replacing Beatrice-Joanna in her father's eyes; he would maintain both his perception of female sexuality, and his identity as a would-be revenger, by acting in an essentially adolescent role that grants him the "father's son" position he has filled throughout the play. But, implicated by his marriage and Beatrice-Joanna's death, his place in this patrilineal system is based on ambivalence: his idealization and denial of Beatrice-Joanna's actions and what they mean.

Alsemero desperately needs to maintain the closet of "sweet secrets," although he never really recognizes the fears and desires projected on the "fallen Eve" locked up in it. He avoids meaningful action, when, for example, he thinks on his marriage: "The bed itself's a charnel, the sheets shrouds / For murdered carcasses; it must ask pause / What I must do in this" (V. iii. 83–85). And he counsels repression when he recommends to Vermandero: "Let it be blotted out; let your heart lose it, / And it can never look you in the face / Nor tell a tale behind the back of life" (V. iii. 182–184). Implied by his language, Alsemero's ambivalence is revealed in his actions — other than bedding Diaphanta and locking first Beatrice-Joanna and then DeFlores in the closet, he does nothing to initiate dramatic action. In the final analysis, Alsemero finds his "right home back," by locking his psyche in a closet of secrets.[6]

The other important male character, DeFlores, speaking in the corrupted private language of the asides, the underside of Courtly Love rhetoric, views Beatrice-Joanna as an "odd feeder" (II. ii. 153). His language and gestures characterize him as driven toward a violent, deadly possession of Beatrice-Joanna, and his view of her character, like Alsemero's, is a projection of his own desires. He would "thrust [his] fingers / Into her sockets" (I. i. 236–237), confusing a vaginal metaphor with, perhaps, a visual reference to her gloves. Anticipating fulfillment of *his* projected erotic intentions, he presents her dead Alonzo's finger, with her betrothal ring still on it. Representations of death and sexual possession are further conflated when, after killing the proxy-bride, Diaphanta, he brings her charred body back for Beatrice-Joanna to see. In these incidents, DeFlores implicates Beatrice-Joanna in the murders through her perceptions. That is, he would have her see what he has seen and done for her favors. Description will not suffice. Distrusting the idealized metaphors of Courtly Love — the public language that Beatrice-Joanna espouses — he consistently produces the content, the bodies, that result from her usage of the play's public language. It is thus DeFlores who interprets and reproduces her metaphoric intentions in the flesh, enacting these connections between language and actions. When Beatrice-Joanna and DeFlores are locked into the closet together, Alsemero assumes fornication; instead, in an attempt

---

[6] For further discussion, see Melanie Klein, *Envy and Gratitude and Other Works, 1946–1963* (New York: Dell, 1975), p. 217. Klein's description of the common male pre-Oedipal movement between the love-object and the authority figure (the mother and father) seems to provide an explanation for Alsemero's psychological realignment with Vermandero.

at ultimate consummation, DeFlores stabs her with his penknife. Finally, stabbing himself and presenting his own body "as a token," he tells the dying Beatrice-Joanna to "make haste"; he would "not go to leave [her] far behind" (V. iii. 175, 177).

In his death speech, DeFlores tells Alsemero of his greedy obsession with Beatrice-Joanna; the taking of her virginity "was so sweet to me / That I have drunk up all, left none behind / For any man to pledge me" (V. iii. 169–171).[7] This is wishful thinking. DeFlores's actions can only be seen as an endless pursuit of absolute consummation, a continuous circling around a deflowered Beatrice-Joanna who by his own definition has been rendered nothing. For this reason, quite literally, he cannot get enough of her. Throughout the play, DeFlores signifies his intentions toward Beatrice-Joanna through violent oral and anal metaphors. He wants to "drink her up," and produces pieces of his murdered victims for her approval.[8] His metaphors indicate an intense egotism that he projects back on Beatrice-Joanna, anticipating that "peace and innocency has turned [her] out / And made [her] one with [him]" (III. iv. 139–140). To DeFlores, as with Alsemero, Beatrice-Joanna is still primarily the imagistic locus for an active psychological exchange of introjected and projected male sexual desires. But if Alsemero creates Courtly Love's version of idealized feminine sexuality, DeFlores designs one for his digestive tract. Beatrice-Joanna's identity remains elusive except in terms of the sexual excitement she generates, one that promises a reunion with Alsemero's and DeFlores's version of the "Other" that is "I."

What Alsemero locks away, DeFlores greedily drinks up. These two male characters would seem to be the play's actual "twins of mischief" (V. iii. 142). Their projections of desire onto Beatrice-Joanna seem to shape the play's rhetoric. Together Alsemero and DeFlores enact two psychological motions involved in the production of Courtly Love rhetoric. In a romance or a single poet's inspirational mode, Alsemero's idealization of Beatrice-Joanna would be complementary to DeFlores's ingestion or internalizing of what she represents as an idealized figure. Split, the two men act out variants of Courtly Love's tragic potential occurring when the source of poetic inspiration may not be as she appears. Frederick Goldin explains that in a harmonious Courtly Love relationship, the lover seeks the "guiding image of his completeness":

> first, that image coincides with the self-image of his class, so that the more he pursues his own desires, the more he is at one with his equal, the more he is part of a community; second, that personal image of his perfection, because it is embodied in the person of the lady, is now capable of responding to him, of loving him and making it possible for him to be at one with the image that guides him. This joy is worth the renunciation of every other joy,

---

[7] This assertion reflects ironically on Alsemero's assumptions that the potion Beatrice-Joanna drank was a "pledge" of her virginity. Alsemero's and DeFlores's perceptions converge metaphorically, leaving Beatrice-Joanna at their center.

[8] Melanie Klein, "The Emotional Life of the Infant," *Envy and Gratitude*. Klein's description of the infant's libidinal responses, fixated on oral and anal functions, is useful in understanding DeFlores's preoccupation with drinking and dead bodies. The infant's sense of producing feces for the mother is both a pleasurable and a frequently conflicted psychological response. According to Klein, cathexis with a death-wish towards the self or mother often occurs.

for it gives inner peace and certainty. Here now is the perfect dream of love: all the aspects of the Courtly man become harmonious and one.[9]

Alsemero constructs a "self-image of his class" which DeFlores would locate inside the psychological boundaries of his body. Like their characteristic languages, these men are psychological doubles, enacting the implications of their rhetoric.

Alsemero fears Beatrice-Joanna's unworthiness to the same degree that DeFlores defines her as such; conversely, DeFlores fears sharing Beatrice-Joanna with the "community" formed through her idealization to the same extent that Alsemero desires access to it. These characters could find completion in each other, and Beatrice-Joanna would still be the vehicle for expressing their desires. Instead, both characters act as though "knowing" Beatrice-Joanna as the "Other" includes seeing a corruption which must be enclosed, termed nothing, and rendered silent. The metaphors which reveal this knowledge deny her an autonomous identity while disclaiming any responsibility for her murder. What does she do to trigger the violent insistence that she has failed to reflect adequately their expectations of harmonious completeness?

In a play where the men see what they want to see, Beatrice-Joanna says: "Would creation — / . . . had formed me man . . . / Oh, tis the soul of freedom . / . . . I should have power / Then to oppose my loathings, nay, remove 'em / For ever from my sight" (II. ii. 107–109, 111–113). Beatrice-Joanna enlists DeFlores as her "man" primarily to dispose of Alonzo, upon whom her "eyes were mistaken" (I. i. 85). Her father is determined to see her married; whether to Alonzo or Alsemero seems to be of little importance so long as the marriage amounts to "the addition of a son" (II. i. 99). She would marry Alsemero, whom she sees "now with the eyes of judgment / And see the way to merit, clearly see it" (II. i. 13–14). In this world, it does not occur to her to act alone; she defines herself through others' perceptions of her, and she is, consequently, powerless "to oppose [her] loathings." She would "see" as the male characters do, but unlike them, she needs an accomplice to turn her dreams into the play's "reality." Accordingly, she always assumes that DeFlores will respond as a courtier to her request for service. The "merit" she sees in Alsemero is his embodiment of the idealized Courtly Love rhetoric; ironically, he becomes her frustrated chivalric lover.

More importantly, she begins to perceive the world around her through male eyes. She becomes the Eve around whom Paradise will collapse. She is initially horrified at DeFlores's serpent-like interpretation of her complicity in Alonzo's murder — she says, "Thy language is so bold and vicious" (III. iv. 123) — but she finally is seduced by her own perceptions of what Alsemero and DeFlores represent. While before her defloration she asks, "Was my creation in the womb so cursed / It must engender with a viper first?" (III. iv. 165–166), she later declaims that "the east [the sunrise] is not more beauteous than [DeFlores's] service" (V. i. 72). She shares with Alsemero the public language that characterizes her perceptions of her world at the same time that she

---

[9] Frederick Goldin, "The Array of Perspectives in the Early Courtly Love Lyric," In Pursuit of Perfection: Courtly Love in Medieval Literature, eds. Joan Farrante, George D. Economous, Frederick Goldin, Esther Quinn, Renata Karlin, Saul N. Brody (Port Washington, N.Y.: Kennikat Press, 1975), p. 56. For a discussion of narcissism in Courtly Love, see Goldin's The Mirror of Narcissus in the Courtly Love Lyric (Ithaca, N.Y.: Cornell University Press, 1967), pp. 50ff.

inures herself to the growing heap of bodies around her. Personifying Alsemero's ambivalence, she incorporates the debased concept of self that DeFlores offers.

Beatrice-Joanna's anger and disappointment with Diaphanta's lust in the marriage bed that should be hers, and her insistence to the end that she has been sexually honorable, do not necessarily indicate her villainy, or even her guilt. Rather, she refuses to relinquish what she perceives as her prerogative in the Courtly Love scenario. As DeFlores works out the details for Diaphanta's death, Beatrice-Joanna declares that she is "forced to love [him] now, / 'Cause [he] provid'st so carefully for my honor" (V. i. 47–48). Here, sex, death, love, and honor become equational terms, and the play's meanings behind the private and public languages converge. Still, she relies on DeFlores to implement those meanings, since she "must trust somebody" (V. i. 15) to sustain her power in a patriarchy. Beatrice-Joanna allows DeFlores to realize her dreams, to act on, and thereby define, her perceptions of what constitutes powerful behavior. For Beatrice-Joanna, DeFlores becomes the active equivalent of the asides in the first four acts; he is the agent of her desire to be as she appears.

Thus, Beatrice-Joanna accepts her role as the "fallen Eve" for the male characters. She voices, manipulates, and incorporates the public and private languages of the play, the languages of male projection that comprise the rhetoric of Courtly Love. Her allegiance to their rhetoric is evidenced not only by her refusal to admit adultery, but also by her insistence that DeFlores has done her only "service," as her "honor fell with him," and then her life (V. iii. 158). By perceiving her world as if, by extension, she could have been "formed a man," she has invested in her own destruction.

The transformation in love that Beatrice-Joanna accomplishes is, finally, one of reflection — she sees herself as a mirror reflecting male desires, as a vehicle for their pleasures. She reflects back upon Alsemero and DeFlores their language through her own; she adheres to the Courtly Love discourse whose underside is enacted for her by DeFlores. In this sense, she embodies the language that characterizes her world, and she unifies in one figure what in the previous acts has been rhetorically split. The asides of the first four acts disappear in the fifth because by then Beatrice-Joanna embodies all the possibilities of Courtly Love that the rhetoric of the play can offer.

Yet, we should not be too quick to argue only for patriarchal harmony in *The Changeling*. Beatrice-Joanna is perceived by the others as being "both of sport and wit, / Always a woman striving for the last hit" (V. i. 126–127). Her "sport" and "wit" are enough to reproduce the play's private and public languages, and to disturb the perfectly narcissistic image both Alsemero and DeFlores want to have mirrored back to them. Her dream of acquiring male prerogative is expressed, as Stilling suggests, in "the language of female rebellion, shown as an impulse toward evil." [10] Because she insists that she speaks the language of Courtly Love and that both Alsemero's and DeFlores's views of her are equivalent to her own perceptions (for which she has "kissed poison . . . stroked a serpent" [V. iii. 66]), her "sporting" discourse becomes the distorted reason for her destruction.

---

[10] Stilling, p. 254.

Beatrice-Joanna dies for the "truth within her," the power of the language she speaks and embodies. Even though she thinks her language includes her in the males' world, her rhetoric becomes the ultimate declaration of "Otherness" that DeFlores and Alsemero would close off in their possession of her. As a screen, as a vehicle of exchange in Courtly Love rhetoric, she actually reflects the opposite of what Alsemero and DeFlores *would* see. She personifies Alsemero's fears that her sexuality will disrupt his tenuous union with Vermandero, his community. To DeFlores she performs his inability to "fill himself up" with another human being, his sense of being alone in his physicality and not part of the male community he serves.[11] Both men define their community, then, in terms of other men: for Alsemero, it is Vermandero, for DeFlores, the men who cannot "pledge" him. Whereas Beatrice-Joanna mirrors what these characters would not see, she is like her counterpart in the subplot, Isabella, who reveals her suitors' folly in pursuing her love by reflecting back to them the roles they have presented to her. But Beatrice-Joanna assumes that her ability to mime, to speak the play's language of love, includes choosing how she will be perceived and possessed.

She does not "see," as Nancy Chodorow puts it, that

> feminine roles are less public or "social," that they exhibit less linguistic and institutional differentiation. . . . Women's roles are thus based on what are seen as personal rather than "social" or "cultural" ties. The corollary to this is that women's roles typically tend to involve the exercise of influence in face-to-face, personal contexts rather than legitimized power in contexts which are categorical and defined by authority. Finally, women's roles, and the biological symbolism attached to them, share a concern with the crossing of boundaries: Women mediate between the social and cultural concerns which men have defined; they bridge the gap and make transitions — especially in their role as socializer and mother — between nature and culture.[12]

Beatrice-Joanna mimes the rhetoric's failure to make the connection between "nature" and "culture," between DeFlores and Alsemero in these terms. But for the male characters, as an image of corrupted nature and failed culture, she also demonstrates the deadly possibilities of their conjunction that must be denied.

Such disintegration and disorder, moreover, threaten *The Changeling* from its first act; the characters are preoccupied with their world's outward symbols of stability —

---

[11] Lacan's "Le Stade du miroir" underlies my discussion here. Without attempting to paraphrase the subtleties of his argument, I would expand it to include the psychodynamics of speech at work in the play. More suggestive, perhaps, is D. W. Winnicott's argument in "Mirror-role of Mother and Family in Child Development," *Playing and Reality* (New York: Basic Books, 1971). Responding to Lacan, Winnicott argues that "the precursor of the mirror is the mother's face" (p. 111), and expressions mediate "the discovery of meaning in a world of seen things" (p. 113). For Winnicott, as for Lacan, infants' assumptions of union with the mother are necessarily disrupted by their autonomous responses to beliefs that they are identical to, and linked with, her. Healthy development depends on these autonomous disruptions of the sense of doubling. In a tragedy like *The Changeling*, where language, plots, and characters double, and "seeing" becomes problematic, the characters might be experiencing "unhealthy" disruptions of the sort Winnicott describes that result in pathological behavior. To the other characters, Beatrice-Joanna may represent the mother's face.

[12] Nancy Chodorow, *The Reproduction of Mothering: Psychoanalysis and the Sociology of Gender* (Berkeley: University of California Press, 1978), p. 180.

Vermandero's castle and Alibius's madhouse. Guarded against strangers, Vermandero explains that "our citadels / Are placed conspicuous to outward view, / On promonts' tops, but within are secrets" (I. i. 167–169). The bridegroom Alonzo's obvious curiosity and his pleasure at finally seeing the "most spacious and impregnable fort" (III. i. 4) the day before his wedding ironically leads him to his death. Nicholas Brooke comments that:

> The Castle and the House are derived from their medieval and renaissance significance as emblems of both the world and the human body. The peculiar imaginative power of DeFlores' leading Alonzo through the dark passages is that the suggestive language long established for him is sustained there; it is also a journey through the organs of a female body to an anal death, *and* a descent into hell.[13]

Vermandero supports this analysis when he says: "An host of enemies entered my citadel / Could not amaze like this: Joanna! Beatrice-Joanna!" (V. iii. 147–148), followed by "We are all there, [hell] circumscribes us here" (V. iii. 164). The analogies between Vermandero's castle and Beatrice-Joanna's body are further reinforced by Beatrice-Joanna's last assertion that her blood is Vermandero's, and that the "common sewer take it from distinction" (V. iii. 153), as though she is merely waste. Seen as the source of their language, Beatrice-Joanna has been kept "secret" as a body to be found out, defended against, and purged — in her father's castle, in Alsemero's physician's closet, and in DeFlores's body — just as Isabella has been locked in her husband's madhouse to save him from cuckoldry. But where Isabella articulates the illusions in the male characters' perceptions ("I have no beauty now, / Nor never had, but what was in my garments" [IV. iii. 135–136]), Beatrice-Joanna is deluded into believing that her language, her garment of speech, corresponds to what the male characters perceive her to be in the flesh.

Beatrice-Joanna's persistent belief in the power of her rhetoric exposes Courtly Love as a linguistic system that must deny women a voice. When the play opens, Beatrice-Joanna's mother is already dead, in "heaven . . . married to joys eternal" (III. iv. 5), and Beatrice-Joanna and Diaphanta join her in deathly silence by the end of the play. In the comic subplot, Alibius, Isabella's husband, interprets Isabella's actions as a reason to "never keep / Scholars . . . wiser than myself" (V. iii. 214–215), not as reason enough to free her from the madhouse. The female characters are consistently forced to the boundaries of the dramatic action, and reduced to what is signified by the male characters. The male characters define the terms of what Chodorow calls social and cultural concerns — language, marriage, and the metaphors that connect them with sexual revenge and death. Beatrice-Joanna particularly disturbs these terms because she doubles, or reproduces and articulates, the pathological connections between Courtly Love and the action of the play. She mediates between those "secrets" of nature and culture which the male characters would not perceive as articulated in their linguistic community. She becomes what Caren Greenberg describes as "the point of intersection between masculine power and pleasure . . . . A sexual battleground important not because of her own intrinsic power, but rather as a mark of the father's power. In this sense, the wife/mother's body fulfills the first requirement

---

[13] Nicholas Brooke, *Horrid Laughter in Jacobean Tragedy* (London: Open Books, 1979), p. 85.

of a language system: it marks something other than itself."[14] As the projection of the male characters' illusions, as the "mark" of a language system, Beatrice-Joanna is what she says—a "prophet to the rest" of her world in her destruction (V. iii. 157).

The last scene of the play reenacts a psychological stasis that characterizes the entire play and reveals the extent to which Beatrice-Joanna marks something other than herself. Alsemero pledges a "son's duty" to Vermandero, who has wanted all along "the addition of a son." Beatrice-Joanna, reinforcing this patriarchal system, tells her father that she "was blood taken from [him] / For [his] better health; look no more upon't, / But cast it to the ground regardlessly" (V. iii. 150–152). DeFlores presents her with a last dead "token"—himself. None of the characters change psychologically as a result of the dramatic action. The audience senses that this scene replicates previous ones—the death scenes of Beatrice-Joanna's mother before the play opens, and Diaphanta's during it—death scenes vigorously denied as meaningful to the participants. The male characters' language, shaped by the "truth" of Beatrice-Joanna's self-affirmation as "Other" in her discourse, reveals the extent of their emotional investments in their perceptions, not only of her, but of their world. Their language, to quote D. W. Winnicott, is "organized to defend against a repetition of 'unthinkable anxiety' or a return to the acute confusional state that belongs to disintegration."[15] The characters employ Courtly Love as a language of power to defend against internal psychological disorder.

Beatrice-Joanna is as "blind" as the other characters. She becomes the "point of intersection" for locating meanings in the play because she represents a dramatic and rhetorical unity that is split in its practice. The asides, which originally were directed towards the audience, become lodged inside the dramatic action—inside Beatrice-Joanna, as her name implies. As Beatrice, she is Courtly Love's Lady; as Joanna, she is a pun, perhaps, on Gehenna, hell.[16] Her name symbolizes the play's rhetorical intentions to signify a spiritual hell. She becomes the focus of the dramatic action, organized to get her off the stage, because she is designated this hell's source.

The transformation in the language of love that does occur, the movement of the asides from the outside to the inside of the play's action, reveals the extent to which Beatrice-Joanna is both outside and inside of her own world. She marks the limits of the play's rhetoric as she embodies it. The tragedy occurs, not because Middleton and Rowley want to point out the depravity inherent in beautiful women, but because Beatrice-Joanna cannot successfully "mediate between the social and cultural categories which men have defined" as inward and outward symbolic experiences; she cannot "bridge the gap and make transitions" between being and seeming in relation to

---

[14] Caren Greenberg, "Reading Reading: Echo's Abduction of Language," *Women and Language in Literature and Society*, ed. Sally McConnell-Ginet, Ruth Borker, Nelly Furman (New York: Praeger, 1980), p. 302.

[15] Winnicott, "The Location of Cultural Experience," *Playing and Reality*, p. 97. Winnicott's description of an infant's creation and use of a transitional object, and the emotional investment in it, has influenced my argument here; in the way Beatrice-Joanna mediates between language and culture, she seems to function as a transitional object for the other characters.

[16] My thanks to Parker Johnson for suggesting this possibility.

her appearance. Possessing no voice, she marks off the cultural boundaries. Her body is defined as a fortress and her language exposes the "gap," the locus of a societal "hell," that a cultural psychology has built upon the "secrets" of the female body, and then used as the referent for its language of love.

Middleton and Rowley point toward this interpretation through Alibius's description of the *danse macabre* his madmen will present to Beatrice-Joanna on her wedding night:

> Only an unexpected passage over
> To make a frightful pleasure, that is all,
> But not the all I aim at; could we so act it,
> To teach it in a wild distracted measure,
> Though out of form and figure, breaking time's head,
> It were no matter, 'twould be healed again
> In one age or other, if not in this.
>
> [III. iii. 270–276]

As a "frightful pleasure," Beatrice-Joanna (and Isabella to a greater extent than I have argued here) shapes the dramatic action of the play, and incorporates its meanings in her embodiment of its split rhetoric. Beatrice-Joanna's "unexpected passage" initiates Alsemero's and the other characters' movements toward a "right home back." They all participate in love's blind transformations. Beatrice-Joanna exposes to the audience the gaps in the drama's language even as she embodies its psychological coherence. She functions as an illusory body of text in which the male characters read the "wild distracted measure" of love's dreams turned nightmares, as though she were both the vehicle for dreaming and the origin of its hells.[17] For the audience, Beatrice-Joanna functions as an image which embodies in her designation as "Other" all the possibilities and limitations of the play's tragic language. She shapes everything and, finally, nothing, worth articulating about love's possessive power. Whether a "frightful pleasure" or an "impure woman," Beatrice-Joanna embodies the site of the interpretation of tragedy.

[17] Greenberg argues that a "mediating text is female – and dead" (p. 303).

Part IV

Performing Gender

Women's Performance Art: Feminism and Postmodernism

Jeanie Forte

Limiting one's critical focus to a particular group of performance artists or their performances has always seemed inappropriate, since that project would appear to perpetrate the very act of defining and categorizing that anything called performance art actively resists. Nevertheless, the overtly political nature of much women's performance art since the 1960s has invited just such a critical distinction, treating feminist performance as a recognizable sub-genre within the field. Through the lens of postmodern feminist theory, women's performance art (whether overtly so or not) appears as inherently political. All women's performances are derived from the relationship of women to the dominant system of representation, situating them within a feminist critique. Their disruption of the dominant system constitutes a subversive and radical strategy of intervention vis à vis patriarchal culture. The implications of this strategy may be understood through readings of feminist theory—especially in relation to performance during the 1970s. Whether or not such considerations must change for the 1980s is taken up at the end of the essay.

Arguably all performance art, particularly in the earlier years, evidenced a deconstructive intent. As the manifestation of a burgeoning postmodernist sensibility, the violent acts of Chris Burden or the enigmatic exercises of Vito Acconci cast into relief the problematic relationship between life and art, between a Renaissance conception of self and a postmodern subject constructed by cultural practices. Performance art made understanding (in any conventional sense) difficult, critical analysis frustrating, and absolute definition impossible. As a continuation of the twentieth-century rebellion against commodification, performance art promised a radical departure from commercialism, assimilation, and triviality, deconstructing the commercial art network of galleries and museums while often using/abusing their spaces. In a very real sense, it is the structures and institutions of modernism which performance art attacks, throwing into doubt the accepted practices of knowledge acquisition and accumulation.

Jeanie K. Forte is a free-lance scholar, director, and dramaturg working in California. She has published in Theater, Women & Performance, High Performance, Modern Drama, *and* Theatre Journal, *as well as the newly revised edition of* Women in American Theatre. *This article derives from a longer work to be published by Indiana University Press entitled* Women in Performance Art: Feminism and Postmodernism.

Within this movement, women's performance emerges as a specific strategy that allies postmodernism and feminism, adding the critique of gender/patriarchy to the already damaging critique of modernism inherent in the activity. In the late 1960s and early 1970s, coincident with the women's movement, women used performance as a deconstructive strategy to demonstrate the objectification of women and its results. In "Waiting" (1972), Faith Wilding rocked slowly in a chair, quietly listing item after item for which she waits as 'woman,' from childhood to old age:

> Waiting for someone to pick me up / Waiting for someone to hold me . . . / Waiting to be somebody / Waiting to wear makeup / Waiting for my pimples to go away . . . Waiting for my children to come home from school / Waiting for them to grow up, to leave home / Waiting to be myself / Waiting for excitement . . . Waiting for my flesh to sag / Waiting for the pain to go away / Waiting for the struggle to end / Waiting for release[1]

Wilding eloquently expressed the frustration of a woman rendered incapable of independent action or thought, forced to wait for her life to happen to her. Always "waiting to be myself," Wilding's monologue shares with her audience the specific status of the objectified, the feeling of selflessness when constructed and delineated by male-dominated society. Initially performed for an audience of women only, the performance also served as a kind of consciousness-raising, feeding the group's awareness of the subtle ways in which women are denied an active role in the constructed path of their own lives.

As a deconstructive strategy, women's performance art is a discourse of the objectified other, within a context which foregrounds the conventions and expectations of modernism. This deconstruction hinges on the awareness that 'Woman,' as object, as a culturally constructed category, is actually the basis of the Western system of representation. Woman constitutes the position of object, a position of other in relation to a socially-dominant male subject; it is that 'otherness' which makes representation possible (the personification of male desire). Precisely because of the operation of representation, actual women are rendered an absence within the dominant culture, and in order to speak, must either take on a mask (masculinity, falsity, simulation, seduction), or take on the unmasking of the very opposition in which they are the opposed, the Other. Michele Montrelay identifies women as the potential "ruin of representation"[2] precisely because of their position within the accepted system. This is an identification informed particularly by semiotics theory and the understanding that "Woman as sign" is the basis of representation without which discourse could not exist.

Women's performance art operates to unmask this function of 'Woman,' responding to the weight of representation by creating an acute awareness of all that signifies Woman, or femininity. The Waitresses, a performance group in Los Angeles, have foregrounded the connections between images of femininity, women's oppression, and the patriarchy: in "Ready to Order?" a performer wore a waitress uniform with

---

[1]Moira Roth, ed., *The Amazing Decade: Women in Performance Art. 1970-1980* (Los Angeles: Astro Artz, 1983), 144.
[2]Michele Montrelay, "Femininity," *m/f: a feminist journal* 1 (1978).

multiple breasts on front, approaching unsuspecting customers in an L.A. diner and asking for their order. In 1979 the group expanded its ranks and marched the streets of L.A. as a band dressed in waitress uniforms, playing kitchen-utensil instruments. Apart from the obvious content regarding the exploitation of women in underpaid labor, these performances evoke an awareness of Woman as a sign, blatantly portraying the master/slave relationship inherent in her exploitation; Woman is merely the negative in relation to Man; a sign for the opposite of man, in service to his needs and dominance. In "Sitting Still" (1970), Bonnie Sherk sat for hours in an overstuffed chair in the middle of a flooded vacant lot, in elegant evening dress and hairdo. Like Wilding, she seemed trapped in a condition of waiting, but her costume also pointedly chose an image of elegant "femininity" for deconstruction: situating herself in relation to the garbage and discarded objects in the lot, her imagery simultaneously foregrounded accepted appearances for women and rejected them. Her stillness and silence also reflected a feeling of helplessness, an immobility as a real woman caught in the cultural signification process that demands certain behaviors in order to be Woman.

For the final scene of a three-week long performance event in Los Angeles created by Suzanne Lacy and Leslie Labowitz, called "Three Weeks in May" (1977), the audience entered a dimly-lit gallery, wherein a massive winged lamb's carcass hung from the center of the room. Above the carcass, four nude women, painted red, crouched quietly on a ledge. On the floor below was a graphic depiction of sexual assault scrawled in chalk on asphalt. Tape recorded voices spoke haltingly of rape and assault experiences. As the culmination of three weeks of rape-awareness performances which included giant maps pinpointing the locations of rapes, the final gallery portion of the event invoked the stark physical reality of the dots on the maps, suggesting the brutalizing effects of the sexual objectification of women. The nude women mutely perched on the ledge bore striking resemblance to the countless nude women hung on the walls of Western museums, deepening the critique of a cultural practice that has made of woman an object, a category, a "sign." Through this piece Lacy and Labowitz demonstrated how such transposition of women into signs (or representations of femininity), endangers the lives of actual women.

The deconstructive nature of women's performance art is thus doubly powerful because of the status of women in relation to representation, a status which, in the performance context, inherently foregrounds the phallocentricity of modernism/patriarchy and its signifying systems. Women performance artists show an intrinsic understanding of culture and signification apparently reached solely through their own feminist consciousness-raising and political acumen; manifesting the metaphor most central to feminism, that "the personal is the political," these performers have used the condition of their own lives to deconstruct the system they find oppressive, and their performance practice shares concerns with recent theory interested in unmasking the system of representation and its ideological alliances.

This type of subversion of the accepted social order goes much deeper than demands for equal pay, demands which are themselves only an acceptance of part of a larger system, of its discourse. As Teresa de Lauretis notes, "Whoever defines the code or the context, has control . . . and all answers which accept that context abdicate the possibility of redefining it."[3] One must be "willing to begin an argument," that is, to confront the language and metaphors which promote women's oppression. By challenging the very discourse of representation, women's performance art begins such an argument, and begins to postulate an alternative discourse, a discourse which shuns the traditional hierarchies built on power and knowledge, the breeding ground of oppression.

Women's performance art has particular disruptive potential because it poses an actual woman as a speaking subject, throwing that position into process, into doubt, opposing the traditional conception of the single, unified (male) subject.[4] The female body as subject clashes in dissonance with its patriarchal text,[5] challenging the very fabric of representation by refusing that text and posing new, multiple texts grounded in real women's experience and sexuality. This strategy is understood particularly in relation to Lacanian psychoanalysis which 'reads' the female body as Lack, or Other, existing only to reflect male subjectivity and male desire. Derived from Freudian conceptions of the psyche, Lacan's model articulates the subject in terms of processes (drives, desire, symbolization) "which depend on the crucial instance of castration, and are thus predicated exclusively on a male or masculine subject."[6] Lacan uses the term "phallus" to designate the privileged signifier, the signifier of power; but he insists that this is not the same as the biological penis, and therefore does not necessarily reside only with males. However, such a distinction ignores the political implications of the terminology. The clear connection between the sexual signifier of privilege and sexual politics has been handled humorously by many women performance artists, as in Vicki Hall's "Ominous Operation" (1971), wherein women were led behind a curtain, later emerging with huge phalluses attached. The changes in the performers' behavior and references to societal power made obvious the relationship between dominance and the biological member. In a similar vein, Pat Oleszko created a giant phallus for her costume, "MacFlasher," which she gleefully revealed to passers-by from under an oversized trenchcoat, punning with notions of penis envy and women's supposed lack.

For Lacan, power relationships are determined by the symbolic order, a linguistically-encoded network of meaning and signification that is internalized with the acquisition of language; and which Lacan sums up as the Name-of-the-Father, recognizing the inherent patriarchy. Theorist Julia Kristeva, by naming woman as the 'semiotic' on which the symbolic order depends, creates a radical inversion of Lacanian theory, effectively negating his paradigm. In describing the semiotic as the 'underside' of symbolic language, she allies it with the maternal, the feminine, although it is not necessarily delineated by sexual difference. This notion nevertheless allows for breaks in meaning in the language structure, a possibility of authentic

---

[3]Teresa De Lauretis, *Alice Doesn't: Feminism, Semiotics and Cinema* (Bloomington: Indiana University Press, 1983), 3.

[4]Dick Hebidge, *Subculture: The Meaning of Style* (London: Methuen), 165.

[5]See Kaja Silverman, *The Subject of Semiotics* (New York: Oxford University Press, 1983), 197, for remarks on the potential dissonance of a speaking subject and its representation.

[6]Josette Féral, "Powers and Difference," in *The Future of Difference*, ed. Eisenstein and Jardine (Boston: G. K. Hall, 1980), 90.

difference articulated as an alternative to the authoritative, Name-of-the-Father lingually-constructed society.[7] It further foregrounds the psychoanalytic foundation of Woman as Other, as a construction necessary for social intercourse in the Western world. Woman has had to be constructed as opposite to man to validate and shore up the dominance of male subjectivity. In "Do not Believe that I am an Amazon," German performance artist Ulrike Rosenbach made her refusal of this Otherness vivid: dressed in a white leotard, she dramatically shot arrows at a madonna-and-child target.[8] While obviously an attack on the oppression of women imbedded in patriarchal Christianity, her performance also illuminated the Amazon myth as a male construction designed to separate woman from man by designating her as not-man, as his opposite.[9]

The opening up of alternative spaces or breaks in the language structure is also implicated in feminists' uncovering of issues that Lacan ignores, such as that of 'the female speaker'—or, how does a woman speak (if it is not possible for her to be subject)?[10] In the Lacanian model, woman, as the culturally constructed, as Other, is trapped in man's self-representation, existing only to reflect back his image of reality, "only as a function of what she is not, receiving upon her denied body the etched-out stamp of the Other, as a signature of her void and a mark of his identity."[11] As Kaja Silverman points out, Lacanian psychoanalysis is reliant on the close interdependence of the terms 'subject' and 'signification,' because "the discourse within which the subject finds its identity is always the discourse of the Other—of a symbolic order which transcends the subject and which orchestrates its entire history."[12] Then how is a woman to speak as subject, to affirm, discover, or insist upon her own identity?

It is precisely this denial of women as 'speaking subjects' that women in performance art both foreground and subvert. The intensely intimate nature of the work, the emphasis on personal experience and emotional material, not 'acted' or distanced from artist or audience, is what most characterizes this alternative, heterogeneous voice. In 1975, in a piece called "Interior Scroll," Carolee Schneemann stood nude in front of a mostly-female audience, ritualistic paint on her face and body. In dim lighting, she began extracting a narrow, rope-like "text" from her vagina, from which she proceeded to "read":

> I met a happy man
> a structuralist filmmaker
> — but don't call me that,
> it's something else I do—
> he said we are fond of you

---

[7]Carolyn Burke, "Irigaray Through the Looking Glass," *Feminist Studies* 7:2 (1981): 111.

[8]RoseLee Goldberg, *Performance: Live Art 1909 to the Present* (New York: Harry N. Abrams, 1979), 114.

[9]For a more extended discussion of the Amazon as a male-constructed image of women, see Sue-Ellen Case, *Feminism and Theatre* (London: MacMillan, in press).

[10]Burke, "Irigaray Through the Looking Glass," 111.

[11]Feral, "Powers of Difference," 89.

[12]Silverman, *Subject of Semiotics*, 194.

Rachel Rosenthal, "Traps," Photo: Daniel J. Martinez.

you are charming
but don't ask us
to look at your films
we cannot
there are certain films
we cannot look at
the personal clutter
the persistence of feelings
the hand-touch sensibility
the diaristic indulgence
the painterly mess
the dense gestalt
the primitive techniques . . .

The filmmaker finishes his remarks by telling Schneemann that she is not "a film-makeress. . . . We think of you as a dancer."[13] This performance vividly links together a number of elements relevant to feminist theory in relation to the postmodern subject. The performance refers to her insistence on "personal clutter," highlighting the feminist perspective on the personal as the political, but also contrasting 'masculine' from 'feminine' modes of addressing the world; not that these are necessarily biolog-

[13]Quoted in Roth, *The Amazing Decade*, 14.

ical modes, but derived from the different ways in which men and women, constructed and conditioned as such, experience the world. As is clear from Schneemann's example, the feminine mode is devalued by the male-dominated art world for its lack of logic, rationality, and distance (attributes Derrida identifies in "phallogocentrism"). Schneemann's "personal clutter" thus defies conventional (male) preference for artistic detachment:

> [Her works] are personal, not only in the usual sense of being based on particular experiences of the author, but in a radically different sense as well; they are conceived as artistic accretions delivered to the reader or viewer by Schneemann from *inside* the emotional environment within which they develop. Wordsworth recollected in tranquility and then wrote; Hemingway sometimes wrote to release the pressure engendered over a period of time by particular past experiences. [Schneemann] wants to use the making of a work to preserve, consider, and reorient the process of the emotion (and the illumination/ confusion it brings) as she experiences it. . . . [She works] from a position of intimacy, not from a position of distance.[14]

This "position of intimacy" is one of the most noteworthy characteristics of women's performance, and one of the primary appeals of the genre for women. As Catherine Elwes (herself a performance artist) notes, "Performance is about the 'real-life' presence of the artist. She takes on no roles but her own. She is author, subject, activator, director, and designer. When a woman speaks within the performance tradition, she is understood to be conveying her own perceptions, her own fantasies, and her own

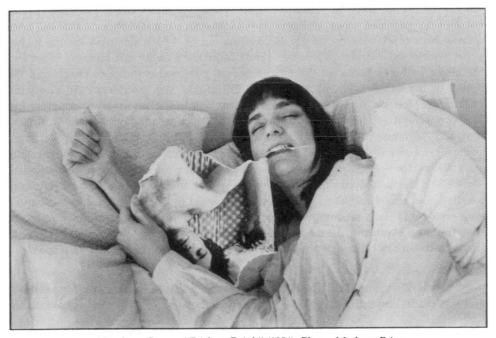

Vanalyne Green, "Trick or Drink" (1984). Photo: Mathew Price.

[14]Scott MacDonald, "Carolee Schneeman's ABC: The Men Cooperated," *AfterImage* 12:9 (1985): 12.

analyses."[15] The performance context is markedly different from that of the stage, in that the performers are not acting, or playing a character in any way removed from themselves; the mode provides women the opportunity for direct address to an audience, unmediated by another author's 'scripting.' Rather than masking the self, women's performance is born from self-revelation as a political move; to quote Manuela Fraire, "The practice of self consciousness is the way in which women reflect politically on their own condition,"[16] and the articulation of self through women's performance cannot help but foreground gender critically. In a Lacanian context, women performance artists thus challenge the symbolic order by asserting themselves as "speaking subjects," in direct defiance of the patriarchal construction of discourse. "A woman performer combines active authorship and an elusive medium to assert her irrefutable presence (an act of feminism) within a hostile environment (patriarchy)."[17] One might paraphrase this as the assertion of subjectivity within a symbolic order hostile to the female subject. If the Lacanian paradigm of the symbolic order is taken as an accurate description of Western culture, then it is debatable whether women (or men, for that matter) can ever "escape" its identifying power; but women performance artists challenge its limitations, even its very foundations, through their direct expression of subjecthood.

The intensely autobiographical nature of women's performance has evidenced the insistence on a woman's ability to 'speak' her subjectivity. In "Deer/Dear" (1978), Nancy Buchanan recounted her horrifying dreams of violence, then related them to the waking nightmare of violence against women through recalling the violence she has herself experienced. In "Trick or Drink" (1984), Vanalyne Green painfully reveals her bulimic past and other addictive behaviors, tracing a childhood obsessed with dieting and shadowed by family alcoholism, all of which she also relates to her experience of the world as a woman. Linda Montano's deliberate blurring of art and life along with her focus on the articulation of personal experience challenges the denial of her subjectivity. In "Three-Day Blindfold," the "performance" consisted entirely of Montano's self-imposed temporary blindness, intended to promote her own consciousness-raising regarding such a physical challenge. As "Chicken-woman," Montano dressed in chiffon and danced wildly in the streets of San Francisco, or on the Golden Gate Bridge, creating an image that had deep personal significance for her. In perhaps her most powerful performance for an audience, "Mitchell's Death," Montano appeared with whitened face, pierced by acupuncture needles, and spoke intensely of her feelings related to her friend and ex-husband's sudden death. Such seemingly disparate works have in common the interest in asserting and exploring personal, lived experience, and are "performed" primarily for herself—in total disregard for any cultural negation of her status as a speaking subject.

By insistently occupying this crucial space of signification as a speaking subject and foregrounding individual, lived experience, the woman performance artist sub-

[15]Catherine Elwes, "Floating Feminity: A Look at Performance Art by Women," in *Women's Images of Men*, ed. Kent and Morreau (London: Writers and Readers Publishing, 1985), 164.

[16]Quoted in De Lauretis, *Alice Doesn't*, 185.

[17]Elwes, "Floating Feminity," 165.

verts the symbolic order's limited parameters for women. "Since signification results in an aphanisis of the real, the speaking subject and its discursive representative— i.e. the subject of the speech [in this case, Woman]—remain perpetually dissimul- taneous, at odds."[18] In other words, actual women speaking their personal experience create dissonance with their representation, Woman, throwing that fictional category into relief and question. Shock waves are set up from within the signification process itself, resonating to provide an awareness of the phallocentricity of our signifying systems and the culturally-determined otherness of women.

However, the personal and autobiographical for women is inextricably linked with female sexuality—"that which is most personal and at the same time most socially determined."[19] The challenge presented by women's autobiographical performance gains strength when seen in conjunction with notions of female sexuality arising from the theoretical work of some feminists. For women, sexuality cannot remain private: since one is constructed as "Woman" through sexuality in relation to male desire, the interrogation of this construction is a political act. The corollary problem in relation to postmodern theories for feminists is that "if language, the symbolic order, is . . . phallocentric, then female drives are by definition incapable of repre- sentation within it."[20] For women performance artists, the assertion of female drives and sexuality is crucial, and their work reclaims the female body from its patriarchal textualization through "writing the body," borrowing the term from French feminist Hélène Cixous.

Cixous agrees with Lacan that it is through language that we acquire patriarchal values, but asserts that it is therefore possible to dismantle the patriarchy through language, specifically by encouraging and exploring women's language, a language rooted in the female body and female sexuality. She sees this 'other' language as both created by and a manifestation of women's sexual difference, and exhorts women to "write the body" in order to speak their subjectivity. For Cixous, "the feminine text cannot fail to be more than subversive," a perspective which echoes Montrelay's earlier remark regarding women as the ruin of representation.[21] Because of the po- sition to which women have been allocated by patriarchal language, they have the potential to generate subversion of that very language from within; but in revolt against the psychoanalytic model of subject construction in which desire is articulated as exclusively male, it is female desire that is most disruptive. As lack, reflecting only man's desire, women are not permitted or even conceived of as having or owning their own desire. Cixous's mandate for women is therefore to terrorize patriarchal discourse by writing from the locus of the inscription of difference, i.e., female sexuality: "anything having to do with the body should be explored."[22]

[18]Silverman, *Subject of Semiotics*, 197.

[19]De Lauretis, *Alice Doesn't*, 184.

[20]Rachel Bowlby, "The Feminine Female," *Social Text* (Spring/Summer 1983): 58.

[21]Hélène Cixous, "The Laugh of the Medusa," in *New French Feminisms*, ed. Marks and de Cour- tivron (New York: Schocken Books, 1981).

[22]Cixous in Helene Wenzel, "The Text as Body/Politics: An Appreciation of Monique Wittig's Writings in Context," *Feminist Studies* 7:2 (1981): 266.

However, many Anglo-American feminists have criticized Cixous's theories, arguing that a Lacanian notion of language precludes "feminine" subversion from within. In this regard, Cixous is often associated with Luce Irigaray, in their similar emphasis on the need to discover and develop a means of expression for women that is not conceived within the phallocentric system of representation, since "all Western discourse presents a certain isomorphism with the masculine sex: the privilege of unity, form of the self, of the visible, of the specularisable, of the erection."[23] Irigaray was herself a Lacanian psychoanalyst until she indirectly criticized his theory in her landmark work, *Speculum of the Other Woman*, which prompted her dismissal from his academy.[24] In referring to the speculum, she challenges the Lacanian "mirror" stage (in which the subject first recognizes himself as distinct from the first Other, the Mother) with the concave, reflective mirror used particularly to view a woman's sexual anatomy. Like Cixous, Irigaray promotes a close identification of women's language with women's sexuality, and sees writing as the arena for new possibilities relating to women's subjectivity.[25] Feminist critic Rachel Bowlby questions the possibility of realizing this aim through simply writing: "if language, the symbolic order, is, as they [Cixous and Irigaray] claim, phallocentric, then female drives are by definition incapable of representation within it."[26] And for Ann Rosalind Jones, establishing a connection between physicality and writing is problematic: "The practice of women's writing is out in the open, for all to see; its basis in the body and id is less certain."[27]

This problem in relation to writing becomes pointedly rhetorical with women's performance art, an activity which challenges the symbolic order on more than just the linguistic level. Cixous's and Irigaray's strategies are much more vividly realized in the context of women's performance than in writing. The very placement of the female body in the context of performance art positions a woman and her sexuality as speaking subject, an action which cuts across numerous sign-systems, not just the discourse of language. The semiotic havoc created by such a strategy combines physical presence, real time, and real women in dissonance with their representations, threatening the patriarchal structure with the revolutionary text of their actual bodies.

Although most women performance artists are probably unfamiliar with Cixous, they employ the strategy of disruption through expression of the female body and sexuality. In the piece by Schneemann already cited, for example, it seems as though her vagina itself is reporting the sexism. Hannah Wilke's pieces have always used her own nude body as her primary "material," foregrounding the conventional uses and abuses of the female body. If the female body has become the locus of the inscription of difference, the "text" by which identity is read, then women's performance art is always the positioning of a female body as subject in direct opposition

[23]Luce Irigaray, "Women's Exile," *Ideology & Consciousness* 1:1 (1977): 64.

[24]See Luce Irigaray, *Speculum of the Other Woman,* trans. Gillian C. Gill (New York: Cornell University Press, 1985).

[25]Burke, "Irigaray Through the Looking Glass," 289.

[26]Bowlby, "Feminine Female," 58.

[27]Ann Rosalind Jones, "French Theories of the Feminine," in *Making a Difference: Feminist Literary Criticism,* ed. Greene and Kahn (London: Methuen, 1985), 106.

to its patriarchal text. Women performers challenge the very fabric of representation by refusing that text and positing new, multiple texts grounded in real women's experience and sexuality.

To dismiss this work as cultural feminism ignores its ramifications within representation and the psychological encoding of the Western signifying systems, and focuses instead on nudity as an assertion of female superiority.[28] Such a critique parallels another common critique of Cixous's work, citing the threat of essentialism, "in which biological difference is made the basis of subjectivity, and of the very forms of representation by which women are oppressed."[29] The insistence on 'writing the body' is an aspect of these theories that creates a problem for many feminists, since it would seem to apotheosize some innate essence that is "woman" and threaten to perpetuate the basis on which the current objectification of women operates.[30] Moreover, the philosophy of cultural feminism lauds that supposed essence, in a simple reversal of terms. Jones chides Franco-feminist critics saying that "every belief about 'what women are' raises political as well as aesthetic questions."[31] Others say it is naive to describe women's subjectivity on the basis of biological traits that might derive from and produce different effects in different social circumstances.[32] And Bowlby warns that "it remains to be shown . . . that the female body is itself productive of a distinctive mode of subjectivity." But through women's performance art, the body speaks both as a sign and as an intervention into language; and it is further possible for the female body to be used in such a way as to foreground the genderization of culture and the repressive system of representation. It is not, as Jill Dolan argues in a recent *Theatre Journal* essay, that the nude female body is meant to stand "somehow outside the system of representation;"[33] rather, the female body's significance within the system affords the performance artist the possibility for frustrating fetishistic practices and asserting an alternative viewing practice. When Rachel Rosenthal had assistants mark her physical "bad points" in "Bonsoir Dr. Schön," it was a means of conquering societal judgements of beauty and of finally recognizing and claiming her body as her own; in short, of peeling away the cultural constructions that had conditioned her self-image. It should be noted that this was only one scene of a larger work that was precisely about sexual politics and personal power.[34]

Dolan's argument ultimately condemns nudity in performance: "From a materialist feminist perspective, the female body is not reducible to a sign free of connotation."[35] Yet women performance artists foreground, this very connotation, pointing to the serious consequences of signification within cultural parameters. Performing nude has, for some performers, provided an opportunity for deepening the critique of centuries of cultural laminations of the body. Far from a "purist" or "self-righteous pose" in service of an asexual philosophy, most female nude performances have

[28]See Jil Dolan, "The Dynamics of Desire: Sexuality and Gender in Pornography and Performance," *Theatre Journal* 39:2 (1987).
[29]Bowlby, "Feminine Female," 62.
[30]Wenzel, "Text as Body/Politics," 266.
[31]Jones, "French Theories," 106.
[32]Beverly Brown and Parveen Adams, "The Feminine Body and Feminist Politics," *m/f* 3 (1979): 33–37.

dealt quite specifically and blantantly with female sexuality and its cultural suppression. Barbara Smith, for example, explores her sexuality publicly, through performance, and her works such as "Feed Me" have raised problems for feminists in the past. The superficial 'content' might seem to be yet another "peep show," but the performance enacts deconstructive strategies when viewed in light of the above discussion. In this all-night event that was part of a group of performances in San Francisco, Smith let it be known that she would remain in a small room for the duration of the 'show,' and that she would interact with whomever wished to see her, on an individual basis. Nude, she greeted each visitor as a friend, briefly encountering them in her room personalized with rugs, cushions, and incense. Her obvious ease with her own sexuality and unabashed exploration of new possibilities boldly asserted her ownership of her body and her desire, allowing for both vulnerability and strength. Definitely not an assertion of female superiority or an erasure of sexuality, Smith's work invited the re-examination of cultural standards as well as participants' own sexualities.

Women's performance actively intervenes into the process of constructing the viewing subject through the disruption of the "male" gaze. Dolan and others have questioned the sexual aspects of these works, asserting that the work merely re-inscribes the body as object, as a source of voyeuristic pleasure. In fact, it is the very choice of the performance art context which denies the accepted path for voyeurism, which subverts the male gaze and the fetishism of the female body.

Much of the feminist theory regarding notions of fetishism has come from the world of film theory, wherein the cinematic image provides a clear paradigm for the workings of fetishism in a patriarchal—and psychoanalytically encoded—culture. The mechanisms of fetishism are rooted in Freudian models, hinging on the fear of castration in males. Woman, as the castrated, provides an opportunity for desire but also of danger: she lacks the penis, implying a threat and the possibility of unpleasure.[36] Since the woman *is* sexual difference, she operates both as an icon (the object of the male gaze for the pleasureable experience of desire) and as a source of anxiety over that difference. As Laura Mulvey pointed out, the male unconscious has two avenues of escape from this anxiety: preoccupation with the re-enactment of the original trauma, which entails investigating the "mystery" that is Woman; or substituting the anxiety with a fetish object, or "turning the represented figure itself into a fetish so that it becomes reassuring rather than dangerous."[37]

The second avenue, fetishistic scopophilia, builds up the physical beauty of the object, transforming it into something satisfying in itself. Unlike voyeurism, which needs narrative, fetishism can exist outside linear time as the erotic instinct is focused

[33]Dolan, "Dynamics of Desire," 159.

[34]Dolan also discusses this work by Rosenthal in the context of cultural feminism, which in her particular case is exceptionally misleading, since Rosenthal in no way believes that women are biologically or spiritually superior to men. Dolan's reference in this context does her a disservice.

[35]Ibid., 160.

[36]See Laura Mulvey, "Visual Pleasure and Narrative Cinema," *Screen* 16:3 (1975).

[37]Ibid., 158.

on the look alone.[38] In Freudian terms, fetishism makes the woman's body a phallic symbol which reconstructs her absent penis, making her temporarily safe for the site of desire. The look of the film camera replicates these two "looks" of patriarchal society in mainstream cinema, as has been demonstrated by feminist film theorists such as Mulvey, E. Ann Kaplan, Mary Ann Doane, Teresa de Lauretis, and others.

Catherine Elwes suggests that, although it is not possible to entirely escape this process, theatre and live entertainment do not provide the perfect illusion necessary for voyeuristic narratives: the fact that performer and spectator occupy the same physical/temporal space makes more difficult the distancing needed for safe fantasizing. In such cases, successful voyeurism depends on predictable outcomes, on the conventions of narrative form which presumably guarantee safety in 'looking.'[39] From this it follows that women's performance art, in totally abandoning and disrupting conventional narrative, thwarts the illusion of distance and exposes the (male) spectator "to the fearful proximity of the performer and the dangerous consequences of his own desires. His cloak of invisibility has been stripped away and his spectatorship becomes an issue within the work."[40]

It is also important to note that the stripper or entertainer is also offering up her body as an object of exchange for *another's* pleasure, with no reference to her own. Her identity, other than that of performer, is erased in service of providing pleasure, in keeping with her fetishistic function within the society. In contrast, women performance artists expose their bodies to reclaim them, to assert their own pleasure and sexuality, thus denying the fetishistic pursuit to the point of creating a genuine threat to male hegemonic structures of women. Instead of the male look operating as the controlling factor (as it does with cinema), the woman performance artist exercises control: "In defining the rules of the game and holding the element of surprise as her trump card, a woman may take unprecedented control of her own image."[41]

In a similar sense, the woman performance artist may work to uncover her own zones of resistance to the patriarchal 'text' of society, exemplifying the search for an alternative to patriarchal discourse, one in which women can speak their own experience, as subjects, from a non-patriarchal frame. Ritualistic elements in women's performance are designed to cathartically shed the patriarchal images of women and embrace new, self-generated images. M. L. Sowers, in the nude, had herself completely buried in beach sand, then slowly, painstakingly emerged in a dramatic and moving personal rebirth. A very private performance, it was witnessed only by her friend and photographer, who documented and gave confirmation to the transformative process. Her nudity and the ceremonial quality of the performance served to reject social or institutional constraints. In a more public performance, Mary Beth Edelson created a ceremony for herself and a large group of women to mourn the

---

[38]Ibid., 158.
[39]Elwes, "Floating Feminity," 172.
[40]Ibid., 172–173.
[41]Ibid., 173.

persecution and murder of witches, those nine million women victimized by a patriarchal society. One of the most predominant images of Woman in culture and literature is that of the witch, the embodiment of the unknown and powerful who threatens male dominance and therefore must be proclaimed evil and destroyed. The fear of witches has often been identified as a fear of female sexuality (again, the Freudian model of the fear of castration comes to mind), and Edelson's ceremony aimed to reclaim female sexuality as a non-threatening life-force.

The female body in performance art, whether nude or not, can also articulate women's sexuality as never before possible, in a most non-essentialist multiplicity of voices. To deconstruct the oppositions based on gender entrenched in patriarchy, women's performance art provides paths to alternatives, to new concepts of difference, subverting the canon of codified sexuality imbedded in centuries of theatre and cultural works, and revealing binary sexuality as another construction complicit in the oppression of women and their full exploration of female sexuality. Bonnie Greer's "Vigil" highlighted the erasure of a black woman's sexuality in her bondage to white culture. In "Leave Her in Naxos," Rachel Rosenthal showed slides of her various lovers, male and female, and discussed intimate aspects of her relationship with each, effectively speaking herself in different sexualities. A group of performance artists identifying themselves as lesbians performed "An Oral Herstory of Lesbianism," in which each spoke of her particular oppression as a lesbian while also frankly revealing sexual intimacies. And Carolee Schneemann's "Meat Joy" (1964) was so graphic in its celebration of female sexual pleasure (contrary to Dolan's notion) with both women and men that one performance was disrupted when an irate male audience member rushed on stage to attack Schneemann.

In reference to patriarchal culture, Annie LeClerc has written: "They invented the whole of sexuality while silencing ours. If we invent ours, they will have to rethink their own."[42] As the creation of alternative points from which to deconstruct traditionally accepted meanings of woman, women's performance art constitutes the continuous "invention" of authentic, heterogenous female sexuality, acting as the concave mirror held up to view women's sex in all its detail and diversity. Although clearly a graphic realization of the theories of Cixous and Irigaray, such strategies should not be disregarded in haste because of the threat of essentialism. As Jane Weinstock notes:

> In defining the woman as 'Other,' doesn't it construct a single point of reference—the male? The woman is simply the opposite, the 'non'—. . . . Perhaps it is becoming necessary to move closer to what has been called the French 'essentialism' in order to escape a position of perpetual otherness. Recent French psychoanalytic and post-psychoanalytic writings on sexual difference have focussed on the female body, or 'female specificity.' Might not this attempt to return the body to the subject lead to a differentiated viewing subject?[43]

Michel Foucault, who was also concerned with forms of resistance to power, described strategies for empowering the subject that amplify this discussion. Foucault

[42]Annie Leclerc, *Parole de Femme* (Paris: Grasset, 1974), 42.
[43]Jane Weinstock, quoted in Maureen Turim, "What is Sexual Difference?" *AfterImage* 12:9 (1985): 5.

Rachel Rosenthal, "L.O.W. in Gaia." Photo: Jan Deen.

characterizes strategies of resistance as struggles which question the status of the governized individual, simultaneously asserting the right to be different and resisting the destruction of community. These strategies oppose the privileges of knowledge, secrecy, deformation, and mystifying representations imposed on people. They are a refusal of abstractions, of economic and ideological violence which ignore who we are or determine who one is: "the main objective of these struggles is to attack . . . a technique, a form of power."[44] Women's performance art is a powerful manifestation of this struggle, as a resistance to the economic and ideological violence done to women. As such it foregrounds the genderization of culture and the over-determination of sexuality, both which are instrumental in the subjugation of women, the repression of female subjectivity.

The charge of individualism has been levelled at performance artists in general, and Foucault's emphasis on the internal workings of power would seem to feed into such critiques, distancing the particular strategy of performance from "real" politics, certainly any politics of coalition. While the history of performance art as a whole might be especially vulnerable to this critique, women's performance art in particular has promoted both collaborative and collective performance, generating numerous performance groups with specific political interventionist goals. However, even apart from the more obvious political stance, women's performance art provides an instance of what Teresa de Lauretis has called the "heterogeneous and heteronomous" face of feminism;[45] that is, both the differences and the commonalities among women are made visible and celebrated. While women performance artists speak their personal, lived experience, and explore the most intimate aspects of their individual lives, their explorations relate directly to the common category of their woman-ness. As women, their relationship to representation is unique, so that the performance context necessarily creates a dissonance with the representations of 'Woman.' Thus the woman performance artist cannot help but assert an image that is simultaneously heterogeneous and heteronomous; singular and yet categorically related to all women.

While I strongly believe in the value of the above perspectives on women's performance, there is a sense in which the terms of this discussion are shifting, "even as we speak." This mobility is a problem endemic to the study of performance art yet is a problem only for the critic/historian—for performance artists, such perpetually shifting sands are a virtue and even a goal. The term "performance art" is rapidly losing any viability as a generic possibility—as performer/dancer Wendy Woodson recently noted, she used to avoid the label performance artist because of its association with the violent, masochistic, and nausea-producing performers (Burden, Stellarc, Paul McCarthy, etc.). Now she eschews it because performance has become slick,

[44]Michel Foucault, "Why Study Power: The Question of the Subject," in *Michel Foucault: Beyond Structuralism and Hermeneutics*, ed. Hubert L. Dreyfus and Paul Rabinow (Chicago: University of Chicago Press, 1982), 211–12.

[45]Teresa de Lauretis, "Feminist Studies: Reconstituting Knowledge," Unpublished ms. (Spring 1985).

commercial, more "theatrical" in a negative, assimilative way.[46] In the past year, I noticed another new trend in performances on both coasts. This trend is toward conventional acting and all the parameters that it implies—which in turn invites assessment of the piece on the basis of the conventional standards by which acting is usually judged, i.e., technique. As Linda Burnham noted in her recent essay for *The Drama Review,* prior performance art may indeed have included role-playing, singing, dancing, whatever, that was frequently not "good" by ordinary standards, but that very discrepancy led viewers to consider a different perspective on the work. The piece was not about "doing something well," but about something else, including the re-examination of those standards.[47] In 1987, performances by Iris Rose of Watchface and John Fleck in "PsychoOpera" depended crucially on the ability to "act well" and on a coherent overall dramatic structure. Instead of deconstructing theatrical convention, performers now seem to court it, encouraging judgement of the work on more technical grounds.

Women performance artists, in general, dominate the field less than in the 1970s—perhaps precisely because of the encroachment of conventional standards of professionalism. However, some performers evidence the shift in focus in a desire for a medium with more visible or permanent results: Laurie Anderson wants to work more with film (despite the lukewarm reception of *Home of the Brave*) and also likes the fact that her performances can be preserved on video and record; Meredith Monk, after remarking in an interview that she wants to make a film, has apparently withdrawn from performance art for a time, focusing instead on chamber music and the production of a new record of vocal works; and Vanalyne Green and Pat Oleszko, among many others, are channeling their energies into film or video rather than performance.[48] Green says that she can manipulate the visual image more completely in the film medium, thus allowing a higher degree of artistic precision. In general, the mid 1980s has brought about a regrouping, perhaps in response to a reactionary political climate, perhaps in the perceived failure of 1970s strategies to achieve more measurable, visible effects.

Rachel Rosenthal, having explored her personal life, has moved to an overt focus on social issues which are not specifically feminist (but which are clearly informed by her feminist sensibility). Recent works have dealt with animal rights, the nuclear threat, pollution, and other, more global issues. Her continued engagement with the deconstructive strategies of performance art combined with her dedicated political consciousness still serves to create some of the most powerful work around in the 1980s. Rosenthal's performance style, always highly theatrical in effects and presentation, was once criticized for its kinship with theatre; now, others seek to emulate the theatrical coherence of her work, but often lack the skills to pull it off.

---

[46]Remark made on a panel discussion of performance art, October 23, 1987, Hampshire College, Amherst, Massachusetts.

[47]Linda Burnham, "Performance Art, *High Performance* and Me," *The Drama Review* 30:1 (1986): 36.

[48]Remarks made in various interviews or conversations with the author: Anderson and Monk, 1983; Green and Oleszko, 1987.

Then there are performers like Karen Finley, whose relatively obscure performance work has suddenly been thrown into the limelight. Banned in London, praised (and then villified) in the *Village Voice,* suddenly invited to performance venues everywhere, Finley's particular brand of violent scatological rant and self-abuse shocked even the jaded New York art scene. Not that other women haven't pursued violent or offensive performance styles, with a conscious feminist agenda; Valie Export, Lydia Lunch, and even Rosenthal have deliberately worked against "pretty" images or conventional aesthetics, frustrating voyeurism, and challenging societal conceptions of women as artists. The violence and/or "disgust" factor in these works fuels the exploration of aesthetics as an ideological trap, one which subjugates women in particular but which also dictates the numbed and plastic tastes of dominant culture.[49] However, in Finley's case, being catapulted into a higher degree of visibility hastened her assimilation into a more commercial audience. In venues other than New York, beer-drinking fraternity boys came to see the naked woman shove yams up her ass and throw obscenities at the crowd. Her work became re-inscribed in the fetishistic process associated with strip-tease or live sex, and not at all the feminist or subversive strategy that theory might endorse. Finley herself seems to have made note of this, and her newest work is reportedly much more direct in its declaration of feminist politics. It even opens with a brilliant bit of critical self-examination: clad in a leopard skin fur coat, Finley yells "Get that dead animal out of my face!" (a remark reportedly made by Rosenthal to Finley on their first encounter); then drops the coat to the floor, revealing her nudity; leaves the stage, and returns clothed to continue the piece.[50]

Finley's apparent re-evaluation of her work and awareness of audience highlights two important issues for women's performance art in the 1980s. The threat and power of assimilation is constant, and most visible in the make-up of the performer's audience; Laurie Anderson's appeal for a mainstream rock audience illustrates this problem—just how much does the work retain any potentially subversive impact once it has achieved commercial viability? To what extent do those commercial endorsements render any radical politics impossible? Yet, if performance artists are doomed to relative obscurity, playing only to audiences of "the converted," how will societal consciousness be raised (or abrased) on a larger scale? Should this even be a conscious goal? One might argue that Anderson's gender-bending appearance and performance style continues to evoke a deconstructive process, however subliminal. Women performance artists meanwhile continue the challenge of cultural deconstruction, actively providing a feminist frame of reference for the re-articulation of difference—and what expression that challenge takes next remains to be seen.

Feminist theory, having discovered in postmodern theory fertile ground both for critical and ideological strategies, thus also discovers a vivid and active voice in woman's performance art. In deconstructing the system of representation, this per-

[49]As Dolan notes, Finley "does not offer herself as a passive object . . . she desecrates herself as the object of [male] desire." See 161–63.

[50]As recounted by Mark Russell, producing director of Performance Space 122, New York, October 1987.

formance practice is paradigmatic as a powerful strategy of intervention into dominant culture. Eminently political regardless of intent, the activity pursues an awareness of the phallocentrism of our signifying systems, and instigates the demolition of genderized identities. Not merely a reflection of feminist theory, women's performance art provides a visible basis for the construction of a feminist frame of reference, articulating alternatives for power and resistance.

Performative Acts and Gender Constitution: An Essay in Phenomenology and Feminist Theory

Judith Butler

Philosophers rarely think about acting in the theatrical sense, but they do have a discourse of 'acts' that maintains associative semantic meanings with theories of performance and acting. For example, John Searle's 'speech acts,' those verbal assurances and promises which seem not only to refer to a speaking relationship, but to constitute a moral bond between speakers, illustrate one of the illocutionary gestures that constitutes the stage of the analytic philosophy of language. Further, 'action theory,' a domain of moral philosophy, seeks to understand what it is 'to do' prior to any claim of what one *ought* to do. Finally, the phenomenological theory of 'acts,' espoused by Edmund Husserl, Maurice Merleau-Ponty and George Herbert Mead, among others, seeks to explain the mundane way in which social agents *constitute* social reality through language, gesture, and all manner of symbolic social sign. Though phenomenology sometimes appears to assume the existence of a choosing and constituting agent prior to language (who poses as the sole source of its constituting acts), there is also a more radical use of the doctrine of constitution that takes the social agent as an *object* rather than the subject of constitutive acts.

When Simone de Beauvoir claims, "one is not born, but, rather, *becomes* a woman," she is appropriating and reinterpreting this doctrine of constituting acts from the phenomenological tradition.[1] In this sense, gender is in no way a stable identity or locus of agency from which various acts proceede; rather, it is an identity tenuously constituted in time—an identity instituted through a *stylized repetition of acts*. Further, gender is instituted through the stylization of the body and, hence, must be understood as the mundane way in which bodily gestures, movements, and enactments of various kinds constitute the illusion of an abiding gendered self. This formulation

Judith Butler is Associate Professor of Humanities at Johns Hopkins University, author of Gender Trouble: Feminism and the Subversion of Identity *(Routledge: 1989).*

[1]For a further discussion of Beauvoir's feminist contribution to phenomenological theory, see my "Variations on Sex and Gender: Beauvoir's *The Second Sex,*" *Yale French Studies* 172 (1986).

moves the conception of gender off the ground of a substantial model of identity to one that requires a conception of a constituted *social temporality*. Significantly, if gender is instituted through acts which are internally discontinuous, then the *appearance of substance* is precisely that, a constructed identity, a performative accomplishment which the mundane social audience, including the actors themselves, come to believe and to perform in the mode of belief. If the ground of gender identity is the stylized repetition of acts through time, and not a seemingly seamless identity, then the possibilities of gender transformation are to be found in the arbitrary relation between such acts, in the possibility of a different sort of repeating, in the breaking or subversive repetition of that style.

Through the conception of gender acts sketched above, I will try to show some ways in which reified and naturalized conceptions of gender might be understood as constituted and, hence, capable of being constituted differently. In opposition to theatrical or phenomenological models which take the gendered self to be prior to its acts, I will understand constituting acts not only as constituting the identity of the actor, but as constituting that identity as a compelling illusion, an object of *belief*. In the course of making my argument, I will draw from theatrical, anthropological, and philosophical discourses, but mainly phenomenology, to show that what is called gender identity is a performative accomplishment compelled by social sanction and taboo. In its very character as performative resides the possibility of contesting its reified status.

I. Sex/Gender: Feminist and Phenomenological Views

Feminist theory has often been critical of naturalistic explanations of sex and sexuality that assume that the meaning of women's social existence can be derived from some fact of their physiology. In distinguishing sex from gender, feminist theorists have disputed causal explanations that assume that sex dictates or necessitates certain social meanings for women's experience. Phenomenological theories of human embodiment have also been concerned to distinguish between the various physiological and biological causalities that structure bodily existence and the *meanings* that embodied existence assumes in the context of lived experience. In Merleau-Ponty's reflections in *The Phenomenology of Perception* on "the body in its sexual being," he takes issue with such accounts of bodily experience and claims that the body is "an historical idea" rather than "a natural species."[2] Significantly, it is this claim that Simone de Beauvoir cites in *The Second Sex* when she sets the stage for her claim that "woman," and by extension, any gender, is an historical situation rather than a natural fact.[3]

In both contexts, the existence and facticity of the material or natural dimensions of the body are not denied, but reconceived as distinct from the process by which the body comes to bear cultural meanings. For both Beauvoir and Merleau-Ponty,

---

[2]Maurice Merleau-Ponty, "The Body in its Sexual Being," in *The Phenomenology of Perception*, trans. Colin Smith (Boston: Routledge and Kegan Paul, 1962).

[3]Simone de Beauvoir, *The Second Sex*, trans. H. M. Parshley (New York: Vintage, 1974), 38.

the body is understood to be an active process of embodying certain cultural and historical possibilities, a complicated process of appropriation which any phenomenological theory of embodiment needs to describe. In order to describe the gendered body, a phenomenological theory of constitution requires an expansion of the conventional view of acts to mean both that which constitutes meaning and that through which meaning is performed or enacted. In other words, the acts by which gender is constituted bear similarities to performative acts within theatrical contexts. My task, then, is to examine in what ways gender is constructed through specific corporeal acts, and what possibilities exist for the cultural transformation of gender through such acts.

Merleau-Ponty maintains not only that the body is an historical idea but a set of possibilities to be continually realized. In claiming that the body is an historical idea, Merleau-Ponty means that it gains its meaning through a concrete and historically mediated expression in the world. That the body is a set of possibilities signifies (a) that its appearance in the world, for perception, is not predetermined by some manner of interior essence, and (b) that its concrete expression in the world must be understood as the taking up and rendering specific of a set of historical possibilities. Hence, there is an agency which is understood as the process of rendering such possibilities determinate. These possibilities are necessarily constrained by available historical conventions. The body is not a self-identical or merely factic materiality; it is a materiality that bears meaning, if nothing else, and the manner of this bearing is fundamentally dramatic. By dramatic I mean only that the body is not merely matter but a continual and incessant *materializing* of possibilities. One is not simply a body, but, in some very key sense, one does one's body and, indeed, one does one's body differently from one's contemporaries and from one's embodied predecessors and successors as well.

It is, however, clearly unfortunate grammar to claim that there is a 'we' or an 'I' that does its body, as if a disembodied agency preceded and directed an embodied exterior. More appropriate, I suggest, would be a vocabulary that resists the substance metaphysics of subject-verb formations and relies instead on an ontology of present participles. The 'I' that is its body is, of necessity, a mode of embodying, and the 'what' that it embodies is possibilities. But here again the grammar of the formulation misleads, for the possibilities that are embodied are not fundamentally exterior or antecedent to the process of embodying itself. As an intentionally organized materiality, the body is always an embodying *of* possibilities both conditioned and circumscribed by historical convention. In other words, the body *is* a historical situation, as Beauvoir has claimed, and is a manner of doing, dramatizing, and *reproducing* a historical situation.

To do, to dramatize, to reproduce, these seem to be some of the elementary structures of embodiment. This doing of gender is not merely a way in which embodied agents are exterior, surfaced, open to the perception of others. Embodiment clearly manifests a set of strategies or what Sartre would perhaps have called a style of being or Foucault, "a stylistics of existence." This style is never fully self-styled, for living styles have a history, and that history conditions and limits possibilities. Consider gender, for instance, as *a corporeal style*, an 'act,' as it were, which is both intentional and performative, where 'performative' itself carries the double-meaning of 'dramatic' and 'non-referential.'

When Beauvoir claims that 'woman' is a historical idea and not a natural fact, she clearly underscores the distinction between sex, as biological facticity, and gender, as the cultural interpretation or signification of that facticity. To be female is, according to that distinction, a facticity which has no meaning, but to be a woman is to have *become* a woman, to compel the body to conform to an historical idea of 'woman,' to induce the body to become a cultural sign, to materialize oneself in obedience to an historically delimited possibility, and to do this as a sustained and repeated corporeal project. The notion of a 'project', however, suggests the originating force of a radical will, and because gender is a project which has cultural survival as its end, the term *'strategy'* better suggests the situation of duress under which gender performance always and variously occurs. Hence, as a strategy of survival, gender is a performance with clearly punitive consequences. Discrete genders are part of what 'humanizes' individuals within contemporary culture; indeed, those who fail to do their gender right are regularly punished. Because there is neither an 'essence' that gender expresses or externalizes nor an objective ideal to which gender aspires; because gender is not a fact, the various acts of gender creates the idea of gender, and without those acts, there would be no gender at all. Gender is, thus, a construction that regularly conceals its genesis. The tacit collective agreement to perform, produce, and sustain discrete and polar genders as cultural fictions is obscured by the credibility of its own production. The authors of gender become entranced by their own fictions whereby the construction compels one's belief in its necessity and naturalness. The historical possibilities materialized through various corporeal styles are nothing other than those punitively regulated cultural fictions that are alternately embodied and disguised under duress.

How useful is a phenomenological point of departure for a feminist description of gender? On the surface it appears that phenomenology shares with feminist analysis a commitment to grounding theory in lived experience, and in revealing the way in which the world is produced through the constituting acts of subjective experience. Clearly, not all feminist theory would privilege the point of view of the subject, (Kristeva once objected to feminist theory as 'too existentialist')[4] and yet the feminist claim that the personal is political suggests, in part, that subjective experience is not only structured by existing political arrangements, but effects and structures those arrangements in turn. Feminist theory has sought to understand the way in which systemic or pervasive political and cultural structures are enacted and reproduced through individual acts and practices, and how the analysis of ostensibly personal situations is clarified through situating the issues in a broader and shared cultural context. Indeed, the feminist impulse, and I am sure there is more than one, has often emerged in the recognition that my pain or my silence or my anger or my perception is finally not mine alone, and that it delimits me in a shared cultural situation which in turn enables and empowers me in certain unanticipated ways. The personal is thus implicitly political inasmuch as it is conditioned by shared social

[4]Julia Kristeva, *Histoire d'amour* (Paris: Editions Denoel, 1983), 242.

structures, but the personal has also been immunized against political challenge to the extent that public/private distinctions endure. For feminist theory, then, the personal becomes an expansive category, one which accommodates, if only implicitly, political structures usually viewed as public. Indeed, the very meaning of the political expands as well. At its best, feminist theory involves a dialectical expansion of both of these categories. My situation does not cease to be mine just because it is the situation of someone else, and my acts, individual as they are, nevertheless reproduce the situation of my gender, and do that in various ways. In other words, there is, latent in the personal is political formulation of feminist theory, a supposition that the life-world of gender relations is constituted, at least partially, through the concrete and historically mediated *acts* of individuals. Considering that "the" body is invariably transformed into his body or her body, the body is only known through its gendered appearance. It would seem imperative to consider the way in which this gendering of the body occurs. My suggestion is that the body becomes its gender through a series of acts which are renewed, revised, and consolidated through time. From a feminist point of view, one might try to reconceive the gendered body as the legacy of sedimented acts rather than a predetermined or foreclosed structure, essence or fact, whether natural, cultural, or linguistic.

The feminist appropriation of the phenomenological theory of constitution might employ the notion of an *act* in a richly ambiguous sense. If the personal is a category which expands to include the wider political and social structures, then the *acts* of the gendered subject would be similarly expansive. Clearly, there are political acts which are deliberate and instrumental actions of political organizing, resistance collective intervention with the broad aim of instating a more just set of social and political relations. There are thus acts which are done in the name of women, and then there are acts in and of themselves, apart from any instrumental consequence, that challenge the category of women itself. Indeed, one ought to consider the futility of a political program which seeks radically to transform the social situation of women without first determining whether the category of woman is socially constructed in such a way that to be a woman is, by definition, to be in an oppressed situation. In an understandable desire to forge bonds of solidarity, feminist discourse has often relied upon the category of woman as a universal presupposition of cultural experience which, in its universal status, provides a false ontological promise of eventual political solidarity. In a culture in which the false universal of 'man' has for the most part been presupposed as coextensive with humanness itself, feminist theory has sought with success to bring female specificity into visibility and to rewrite the history of culture in terms which acknowledge the presence, the influence, and the oppression of women. Yet, in this effort to combat the invisibility of women as a category feminists run the risk of rendering visible a category which may or may not be representative of the concrete lives of women. As feminists, we have been less eager, I think, to consider the status of the category itself and, indeed, to discern the conditions of oppression which issue from an unexamined reproduction of gender identities which sustain discrete and binary categories of man and woman.

When Beauvoir claims that woman is an "historical situation," she emphasizes that the body suffers a certain cultural construction, not only through conventions that sanction and proscribe how one acts one's body, the 'act' or performance that one's body is, but also in the tacit conventions that structure the way the body is culturally perceived. Indeed, if gender is the cultural significance that the sexed body assumes, and if that significance is codetermined through various acts and their cultural perception, then it would appear that from within the terms of culture it is not possible to know sex as distinct from gender. The reproduction of the category of gender is enacted on a large political scale, as when women first enter a profession or gain certain rights, or are reconceived in legal or political discourse in significantly new ways. But the more mundane reproduction of gendered identity takes place through the various ways in which bodies are acted in relationship to the deeply entrenched or sedimented expectations of gendered existence. Consider that there is a sedimentation of gender norms that produces the peculiar phenomenon of a natural sex, or a real woman, or any number of prevalent and compelling social fictions, and that this is a sedimentation that over time has produced a set of corporeal styles which, in reified form, appear as the natural configuration of bodies into sexes which exist in a binary relation to one another.

II. Binary Genders and the Heterosexual Contract

To guarantee the reproduction of a given culture, various requirements, well-established in the anthropological literature of kinship, have instated sexual reproduction within the confines of a heterosexually-based system of marriage which requires the reproduction of human beings in certain gendered modes which, in effect, guarantee the eventual reproduction of that kinship system. As Foucault and others have pointed out, the association of a natural sex with a discrete gender and with an ostensibly natural 'attraction' to the opposing sex/gender is an unnatural conjunction of cultural constructs in the service of reproductive interests.[5] Feminist cultural anthropology and kinship studies have shown how cultures are governed by conventions that not only regulate and guarantee the production, exchange, and consumption of material goods, but also reproduce the bonds of kinship itself, which require taboos and a punitive regulation of reproduction to effect that end. Levi-Strauss has shown how the incest taboo works to guarantee the channeling of sexuality into various modes of heterosexual marriage,[6] Gayle Rubin has argued convincingly that the incest taboo produces certain kinds of discrete gendered identities and sexualities.[7] My point is simply that one way in which this system of compulsory heterosexuality is reproduced and concealed is through the cultivation of bodies into discrete sexes with 'natural' appearances and 'natural' heterosexual dispositions. Although the enthnocentric conceit suggests a progression beyond the mandatory structures of kinship relations as described by Levì-Strauss, I would suggest, along with Rubin, that contemporary gender identities are so many marks or "traces" of

---

[5]See Michel Foucault, *The History of Sexuality: An Introduction*, trans. Robert Hurley (New York: Random House, 1980), 154: "the notion of 'sex' made it possible to group together, in an artificial unity, anatomical elements, biological functions, conducts, sensations, and pleasures, and it enabled one to make use of this fictitious unity as a causal principle . . .".

[6]See Claude Levì-Strauss, *The Elementary Structures of Kinship* (Boston: Beacon Press, 1965).

[7]Gayle Rubin, "The Traffic in Women: Notes on the 'Political Economy' of Sex," in *Toward an Anthropology of Women*, ed. Rayna R. Reiter (New York: Monthly Review Press, 1975), 178–85.

residual kinship. The contention that sex, gender, and heterosexuality are historical products which have become conjoined and reified as natural over time has received a good deal of critical attention not only from Michel Foucault, but Monique Wittig, gay historians, and various cultural anthropologists and social psychologists in recent years.[8] These theories, however, still lack the critical resources for thinking radically about the historical sedimentation of sexuality and sex-related constructs if they do not delimit and describe the mundane manner in which these constructs are produced, reproduced, and maintained within the field of bodies.

Can phenomenology assist a feminist reconstruction of the sedimented character of sex, gender, and sexuality at the level of the body? In the first place, the phenomenological focus on the various acts by which cultural identity is constituted and assumed provides a felicitous starting point for the feminist effort to understand the mundane manner in which bodies get crafted into genders. The formulation of the body as a mode of dramatizing or enacting possibilities offers a way to understand how a cultural convention is embodied and enacted. But it seems difficult, if not impossible, to imagine a way to conceptualize the scale and systemic character of women's oppression from a theoretical position which takes constituting acts to be its point of departure. Although individual acts do work to maintain and reproduce systems of oppression, and, indeed, any theory of personal political responsibility presupposes such a view, it doesn't follow that oppression is a sole consequence of such acts. One might argue that without human beings whose various acts, largely construed, produce and maintain oppressive conditions, those conditions would fall away, but note that the relation between acts and conditions is neither unilateral nor unmediated. There are social contexts and conventions within which certain acts not only become possible but become conceivable as acts at all. The transformation of social relations becomes a matter, then, of transforming hegemonic social conditions rather than the individual acts that are spawned by those conditions. Indeed, one runs the risk of addressing the merely indirect, if not epiphenomenal, reflection of those conditions if one remains restricted to a politics of acts.

But the theatrical sense of an "act" forces a revision of the individualist assumptions underlying the more restricted view of constituting acts within phenomenological discourse. As a given temporal duration within the entire performance, "acts" are a shared experience and 'collective action.' Just as within feminist theory the very category of the personal is expanded to include political structures, so is there a theatrically-based and, indeed, less individually-oriented view of acts that goes some of the way in defusing the criticism of act theory as 'too existentialist.' The act that gender is, the act that embodied agents *are* inasmuch as they dramatically and actively embody and, indeed, *wear* certain cultural significations, is clearly not one's act alone. Surely, there are nuanced and individual ways of *doing* one's gender, but *that* one does it, and that one does it *in accord with* certain sanctions and proscriptions, is clearly not a fully individual matter. Here again, I don't mean to minimize the effect

[8]See my "Variations on Sex and Gender: Beauvoir, Wittig, and Foucault," in *Feminism as Critique*, ed. Seyla Benhabib and Drucila Cornell (London: Basil Blackwell, 1987 [distributed by University of Minnesota Press]).

of certain gender norms which originate within the family and are enforced through certain familial modes of punishment and reward and which, as a consequence, might be construed as highly individual, for even there family relations recapitulate, individualize, and specify pre-existing cultural relations; they are rarely, if ever, radically original. The act that one does, the act that one performs, is, in a sense, an act that has been going on before one arrived on the scene. Hence, gender is an act which has been rehearsed, much as a script survives the particular actors who make use of it, but which requires individual actors in order to be actualized and reproduced as reality once again. The complex components that go into an act must be distinguished in order to understand the kind of acting in concert and acting in accord which acting one's gender invariably is.

In what senses, then, is gender an act? As anthropologist Victor Turner suggests in his studies of ritual social drama, social action requires a performance which is *repeated*. This repetition is at once a reenactment and reexperiencing of a set of meanings already socially established; it is the mundane and ritualized form of their legitimation.[9] When this conception of social performance is applied to gender, it is clear that although there are individual bodies that enact these significations by becoming stylized into gendered modes, this "action" is immediately public as well. There are temporal and collective dimensions to these actions, and their public nature is not inconsequential; indeed, the performance is effected with the strategic aim of maintaining gender within its binary frame. Understood in pedagogical terms, the performance renders social laws explicit.

As a public action and performative act, gender is not a radical choice or project that reflects a merely individual choice, but neither is it imposed or inscribed upon the individual, as some post-structuralist displacements of the subject would contend. The body is not passively scripted with cultural codes, as if it were a lifeless recipient of wholly pre-given cultural relations. But neither do embodied selves pre-exist the cultural conventions which essentially signify bodies. Actors are always already on the stage, within the terms of the performance. Just as a script may be enacted in various ways, and just as the play requires both text and interpretation, so the gendered body acts its part in a culturally restricted corporeal space and enacts interpretations within the confines of already existing directives.

---

[9]See Victor Turner, *Dramas, Fields, and Metaphors* (Ithaca: Cornell University Press, 1974). Clifford Geertz suggests in "Blurred Genres: The Refiguration of Thought," in *Local Knowledge, Further Essays in Interpretive Anthropology* (New York: Basic Books, 1983), that the theatrical metaphor is used by recent social theory in two, often opposing, ways. Ritual theorists like Victor Turner focus on a notion of social drama of various kinds as a means for settling internal conflicts within a culture and regenerating social cohesion. On the other hand, symbolic action approaches, influenced by figures as diverse as Emile Durkheim, Kenneth Burke, and Michel Foucault, focus on the way in which political authority and questions of legitimation are thematized and settled within the terms of performed meaning. Geertz himself suggests that the tension might be viewed dialectically; his study of political organization in Bali as a "theatre-state" is a case in point. In terms of an explicitly feminist account of gender as performative, it seems clear to me that an account of gender as ritualized, public performance must be combined with an analysis of the political sanctions and taboos under which that performance may and may not occur within the public sphere free of punitive consequence.

Although the links between a theatrical and a social role are complex and the distinctions not easily drawn (Bruce Wilshire points out the limits of the comparison in *Role-Playing and Identity: The Limits of Theatre as Metaphor*[10]), it seems clear that, although theatrical performances can meet with political censorship and scathing criticism, gender performances in non-theatrical contexts are governed by more clearly punitive and regulatory social conventions. Indeed, the sight of a transvestite onstage can compel pleasure and applause while the sight of the same transvestite on the seat next to us on the bus can compel fear, rage, even violence. The conventions which mediate proximity and identification in these two instances are clearly quite different. I want to make two different kinds of claims regarding this tentative distinction. In the theatre, one can say, 'this is just an act,' and de-realize the act, make acting into something quite distinct from what is real. Because of this distinction, one can maintain one's sense of reality in the face of this temporary challenge to our existing ontological assumptions about gender arrangements; the various conventions which announce that 'this is only a play' allows strict lines to be drawn between the performance and life. On the street or in the bus, the act becomes dangerous, if it does, precisely because there are no theatrical conventions to delimit the purely imaginary character of the act, indeed, on the street or in the bus, there is no presumption that the act is distinct from a reality; the disquieting effect of the act is that there are no conventions that facilitate making this separation. Clearly, there is theatre which attempts to contest or, indeed, break down those conventions that demarcate the imaginary from the real (Richard Schechner brings this out quite clearly in *Between Theatre and Anthropology*[11]). Yet in those cases one confronts the same phenomenon, namely, that the act is not contrasted with the real, but *constitutes* a reality that is in some sense new, a modality of gender that cannot readily be assimilated into the pre-existing categories that regulate gender reality. From the point of view of those established categories, one may want to claim, but oh, this is *really* a girl or a woman, or this is *really* a boy or a man, and further that the *appearance* contradicts the *reality* of the gender, that the discrete and familiar reality must be there, nascent, temporarily unrealized, perhaps realized at other times or other places. The transvestite, however, can do more than simply express the distinction between sex and gender, but challenges, at least implicitly, the distinction between appearance and reality that structures a good deal of popular thinking about gender identity. If the 'reality' of gender is constituted by the performance itself, then there is no recourse to an essential and unrealized 'sex' or 'gender' which gender performances ostensibly express. Indeed, the transvestite's gender is as fully real as anyone whose performance complies with social expectations.

Gender reality is performative which means, quite simply, that it is real only to the extent that it is performed. It seems fair to say that certain kinds of acts are usually interpreted as expressive of a gender core or identity, and that these acts either conform to an expected gender identity or contest that expectation in some

---

[10]Bruce Wilshire, *Role-Playing and Identity: The Lmits of Theatre as Metaphor* (Boston: Routledge and Kegan Paul, 1981).

[11]Richard Schechner, *Between Theatre and Anthropology* (Philadelphia: University of Pennsylvania Press, 1985). See especially, "News, Sex, and Performance," 295–324.

way. That expectation, in turn, is based upon the perception of sex, where sex is understood to be the discrete and factic datum of primary sexual characteristics. This implicit and popular theory of acts and gestures as *expressive* of gender suggests that gender itself is something prior to the various acts, postures, and gestures by which it is dramatized and known; indeed, gender appears to the popular imagination as a substantial core which might well be understood as the spiritual or psychological correlate of biological sex.[12] If gender attributes, however, are not expressive but performative, then these attributes effectively constitute the identity they are said to express or reveal. The distinction between expression and performativeness is quite crucial, for if gender attributes and acts, the various ways in which a body shows or produces its cultural signification, are performative, then there is no preexisting identity by which an act or attribute might be measured; there would be no true or false, real or distorted acts of gender, and the postulation of a true gender identity would be revealed as a regulatory fiction. That gender reality is created through sustained social performances means that the very notions of an essential sex, a true or abiding masculinity or femininity, are also constituted as part of the strategy by which the performative aspect of gender is concealed.

As a consequence, gender cannot be understood as a *role* which either expresses or disguises an interior 'self,' whether that 'self' is conceived as sexed or not. As performance which is performative, gender is an 'act,' broadly construed, which constructs the social fiction of its own psychological interiority. As opposed to a view such as Erving Goffman's which posits a self which assumes and exchanges various 'roles' within the complex social expectations of the 'game' of modern life,[13] I am suggesting that this self is not only irretrievably 'outside,' constituted in social discourse, but that the ascription of interiority is itself a publically regulated and sanctioned form of essence fabrication. Genders, then, can be neither true nor false, neither real nor apparent. And yet, one is compelled to live in a world in which genders constitute univocal signifiers, in which gender is stabilized, polarized, rendered discrete and intractable. In effect, gender is made to comply with a model of truth and falsity which not only contradicts its own performative fluidity, but serves a social policy of gender regulation and control. Performing one's gender wrong initiates a set of punishments both obvious and indirect, and performing it well provides the reassurance that there is an essentialism of gender identity after all. That this reassurance is so easily displaced by anxiety, that culture so readily punishes or marginalizes those who fail to perform the illusion of gender essentialism should be sign enough that on some level there is social knowledge that the truth or falsity of gender is only socially compelled and in no sense ontologically necessitated.[14]

---

[12]In *Mother Camp* (Prentice-Hall, 1974), Anthropologist Esther Newton gives an urben ethnography of drag queens in which she suggests that all gender might be understood on the model of drag. In *Gender: An Ethnomethodological Approach* (Chicago: University of Chicago Press, 1978), Suzanne J. Kessler and Wendy McKenna argue that gender is an "accomplishment" which requires the skills of constructing the body into a socially legitimate artifice.

[13]See Erving Goffmann, *The Presentation of Self in Everyday Life* (Garden City: Doubleday, 1959).

[14]See Michel Foucault's edition of *Herculine Barbin: The Journals of a Nineteenth Century French Hermaphrodite*, trans. Richard McDougall (New York: Pantheon Books, 1984), for an interesting display

III. Feminist Theory: Beyond an Expressive Model of Gender

This view of gender does not pose as a comprehensive theory about what gender is or the manner of its construction, and neither does it prescribe an explicit feminist political program. Indeed, I can imagine this view of gender being used for a number of discrepant political strategies. Some of my friends may fault me for this and insist that any theory of gender constitution has political presuppositions and implications, and that it is impossible to separate a theory of gender from a political philosophy of feminism. In fact, I would agree, and argue that it is primarily political interests which create the social phenomena of gender itself, and that without a radical critique of gender constitution feminist theory fails to take stock of the way in which oppression structures the ontological categories through which gender is conceived. Gayatri Spivak has argued that feminists need to rely on an operational essentialism, a false ontology of women as a universal in order to advance a feminist political program.[15] She knows that the category of 'women' is not fully expressive, that the multiplicity and discontinuity of the referent mocks and rebels against the univocity of the sign, but suggests it could be used for strategic purposes. Kristeva suggests something similar, I think, when she prescribes that feminists use the category of women as a political tool without attributing ontological integrity to the term, and adds that, strictly speaking, women cannot be said to exist.[16] Feminists might well worry about the political implications of claiming that women do not exist, especially in light of the persuasive arguments advanced by Mary Anne Warren in her book, *Gendercide*.[17] She argues that social policies regarding population control and reproductive technology are designed to limit and, at times, eradicate the existence of women altogether. In light of such a claim, what good does it do to quarrel about the metaphysical status of the term, and perhaps, for clearly political reasons, feminists ought to silence the quarrel altogether.

But it is one thing to use the term and know its ontological insufficiency and quite another to articulate a normative vision for feminist theory which celebrates or emancipates an essence, a nature, or a shared cultural reality which cannot be found. The option I am defending is not to redescribe the world from the point of view of women. I don't know what that point of view is, but whatever it is, it is not singular, and not mine to espouse. It would only be half-right to claim that I am interested in how the phenomenon of a men's or women's point of view gets constituted, for while I do think that those points of views are, indeed, socially constituted, and that a reflexive genealogy of those points of view is important to do, it is not primarily the gender episteme that I am interested in exposing, deconstructing, or reconstructing.

---

of the horror evoked by intersexed bodies. Foucault's introduction makes clear that the medical delimitation of univocal sex is yet another wayward application of the discourse on truth-as-identity. See also the work of Robert Edgerton in *American Anthropologist* on the cross-cultural variations of response to hermaphroditic bodies.

[15]Remarks at the Center for Humanities, Wesleyan University, Spring, 1985.

[16]Julia Kristeva, "Woman Can Never Be Defined", trans. Marilyn A. August, in *New French Feminisms*, ed. Elaine Marks and Isabelle de Courtivron (New York: Schocken, 1981).

[17]Mary Anne Warren, *Gendercide: The Implications of Sex Selection* (New Jersey: Rowman and Allanheld, 1985).

Indeed, it is the presupposition of the category of woman itself that requires a critical genealogy of the complex institutional and discursive means by which it is constituted. Although some feminist literary critics suggest that the presupposition of sexual difference is necessary for all discourse, that position reifies sexual difference as the founding moment of culture and precludes an analysis not only of how sexual difference is constituted to begin with but how it is continuously constituted, both by the masculine tradition that preempts the universal point of view, and by those feminist positions that construct the univocal category of 'women' in the name of expressing or, indeed, liberating a subjected class. As Foucault claimed about those humanist efforts to liberate the criminalized subject, the subject that is freed is even more deeply shackled than originally thought.[18]

Clearly, though, I envision the critical genealogy of gender to rely on a phenomenological set of presuppositions, most important among them the expanded conception of an "act" which is both socially shared and historically constituted, and which is performative in the sense I previously described. But a critical genealogy needs to be supplemented by a politics of performative gender acts, one which both redescribes existing gender identities and offers a prescriptive view about the kind of gender reality there ought to be. The redescription needs to expose the reifications that tacitly serve as substantial gender cores or identities, and to elucidate both the act and the strategy of disavowal which at once constitute and conceal gender as we live it. The prescription is invariably more difficult, if only because we need to think a world in which acts, gestures, the visual body, the clothed body, the various physical attributes usually associated with gender, *express nothing*. In a sense, the prescription is not utopian, but consists in an imperative to acknowledge the existing complexity of gender which our vocabulary invariably disguises and to bring that complexity into a dramatic cultural interplay without punitive consequences.

Certainly, it remains politically important to represent women, but to do that in a way that does not distort and reify the very collectivity the theory is supposed to emancipate. Feminist theory which presupposes sexual difference as the necessary and invariant theoretical point of departure clearly improves upon those humanist discourses which conflate the universal with the masculine and appropriate all of culture as masculine property. Clearly, it is necessary to reread the texts of western philosophy from the various points of view that have been excluded, not only to reveal the particular perspective and set of interests informing those ostensibly transparent descriptions of the real, but to offer alternative descriptions and prescriptions; indeed, to establish philosophy as a cultural practice, and to criticize its tenets from marginalized cultural locations. I have no quarrel with this procedure, and have clearly benefited from those analyses. My only concern is that sexual difference not become a reification which unwittingly preserves a binary restriction on gender identity and an implicitly heterosexual framework for the description of gender, gender identity, and sexuality. There is, in my view, nothing about femaleness that is waiting to be expressed; there is, on the other hand, a good deal about the diverse

[18]Ibid.; Michel Foucault, *Discipline and Punish: The Birth of the Prison* trans. Alan Sheridan (New York: Vintage Books, 1978).

experiences of women that is being expressed and still needs to be expressed, but caution is needed with respect to that theoretical language, for it does not simply report a pre-linguistic experience, but constructs that experience as well as the limits of its analysis. Regardless of the pervasive character of patriarchy and the prevalence of sexual difference as an operative cultural distinction, there is nothing about a binary gender system that is given. As a corporeal field of cultural play, gender is a basically innovative affair, although it is quite clear that there are strict punishments for contesting the script by performing out of turn or through unwarranted improvisations. Gender is not passively scripted on the body, and neither is it determined by nature, language, the symbolic, or the overwhelming history of patriarchy. Gender is what is put on, invariably, under constraint, daily and incessantly, with anxiety and pleasure, but if this continuous act is mistaken for a natural or linguistic given, power is relinquished to expand the cultural field bodily through subversive performances of various kinds.

Gender Ideology and Dramatic Convention in Progressive Era Plays, 1890–1920

Judith L. Stephens

In her essay, "Ideology and the Cultural Production of Gender," Michele Barrett suggests new methods for studying relations between literature, gender ideology, and social change. Defining ideology as "the process of producing meaning," Barrett isolates several processes by which literary texts reproduce gender ideology within a given social formation.[1] Two of these processes, "compensation" and "recuperation," seem particularly useful in providing the basis for a materialist feminist analysis of Progressive era plays. Since compensation refers to the presentation of imagery and ideas that tend to elevate the "moral value" of femininity and recuperation refers to the process of negating and defusing challenges to the historically dominant meaning of gender in particular periods, Progressive era dramas, which characteristically adhered to the conventional belief in the moral superiority of females while simultaneously addressing issues arising from women's changing position in society, can be newly appreciated as a site of struggle over the meaning of gender.[2]

Certain dramas of the Progressive era (1890–1920) are particularly suited to a feminist analysis because they addressed issues that grew out of contemporary social movements dedicated to changing women's position in society. However, this essay will attempt to demonstrate how presenting such issues within the confines of certain dramatic conventions served the processes of compensation and recuperation and thereby reproduced dominant gender ideology. Recognizing the presence of compensation and recuperation in Progressive era plays can provide an understanding of how drama, as cultural practice, can both challenge and reinforce dominant gender ideology in periods of social change.

Judith Stephens is Associate Professor in the Department of Speech Communication at the Pennsylvania State University, the Schuylkill Campus. She has previously published dramatic criticism in Theatre Journal, Theatre Annual, The Cue, Text and Performance, *and* Women in American Theatre.

---

[1] Michele Barrett, "Ideology and the Cultural Production of Gender," in *Feminist Criticism and Social Change: Sex, Class, and Race in Literature and Culture,* ed. Judith Newton and Deborah Rosenfelt (New York: Methuen), 65–85.

[2] Ibid., 83.

Earlier studies by theatre scholars have established different feminist approaches to reading nineteenth- and early twentieth-century dramatic texts. Kathleen McLennan has examined Steele MacKaye's *Marriage* (1872) as a challenge to the nineteenth-century ideology of domesticity.[3] Rosemarie Bank has demonstrated how female characters often play an active and crucial role in late nineteenth- and early twentieth-century melodramas, challenging the popular stereotype of the passive, helpless, melodramatic heroine.[4] Lois Gottlieb examined how the term "feminist" applies to the plays of Rachel Crothers.[5] The intent of this essay is not to refute these earlier valuable studies but to offer an additional feminist approach for studying dramatic texts from this period.

Social Reform and Gender Ideology

The feminist tradition inherited by leaders of the Progressive era was a tradition marked by ties to religion, family, and a sense of moral duty. According to Ellen Dubois, the earlier reform societies of the 1830s and 1840s had claimed the moral reform of society as a "self-consciously female endeavor," and Alice Rossi found that "in both social origins and the deepest premises of their thinking, most early native born American feminists were profoundly conservative and moralistic."[6] Given this set of circumstances, it is not surprising to learn the female reformers of the Progressive era openly embraced the moral hegemony nineteenth-century ideology bestowed upon middle-class women.

Nineteenth-century middle-class ideology constructed an image of Woman as a morally superior being especially suited for protecting her (female) domestic sphere from the corruption of society or the (male) work place.[7] Accepting this conventional belief which, on the one hand, relegated women and men to separate spheres but, on the other, gave females special sanctifying powers, women reformers of the Progressive era successfully argued for a logical extension of those powers from the private sphere of the home into the wider public sphere of society. Known to historians as moral reformers and generally acknowledged as representing a strain of nineteenth-century feminism, women such as Carrie Chapman Catt, Anna Howard Shaw, Florence Kelly, and Lillian Wald argued that women could weed out corruption and ultimately reform society if given the chance to extend their housecleaning and sanctifying talents into the public arena. Many contemporary female reformers

---

[3]Kathleen McLennan, "Marriage in America's Gilded Age," *Theatre Journal* 37 (1985): 345–56.

[4]Rosemarie K. Bank, "The Second Face of the Idol: Women in Melodrama," in *Women in American Theatre*, ed. Helen Kirch Chinoy and Linda Walsh Jenkins (New York: Crown Press, 1981), 238–43.

[5]Lois Gottlieb, "Looking to Women: Rachel Crothers and the Feminist Heroine," in Chinoy and Jenkins, *Women in American Theatre*, 137–45.

[6]Ellen Dubois, "Women's Rights and Abolition: The Nature of the Connection," in *Anti Slavery Reconsidered: New Perspectives on The Abolitionists*, ed. Lewis Perry and Michael Fellman (Baton Rouge: Louisiana State University Press, 1979), 245 and Alice Rossi, ed., *The Feminist Papers: From Adams to de Beauvoir* (New York: Columbia University Press, 1973), 248.

[7]Barbara Epstein, *The Politics of Domesticity: Women, Evangelism, and Temperance in Nineteenth Century America* (Middletown: Wesleyan University Press, 1981) and Kathryn Kish Sklar, *Catherine Beecher: A Study in American Domesticity* (New Haven: Yale University Press, 1973).

adopted the same premise and language. Jane Addams encouraged women to become involved with municipal government by comparing it to "housekeeping on a large scale"; Charlotte Perkins Gilman asked women not to limit their nurturing ability to a nuclear family but to assume their full duty as "mothers of the world"; socialist editor Josephine Conger-Kaneko suggested women's sphere was not confined to the thing misnamed "home" but extended to the larger sphere of world services; and proponents of higher education for women, such as Alice Freeman Palmer and M. Carey Thomas, argued for its acceptance on the grounds that it would serve "the best interests of the family."[8] Temperance leader Frances Willard won wide support for her cause by adopting such mottos as "Home Protection," and she proclaimed that, "woman will bless and brighten every place she enters and will enter every place."[9] Using such traditional language and imagery, the female reformers of the Progressive era worked to expand woman's sphere of action and influence. Ironically, dominant gender ideology was appropriated by a movement dedicated to changing middle-class women's position in society.

Whether the Progressive era included significant progress for women is still debated today, with some feminists defending the female reformers for asserting women's right to a public voice and others viewing their achievements as "hollow victories."[10] Perhaps the reason for the lingering debate stems from the contradictory position female reformers assumed by basing their argument to change their position in society on a conventional belief which had served to limit their opportunities and power.

Dramatic Conventions and Gender Ideology

Just as female reformers assumed a contradictory stance in their struggle for change, dramas of the Progressive era that addressed women's position in society often appeared to champion the cause of women's rights but, by adhering to standard dramatic conventions, they inherently contained an imperceptible counterargument which served to reinforce the status quo.

The morally superior female is a dominant, even characteristic, figure in nineteenth-century drama. During the Progressive era, theatre audiences accepted the growing tendency of playwrights to deal with current social issues, but these issues were presented through the conventions of traditional dramatic form. According to Garth Wilson, "liberation from old tastes and habits was slow and most playwrights were

---

[8]Jane Addams, "Utilization of Women in City Government," in Alice S. Rossi, ed., *The Feminist Papers: From Adams to de Beauvoir* (New York: Columbia University Press, 1973), 605; Charlotte Perkins Gilman, "Women and Economics" in Rossi, 588; Josephine Conger-Kaneko, "Women and Socialism," *Progressive Woman* 5 (1911): 8; Alice Freeman Palmer and M. Carey Thomas quoted in Sheila M. Rothman, *Woman's Proper Place: A History of Changing Ideals and Practices, 1870 to the Present* (New York: Basic Books, 1978), 107, 108.

[9]Frances Willard, quoted in Rothman, *Women's Proper Place*, 67 and in Eleanor Flexner, *Century of Struggle: The Women's Rights Movement in the United States* (Cambridge: Belknap Press, 1959), 183.

[10]See Carroll Smith-Rosenberg, *Disorderly Conduct: Visions of Gender in Victorian America* (New York: Knopf, 1985) and Ann Douglas, *The Feminization of American Culture* (New York: Knopf, 1977), 45. For an assessment of the connection between moral reformers and socialism see Mari Jo Buhle, *Women and American Socialism, 1870–1920* (Urbana: University of Illinois Press, 1981).

still devoted to the devices and methods of melodrama which had influenced dramatists for a hundred years."[11] The idea that drama should present a moral view of life remained a basic tenet. Even the more progressive critics of the period, such as Brander Matthews and Clayton Hamilton, who championed the new Ibsen-like realism over the strict Victorian standards of William Winter, supported the traditional view of drama as a story incorporating conflict, crisis, and resolution involving characters faced with moral decisions.[12] While the conventions of the drama focused attention on characters faced with moral decisions, prevailing ideology dictated the most moral or "right" decision must be made by the female. Rosemarie Bank found even the most "liberal minded" critics of the period subscribed to a belief in the morally superior female.[13] In a review of *Margaret Fleming*, B. O. Flower wrote in *Arena*, "it is an incontestable fact that woman is ethically, infinitely superior to man; her moral perceptions are firmer and stronger, her unselfishness is far greater, her spiritual nature deeper and richer than that of her brothers."[14] The dominant theory of the drama joined with the prevailing belief in women's moral superiority to exert a strong influence in determining the bounds within which the meaning of gender was constructed and negotiated in Progressive era dramas.

The moralistic nature and conventional structure of melodrama were conducive to presenting the morally superior female and thereby reproduced dominant gender ideology of the period. The following discussion will demonstrate how these dramatic conventions served the processes of compensation and recuperation in plays that addressed women's changing position in society. The plays chosen for discussion were selected from a growing list of Progressive era plays singled out by critics as significantly involving issues affecting women. That list appears at the end of this essay. The five plays chosen for discussion have been acknowledged for their feminist tendencies and are familiar to theatre scholars. I have chosen to discuss James Herne's *Margaret Fleming* (1890) and Rachel Crothers's *A Man's World* (1909) because they are recognized for their challenge to the sexual double standard. Herne's *Sag Harbor* (1899) and Crothers's *He and She* (1911) were chosen because both deal with combining the responsibilities of motherhood with female independence. Finally, I have chosen to include Susan Glaspell's *Trifles* (1916) because it addresses the consequences of assigning separate spheres to men and women and demonstrates how an avowedly feminist play, written for a noncommercial theatre, still served to reinforce dominant gender ideology.

The Double Standard

During the Progressive era, the position of the moral reformers on the double standard was not that women should have the same sexual freedom as men but that

---

[11]Garth Wilson, *Three Hundred Years of American Drama and Theatre: From Ye Bare and Ye Cubb to Hair* (Englewood Cliffs: Prentice Hall, 1973), 243.

[12]See Brander Matthews, *A Study of the Drama*, 1910, *The Development of the Drama*, 1903 and *Principles of Playmaking*, 1919; Clayton Hamilton, *The Theory of the Theatre and Other Principles of Dramatic Criticism*, 1939, *Studies in Stagecraft*, 1914, and *Problems of the Playwright*, 1917.

[13]Rosemarie K. Bank, "The Image of Women in Plays of the Progressive Era," paper presented at the annual convention of the American Theatre Association, Toronto, 1985.

[14]B.O. Flower, "The Era of Women," *Arena* 4 (1891), 382.

men and women should be judged by a single standard, the "most moral" standard (strict fidelity to one's spouse), which was then only applied to women. *Margaret Fleming* and *A Man's World* both espouse this view and include final scenes in which each heroine delivers a monologue denouncing the double standard.[15] While both Herne and Crothers were credited with presenting a feminist view that challenged the status quo, the fact that dramatic convention forced the issue to be placed within the context of a female facing a moral decision served the processes of compensation and recuperation and thereby reinforced dominant gender ideology.

Margaret Fleming's major decision in the play is to take back Philip, her repentant husband, and to raise his illegitimate son, along with their daughter, as their own. Within the context of the play, Margaret's decision is not portrayed as a submissive or self-sacrificing gesture but is carefully constructed to demonstrate her courage and strength, as well as her moral leadership. It is clear from her dialogue in the final scene that her decision does not include forgiveness for Philip but simply reflects what she feels is "best" for them to do. Philip concedes to Margaret's moral leadership and gives her the power to determine their future when he asks, "What do you want me to do? Shall I go away? . . . I want to do whatever you think is best." Margaret replies, "it is best for both of us to remain here and take up the old life together" (543).

Although in the original version Margaret had refused to be reunited with Philip, Mrs. Katherine Herne, who acted the part of Margaret, and who, according to A. H. Quinn, had taken an active role in the original creation of the play, approved of the new version and felt that "given the character of Margaret and the personality of Philip, they would be reunited."[16] With either ending, Margaret is shown to provide the moral leadership and make the "right" or most moral decision within the context of the play. Such presentation of ideas and images that emphasized the moral worth of femininity served the process of compensation by convincing females they actually possessed an important source of power. In her essay, Barrett cites examples from "the plethora of practices which, in the context of systematic denial of opportunities for women, attempt to 'compensate' for this by a corresponding ideology of moral worth."[17] She specifically notes "the ideology of domesticity," with its intense moral and sentimental elevation of the family home, was developed in the stultifying ethos of Victorian restrictions on female activity.

In addition to compensation, *Margaret Fleming* serves the process of recuperation because it appears to challenge the status quo while, on a more subtle level, it works to defuse that challenge. The play appears to challenge the status quo by portraying a strong female character who seems to determine the events of the play while presenting "the female view" on a contemporary controversial issue. But the conventions of the drama undermine the challenge by presenting the issue in a framework

[15]James Herne, *Margaret Fleming*, in *Representative American Plays*, ed. Arthur Hobson Quinn (New York: Appleton-Century-Crofts, 1953) and Rachel Crothers, *A Man's World* in *Plays by American Women: 1900–1930*, ed. Judith Barlow (New York: Applause, 1985). Citations from these sources are documented within the text.

[16]Quinn, *Representative American Plays*, 516.

[17]Barrett, "Ideology and Cultural Production of Gender," 81.

constructed to focus ultimately on an individual moral decision with the female character positioned to provide the moral leadership. Margaret appeared to be a new type of heroine because her character seemed to determine the events of the play instead of being manipulated by the plot, but by confining her power to moral influence, the drama reinforces dominant gender ideology and takes away with one hand what it gives with the other.[18] In the final act of the play, Dr. Larkin, who seems to be a spokesman for the author, tells Margaret: "this world needs just such women as you." Dr. Larkin is saying that the world needs the influence of Margaret's moral leadership, but this view, which is the same one presented by the female moral reformers, contains an inherent concession to dominant gender ideology and thus inadvertently reinforces the status quo.

In contrast to Margaret, Frank Ware in a *A Man's World*, by Rachel Crothers, is a heroine whose major decision is to reject her long-time companion when she learns he has fathered an illegitimate child. For this reason the play was acclaimed for taking an ever stronger feminist stance than *Margaret Fleming*. Frank's decision to reject Malcolm Gaskell was seen as a daring reversal of the usual pattern in which "erring men easily won forgiveness from their mates."[19] The play aroused enough controversy to prompt a response by contemporary playwright Agustus Thomas, who wrote *As A Man Thinks* in defense of the double standard.

The process of compensation is at work here because Frank, like Margaret Fleming, is presented as moral leader. Her decision to reject Gaskell is presented as the most moral, noble, or the "right" decision within the context of the play. Unlike Philip Fleming, Gaskell is unrepentant; he refuses to acknowledge any wrong doing and feels he has simply "led a man's life" (68). When Frank asks him to consider the irresponsibility of his actions, Gaskell replies: "No! Don't try to hold me to account by a standard that doesn't exist. Don't measure me by your theories. If you love me, you'll stand on that and forget everything else" (69). Frank's rejection of Gaskell is accepted by the audience as the moral or "right" decision because of his unrepenting attitude. Philip accepted Margaret's moral leadership, realized the "iniquity" of his behavior, and was "saved" while Gaskell refused to grant Frank Ware such power and is justifiably rejected.

The process of recuperation is served in that Frank Ware is portrayed as an intelligent, independent, modern woman striking a blow against the double standard but her power is ultimately couched in terms of moral leadership. Progressive era dramas such as *It's A Man's World* and *Margaret Fleming* easily incorporated contemporary feminist arguments against the double standard, but such challenges to the status quo were obliquely diffused by conventions that upheld middle-class society's definition of and insistence on women's moral superiority.

---

[18]Margaret Fleming is traditionally recognized as a progressive heroine in the portrayal of women in American drama. Laurilyn Harris, "Atypical Ingenues and Other Iconoclastic Females in 19th Century American Drama," paper presented at the National Educational Theatre Conference, New York, 1986.

[19]Judith Barlow, "Introduction," *Plays by American Women*, xviii.

Motherhood

Both *Sag Harbor* and *He and She* demonstrate the family's dependency on the mother's moral leadership.[20] Although Martha in *Sag Harbor* is a full-time wife and mother and Ann Herford in *He and She* is juggling the demands of wife, mother, and successful professional artist, both women fulfill the function of moral leader within their own homes.

In the final act of *Sag Harbor*, Martha decides she is not dependent on her husband but, if necessary, is fully capable of raising their son on her own. She is portrayed as the strongest character because she is the only one capable of rising above the petty love triangle created through the devotion shown to her by both her husband, Ben, and his younger brother, Frank. Jealousy, bitterness, and suspicion between the two brothers results in Ben threatening to leave Sag Harbor so that Martha and Frank can be left alone together. Martha resolves the conflict by accepting her husband's decision to leave and vows to send Frank away too. When asked who will carry on the family business, she answers: "I will—best I can . . . I'm not going to sit down here and eat my heart out because my husband doesn't choose to live with me. I've got a child to bring up and educate and I'm going to do it . . ." (234). Herne's stage directions read that Ben and Frank both "stare at Martha, amazed at the fearless spirit she is showing for the first time in her life." This climactic scene, which demonstrates previously hidden independence and assertiveness, appears to grant her a new dimension of power. The scene also is consistent with the contemporary suffragist/feminist argument that declared motherhood required strength and independence from women, not dependency.[21] But recuperation is subtly at work here because Martha's new-found courage and independence are championed within the safe confines of a mother's devotion to her child. On the one hand, the play espouses the "modern woman's" argument that said motherhood fostered independence and assertiveness in women instead of a need for protection, but on the other hand, it reestablishes the conventional boundaries within which these qualities can be displayed. Martha's startling scene of independence permanently ends the rivalry between the two brothers, and it becomes unnecessary for her to carry out her threat.

Compensation occurs because Martha retains her role as a moral leader for the family. She remains an elevated figure who knows what is "best" for everyone concerned.

In contrast to Martha, Ann Herford in *He and She* is a wife and mother with a professional career but, like Martha, she also provides the moral leadership within her home. Ann's decision, in the final moments of the play, is to give up the prestigious commission she has won in order to devote her full attention to her troubled teenage daughter. When her husband, who had also entered the artistic competition,

---

[20]James Herne, *Sag Harbor*, in *Shore Acres and Other Plays* (New York: Samuel French, 1928) and Crothers, *He and She*, in Quinn, *Representative American Plays*. Citations from these sources are documented in the text.

[21]Elizabeth Cady Stanton, "Motherhood," in Rossi, *The Feminist Papers*, 396–401 and Aileen Kraditor, *The Ideas of the Women's Suffrage Movement, 1890–1920* (New York, Columbia, 1965), 114–15.

reminds her she will always regret giving up the commission, Ann answers: "It's my job. She is what I've given to life. If I fail her now my whole life is a failure. There isn't any choice, she's part of my body, part of my soul" (928).

A common argument against middle-class women working outside the home was that if mothers were to devote their energies to maintaining a professional career, the home and family life would necessarily be neglected. It is easy to understand how Ann Herford is a refutation of that argument, and in this sense she is a "feminist heroine" in the Progressive era. But when Ann is compared to Martha of *Sag Harbor*, it appears the power granted to both females is negotiated under very similar conditions. Martha's climactic scene was constructed to show she possessed an underlying spark of independence and an ability to work in the public sphere. This liberating scene is *acceptable*, and her character remains admirable in the eyes of the public because her motherly devotion and moral leadership were previously established throughout the play. Ann's climactic scene of moral decision was constructed to convince the audience she possessed true motherly devotion. This scene of recuperation is *necessary* because her independence and ability to compete in the male domain has automatically brought her motherly devotion and moral leadership into doubt. Compensation occurs because Ann retains her moral leadership, but the price she is forced to pay (giving up the commission) is the work of recuperation which, again, takes away with one hand what it has given with the other. Through the character of Ann Herford, Rachel Crothers championed the feminist cause by presenting a woman who was able to compete successfully in a male-dominated profession, but this portrayal of female victory apparently demanded a simultaneous reassurance that the "new woman" would not sacrifice her traditional responsibility of providing moral leadership in the home. If a choice *had* to be made between successful artist and ideal mother, the new woman must prove she is a true woman and choose the latter. Such oscillation between a desire to champion feminist arguments and loyalty to dominant gender ideology established the boundaries within which dramas could challenge conventional views of motherhood.

Separate Spheres

Trifles, by Susan Glaspell, focuses on the decision of two farm women, Mrs. Hale and Mrs. Peters, to conceal evidence that would implicate another farm wife in the investigation of her husband's murder.[22] As with the previous plays, their decision is presented as the moral or "right" decision, even though it is understood to go clearly against conventional law.

While the Sheriff and County Attorney search through the farmhouse looking for evidence of a break-in or struggle, Mrs. Hale and Mrs. Peters notice many clues of disruption in the wife's canning, housekeeping, and needlework. Through the accumulation of these details the women begin to solve the murder mystery on their own. By slowly making the audience aware of the wife's frustration, isolation, and difficult life with her husband, Glaspell creates understanding for the women's de-

[22]Susan Glaspell, *Trifles*, in Barlow, *Plays by American Women*, 70–86.

cision to conceal the evidence. As they debate with their own consciences, Mrs. Peters points out, "The law has got to punish crime," but Mrs. Hale reminds her of the wife's predicament and total isolation, saying, "That was a crime! Who's going to punish that?" (84).

Further support for the women's decision is created through the portrayal of the condescending attitude of the two men. As the Sheriff and County Attorney scoff at the women's preoccupation with the "trifles" of housekeeping, Mrs. Hale and Mrs. Peters proceed to solve the mystery and conceal their evidence. In portraying this situation, Glaspell is saying that women have a certain knowledge or wisdom that men do not want or value. By their decision, Mrs. Hale and Mrs. Peters disrupt or subvert conventional law, but they maintain the image of moral leaders by adhering to an alternate or "higher" moral code.

Karen K. Stein has suggested that *Trifles* is a feminist document because it sympathetically explores the lives of women who would normally be minor figures in a play.[23] Other feminist critics have praised it because it presents and shows the value of a specifically female point of view.[24] I am suggesting that, in addition to these views, the play also colludes with dominant gender ideology, and, in this respect, refutes its own argument. Compensation is at work here because the women's moral superiority enables them to go against or to subvert conventional law and still be "right." However, recuperation is served in that "women's law" is pitted against "men's law," and thus the play perpetuates the idea of separate spheres. By finding and concealing the incriminating evidence, the women win their own individual victory, but the system continues intact. It is as if Mrs. Hale and Mrs. Peters are playing out the standard "What Every Woman Knows" role, encouraging a smug complacency in their moral superiority, knowing they secretly have the "real power" while "permitting" the men to remain and function in socially acknowledged positions of power. The play perpetuates the romantic notion that each woman can secretly and individually subvert the larger system, if she so desires. Like the other plays discussed in this essay, *Trifles* both challenged and reinforced the dominant gender ideology of the period.

Conclusion

The five texts discussed in this essay demonstrate that the structure of melodrama with its emphasis on moral choice was especially adapted to reinforcing the prevailing belief in women's moral leadership. Because of this unique set of circumstances, progressive dramas of the period commonly expressed the same arguments the moral reformers were presenting to society. However, while appearing to challenge the

[23]Karen F. Stein, "The Women's World of Glaspell's *Trifles*," in Chinoy and Jenkins, *Women in American Theatre*, 251.

[24]Rachel France, "Apropos of Women and The Folk Play," in Chinoy and Jenkins, *Women in American Theatre*, 151; Linda Walsh Jenkins, "Locating the Language of Gender Experience," *Women and Performance: A Journal of Feminist Theory* 2 (1984): 12; Karen Malpede, "Susan Glaspell," in *Women in Theatre: Compassion and Hope* (New York: Drama Book Publishers, 1983), 146; and Barlow, xxii.

status quo, both the dramas and female reformers were operating on a basic assumption that served to uphold dominant gender ideology.

Although the females in these plays are very different from one another and at times make opposite choices, they share a common power to determine what will be seen as "right" or "wrong" within the context of the play. Whether the female is a wife and mother with a professional career, such as Ann in *He and She*, or a full-time homemaker, such as Martha in *Sag Harbor*, whether she is a woman who takes back the so-called "errant male," such as Margaret Fleming, or rejects him, such as Frank in *A Man's World*, she retains the role of moral leader. She persists in this role even when she defies conventional law, like the farm wives in *Trifles*. Such elevation of the moral worth of femininity serves the process of compensation by suggesting females possess an important power. The representation of the morally superior female projected a powerful figure in Progressive era dramas, but this same representation served to reinforce dominant gender ideology.

The process of recuperation is also at work because while each play appears to champion "the female cause," it is also reinforcing dominant gender ideology. Specifically, each play espouses the views put forth by the female reformers on contemporary issues concerning women: there should be a single standard of sexual morality applied to both men and women, motherhood demands self-reliance instead of dependency, mothers who are also professional career women will not neglect their responsibility within the home, and men who trivialize what they see as "women's sphere" are denying themselves an important source of knowledge and insight. However, like the female reformers, Progressive era plays presented their argument for changing women's position in society through a framework that functioned to control the limits of change. Like ideology, the functioning of dramatic convention is often hidden, and what appears to the reader/spectator as an engaging story which challenges social convention may also contain a more subtle counterargument which serves to recoup any ground lost in the direction of significant change. Elin Diamond has noted an important intersection of gender, ideology, and the theatre experience:

> Gender refers to the words, gestures, appearances, ideas and behavior that dominant culture understands as indices of feminine or masculine identity. When spectators 'see' gender they are seeing (and reproducing) the cultural signs of gender and by implication, the gender ideology of a culture. Gender in fact provides a perfect illustration of ideology at work since 'feminine' or 'masculine' behavior usually appears to be a natural—and thus fixed and unalterable—extension of biological sex.[25]

When Progressive era audiences saw the representation of the morally superior female on stage, they accepted her as a natural fact—as an index of feminine identity. This essay has demonstrated how Progressive era plays reinforced such gender ideology by their moralistic nature and conventional structure even as they incorporated ideas intended to effect "progress for women." The plays were celebrated for presenting ideas that called for social change while the working of the apparatus,

---

[25]Elin Diamond, "Brechtian Theory/Feminist Theory: Towards a Gestic Feminist Criticism," *The Drama Review* 32 (1988): 84.

within which such ideas were constructed and negotiated, was ignored. In Jill Dolan's view, the materialist feminist project is to reveal the complicity of the representational apparatus in maintaining sexual difference.[26] As the five plays discussed in this essay demonstrate, the insight resulting from such revelation permits a new appreciation of drama as a site of struggle over the meaning of gender during periods of social change.

Progressive Era Plays Concerning Issues Affecting Women

Year	Author	Title
1890	James A. Herne	*Margaret Flemming*
1895	Sydney Grundy	*The New Woman*
1896	Martha Morton	*A Bachelor's Romance*
1897	Charles Hoyt	*A Contented Woman*
1899	James A. Herne	*Sag Harbor*
1906	William Vaughn Moody	*The Great Divide*
1906	Langdon Mitchell	*The New York Idea*
1906	Rachel Crothers	*The Three of Us*
1906	Clyde Fitch	*The Woman in the Case*
1908	Eugene Walter	*The Easiest Way*
1909	Clyde Fitch	*The City*
1909	Rachel Crothers	*A Man's World*
1910	William Vaughn Moody	*The Faith Healer*
1910	Elizabeth Robins	*Votes for Women*
1911	Agustus Thomas	*As A Man Thinks*
1911	Rachel Crothers	*He and She*
1913	Alice Brown	*Children of the Earth*
1913	William Hurlbut	*The Strange Woman*
1913	Bayard Veiller	*The Fight*
1913	Anne Crawford Flexner	*The Marriage Game*
1916	Susan Glaspell	*Trifles*
1916	Clare Kummer	*Good Gracious Annabelle*
1917	Jesse Lynch Williams	*Why Marry?*
1918	Susan Glaspell	*Woman's Honor*
1918	Charlotte E. Wells and Dorothy Donnelly	*The Riddle: Woman*
1918	Arlene Van Ness Hines	*Her Honor the Mayor*
1919	Zoe Atkins	*Declasse*
1919	Rachel Barton Butler	*Mama's Affair*

[26]Jill Dolan, *The Feminist Spectator as Critic* (Ann Arbor: UMI, 1988), 101.

Travesty and Transgression: Transvestism in Shakespeare, Brecht, and Churchill

Anne Herrmann

> The woman shall not wear that which
> pertaineth unto a man, neither shall
> a man put on a woman's garment; for
> all that do so are an abomination
> unto the Lord thy God.
> —Deuteronomy (22:5)

> This earth that beareth and
> nourisheth us, hath been turned into
> a Stage, and women have come forth
> acting the parts of men.
> —Francis Rous (1624)

> We're all born stark naked;
> To dress is bizarre.
> And that's the reason why
> Everybody's in drag.
> —"You Are What You Wear," Lynn Lavner (1988)

In Marguerite Duras's *The Lover* (1984), the first person narrator recalls her image at fifteen and a half crossing the Mekong on a ferry that takes her to school in Saigon. She is wearing a silk dress that used to belong to her mother, gold lamé evening shoes, and a "flat-brimmed hat, a brownish-pink fedora with a broad black ribbon." "The crucial ambiguity of the image," she suggests, "lies in the hat." Like the shoes, the hat must have been a discount item:

> But why was it bought? No woman, no girl wore a man's fedora in that colony then. No native woman, either. What must have happened is: I try it on just for fun, look at myself in the shopkeeper's glass, and see that there, beneath the man's hat, the thin awkward shape, the inadequacy of childhood, has turned into something else. Has ceased to be a harsh, inescapable imposition of nature. Has become, on the contrary, a provoking choice

---

Anne Herrmann is an Associate Professor of English and Women's Studies at the University of Michigan at Ann Arbor. She is the author of The Dialogic and Difference: 'An/Other Woman' in Virginia Woolf and Christa Wolf *and is currently working on transvestism and transsexualism in 20th century film, fiction and photography.*

---

of nature, a choice of the mind. Suddenly it's deliberate. Suddenly I see myself as another, as another would be seen, outside myself, available to all, available to all eyes, in circulation for cities, journeys, desire. I take the hat, and am never parted from it. Having got it, this hat that all by itself makes me whole, I wear it all the time. With the shoes it must have been much the same, but after the hat. They contradict the hat, as the hat contradicts the puny body, so they're right for me. I wear them all the time too, go everywhere in these shoes, this hat, out of doors in all weathers, on every occasion. And to town.[1]

The ambiguity of living in a French colony in Indochina, of belonging to the colonizer yet being poor, of spending afternoons with a lover instead of in school, is figured as a gendered contradiction between the excessively feminine shoes and the necessarily masculine hat. The particular style of the hat cannot be attributed to either historical or cultural differences. The narrator's own invention, it simultaneously splits between viewer and viewed, and makes whole. The shoes contradict the hat, but the hat contradicts the wearer; "the puny body," an unwanted act of nature, has become a cultural artifact. By putting on the hat, the narrator deliberately inscribes herself as desiring because she sees herself as desirable. She transgresses the boundaries of age, nationality, and sexual difference signified by a single item of clothing meant for someone else. The result is not an androgynous figure by an anomalous one; the object, for her, is not to resolve the contradictions but to proliferate them.

The three plays I have chosen for comparison, Shakespeare's *As You Like It* (1599–1600), Bertolt Brecht's *The Good Woman of Setzuan* (1938–40), and Caryl Churchill's *Cloud Nine* (1979), use transvestism as a dramatic device to figure historicized forms of social transgression. Such transgression never takes the form of travesty itself; that is, cross-dressing as such is not coded as violation. Rather, the vacillation between masculine and feminine serves as a metaphor for a particular social contradiction, the struggle between the natural and the unnatural, the good and the bad, sexuality as sinful and as political. In its historicized context, the conflict takes the form of two competing social formations: in Shakespeare the court and the forest, in Brecht socialism and capitalism, in Churchill hetero- and homosexuality. Structurally, the transvestite functions as mediator between the symbols of these formations—"father" and son, tobacco store and tobacco factory, Victorian and contemporary England.

In addition to mediating between social contradictions, the use of transvestism coincides with the violation of dramatic conventions: *As You Like It* ends with four comic marriages (instead of the usual one or two) and includes an epilogue which exposes the true sex of the actor. *The Good Woman of Setzuan* and *Cloud Nine* both have two endings, depending on the original place of performance.[2] In Brecht, gods appear on earth and disappear into heaven through a reverse *deus ex machina*, and in Churchill, racial as well as sexual boundaries are crossed when a white actor plays a black. In each case the play ends by foregrounding its own open-endedness—

---

[1]Marguerite Duras, *The Lover*, trans. Barbara Bray (New York: Random House, 1985), 12–13.

[2]In Brecht's case the misunderstandings created by the Viennese premiere of *The Good Woman of Setzuan* led him to add an epilogue; in the case of *Cloud Nine*, the New York production sought for a more pronounced "emotional climax" by ending with Betty's self-discovery instead of the beginning of a new relationship.

suggesting that if beneath the disguise there is a real self it is a sexed one, not an essential but a desiring, sexual subjectivity.

"Motley's the only wear"

—Shakespeare

On 25 January 1620, John Chamberlain wrote in a letter to Dudley Carleton:

> Yesterday the bishop of London called together all the Clergie about this towne, and told them he had expressed commaundment from the King to will them to inveigh vehemently and bitterly in theyre sermons, against the insolencie of our women and theyre wearing of *brode brimd hats*, pointed dublets, theyre haire cut short or shorne, and some of them stilettaes or poinards, and such other trinckets of like moment: adding withall that yf pulpit admonitions will not reforme them he would proceed by another course: the truth is the world is very far out of order, but whether this will mende yt God knowes.[3]

Why King James I sought to extinguish a female transvestite movement which began in the 1570s, experienced a revival in 1606–1607 and reached its height in 1620, and which was publicly debated in two anonymous pamphlets, *Hic mulier: or, The Man-Woman; Being a Medecine to cure the Coltish Disease of the Staggers in the Masculine-Feminines of our Times* and *Haec-Vir; or The Womanish Man: Being an Answere to a late Book intituled Hic-Mulier*, will never be known.[4] What is known is that the king turned to the authority of the church, a church whose members at the beginning of the movement had argued in anti-theatrical tracts against male cross-dressing. The most cited of these tracts are Stephen Gossen's *The School of Abuse* (1583) which claims that cross-dressing will "adulterate" gender. Men who play the parts of women become like women; and if men become like women, then clothes constitute rather than signify the sex of the subject, suggesting an inherently unstable sexual identity and/ or subjectivity.[5]

In the early 1590s John Rainolds, a learned Puritan, William Gager, the leading writer of academic drama at Oxford, and Alberico Gentili, England's most reknowned jurist, engaged in a debate (in Latin) over whether Deuteronomy 22:5 applied to actors, specifically university actors who played in private theaters. Rainolds argued that it did, Gentili that it did not, and Gager that it was wrong for men to wear women's clothing unless they did so to save their lives or benefit their country.[6] Sex

---

[3]*The Letters of John Chamberlain*, ed. Norman Egbert McClure (Philadelphia, 1939), II, 287–87. Quoted in Linda T. Fitz, " 'What says the Married Woman?': Marriage Theory and Feminism in the English Renaissance," *Mosaic* 13:2 (1980): 15. Emphasis added.

[4]See Linda Woodbridge, *Women and the English Renaissance: Literature and the Nature of Womankind, 1540–1620* (Urbana: University of Illinois, 1984), 139–51. See also Sandra Clark, "*Hic Mulier, Haec Vir*, and the Controversy over Masculine Women," *Studies in Philology* 82:2 (1985): 157–83.

[5]See Laura Levine, "Men in Women's Clothing: Anti-theatricality and Effeminization from 1579 to 1642," *Criticism* 28:2 (1986): 121–41.

[6]J. W. Binns, "Women or Transvestites on the Elizabethan Stage?: An Oxford Controversy," *Sixteenth Century Journal* 5:2 (1974): 100.

differences were seen by all as "natural," God-ordained. Transgressing natural distinctions meant transgressing social and moral ones. Both women dressing as men (on the streets) and men dressing as women (on the stage) led to unnatural behavior, particularly behavior that was sexually "unnatural." Women became sexually aggressive and socially undesirable, taking on the identity of "roaring girls," that is, pickpockets or ruffians;[7] men became effeminate and sexually aroused the male members of their theater audience. In the Renaissance, the androgyne was "the erotically irresistible effeminate boy."[8] The object, then, was to contain the contradiction between the essential sex and the lack of an essential gender in order to prevent its proliferation. As soon as female cross-dressers appeared on the streets of London, they ceased to appear on the Shakespearean stage. The first professional English actress made her debut in 1660.[9]

In *As You Like It*, even before Rosalind dresses as Ganymede, two forms of doubling without disguise establish gendered subject positions which distinguish between masculine and feminine without relying on sexual stereotypes. Orlando begins the play by lamenting that the unfair treatment he received from his brother Oliver results in a misleading single self which in fact conceals two: the gentleman by birth and the rustic by education. Afraid that the latter will usurp the former, he invokes the natural bond with his father against the unnatural bond between brothers. To Adam, his surrogate father, he says: "the spirit of my father, which I think is within me, begins to mutiny against this servitude,"[10] inflicted by the older brother who has usurped the place of the father. The body of Orlando contains the spirit of the father which begins to rebel against the brother, who insists on containing that spirit in a singularly physical existence: "I, his brother, gain nothing under him but growth, for the which his animals on his dunghills are as much bound to him as I" (1. 1. 13–15). Even though Orlando protests against this purely physical increase, his mutiny takes the form of a wrestling match. His brother then reads Orlando's physical superiority as mental prowess by imagining him as doubly devious, precisely because there is no attempt to disguise his desire to repossess his social position.

In contrast with Orlando, caught between man and beast, Rosalind partakes of an external doubling where two appear as one. Rosalind and Celia, although merely cousins, share a love that (unlike the perverted bond between brothers) is "dearer than the natural bond of sisters" (1. 2. 266). Even though not blood-linked, they have been raised together, creating a bond more "natural" and more permanent than

---

[7]See Paula S. Bergren, " 'A Prodigious Thing': The Jacobean Heroine in Male Disguise," *Philological Quarterly* 62:3 (1983): 383–402; Patrick Cheney, "Moll Cutpurse as Hermphrodite in Dekker and Middleton's *The Roaring Girl*," *Renaissance and Reformation* 7:2 (1983): 120–34; Mary Beth Rose, "Women in Men's Clothing: Apparel and Social Stability in *The Roaring Girl*," *English Literary Renaissance* 14:3 (1984): 367–91.

[8]Lisa Jardine, *Still Harping on Daughters: Women and Drama in the Age of Shakespeare* (New Jersey: Barnes and Noble, 1983), 17. See also Phyllis Rackin, "Androgyny, Mimesis, and the Marriage of the Boy Heroine on the English Stage," *PMLA* 102:1 (1987): 29–41.

[9]See Katharine Eisaman Maus, " 'Playhouse Flesh and Blood': Sexual Ideology and the Restoration Actress," *ELH* 46:4 (1979): 595–617.

[10]*As You Like It* (Signet), I, i. 21–22. Subsequent references will appear in the text.

kinship. When Celia's father attempts to separate them by suggesting that the adopted daughter has begun to outshine the "real" one, Celia responds:

If she be a traitor,
Why, so am I. We still have slept together,
Rose at an instant, learned, played, eat together;
And wheresoe'er we went, like Juno's swans,
Still we went coupled and inseparable.

[1. 3. 70–74]

While the Duke seeks to turn the two girls into rivals, Celia insists that they are one and the same, and therefore indivisible. Not only has Celia already promised to share her inheritance with Rosalind, but she is willing to relinquish it altogether in order to follow her twice dispossessed "sister" into exile.

Here the difference between the masculine and feminine subject position lies in the difference between the divided and doubled self. The divided self rests on a hierarchy of two terms (like Duke Senior and Duke Frederick, the banished ruler and his usurper) where the disenfranchised term must be restored to its rightful place, the rustic must give way to the gentleman. The doubled self, in contrast, has two parts (or "sisters") which reflect each other and thus become suitable substitutions. In order for the doubled self to enter representation as more than a mimetic repetition, it must divide itself by means of heterosexual difference (thus Ganymede and Aliena). Although both "couples" are banished, the male "couple" requires the restitution of one term, while the female one requires the relinquishment of the bond, figured as the difference between reclaiming and renouncing one's patrimonial inheritance.

For the two women, "falling in love" replaces wrestling as a sport, although, like wrestling, it will divide them since they cannot fall in love with each other. This arrangement is guaranteed by their "naturalized" relationship based on two terms which are not differentiated enough to engage in competition and cannot thus act as complements (except in play or performance in the forest). Instead, Rosalind falls in love with Orlando, prefiguring the verbal match they will have as lovers in Arden. There, the love joust takes place between two men (Orlando and Ganymede as well as two boy players), one of whom plays a woman (Rosalind who dresses as Ganymede in order to play Rosalind). Male homoeroticism, as "unnatural" as the bond between brothers and as "sporty" as the fight between wrestlers, is veiled by the doubled costume of the woman which offers a form of heterosexual legitimation. Rosalind's role as transvestite is likewise prefigured in her dual relationship to "wrestling": she is both wrestler, when Celia encourages her to "wrestle with thy affections" (1. 3. 21) and wrestled, when she says to Orlando:

Sir, you have wrestled well, and overthrown
More than your enemies.

[1. 2. 243–44]

Here the other man is portrayed as antagonist (like the brother) in contrast to the "friend" (or lover) Orlando will find in Ganymede. While men function in terms of contradictions, women function as imitations of each other unless they become men.

When Rosalind does put on her male attire (since a woman alone was a woman to be raped), there is division with the aid of disguise. Disguise is less deceptive than duplicity because it relies on visual rather than linguistic signifiers. Unlike the fictions created by Oliver against Orlando and by Duke Frederick against Rosalind—whereby words are used to fabricate lies enforced as truth by the authority of the speaker—visual disguise presents only one view to the viewer at a time. Without deceit, the signs of masculine and feminine take the form of sexual stereotypes. Even though Rosalind says herself that "a swashing and martial outside" (1. 3. 118) provides only the deceptive appearance of manly courage, crying and fainting reveal her as a "true" woman. By suggesting that through her disguise "Rosalind becomes 'brother' to herself,"[11] Joel Fineman not only privileges the familial bond the play constitutes as perverted (even if finally restored), but also creates a distinction between "feminine" as "natural" and therefore susceptible to mimesis, and "masculine" as deceptive (both politically and dramatically) and therefore suitable for performance.[12] It is this distinction that offers a profounder difference between the sexes than the signifiers of social roles, or sexual stereotypes.

In the forest, Rosalind further "naturalizes" the feminine by mimicking the words of the misogynist. In response to Orlando's suggestion that her way of speaking might be too refined for a place so removed from the court, she says:

> I have been told so by many. But indeed an old religious uncle of mine taught me to speak, who was in his youth an inland man; one that knew courtship too well, for there he fell in love. I have heard him read many lectures against it; and I thank God I am not a woman, to be touched with so many giddy offenses as he hath generally taxed their whole sex withal.
>
> [3. 2. 338–345]

Rosalind seeks to emulate the paternal figure, who in this case is not the displaced ruler but the scorned lover, and does so as disciple. Thus she imitates her model by "reading his many lectures," rather than by performing in his place, as son. In the forest the opponent is not another man but woman, made less threatening by the fact that she is played by a man. Rosalind reinforces her disguise through deception—not only is she not a woman but she thanks God she never was one. And in contrast to "man," who appears as contradiction, whether in love or not, corruption contaminates the entire "weaker sex."

If Rosalind breaks her "sisterly" bond with Celia in order to establish an "unnatural" one (both false and homoerotic) with Orlando, what role does Celia play, once one

---

[11] Joel Fineman, "Fratricide and Cuckoldry: Shakespeare's Doubles" in Murray M. Schwartz and Coppelia Kahn, eds., *Representing Shakespeare: New Psychoanalytic Essays* (Baltimore: Johns Hopkins, 1980), 79.

[12] I am endebted to Wolfgang Iser for proposing this distinction, although he does not consider it in gendered terms: "If representation arises out of bridging difference, it can no longer be conceived of in terms of mimesis, but must be construed in terms of performance, for each act of difference-removal is a form of production, not of imitation. Furthermore, the fact that performance is a means of bringing something about suggests a process of staging, and this endows it with an intangible quality." "The Dramatization of Double Meaning in Shakespeare's *As You Like It*," *Theatre Journal* 35:3 (1983): 330.

concludes, as Sue-Ellen Case does, that: "The fictional 'Woman' (the character of Rosalind) simply mediates and enhances the homoerotic flirtation between two males."[13] Celia, the one who relinquishes her inheritance but not her sex, is the one who questions Rosalind's identification with and appropriation of masculinist values. This begins even before Rosalind cross-dresses, when she falls in love with Orlando and justifies her feelings by saying: "The Duke my father loved his father dearly." Celia responds: "Doth it therefore ensue that you should love his son dearly? By this kind of chase, I should hate him, for my father hated his father dearly; yet I hate not Orlando" (1. 3. 29–33). Just as Celia breaks with her father in order to follow her "sister," she suggests breaking bonds of kinship in order to pursue the alternative model provided by female friendship (or love). Celia seeks to distinguish between adopting masculine attributes (for survival) and mimicking the misogynist (for play or prowess). Shortly before Rosalind faints, Celia chastizes her for betraying her own sex: "You have simply misused our sex in your love-prate. We must have your doublet and hose plucked over your head, and show the world what the bird hath done to her own nest" (4. 1. 192–195). Becoming a traitor to one's own sex exceeds the treachery perceived by the father—outshining one's sex—which serves as the initial reason for banishment. Celia's defense of her sex, potentially subversive, is contained as conservative because she represents an imitative, same-sex reflection of the cross-dressed heroine who has learned to play with gender distinctions by assuming masculine privilege.

Ultimately it is Touchstone—the fool, not the transvestite—who functions as third term in the form of transgressor, using language to manipulate marriage as that institution which keeps sexual difference in place or at bay. For Wolfgang Iser the fool "is always his own double without ever having to disguise himself"[14] and for Terry Eagleton he "is pure transgression . . . because he appears to lack a body . . . ."[15] It is his "motley coat" (an incongruous mixture of colors and materials) that provides the alternative to male and female dress because the wearer of that coat knows the duplicity of language and can thus manipulate the linguistic performance of the marriage ceremony.[16] He would have it both ways at once, a doubleness based not on disguise, but on the instability of meaning. He knows that every signifier has more than one signified, just as every situation can offer more than one referent. This becomes most apparent when asked whether he likes the life of a shepherd, to which he answers:

> Truly, shepherd, in respect of itself, it is a good life; but in respect that it is a shepherd's life, it is naught. In respect that it is solitary, I like it very well; but in respect that it is private, it is a very vile life. Now in respect it is in the fields, it pleaseth me well; but in

[13]Sue-Ellen Case, *Feminism and Theatre* (New York: Methuen, 1988), 23.

[14]Iser, 316.

[15]Terry Eagleton, *William Shakespeare* (Oxford: Basil Blackwell, 1986), 33.

[16]For an interesting reading of marriage as a non-referential linguistic operation, see Nelly Furman, "The Politics of Language: Beyond the Gender Principle?" in Gayle Greene and Coppelia Kahn, eds., *Making a Difference: Feminist Literary Criticism* (London: Methuen, 1985), 59–79.

respect it is not in the court, it is tedious. As it is a spare life, look you, it fits my humor well; but as there is no more plenty in it, it goes much against my stomach.

[3. 2. 13–21]

A single situation is described with a potentially limitless set of oppositions which seem to cancel each other out and thus mean nothing at all. On the one hand, "solitary" and "private" both refer to the separation or isolation of the individual from the community; on the other hand, they are juxtaposed to create a contradiction: is he secluded or is he lonely? What initially appears as nonsense ultimately offers a lesson in linguistics. As long as this word-play remains in the realm of what Touchstone calls "philosophy," it matters little whether meaning is ever stabilized. He nevertheless attempts to transfer this doubleness to the marriage ceremony, the ritual which seeks to arrest sexual indeterminacy by legitimizing the heterosexual couple. Knowing that a whore can become a wife only in name, the fool attempts to arrange an illegal ceremony with Audrey (a country girl) that would pronounce him husband and release him from that pronouncement at the same time. Audrey, no longer a virgin and thus indifferent to whether she is pronounced "wife," sets as little store by the ceremony as Touchstone does. Yet she does so out of a lack of understanding of the figurative: "I do not know what poetical is. Is it honest in deed and word? Is it a true thing?" (3. 3. 16–17) Honesty becomes equated with the "natural" as that which is (hetero)sexually explicit rather than (homosexually) implicit.

Louis Montrose suggests: "Marriage, the social institution at the heart of comedy, serves to ease or eliminate fraternal strife. And fraternity, in turn, serves as a defense against the threat men feel from women."[17] If this is the case, then Rosalind, as "her own 'brother,' " will ease the strife between actors and characters by coordinating the four marriages "to make these doubts all even" (5. 4. 25). Yet the homoeroticism contained by these social roles makes its reappearance in the epilogue, where Rosalind reveals her true sex as masculine: "If I were a woman, I would kiss as many of you as had beards that pleased me, complexions that liked me, and breaths that I defied not; and I am sure, as many as have good beards, or good faces, or sweet breaths, will, for my kind offer, when I make curtsy, bid me farewell" (Epilogue 17–22). The audience knows he is not a woman, that he is a boy actor playing a woman's part. This becomes the most transgressive moment in the play because it suggests that the sport, whether athletic or erotic, takes place, both candidly and confidentially, between men. This is the social contradiction *As You Like It* addresses, placing cross-dressed heroines on the stage at the moment when they ceased to appear on the streets, thereby reinforcing the fact that its point of address was men, not women.

"Shakespeare never flew in the air."

—Brecht

In Brecht, the transgressive moment when the actor reveals his or her true sex forms the basis for an elaborate dramaturgy.[18] Founded on a deliberate "alienation

---

[17]Louis Adrian Montrose, " 'The Place of a Brother' in *As You Like It:* Social Process and Comic Form," *Shakespeare Quarterly* 32:1 (1981): 51.

effect" (*Entfremdung*) or "making the familiar strange," the motivation behind the "A-effect" is not an erotic, but a political one: "The object of the A-effect is to alienate the social gest underlying every incident. By social gest is meant the mimetic and gestural expression of the social relationships prevailing between people of a given period." To achieve this effect, the actor must not become his or her character, but speak it "like a quotation," making it appear strange by looking at it strangely him or herself:

> Because he doesn't identify himself with him he can pick a definite attitude to adopt towards the character whom he portrays, can show what he thinks of him and invite the spectator, who is likewise not asked to identify himself, to criticize the character portrayed. The attitude which he adopts is a socially critical one. . . . In this way his performance becomes a discussion (about social conditions) with the audience he is addressing. He prompts the spectator to justify or abolish these conditions according to what class he belongs to.[19]

The lack of identification between actor and character is neither a function of historical necessity nor an opportunity for veiled eroticism, but rather a conscious attempt to "denaturalize" social formations in order to make their arbitrary constructions more visible. The most obvious device for achieving this effect would be to play a character of the opposite sex.

In *The Good Woman of Setzuan* (originally *Der gute Mensch von Sezuan*, which leaves the sex of the protagonist indeterminable) the good Shen Te becomes her evil cousin Shui Ta in order to preserve the monetary gift from the gods which she has traded for a tobacco store. Because of her generosity, she fails to make a profit and, heeding the advice of her exploiters, not only invokes the authority of the cousin but actually embodies him by appearing as a man. In a lyric entitled "The Song of Defense-lessness," which Shen Te sings carrying the mask of Shui Ta, both characters ask why even the gods are defenseless against a world which is so evil that it has become impossible to be good. Not the threat of rape, but the spector of economic insolvency forces a female character to acquire the clothes traditionally reserved for the masculine.

Conceived as a parable, the play portrays Shen Te less as a psychological subject than as a subject position (accentuated by the mask borrowed from Chinese theater[20]), a subject position conceivable only in its relation to the masculine. Initially Shen Te is juxtaposed to Wong, the waterseller, who, like the prostitute, must sell a commodity most people manage to acquire for free — water from floods or rainfall and sex through seduction or marriage. Although Shen Te sells herself for a living, she is still con-

---

[18]For a reading of *"The Good Person of Setzuan* as a redaction of *As You Like It,"* see Helen M. Whall, "The Case is Altered: Brecht's Use of Shakespeare," *University of Toronto Quarterly* 51:2 (Winter 1981/2): 138–47. See also Margot Heinemann, "How Brecht Read Shakespeare" in Jonathan Dollimore and Alan Sinfield, eds., *Political Shakespeare: New Essays in Cultural Materialism* (Manchester: University of Manchester, 1985), 202–30.

[19]"Short Description of a New Technique of Acting" in *Brecht on Theatre: The Development of an Aesthetic,* trans. John Willett (London: Methuen, 1964), 139. See also "The Author as Producer" in Walter Benjamin, *Understanding Brecht,* trans. Anna Bostock (London: NLB, 1973), 100.

[20]See "Alienation Effects in Chinese Acting" in *Brecht on Theatre,* 91–99.

sidered good, unlike the waterseller who sells water from a cup with a false bottom. Sexual difference is used to figure an economic difference, while the difference between the sexes is neither economic or sexual, but moral. Morality, although differentiated from the hypocritical sexual standards of the bourgeoisie, is largely predicated on psychological differences that lie at the core of sexual stereotypes. Sexual difference is not determined by the commodity one sells—sex or water—but by one's faith in goodness: Wong disappears thinking that even Shen Te's goodness will fail when it comes to offering the gods a place for the night, while Shen Te would like to be good, although she admits that economic necessity often makes it unfeasible. While Wong fears that the gods will discover Shen Te's true profession, the gods are afraid that someone will misread their monetary compensation for a night's lodging as a sex trade. Brecht privileges prostitution (a financial transaction necessitated by poverty) over marriage, because the latter is founded on deception as the corruption of neither money nor sex, but of (heterosexual) love.

In this play marriage does not "make all this matter even"; rather it makes matters worse because it involves the "deadliest weakness" (a weakness deadlier than goodness)—love. Like Audrey, Shen Te no longer has her virginity to sell and instead exchanges her honesty in the form of material generosity. Vulnerability does not stem from an inability to distinguish between the literal and the figurative, but from Shen Te's willingness to sacrifice her own source of livelihood in order to guarantee her husband's reemployment as flyer. (Like Rosalind, she plays the man in order to restore "true manhood" to her lover). Rather than providing an end to the play, the reward for revealing one's true sex, the wedding ceremony interrupts it in the middle and the play does not even offer one union. Marriage provides the moment when the impossibility of appearing as both sexes at once obstructs the nuptial knot: Yang Sun will not pronounce his vows until the cousin appears with the money which he will use as a bribe to acquire the job of a pilot; Shui Ta will not appear until Yang Sun displays two plane tickets and ensures that he plans to take Shen Te with him, and not his mother. The complexity of these gendered subject positions is once again juxtaposed to the simplicity of sexual stereotypes. Like the "uncle" who teaches Rosalind that all women are guilty of "giddy offenses," Yang Sun represents women from the point of view of the misogynist: "Shen Te is a woman; she *is* devoid of common sense. I only have to lay my hand on her shoulder, and church bells ring."[21] While waiting for the wedding to take place, Yang Sun attempts to determine what kind of wife Shen Te will make by testing her "home economics": can she make five cups of tea with three leaves; can she sleep alone on a mattress the size of a book? Meanwhile, Shen Te tries to explain to Yang Sun that "my cousin can't be coming. . . . My cousin can't be where I am" (93). Unlike Wong, who remains Shen Te's best friend, both Shui Ta and Yang Sun become "her worse enemy" because they prevent her from being a "true" woman, kind and in love, and still surviving economically. Being a woman prohibits marriage from taking place; economics perverts marriage into a form of psychological prostitution.

[21]Bertolt Brecht, *The Good of Setzuan*, revised English version Eric Bentley (New York: Grove, 1965), 80. Subsequent references will appear in the text.

The disguise prevents the transvestite from mediating between herself and her lover (although both Shen Te and Shui Ta attempt to negotiate with Yang Sun in the name of the other); worse yet, the disguised is accused of being a murderer. Again, it is not the act of cross-dressing which transgresses, but the disappearance of the female subject. First Yang Sun hears someone sobbing in the back room; then Shen Te's clothes are found under the table in Shui Ta's office. Brought to the trial which replaced the wedding as the end of the play, Shui Ta reveals himself as both Shen Te and Shui Ta and defends herself as follows:

> Your injunction
> To be good and yet to live
> Was a thunderbolt:
> It has torn me in two
> I can't tell how it was
> But to be good to others
> And myself at the same time
> I could not do it . . .

[136]

Here the split subject embodies neither a mimetic doubling nor a division which can be restored; rather, it represents divisiveness as the symptom of a capitalist system in which moral goodness and economic survival are mutually exclusive. Like Rosalind, Shen Te abandons her sex, this time by making her disguise permanent. And yet it is the impermanence of the clothes—Shui Ta's trousers hanging on Shen Te's clothesline—that finally gives her away.

The body would seem a more stable signifier than the clothes that simply signify it. Yet even as Shen Te becomes increasingly pregnant, it is not her body that betrays her (Shui Ta simply gets fatter as his wealth grows) but her emotional weakness. Like Rosalind's fainting at the news of Orlando's wounding, Shen Te sobs in the back room when she hears that the father has learned of his illegitimate child. Physical weakness can be hidden behind the bravado of the opposite sex, but emotional weakness reveals the true difference between the sexes. This distinction establishes the "good" mother and "bad" father based on the "natural" difference produced by their respective participation in biological reproduction. Unlike Shakespeare, who blurs the difference in social status between the boy actor and the unmarried woman, Brecht conflates social and sexual differences by relying on biology when he makes Shen Te grow large with child. Shen Te abandons herself to her faithless lover at the very moment she reproduces herself in her child; yet that child, a son, reproduces the father, the former flyer who has risen in the world as tobacco factory foreman.

The third term in Brecht's play are the gods, traditionally invoked to mediate in the disputes between men, here called to preside at the trial of the man who apparently has done away with "the good woman." The ethereal gods represent the bourgeois alternative to earthly contradictions, and are figured as inept, uninformed figures who know less about earth than those who live on it. Not having created it, they are trying to maintain the world as it is through their arbitrary "book of rules." Convinced that if they find the exception to the rule (i.e., a good person) the rules

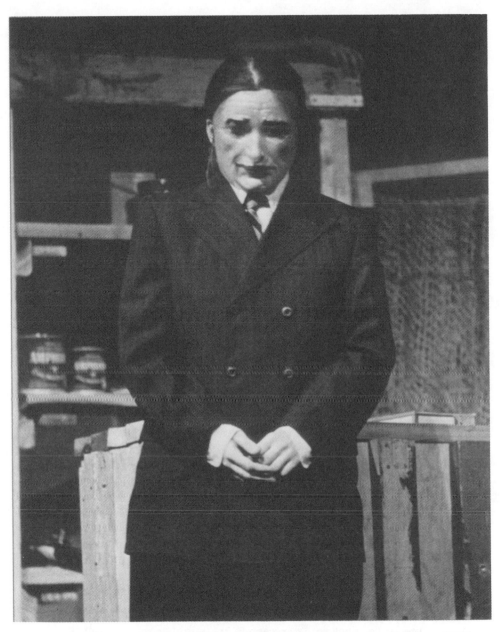

Maureen Sullivan as Shen Te in *The Good Woman of Setzuan*, University of Michigan (1975).
Photo: Paul Klinger.

need not be changed, they leave Shen Te crying for help. Unlike Shakespeare's fool, these gods are truly foolish, because they adhere to the literal meaning of the law. The most they can offer is a benevolent reading of the "rules" when Shen Te yells that she needs the help of her evil cousin at least once a week and they respond that once a month should suffice. The contradiction between the sexes is left unresolved and the play ends with the existence of morality in question.

The epilogue (to be spoken by either Shen Te or Wong, but not in character) likewise addresses itself to the audience, although not to "conjure," but to implore. Both epilogues reflect on their own breaks with dramatic convention: Rosalind appears as a woman when the last word should be had by a man, and *The Good Woman of Setzuan* offers no closure when a play should have an ending:

> You're thinking, aren't you, that this is no right
> Conclusion to the play you've seen tonight?
> After a tale, exotic, fabulous,
> A nasty ending was slipped up on us.
> We feel deflated too. We too are nettled
> To see the curtain down and nothing settled.
> How could a better ending be arranged?
> How could one change people? Can the world be changed?
> Would new gods do the trick? Will atheism?
> Moral rearmament? Materialism?
> It is for you to find a way, my friends,
> To help good men arrive at happy ends.
> *You* write the happy ending to the play!
> There must, there must, there's got to be a way!
>
> [141][22]

Unlike the boy player who attempts to seduce the male members of his audience, this actor desperately seeks the audience's assistance. The relationship is not erotic, based on the conditional ("if"), but political, grounded in the interrogative. The solution to the binariness of sexual difference is no longer displaced onto homo-eroticism; it lies in dramatic closure as the solution to "naturalized" social relations. If the feminine represents the possibility of a socialist revolution, what then is the connection between Shen Te and the women of that utopian social order?

Considering the historical moment during which Brecht wrote this play, it is apparent that Shen Te as the "eternal feminine" becomes divided between the "mas-

---

[22]It is interesting to note that the following lines were omitted from the English translation:
> Dabei sind wir doch auf Sie angeweisen
> Dass Sie bei uns zu Haus sind und geniessen.
> Wir können es uns leider nicht verhehlen:
> Wir sind bankrott, wenn Sie uns nicht empfehlen!
> Vielleicht fiel uns aus lauter Furcht nichts ein.
> Das kam schon vor. Was könnt die Lösung sein?
> Wir konnten keine finden, nicht einmal für Geld.

Brecht, *Der Gute Mensch von Sezuan* (Berlin: Suhrkamp, 1955), 143. By establishing a greater dependency between actor and audience and thus a greater vulnerability on the part of the cast, the economic metaphors begin to function almost like the sexual ones in Shakespeare.

culinized" New Woman and a historically specific exploitation of motherhood. Not only does the play's ending take the form of an admonition as opposed to a seduction, but, as Sue-Ellen Case has pointed out, in Brecht "the mothers are defined by their mothering roles and have no sexual definition."[23] By placing the mother in the female subject position, Brecht not only desexualizes her, but also insists on biological differences as they were used and misused by both the sex reformers of the Weimar Republic (1918–1933) and the Nazis of the Third Reich (1933–1945). Atina Grossman describes the New Woman as she appeared in Germany after World War I:

> The New Woman was not only the intellectual with a Marlene Dietrich-style suit and short mannish haircut or the young white-collar worker in a flapper suit. She was also the young married factory worker who cooked only one warm meal a day, cut her hair short into a practical Bubikopf, and tried with all available means to keep her family small.[24]

As women entered the work force in greater numbers and were required to relocate responsibilities assumed by social services into the private home during the Depression, sex reformers were intent on "rationalizing" women's double burden on the one hand by reducing birth rates through available birth control and legal abortion, and on the other hand by improving women's sex lives.[25] Both approaches were based on biological distinctions between the sexes, on women's unique sensibility, and on their entitlement to a separate "Lebensraum."[26] Sex reform carried with it greater control of sexual deviance; those unfit to marry came "close to the malicious stereotype of the New Woman: short, dark hair, dressed in a unisex shirt, distinctly unmaternal—the image not only of the prostitute but also of the Jewess and the lesbian."[27]

When the Nazis came to power they simply turned birth control counseling centers into racial hygiene clinics and carried the sex reform movement's eugenics goals to their unthinkable conclusion. Women were hailed as "mothers of the race" or guilty of "racial degeneration." The Nazis were intent both on raising the rate of childbirth and enforcing the sterilization of "asocials," which included prostitutes, women of

---

[23]Sue-Ellen Case, "Brecht and Women: Homosexuality and the Mother" in John Fuegi, Gisela Bahr and John Willett, eds., *Brecht: Women and Politics*, Brecht Yearbook 12 (Detroit: Wayne State, 1985), 66.

[24]Atina Grossmann, "The New Woman and the Rationalization of Sexuality in Weimar Germany" in Ann Snitow, Christine Stansell, and Sharon Thompson, eds., *Powers of Desire: The Politics of Sexuality* (New York: Monthly Review, 1983), 156. See also Grossmann, " 'Satisfaction is Domestic Happiness': Mass Working-Class Sex Reform Organizations in the Weimar Republic" in Michael N. Dobkowski and Isidor Walliman, eds., *Towards the Holocaust: The Social and Economic Collapse of the Weimar Republic* (Westport: Greenwood, 1983), 265–93.

[25]See Atina Grossmann, "Abortion and Economic Crisis: The 1931 Campaign Against Paragraph 218" in Renate Bridenthal, Atina Grossmann, and Marion Kaplan, eds., *When Biology Became Destiny: Women in Weimar and Nazi Germany* (New York: Monthly Review, 1984), 66–86.

[26]Claudia Koonz, "The Competition for Women's *Lebensraum*, 1928–1934" in Bridenthal, 199–236. See also Koonz, "Some Political Implications of Separatism: German Women Between Democracy and Nazism, 1928–1934," in Judith Freidlander, Blanche Wiesen Cook, Alice Kessler-Harris, and Carroll Smith-Rosenberg, eds., *Women in Culture and Politics: A Century of Change* (Bloomington: Indiana University, 1986), 269–85.

[27]Grossmann, "The New Woman," 167.

"inferior character," and those of "alien race."[28] Even though women acquired the vote in 1918 (as a reward for their war effort, not their suffrage struggle), parties of the right, from the Catholic Center party to the National Socialists, were much more successful at attracting women's votes because they encouraged women to participate in politics in order to preserve and enhance their traditional roles as wife and mother.[29] Neither the Communist nor the Socialist party was able to offer a competing conceptual framework. When it came time to mobilize women for war, propagandistic images of women changed, but not basic beliefs about women's nature, which continued to fuel the extension of the maternal role into the public sphere.[30]

Brecht, who more than other theorists has insisted upon the need to historicize social formations, continues to metaphorize and idealize the mother at the very moment in history when she is most exploited as purely biological function. Sara Lennox has suggested that Brecht's dramaturgy is predicated on an "instrumentalism" which necessarily regards women "as demonstration objects rather than subjects in their own right."[31] If the "A-effect" is meant to afford critical distance so as to imagine a different set of social relations, then those arrangements do not include sexual arrangements, just as "the half-Westernized city of Setzuan" serves to promote geographical distance in the service of parable, not history. Like Shakespeare, who ceased to put cross-dressed heroines on stage once they began to appear on the streets, Brecht used his woman figures to embody Communist Party policy at a particular historical moment.[32] The discrepancy between women on stage and their roles on the stage of history reinforces the role of the cross-dressed heroine as metaphor. Even after women have been allowed onto the theatrical stage and have succeeding in winning the vote, they still appear politically as the "woman question," tangential to the electoral process yet crucial to consolidating the power of (white male) political parties.

"You can't separate fucking and economics."

—Churchill

The work of Caryl Churchill marks the appearance of a female playwright who identifies herself as a socialist-feminist and uses cross-dressing to question the cat-

---

[28]Gisela Bock, "Racism and Sexism in Nazi German: Motherhood, Compulsory Sterilization, and the State" in Bridenthal, 271–96. See also Bock, " 'No Children at Any Cost': Perspectives on Compulsory Sterilization, Sexism and Racism in Nazi Germany" in Friedlander, 286–98.

[29]See Renate Bridenthal and Claudia Koonz, "Beyond *Kinder, Küche, Kirche:* Weimar Women in Politics and Work" in Bridenthal, 33–65.

[30]"Public images, unlike basic beliefs about woman's nature, can change quickly in response to economic need. The economic role and the popular image of women may change drastically in the course of a modern war, but basic ideas about women's proper sphere, characterized by cultural lag even in the case of long-term economic developments, change little. Of course, the war was too short a span of time to expect fundamental changes in people's attitudes. The German and American cases show that public images can adapt to the need for women in jobs previously reserved for men without challenging traditional assumptions." Leila J. Rupp, *Mobilizing Women for War: German and American Propaganda, 1930–1945* (Princeton: Princeton University, 1978), 174–75.

[31]Sara Lennox, "Women in Brecht's Works," *New German Critique* 14 (Spring 1978): 93, 91.

[32]See Lennox, 88.

egories that legitimize not only patriarchy and capitalism, but also colonialism. Since many of her plays do not revolve around a central character, she herself becomes the center of a discourse which figures the "female playwright" as oxymoron, a woman occupying the position of a man. Mel Gussow, in a review in the *New York Times* of her most recent play, *Serious Money*, writes the following:

> Just as her work has its contradictions, Ms. Churchill is herself a paradox. Her plays are outrageous, even scandalous and the language, as in "Serious Money," can be scabrous. The playwright, however, is no wild-eyed weird sister, but a genteel woman with a kind of regal reserve, The British director William Gaskill thinks she has a 'classic English beauty'—with her graying hair and high cheekbones. Married to a lawyer and the mother of three sons (they are 24, 22 and 17), she has a close circle of friends. Outside of that circle, she is so aggressively shy that, next to her, Woody Allen would seem like an ebullient self-promoter.[33]

On the one hand, Churchill has illegitimately appropriated the language of men, language which is "outrageous," "scandelous," "scabrous"; on the other hand she is relegitimized through her association with men: her husband, her sons, a male director, Woody Allen. The unthinkable is "the wild-eyed weird sister" she might either be or be a part of, simply by gender association. Fortunately she is seen as neither politically nor sexually aggressive, but only as "aggressively shy," and if her language in "manly," she at least carries the "graying hair" of male royalty. By taming her physically, by domesticating her socially, the words of the female professional become audible.

This review appears four years after the *The New York Times Magazine* presented a cover story entitle "Women Playwrights: New Voices in the Theater." At that time Mel Gussow wrote: "In order to trace the reasons for the proliferation of plays by women, one must begin with the women's movement itself, which nurtured the belief that there is no profession or artistic discipline—from movie making to monumental sculpture—that should be exclusive of men" and "The increase in number of women playwrights is part of a larger pattern in which women are assuming roles of authority and creativity in all aspects of the theater."[34] As long as women are represented as a group separate from men, democratic liberal politics can provide the impression that one is experiencing and/or witnessing historical progress; as soon as a woman appears alone, she leaves her sex and must be demonized or turned into an honorary man.

Churchill further exploits "Brechtian techniques" by exploring capitalism in its relation to sexism and colonialism,[35] and by encouraging actors to examine not only

---

[33]Mel Gussow, "Genteel Playwright, Angry Voice," *New York Times*, 22 November 1987, Arts and Leisure section.

[34]Mel Gussow, "Women Playwrights: New Voices in the Theater," *New York Times*, 1 May 1983, Magazine. For a history of women's theatre see Case, *Feminism and Theatre* and Michelene Wandor, *Carry on, Understudies: Theatre and Sexual Politics* (London: Routledge and Kegan Paul, 1986).

[35]See, for instance, Janelle Reinelt, "Beyond Brecht: Britain's New Feminist Drama," *Theatre Journal* 38:2 (1986): 154–63.

their characters but also their own sexual identities. *Cloud Nine* was written for the British Joint Stock Theatre Group, where the cast, playwright, and director held three-week workshops during which they read relevant texts, did consciousness-raising exercises, and improvised. One such exercise involved

> a game in which numbers and images (jacks, queens, etc.) on playing cards represented varying degrees of power; red and black respectively represented male and female. Players arbitrarily received cards assigning them numerical power as well as a sexual identity; they were then to improvise situations and interact according to their given power. Repeatedly, actors who received cards identifying them as males would assert more power than those who received cards identifying them as females; assigned gender outweighed off-stage sexual identity as well as numerical scores.[36]

Consciousness–raising exercises have replaced dramatic theory as a way of producing "alienation effects" by making visible the interpenetration of theatrical and social roles. This involves not only assuming roles of the opposite sex or of another race, but also playing two different roles from one act to the next.

The disjuncture between actor and character becomes reinforced by the discontinuity between Act I, which takes place in a British colony in Africa during Queen Victoria's reign, and Act II, which takes place in London in the 1970s. Although Act II takes place one hundred years later, the characters are only twenty-five years older. Not only does Churchill "historicize" racial, sexual, and class oppression, but she puts into question "history" as a coherent, truth-telling narrative. Elin Diamond, in "Refusing the Romanticism of Identity: Narrative Interventions in Churchill, Benmussa, Duras" suggests: "To understand history as narrative is a crucial move for feminists, not only because it demystifies the idea of disinterested authorship, but because the traditionally subordinate role of women in history can be seen as the legacy of narrative itself."[37] Thus it becomes not a question of whether women have been excluded from history or how they might be included, but a question of how history *a priori* inscribes the white male subject through a story of power and legitimation. It is this story that Churchill puts into question (as Diamond argues further) by preventing the spectator from producing a coherent narrative within the boundaries of the play's dramatic structure.

The gendered subject positions encountered in Shakespeare (male division vs. female doubling) and in Brecht (Shen Te's relation to her "best friend" vs. her "worst enemies") take on an even more complex configuration in Churchill. The play begins with Clive, the Victorian father/husband/subject, introducing his wife: "My wife is all I dreamt a wife should be, / And everything she is she owes to me."[38] The referent of this statement is not only the ideology of Victorian sexual arrangements but also the male actor who plays the part of Clive's wife, Betty. Betty responds:

---

[36]Helene Keyssar, *Feminist Theatre* (New York: Grove, 1985), 93–94.

[37]Elin Diamond, "Refusing the Romanticism of Identity: Narrative Interventions in Churchill, Benmussa, Duras," *Theatre Journal* 37:3 (1985): 276.

[38]Caryl Churchill, *Cloud Nine* (New York: Methuen, 1984), 3–4. Subsequent references will appear in the text.

I live for Clive. The whole aim of my life
Is to be what he looks for in a wife.
I am a man's creation as you see,
And what men want is what I want to be.

[4]

To be "a man's creation" means to conform to masculine expectations not by mimicking the misogynist or murdering the feminine, but by leaving nothing to the woman except the name and the clothes. Like Touchstone's "wife," this "wife" is the product of a linguistic operation which unmasks rather than secures her as masculine/marital construct. The lack of correspondence between actor and character is replaced by the enunciated correlation between "what men want" and "what I want to be." The "alienation effect" produced by this disjuncture reinforces the fact that characters *are* their discourses and that their discourses are often someone else's. Sexual stereotypes are parodied and deception virtually disappears.

For further clarification, I will trace the trajectory of a single actor who plays two characters, and of the two characters who appear first in Act I and then as twenty-five years older in Act II. In the New York production, the same actor plays Edward the son in Act I and Victoria the daughter in Act II. In Act I Edward is played by a woman, while Victoria is played by a doll. Churchill herself attributes this technique not to Shakespeare, but to "the English tradition of women playing boys (e.g. PETER PAN)" (viii). At the same time, Edward is gay; that is, homosexuality becomes an issue for the character, not an issue suppressed in the relation between boy actors or veiled in the relation between actor and audience. Male homosexuality in the Victorian period is of course associated with effeminacy, made explicit in Edward's relationship to the doll of his sister Victoria (played by a doll). The controversy over the doll (since the sister *is* a doll she can do little to enter the controversy) has to do with whether Edward is playing with or minding the doll: if he minds the doll, he is beginning to learn his social role as a man; if he plays with it, then he is adopting a feminine role and must be dealt with accordingly. Gender roles (as in Shakespeare) are represented in terms of specular images: Edward must not play with, that is, identify with the doll, otherwise he will grow up to be a girl, like his sister, while his sister has internalized her role so well (without even having to learn it) that she does not even play with the doll but is one.

Unlike the veiled homoeroticism in Shakespeare and the suppression of sexuality in Brecht, homosexuality appears as explicit content in *Cloud Nine*. It is treated both historically (differently transgressive in the nineteenth century than in the twentieth) and as the form of sexuality that has politicized sexual arrangements in general. In Act I homosexuality is still associated with deception. On the one hand, Harry Bagley (Edward's "uncle"/lover) represents Victorian hypocrisy by pretending to love "woman" while preferring sex with men. On the other hand, lying as a form of justification legitimizes not (Shakespmean) primogeniture but the interpenetration of sexism and racism. Edward accuses Joshua, the Black native, of stealing his mother's necklace when he has actually taken (not stolen) it from his mother in order to give it to Bagley. The impermissibility of a "feminine" gesture from one man to another must be blamed on a social inferior, who in this case is racially other. But since this configuration of gestures and words is attributed to Edward's youth (instead of to a network of sexual and racial oppression), when Joshua destroys the (doll's) doll and Edward rightly accuses him, his father no longer believes him. This results in the death of the father, the end of the Empire and the curtain of Act I.

Act I also ends with a marriage between Bagley, the gay explorer, and Ellen, the lesbian governess. The wedding scene once again bisects rather than ends the play, but this time no longer grounded in the romantic illusion of love. Clive insists that Bagley get married: "Rivers will be named after you, it's unthinkable" (53), in order to hide the "perversion," the "sin," the "disease," he calls "effeminacy." Ellen agrees to the marriage, since she is in love with Betty and will be forced to leave her employer as soon as Edward grows up. Initially Bagley asks Mrs. Saunders, "the woman of spirit" (who lives on in Africa as a widow and plans to return to England to introduce threshing machines) to marry him, but she refuses since the only part of marriage she liked was the sex. The only part of marriage Ellen dislikes is the sex, which Betty in turn explains to her: "You must keep still. . . . Ellen, you're not getting married to enjoy yourself" (57). The choice between Mrs. Saunders and Ellen is reinforced as exclusive by the fact that they are played by the same actress (like Shen Te and Shui Ta) and therefore cannot appear at the wedding together. Even more importantly, as women who are equally uninterested in marriage and might potentially be interested in each other, they can literally never meet.

In Act II, Edward continues to play the "effeminate" part by playing the role of the "wife" in the live-in relationship with first, his lover Gerry (who occasionally prefers anonymous sex) and then with his sister Victoria and Lin (who themselves are involved with each other). The "wife" is no longer a linguistic operation; rather, it involves a role that necessarily must be performed within the family unit (given the present social arrangements), but not by someone of a particular biological sex or an assigned place in a kinship system. Victoria, in contrast, has developed from a doll into a feminist. The figure who had no voice now speaks with the voice of critical commentary. In response to Lin who says "I hate men," Victoria answers: "You have to look at it in a historical perspective in terms of learnt behavior since the industrial revolution" (68). The daughter retains a relation to the patriarch, no longer silenced by him but offering theoretical explanations of his institutions.

Betty, the middle-aged divorcee, offers the third term in a world where the taboos surrounding who can enter a relationship with whom have been almost completely broken. She represents the woman alone, who has severed all old ties and forged no new ones, who has sex with herself and thus eliminates the social constructions which determine all sexual relationships. She is the mother who is totally absent in Shakespeare, who replaces the wife in Brecht, and now appears for the first time as a transgressive figure. Her transgression (masturbation) need not be contained and her contradictions will not be solved outside of her personal history. The relationship she commences with a gay man, Gerry—with whom she enters into conversation at the end of the British version of the play—cannot be coded as transgressive because it is *a priori* not sexual.

The most transgressive moment in the play is finally the most parodic:

Jim Vezina as Betty and Mark O'Brien as Harry Bagley in *Cloud Nine*, Eastern Michigan University Theatre (1985). Photo: Dick Schwarz.

> Edward: I like women.
> Victoria: That should please mother.
> Edward: No listen Vicky. I'd rather be a woman. I wish I had breasts like that, I think
>   they're beautiful. Can I touch them?
> Victoria: What, pretending they're yours?
> Edward: No, I know it's you.
> Victoria: I think I should warn you I'm enjoying this.
> Edward: I'm sick of men.
> Victoria: I'm sick of men.
> Edward: I think I'm a lesbian.
>
>   [92]

This moment puts the very notion of transgression into question. The scene takes the audience back to the one with the doll: is Edward playing with it or minding it? Here the question becomes, are the breasts his or his sister's (and since the question concerns body parts, the answer should be clearer). Does Edward want to be like his sister or be his sister? Does the fact that they are both "sick of men" make them the same? Can a man be a "lesbian" (as the logical conclusion of his feelings about men) or is being a lesbian instead biological? How can "lesbian" refer to both an "effeminate" man and a "masculine" woman? Should the incest taboo be the only one left unbroken (even between consenting adults)?

In Churchill the actor no longer simply comments on the character, but places the very notion of a character in question. Cross-dressing takes place as the disjuncture between body and text, not on the level of who is permitted on stage nor of how to appear on stage as two characters simultaneously. Rather, the discrepancy between actor and character separates the signifier from the signified, pointing this time to the significance of language in the construction of the sex-gender system.

When the "earth . . . hath been turned into a Stage, and women have come forth acting the parts of men,"[39] then the question is not why women dress as men, but why the metaphor of the stage. "New historicism" rereads the Renaissance theater against the "theater" of Renaissance politics, that is, gender and power relations. "Postmodernism" speaks in terms of performance reality as linguistic impersonation. Nazism provided the most extravagent performance of this century, captured in the films of Leni Riefenstahl. On the one hand, if it is only a performance, then one can leave it and return to the real, the everyday. On the other hand, if the performance is all there is, who will write the parts? Shakespeare, Brecht, and Churchill have all written a part for the cross-dressed heroine, and yet in none of these plays does her cross-dressing alter or reconstruct the female subject. In Shakespeare the female character is assimilated by the boy player; in Brecht the female character is appropriated by her male double; and in Churchill the character becomes a gay man, although the actress goes on to play a middle-class feminist. The transgressive figure nevertheless shifts from the fool to the gods to the middle-aged woman, thereby shifting the site of contradiction from the cross-dressed figure (which will always

---

[39]Francis Rous, *Oile of Scorpions* (London, 1624), pp. 173–74. Quoted in Susan C. Shapiro, "Amazons, Hermaphrodites, and Plain Monsters: The 'Masculine' Woman in English Satire and Social Criticism from 1580–1640," *Atlantis* 13:1 (Fall/Autumn, 1987): 73.

"be appropriated by the 'masculine' ") to the female figure as the product of a particular historical moment.

Eagleton has suggested: "If representation is a lie, then the very structure of the theatrical sign is strangely duplicitous, asserting an identity while manifesting a division, and to this extent it resembles the structure of metaphor."[40] The theater as metaphor, the theatrical sign resembling the structure of metaphor, the feminine as the metaphor for that division, are these all signs of duplicity or of proliferation? The cross-dressed heroine, as metaphor, points to the limits of metaphorical structures that rely on an unexamined assumption of gendered distinctions. As theatrical sign, she points to the disjuncture between body and clothes, between clothes as signifying and/or constituting the subject. In Shakespeare and Brecht she stands in for something else; in Churchill where she stands—whether on her high-heeled shoes or under the broad-rimmed hat—is itself the question.

[40]Eagleton, 3–4.

The Female Entertainment Tradition in Medieval Japan: The Case of *Asobi*

Yung-Hee Kim Kwon

The role of women in the field of performing arts and entertainment in Japan has been long and indispensable. Particularly prominent was the contribution made by women during the Heian period (794–1192) and down through the medieval period. During these fertile periods in the development of Japanese cultural history, women, especially on the low rung of the social ladder, had a large share in giving life to a variety of genres and carrying the burden of sustaining them. For example, the creation of the celebrated *kabuki* theatre in Japan is credited to a woman named Okuni, who lived in the early seventeenth century.[1] Okuni, however, is one of only a few exceptional cases of women whose names have been identified and transmitted to the present. Across the centuries, there have been a multitude of anonymous female performers who staged their talents as dancers, singers, and itinerant reciters of religious stories with the visual aid of illustrations in the countryside, mountain temples, and city streets, thereby keeping their respective performing arts traditions alive and memorable. Without their presence, much of the texture and color of the pre-modern literary and performing arts traditions in Japan would have been impoverished.

Yet it appears that these women's artistic achievements, their functions, mode of life, and their interrelationships have never been seriously examined or assessed. Set against the scope and diversity of their participation in the performing arts and the immensity of the implications of their activities, the dearth of studies in this area is all the more glaring. This situation necessitates a vigorous exploration of their work—not simply to do justice to the legacy bequeathed by these women artists, but also to address the larger issue of the intricate relationship between women and entertainment in the social and cultural milieu of medieval Japan. In this connection,

Yung-Hee Kim Kwon is an Assistant Professor of Japanese in the Department of East Asian Languages and Literatures at Ohio State University. She has published articles on Japanese popular songs which flourished during the medieval period.

All the Japanese names are given in order of last name first followed by the given name observing the customary Japanese practice.

[1] James R. Brandon, William P. Malm, and Donald H. Shively, *Studies in Kabuki: Its Acting, Music, and Historical Context* (Honolulu: University Press of Hawaii, 1978), 5.

the present study represents an effort to bring to light one of the earliest links in this long and fascinating chain of the female entertainment tradition in Japan and to acquaint the readers with this important subject.

The primary focus of this study concerns a group of women called *asobi*, with occasional reference to other women who belonged to a similar social class and engaged in a comparable area of entertainment. *Asobi* were, simply put, professional female singers of low social status who flourished during the eleventh and twelfth centuries in Japan. Their main distinction came from their expertise in *imayō*, a popular song genre of plebeian origin, which began to gain currency during the late tenth century. By the late twelfth century, it enjoyed a sweeping popularity among both the aristocrats and the common people. As the *imayō* genre flourished, so thrived *asobi*, carving their artistic niche in the society and life of the people they entertained.

Imayō songs had a wide spectrum of subjects and themes. The repertoire included songs on elevated themes such as Buddhist doctrines as well as songs on snails, dragonflies, and grasshoppers, which appear to be children's songs, although they may have possessed deeper implications than those they appear to represent. Within this spectrum, *imayō* songs paid tribute to the Buddha, his disciples, eminent Buddhist saints, and mountain ascetics; then, in the next breath, they celebrated woodcutters, fishermen, gamblers, potters, barrier-keepers, Shinto shrine priestesses, and courtesans. When we add different kinds of trees, birds, animals, clothing, and accessory items to this list, the variety of topics the *imayō* genre touched upon reaches kaleidoscopic dimensions. This juxtaposition of the high and low, sacred and profane, serious and light, as well as men and women—a comprehensive coverage speaking to every level of humanity—may have been the main source for the immense following that *imayō* commanded. After a successful career of two centuries, however, *imayō*'s popularity suffered a radical decline with the demise of the Heian civilian government and subsequent establishment of the Kamakura military regime at the very end of the twelfth century.[2] With the decline of *imayō* as a song genre by the mid–Kamakura period in the late thirteenth century, the tradition of *asobi* as *imayō* singers died out.

In spite of their decline, there are a number of reasons why the significance of *asobi* in the history of performing arts in Japan cannot be ignored. For one, *asobi* were the first private performing artists ever identified by formal, specific group designations. They were also the first known female artist groups who specialized in one single performing arts genre. Furthermore, their development as a social unit reveals that they were products of a much larger and more complex historical process in which their social status was inverted, demoting them from the political and religious center of society to the margin of servitude. The combination of these factors makes the *asobi* study imperative, not only for the intrinsic interest of the topic itself, but also for the impact the study would have on an accurate appraisal of women's true position in the broader context of the cultural history of Japan.

---

[2]The Kamakura government was established by a military general, Minamoto Yoritomo (1147–1199), who moved the capital from Heian-kyō, the present-day city of Kyoto, to Kamakura near the present-day Tokyo. The Kamakura period lasted from 1192–1333.

One of the most intriguing facts about these female entertainers is the etymological and social origins of their nomenclature, *asobi*. Japanese scholars trace its origin to as far back as a goddess by the name of Ameno-uzume-no-mikoto, who appears in the myths concerning the founding of the Japanese nation. These mythic cycles are included in the *Kojiki* (Record of Ancient Matters), the earliest dynastic chronicle of Japan, a partially mythical and partially historical record, completed in 712 A.D.[3] One of these myths relates a famous narrative about the Sun Goddess Amaterasu from whom the Japanese claim their descent and her relationship with Ameno-uzume-no-mikoto. To briefly outline the account, Amaterasu had a brother called Susano-o-no-mikoto, whose repeated pranks enraged Amaterasu, finally driving her to enter a rock cave and to remain in it. Since Amaterasu was the Sun Goddess, her retreat into the cave brought on a total darkness to this celestial realm. Ameno-uzume-no-mikoto became pivotal in inducing Amaterasu from the rock cave. As the story goes, Ameno-uzume danced herself into an ecstasy in the presence of the myriad gods gathered in front of the rock cave. Divinely possessed, she became half-naked exposing her breasts and lower body to public view. Sighting this spectacle, the assembled deities burst into laughter, which in turn served as a lure to draw Amaterasu out from her seclusion as she, out of curiosity, opened the rock gate and peeked out to see why the gods were having such a good time.[4] Ameno-uzume's ingenious act, which is in essence a shamanistic exorcism, is labelled as *"asobi"* in the *Kojiki*.[5] Her action has been interpreted as the archetypal funerary ritual performed to appease the soul of the dead.[6] The point of significance in this dramatic skit is that *asobi*'s primary function was that of a priest, specifically designed to deal with death and to effect a relief from its threat of disintegration, chaos, and communal paralysis. That is to say, her function was to bring about a collective or social renewal or resurrection through transformational magic. In a way she was a prototype of a religious cleric performing a healing rite.

Another crucial aspect to note here is that, although Ameno-uzume's act was clearly of a religious order, it simultaneously included a dimension of entertainment. Its affective power transformed the emotional state of its audience and in the end successfully accomplished the intended mission of restoring normalcy by relieving them from the threat of annihilation and the accompanying feeling of despair. In sum, what emerges out of this episode is an archetypal image of the *asobi* with a dual or combined function of a priest and entertainer, mediating between the two worlds of light and darkness, order and chaos, and ultimately, life and death.

---

[3]The compilation of *Kojiki* was ordered by the Empress Gemmei (r. 707–715) based on the earlier work begun by the Emperor Temmu (r. 673–686). The same myths are repeated with variations in the *Nihonshoki* (720), another imperially commissioned dynastic history completed during the reign of the Empress Genshō (r. 715–724).

[4]See *Kojiki*, trans. Donald L. Philippi (Princeton: Princeton University Press, 1969), 81–86.

[5]Ibid., 85.

[6]Origuchi Shinobu, *Origuchi Shinobu Zenshū: Nōto Hen* (Collected Works by Origuchi Shinobu: Notes Section) (Tokyo: Chūō Kōronsha, 1971), 5: 16. For many years, a number of theories has been offered as interpretations of this myth. To name a few best-known propositions: the theory of solar eclipse, storm, winter equinox, or political upheaval. However, the position promoted by Origuchi Shinobu which takes it as the funerary rite has been accepted as the orthodox line.

Up to early in the eighth century, the special lineage group that served as the royal morticians was called *asobi-be*, and it claimed Ameno-uzume as its ancestor.[7] The mainstay of the *asobi-be* were females (with assistance coming from male members of the group)[8] and it appears that the lineage was succeeded to female clan members.[9] They had exclusive access to the royal coffin in its temporary enshrinement, ministering to the needs of the occasion, usually performing ritual dance, and uttering incantatory formulas.[10] These professional skills were secretly transmitted to succeeding generations within the group. Since the *asobi-be* members delivered such critical services at the time of death at the imperial court, they were granted the privilege of lifelong immunity from the conscript labor and taxes and accordingly enjoyed special status.

However, in the wake of the promulgation of the Taihō Reform Code in 701 (later reinforced by the Yōrō Code in 718), an unsavory view towards the *asobi-be* began to emerge. These reforms were an ambitious move taken by a coterie of political leaders who attempted to consolidate the power of the central government by adopting the legal and administrative system of China, much of which was based on Confucianism. Their aim was to transform their indigenous society into a far more civilized nation patterned after the Chinese model and to enhance the authority of the throne. The results of these reformatory measures soon began to appear in a number of areas in Japanese life but the changes were not always auspicious. Especially hard-hit was the *asobi-be*. For instance, the "Article on the Funeral" in the Yōrō code describes *asobi-be* as follows: "*Asobi-be* are groups of people engaged in funeral services, exempt from taxes and conscript labor. Since they live without working and are allowed to move freely around, they are called *asobi-be*."[11] To the Taihō Code authorities who envisioned an absolute monarchical system based on revenues from agriculture and on the Confucian ethic of hard work, the *asobi-be* who were exempt from agrarian production and conscript labor, most probably due to the gravity of their responsibility for taking care of the royal deaths and due to the ritual pollution from their contact with the dead, appeared to be non-productive loafers. In fact, the Taihō Code had as its aim to turn the whole country into a tax-based economy, especially levied on the farming population, and as a consequence, succeeded in triggering a mass exodus from the peasantry into the mountains and temples to avoid the taxes and forced labor.[12] In this context, the *asobi-be*'s services which were disengaged from direct national revenue production, and by association, from the maintenance of the power structure, began to carry a negative implication as non-essential and dispensable activities. Consequently, the *asobi-be* as a whole became a superfluous and expendable component of the society. In this sense, the Taihō era

[7]Gorai Shigeru, "Asobi-be Kō," (A Study on the *Asobi-be*), *Bukkyō Bungaku Kenkyū* (Studies on Buddhist Literature), 1 (1963): 42.

[8]Gorai Shigeru, *Nihon Joseishi* (History of Japanese Women), ed. Joseishi Sōgō Kenkyūkai (Association for Research on Women's History) (Tokyo: Tokyo Daigaku Shuppan, 1982), 2: 109.

[9]Gorai, "Asobi-be Kō," 42.

[10]Gorai, *Nihon Joseishi*, 2: 108.

[11]Nakamura Tarō, *Nihon Fujoshi* (History of Japanese Shamaness) (Tokyo: Ōokayama Shoten, 1930), 217.

[12]G. B. Sansom, *Japan: A Short Cultural History* (Stanford: Stanford University Press, 1978), 175.

marks the beginning of the present-day connotation of "*asobu*" or "*asobi*," which means "play" in Japanese implying labor-free and pleasure-oriented activity, and also the beginning of the derogatory implications for the designation of the *asobi-be* as a social group.

As the spirit of the Taihō Reform became entrenched and the Buddhist establishment which consisted mostly of males, started to take over the funeral operations, *asobi-be* irrevocably lost their status. It is believed that by the mid-eighth century, the *asobi-be* as a court functionary ceased to exist.[13] Consequently, among these women, who had no land basis or special mundane skills, many began to take up the itinerant mode of life, turning increasingly to performing arts and often to prostitution. Thus, the *asobi-be*, once positioned at the center of the political and religious sphere as crisis-controllers and chief catalysts between the transcendental and the mundane world underwent a radical displacement until they found themselves in a position of catering to the whimsical humors of men. This downfall also meant that the *asobi-be*'s originally subsidiary variant paths now came to the fore, while their canonical functions became totally alienated from them. Eventually, they became outcasts from the milieu they once helped form, and were reduced to render services of a secondary nature to its institutions in order to validate their existence. Seen in this context, *asobi* of the twelfth century were the progenies of the ancient shamaness, who as a result of a complex interplay of religious, ideological, and political factors, experienced a drastic dislocation both in their status and function and found themselves at the periphery of their society.

It is not entirely clear when *asobi* abandoned their wandering style of life to take up permanent domiciles. However, according to the "Yūjoki" (ca. 1087), a short tract by Ōe no Masafusa (1041–1111),[14] which is by far the most detailed document on *asobi* available from the Heian period, the *asobi* group had already formed permanent settlements by the late eleventh century.[15] The areas where *asobi* established their settlements were chiefly on the transportational strategic points along the waterways, where travelers, merchants, and cargo ships sought lodging. The most fabled *asobi* colonies concentrated at Eguchi along the Yodo River, and Kanzaki and Kanishima on the Kanzaki River, a tributary of the Yodo River, which served as the main passageway to the capital of Heian-kyō from the inland sea. *Asobi*'s attraction and demand grew in direct proportion to the prosperity of these ports as they served as the collection points and conveyers of the luxury items gathered from various regions throughout the country to supply the ever-increasing fastidious and expensive tastes of aristocrats in the capital at Heian-kyō. In fact, the "Yūjoki" describes the flourish of *asobi* during this period as follows: "Kanzaki and Kanishima of the Settsu Province are lined with the *asobi* quarters one door after another."[16]

[13]Gorai, "Asobi-be Kō," 46.

[14]One of the most learned scholars of Chinese classics and poet of his time.

[15]"Yūjoki," *Gunsho Ruijū* (Classified Collection of Japanese Classics), comp. Zoku Gunsho Ruijū Kanseikai (Association for the Completion of the Gunsho Ruijū Sequel) (Tokyo: Zoku Gunsho Ruijū Kanseikai, 1959), 9: 323–24.

[16]Ibid., 9: 323.

As a group, *asobi* seemed to have maintained a loose internal structure headed by a female leader at the top.[17] These head mistresses are believed to have reached such positions by virtue of their superiority in their *imayō* skill and their personal charm as courtesans.[18] It is not known exactly what functions these leaders had, but presumably these women were charged to protect their group members from undue exploitation by customers, to maintain certain order within the group, and sometimes to supervise the distribution of goods among themselves.[19]

In addition to this organizational protection, *asobi* sought further safeguard for their business prosperity in the worship of a deity by the name of *hyakudaifu*. This *hyakudaifu* worship is a phallic cult which has as its object of veneration a representation of the male sexual organ made of wood or paper, and sometimes found among stones. The "Yūjoki" records that *asobi* kept hundreds and thousands of these objects.[20] The cultic practice stems from the belief that by praying to and honoring the *hyakudaifu* these courtesans could ensure continuing success in drawing male customers.

Hyakudaifu worship was not simply confined to a realm of private observances. Besides keeping a large stock of phallic shaped objects for their personal worship, *asobi* made it a point to go on pilgrimages to the shrines famous for the *hyakudaifu* practice. Most well-known among them were the Hirota Shrine[21] and the Sumiyoshi Shrine[22] where *asobi* periodically paid visits.[23] Coincidentally, these shrines, especially, the Sumiyoshi Shrine, also happened to be the favorite destination for religious pilgrimages by aristocrats from the capital.[24] Thus these holy centers became a vortex where *asobi* and the aristocrats converged, each group coming from separate ways and harboring different sets of aspirations. However, these seemingly unrelated pilgrimages did not end without affecting one another. A curious interaction between *asobi* and the nobles was played out, taking one of the most secular and profane forms of carnal and material transactions. In turn, such beneficial results of visiting these shrines reinforced and successfully promoted the *hyakudaifu* cult among *asobi*. The shrines also benefited from this liaison, because the more visits by the affluent aristocrats drawn by *asobi* attraction meant the more income in the form of offerings from both groups of pilgrims. This triangular symbiotic interdependence among *asobi*, the shrines, and the aristocrats, undergirded the *hyakudaifu* worship practiced at the shrines, and produced an intriquing coalescence of diverse interests in a most unlikely setting and conditions. Each component in this relationship sought the presence of

[17]Watanabe Shōgo, *Ryōjin Hishō no Fūzoku to Bungei* (The Folk Customs and Literary Arts of *Ryōjin Hishō*) (Tokyo: Miyai Shoten, 1981), 35.

[18]Takigawa Masajirō, *Yūkōjofu, Yūjo, Kairaijo* (Women Entertainers in Ancient Times: *Yūkōjofu, Yūjo, and Kairaijo*) (Tokyo: Shibundō, 1965), 119.

[19]Watanabe, *Ryōjin Hishō*, 35.

[20]*Gunsho Ruijū*, 9: 323–24.

[21]It is located in the present-day City of Nishi-no-miya in the Hyōgo Province, to the west of the Eguchi and Kanzaki area.

[22]One of the most renowned shrines in Japan, it is located in the present-day Osaka City to the south of the Eguchi and Kanzaki area.

[23]*Gunsho Ruijū*, 9: 323.

[24]For related details, see notes 29–38.

the others, making their respective pursuit of interests into an inseparably woven single entity.

The regular trademark of *asobi* consisted in the peculiar manner in which they carried on their business. Even though these women settled along the river or seaport areas, they enticed their potential customers by singing from their boats. Once their patrons got on board, *asobi* entertained them by singing *imayō* and conducted their transactions floating on the water. An average *asobi* boat in action carried at least three members on board: one principal *asobi* who entertained the guests by singing while beating on a small drum; an apprentice *asobi* who held a huge parasol to shelter her mistress and looked to her needs; and an elderly, retired *asobi* who was in charge of rowing the boat.[25] On this exotic mode of *asobi* entertainment, "Yūjoki" glosses as follows:

> *Asobi* row their small boats toward the passenger boats and invite the travelers to their beds. Their singing makes the mountain clouds stop and their rhymes are on the wings over the river. Along the isles with rushes and breakers, hordes of fishermen and merchant ships throng in stern to stern toward the *asobi* boats with no empty space left on the water. Up from the aristocrats down to the commoners, none hesitates to lavish their love on these women. Some of them marry as wives and some become concubines to be cherished until their death. Even wise men and men of character cannot help visiting them. Under the heaven, this must be the best pleasure resort.[26]

What has to be stressed here is that the primary point of *asobi*'s distinction was their superb skill in singing *imayō*. Lacking this musical qualification, other courtesans at Eguchi or Kanzaki were simply called *yahochi*, meaning a mere prostitute, not *asobi*.[27] Additionally, the reason why these *asobi* could so openly solicit their customers during the broad daylight and among crowds of onlookers was because they were performing artists in their own right.[28]

The magnetism of *asobi* was such that some of the contemporary nobles did not hesitate to declare that the pleasure derived from the tryst with *asobi* cruising along the river on the gently rocking boat was on par with the excitement on their wedding night.[29] A number of historical records, especially the diaries and letters by the Heian court nobles, are sprinkled with references to the attractions felt by the aristocrats to *asobi*.[30] These documents show that frequently, under the pretense of making pilgrimages to shrines and temples, high court nobles and even imperial family

---

[25]Takigawa, *Yukōjofu*, 121.

[26]*Gunsho Ruijū*, 9: 323.

[27]Takigawa, *Yūkōjofu*, 4.

[28]Ibid., 114–15.

[29]Refer to poem no. 720 on *asobi* by Ōe Koretoki (955–1010), in *Wakan Rōeishū* (Poems in Chinese and Japanese for Recitation), ed. Kawaguchi Hisao and Shida Nobuyoshi, *Nihon Koten Bungaku Taikei* (Great Series in Japanese Classics) (Tokyo: Iwanami Shoten, 1980), 73: 236.

[30]Some of the better known sources for information in this area are: *Nihon Kiryaku* (A Condensed History of Japan), a historical compilation of the late Heian period in 34 volumes; *Meigō Ōrai* (1066) (Meigō's Correspondence), a collection of letters by its author, Fujiwara Akihira (989–1066), mid-Heian scholar and writer of Chinese poetry; and *Chōshūki* (Record of Long Autumn), a diary by Minamoto Morotoki (1077–1136), a Heian courtier.

members made detour excursions to *asobi* centers in Eguchi or Kanzaki in pursuit of the pleasure and entertainment these women provided.

The list of these highborn visitors contains such illustrious figures as the Emperors Ichijō (r. 986–1011), Go-Sanjō (r. 1068–1072), Fujiwara Michinaga (966–1027), the most powerful imperial regent in Japanese history, and his son, Yorimichi (992–1074). For instance, in the year of 1000, on the way from pilgrimage to the Sumiyoshi Shrine, Michinaga in company with Empress Dowager Tōsanjō-in, who was his sister and mother of the Emperor Ichijō, dropped by Eguchi, where he is reported to have given favor to an *asobi* named Kokannon.[31] Later, in the year 1031, Yorimichi followed exactly the same path as his father took to pay a visit to the Sumiyoshi Shrine and to Eguchi thereafter, and fell in love with an *asobi* by the name of Nakanogimi at Eguchi.[32]

Such visits from the high and mighty were coveted by these women because they were often accompanied by material donations of incredible magnitude by contemporary standards. Some of these bounteous gifts from the nobility reached hundreds of bushels of rice and hundreds of skeins of silk. To cite a few examples, the Emperor Ichijō on his visit in 1023 to Eguchi from his pilgrimage to Mt. Kōya[33] bestowed 100 *koku* (500 bushels) of rice to the groups of *asobi* that crowded upon the imperial barge on the Yodo River, taking pity on them.[34] On the occasion of Michinaga's visit to Eguchi mentioned above, the Empress Dowager Tōsanjō-in granted 100 *koku* of rice to *asobi*, while Michinaga gave 50 *koku*.[35] Yorimichi, the most spendthrift of all, dispensed 200 skeins of silk and 200 *koku* of rice on his visit to the Eguchi and Kanzaki areas in 1031.[36] The enormity of these gifts no doubt far surpassed the petty rewards paid by ordinary customers.

In rare cases, the relationship between the nobility and *asobi* went beyond the temporary infatuation and developed into a life-long commitment. A case in point is an *asobi* by the name of Tamba-no-tsubone.[37] She captured the attention of the Emperor Go-Shirakawa (1127–1192), an unrivaled patron of *imayō* and its long-time practitioner, and became one of his secondary wives bearing him a prince. This was an inconceivable honor for a woman of ignoble birth but was made possible by her skills in *imayō* singing. She even makes an appearance in the Emperor's personal memoir,[38] which revolves around his extraordinary involvement in the *imayō* genre, while none of his numerous regular consorts is ever mentioned in it.

---

[31]*Gunsho Ruijū*, 9: 324.

[32]Ibid.

[33]The mountain range in the present day Wakayama Prefecture where the Kogōbuji Temple, the center of the Shingon Buddhism, is located.

[34]Watanabe, *Ryōjin Hishō*, 37.

[35]Ibid.

[36]It was during his visit to Eguchi on his way from the pilgrimage to Mt. Kōya in 1048. See Watanabe, *Ryōjin Hishō*, 39–40.

[37]Her father seemed to have been an aristocrat but her mother was obviously an *asobi* herself. See Watanabe, *Ryōjin Hishō*, 43.

[38]See Shida Nobuyoshi, ed., *Ryōjin Hishō* (Secret Selection of Music), Nihon Koten Bungaku Taikei (Iwanami Shoten, 1980), 454. The memoir is Book 10 in *Ryōjin Hishō Kudenshū* (The Oral Transmission

In considering *asobi*'s station in the Heian society, it is impossible to bypass the monumental mediation played by this Emperor Go-Shirakawa. The Emperor's patronage resulted in the elevation of the *imayō* art from the rubric of commoner's entertainment to a musical realm refined and sophisticated enough to suit the taste of aristocrats. There was a fanatical streak in the Emperor's cultivation and promotion of *imayō* including its main propagators, *asobi*. His infatuation turned out to be an enduring commitment lasting throughout his lifetime, not a frivolous dilettante's dabbling in popular music, a fact he reminisces in his memoir as follows: "I have been fond of *imayō* ever since my youth and have never neglected it since that time."[39]

Thus, the Emperor Go-Shirakawa's absorption in the art of *imayō*, begun at young age, took him to arduous paths of training spanning over a few decades. As he pens at great length in his memoir, Go-Shirakawa spent countless months and years in cultivating his skills in *imayō* singing long before his ascension to the throne. It was not unusual for him to forego sleep for days on end and endure painful physical discomforts in an effort to master the art. The extent to which the Emperor went to train himself in the art of *imayō* closely resembles a religious ascetic's willing subjection to the most grueling regimen. He recalls this commitment in his memoir as follows:

> Ignoring both summer's heat and winter's cold, and favoring no one season over another, I spent my waking hours in singing; no day dawned without my having spent the whole night singing. Even at dawn, with the shutters still unopened, I kept on singing, oblivious of both sunrise and noon. Hardly distinguishing day from night, I spend my days and months in this manner.
>
> On occasion I gathered together some people to dance and enjoy the singing. At times we gathered in groups of four or five, or seven or eight, simply to sing *imayō*. Sometimes I set up a schedule for my close retainers to take turns as my singing partners as I practiced *imayō* day and night. . . . Three times I lost my voice. Twice I sang to the point where, even as I tried to follow the set rules as closely as possible, I could no longer produce a sound. Straining my voice in this way gave me a sore throat and made it painful even to swallow water. In spite of this affliction, I still managed to keep on singing.
>
> Sometimes, after first practicing for seven, eight, fifty, or one hundred days, I continued singing for even a thousand days in a row. Although there were times when I did not sing during the day, no dawn broke without my singing.[40]

This total absorption on the part of the Emperor in *imayō*, a product of the populace, to the exclusion of the more orthodox courtly art of composing poems and other elegant aesthetic pursuits befitting the imperial personage, was regarded as an anomaly by the court and even brought to the emperor an unsavory reputation. However, such criticism did not deter his dedication to *imayō*. On the contrary, he summoned to his imperial residence *imayō* singers of low social status, especially women from the *asobi* group, to give him musical instructions. One such early teacher of his

---

of Secret Selection of Music), a collection of materials on the musical aspects of *imayō* compiled by the Emperor. For an English translation and introduction, see my article, "The Emperor's Songs: Go-Shirakawa and *Ryōjin Hishō Kudenshū*," *Monumenta Nipponica* 41 (1986): 261–98.

[39]Kwon, "The Emperor's Songs," 272.

[40]Ibid., 273.

was a woman by the name of Kane, who was a lady-in-waiting in the service of his mother and who was of obviously *asobi* background coming from the Kanzaki area.[41]

Even after ascension to the throne, Emperor Go-Shirakawa's dedication to *imayō* did not slacken. On the contrary, his training in *imayō* leaped to a new dimension when in the year 1157 he invited to his court an *imayō* expert by the name of Otomae, an elderly woman in her seventies, who came from a similar background as his early teachers. Once he submitted himself to Otomae's guidance, the Emperor had to undergo a trying process of relearning his entire repertoire according to her musical style, for she came from the most authentic *imayō* lineage. Over a decade, the teacher-disciple relationship between the Emperor and Otomae continued and it culminated in Go-Shirakawa becoming the sole successor to Otomae's school of *imayō* by receiving a complete oral transmission from her.

Go-Shirakawa's deep devotion to his teacher is legendary and his esteem and affection for his aged teacher was summarily expressed in his visit to her sickbed when she was nearing the end of her life. At her sickbed, out of his desire to comfort her, the emperor even sang an *imayō* song on the healing power of the Buddha, and to please her, he repeated the song, which moved his teacher to tears.[42] The abiding relationship between the Emperor and Otomae went beyond the latter's lifetime. The following moving account in his memoir on the death of his teacher reveals one of the most disarming features of the Emperor as a private person and at the same time eloquently exemplifies the power of art to remove class barriers and put individuals on one human continuum:

> Although death at her age[43] was not something to be mourned over, my grief was boundless because I had known her for so many years. It was not the first time that I grieved for those who had gone ahead of me, but my memories of her would not go away. She had been my teacher from whom I had learned so much, and so at the news of her death I started reading the sutra in the morning to purify the six roots of evil,[44] and in the evening I read the Amida Sutra[45] continuously for fifty days to pray for her rebirth in the Western Pure Land.[46]

On the first anniversary of Otomae's death, the Emperor Go-Shirakawa conducted a special memorial service, accentuating it by singing himself the *imayō* songs he had learned from her. Thereafter, annually without fail he offered memorial services on her behalf. That Otomae held a special place in Go-Shirakawa's music career and possibly, his inner life, is further confirmed by the fact that approximately one-third of his memoir is allocated to the anecdotes and stories related to her or told by her to the Emperor. Furthermore, it is generally believed that the largest extant *imayō*

[41]Ibid., 273–74.

[42]Ibid., 276.

[43]Otomae died in 1169 and she was said to be eighty-four years old at the time.

[44]Also called six sensory organs, they are the eyes, ears, nose, tongue, body, and mind. In Buddhism, they are regarded as the source of earthly desires which need to be purified.

[45]As one of the three basic Pure Land Buddhist scriptures, it describes the blessing of Amida Buddha and his Pure Land of Perfect Bliss in the western region of the universe. It further asserts that one can attain rebirth in this Pure Land by solely relying on Amida.

[46]Kwon, "The Emperor's Song," 283.

lyric collection called *Ryōjin Hishō* (Secret Selection of Music) compiled by the Emperor Go-Shirakawa was inspired by Otomae.[47] The compilation project was presumably launched soon after Otomae began to give him music lessons and was apparently undertaken in his effort to commit to writing the oral instruction he received from his teacher. It was completed in 1179 taking him over two decades spurred on as he was even after her death. Without the Emperor's toil through half of his adult life to collect *imayō* songs, the harvest of the plebeian culture, which is scarce in the first place, would never have been transmitted to the present.

The relationship between the Emperor Go-Shirakawa and his teacher of humble birth is indeed a unique and rare phenomenon in the history of the royal family in Japan, never precedented or repeated. What brought Otomae to her remarkable association with the Emperor and to the exalted position of the royal music instructorship was first and foremost her artistic renown as a consummate *imayō* singer. In the intensely class-conscious Heian society, where birth and rank determined the worth of an individual, Otomae would not have been at all able to come to such a close proximity to the imperial personage and court life had it not been for her supreme musical virtuosity. Assuredly, *imayō* was her sole but powerful key to gain entrance into the exclusive aristocratic society.

Under the Emperor Go-Shirakawa's sponsorship, a number of *imayō* concerts, or *imayō* symposia, so to speak, were held at his own palace to which *asobi* were invited to participate. These occasions provided opportunities for these women to freely mingle with the high court nobles, almost on equal footing. In these gatherings when actual *imayō* performance was required, these *asobi* became the center of the stage. Along with their performing engagements, these singers took an active part with the courtiers in informal, critical discussions on *imayō* art, sharing their esoteric knowledge of *imayō*. In such exchanges, these *asobi* took advantage of the opportunity to show their pride in their profession and schooling and took pleasure in demonstrating their competence.[48] What emerges most significantly out of these events is that through the medium of music, an intercommunication between the high and low cultures was achieved creating a qualitatively new milieu that could have never existed in the regular aristocratic cultural context.

In the meticulously stratified Japanese society, these women occupied only a marginal space, and often the other art they practiced was prostitution. Yet their artistry in *imayō* brought them into a high level contact with aristocrats and to the heart of aesthetic life of the elite society. We may even venture to say that *imayō* art served for *asobi* as an instrument to restore them to their former lost status and, sporadic and ephemeral though that may have been, made them enjoy their onetime privilege of being near the hub of power and status. In essence, what they could not retrieve in the real political or religious arena, they recovered by means of their artistic excellence. In the end, their lost status as a priestly caste was redeemed in the act of entertainment.

---

[47]Konishi Jin'ichi, *Ryōjin Hishō Kō* (A Study on *Ryōjin Hishō*) (Tokyo: Sanseidō, 1941), 43–44.
[48]Kwon, "The Emperor's Song," 276–81.

Asobi's ascendancy and acceptance into the court circle testify that there existed a positive dialectic operating between the high and low cultures in the Heian society. In this process, *asobi* experienced a transformation in their modality of existence from one of marginality to that of centrality, albeit temporary and tenuous. *Asobi*'s masterful control of some of the culturally-valued constructs of their society catapulted them into the rarified realm of the privileged few and enabled them to justify their being. In such aesthetic rectification of the *asobi*'s reality, one can see the paramount instrumentality of art. The case of *asobi*, however, is not to be settled simply as an illustration of vindication or elevation of status of a class of women by the catalytic mediation of art. It is because the totality of the issue of *asobi* is linked to far deeper questions about the dynamics involving women and entertainment, power structure and prostitution, and ritual and performing arts, and finally to the overarching question about the role and position of women stipulated by these powerful variables. It is, therefore, hoped that the present exercise at an identification and clarification of the actuality of a group of women engaged in the entertainment enterprise in medieval Japan serves as a germinal ground for a further discourse on these epistemological topics, possibly a tortuous task but potentially an illuminating and rewarding work.